# Latinos in New England

# Latinos *in* New England

*Edited by* Andrés Torres

Temple University Press
**PHILADELPHIA**

This book is dedicated to the memory of Mauricio Gastón (1947–1986) and to Latina and Latino Youth of New England: future leaders of our Community

Andrés Torres is Research Associate at the Center for Puerto Rican Studies, Hunter College, City University of New York. Until recently he was Director of the Mauricio Gastón Institute for Latino Community Development and Public Policy at the University of Massachusetts at Boston. He is past president of the Puerto Rican Studies Association and is the author of several books, including *The Puerto Rican Movement: Voices from the Diaspora (Temple)*.

Temple University Press
1601 North Broad Street
Philadelphia PA 19122
*www.temple.edu/tempress*

*F*
*15*
*,S75*
*L38*
*2006*

∞ The paper used in this publication meets the requirements of the American National Standard for Information Sciences—Permanence of Paper for Printed Library Materials, ANSI Z39.48-1992

Library of Congress Cataloging-in-Publication Data

Latinos in New England / edited by Andrés Torres.
   p. cm.
Includes bibliographical references and index.
ISBN 1-59213-416-5 (cloth : alk. paper)— ISBN 1-59213-417-3 (pbk. : alk. paper)
   1. Hispanic Americans—New England—Social conditions.   2. Hispanic Americans—New England—Economic conditions.   3. Hispanic Americans—New England—Politics and government.   4. Hispanic Americans—New England—Ethnic identity.   5. Hispanic Americans—New England—Cultural assimilation.   6. New England—History.   I. Torres, Andrés 1947–

F15.S75L38   2006
305.868'074—dc22                                                   2005056049

2   4   6   8   9   7   5   3   1

# Contents

**Part III: Identity and Politics**

*Photographs follow page 222*

# Tables and Figures

## Tables

## Figures

# Acknowledgments

I am grateful to many collaborators for helping to make this book possible. The Mauricio Gastón Institute for Latino Community Development and Public Policy was my home during the years this anthology came to fruition. Without the dedication and support of the institute's core staff this project would not have been realized. Mary Jo Marion was a talented, busy, and gracious Associate Director throughout my tenure. Gissell Abreu, Paloma Britt, and Hedy Castaño, assured that our numerous initiatives and activities were kept on track. On several occasions, each of them pitched in when the process of manuscript preparation was threatened with gridlock. Professor Jorge Capetillo, as faculty researcher, contributed valuable studies and good cheer.

Dr. Miren Uriarte has been a key supporter over the years, and a leading figure in the community of scholars that works closely with the Gastón Institute. The organization has continually benefited from the volunteer efforts and political wisdom of its Advisory Board, chaired by Nelson Merced. Grateful appreciation is also due to the University of Massachusetts Boston, home to the institute since 1989.

New England is hardly a prime region for studies about the Latino experience. California, the South West, and New York are in the limelight. Nevertheless, there was an enthusiastic response to the call for submissions to this publication. This is testimony to the growing cadre of Latino-focused researchers in the region, and to the burgeoning interest in Latino issues as the Hispanic population increases in numbers and influence. I am deeply thankful to each of the contributing authors. They labored diligently and creatively to produce a quality collection, making their research available for and accessible to a wide audience. Their cooperation in meeting deadlines and their collegial interactions are greatly appreciated.

Other individuals helped push this project along. Daniel Vásquez created special tables that focused on Latino populations in New England. With customary expertise and reliability, Angel Amy Moreno helped coordinate the photography section. Leslie Bowen, Carlos Bock Maldonado, and Carmen Vivian Rivera helped with the manuscript at critical junctures. Thanks also to others who provided materials, advice, and other forms of support: Ramón Borges-Méndez, Melissa Colón, Linda Delgado, James Green, Ramona Hernández, Marta Monteiro-Sieburth, and Jaime Rodríguez. Jim O'Brien, who I have relied on in the past, produced the index. During my stint as director of the institute I was able to count on many colleagues for moral and material support, especially at the College of Public and Community Services, the Asian American Studies Institute, and the William Monroe Trotter Institute. I also extend special thanks to Robert J. Hildreth who, during my time, has been a steadfast and generous donor to the Institute's work.

I am happy that Temple University Press is publishing this work. Dating back to my previous association with Doris Braendel, I have enjoyed collaborating with the Press. For their assistance with the present anthology, I thank Janet Francendese, Will Hammell, Gary Kramer, Peter Wissoker, Dave Wilson, and the production and marketing staffs. I am also appreciative of Kim Hoag for her diligent oversight of the production process.

The final phase of the manuscript preparation process found me in a state of hectic transition. Leaving the Boston area and not yet settled in my new home in New York, I constantly fretted that some catastrophe might derail the manuscript's progress. Fortunately, this editor's nightmares were limited to the imagination. For this I am grateful to my brothers-in-law and their wives, Philip and Terri, Ruben and Nicki. Over the course of several weeks in limbo, they provided me with a writer's sanctuary, reliable technology, and warm company. As always, my wife Carmen Vivian, and my children, Rachel and Orlando, have been my principle cheerleaders. As well as John, Jaclyn, David and Jonathan. ¡Gracias, familia! ¡Gracias, todos!

# Latinos in New England: An Introduction

Andrés Torres

When the United States declared war on Mexico, more than a century and half ago, did anyone imagine that this act would ultimately bond this country into a permanent relation with our southern neighbor? It was a war of conquest, supported by the logic of Manifest Destiny and by the economic interests that desired the extension of slave-owning territories. U.S. imperial might (and Mexican internal division) dictated an easy victory, leading to the appropriation of half the land formerly belonging to Mexico. To this day Mexican-Americans can claim, with a measure of historical accuracy, "we didn't cross the U.S. border, the U.S. border crossed *us*."

A little-known episode of the so-called Mexican War, which has ironic relevance to the present anthology, concerns the story of the *San Patricios*. This was a brigade of mostly Irish Americans who had been recruited to fight in the invading army, but who abandoned the U.S. side to join with the Mexicans. Like their putative enemy, these Irish had been colonial subjects and were Catholic. In the gateway cities of Boston and New York, the newcomers had been subjected to ethnic and religious discrimination. South of the border, they were enticed with promises of land and freedom if they joined the Mexican Army.[1]

When U.S. victory came, the *San Patricios* met a tragic ending, most of them executed or jailed for desertion. North of the Rio Grande history treats them as an embarrassing chapter; in Mexico City a monument preserves their names in honor for their gallantry in battle. In 1997 the Mexican and Irish governments issued commemorative stamps of the St. Patrick's Battalion.

Decades later history would record another interesting link of a Hispano-Yankee character. José Martí, writer and freedom fighter, was a leading figure in the Cuban independence struggle. In 1869 the Spanish authorities exiled him from his homeland, after which he lived many years in Latin America and in New York City. Though he was skeptical of

U.S. intentions in the Caribbean, he was an admirer of this country's democratic ideals.

Martí was attracted to the writings of Ralph Waldo Emerson, the famous New England essayist and philosopher. A democrat and humanist, Emerson was an active Abolitionist and had opposed the U.S. war on Mexico. Martí wrote about Emerson, showing his Latin American readers that there was another side to the bellicose Giant of the North.[2]

In the early twentieth century, by which time the United States had replaced Spain as the dominant foreign influence in Latin America, a young Puerto Rican was studying at Harvard. His records reveal how active Pedro Albizu Campos was while living in Cambridge. In June of 1916, he wrote, "I have given lectures in Boston and other cities on Latin-American questions. This year I was invited to speak at the Convention of New England Immigration Secretaries. I spoke on the Monroe Doctrine at the Boston Social Science Club... [and gave] the welcome address at the reception given to all foreign students at Harvard."

Like Martí, Albizu Campos was inspired by the democratic strain in U.S. history. After this country entered World War I, he wrote in the *Harvard Crimson* of "our [Puerto Ricans'] loyalty to the United States." He was still concerned, however, that U.S. power was impeding Puerto Rico's autonomy, two decades after the Spanish-American War. "We want Americans to know the facts of our situation that they may be true to themselves and find a just solution for our relations."[3]

It may be that these are but tenuous connections, individual stories plucked out of the historical record. Yet I hope they demonstrate some symbolic precedence to a reality that can no longer be denied. Latin America's children—her Latinas and Latinos—are a permanent fixture in New England.

This book assembles new writings from experts who examine the Latino impact on New England, perhaps the most tradition-bound area of the United States. A "blue state" region perceived as a stalwart liberal zone, many are paying attention to this part of the country as a new testing ground for social and economic policies that will challenge the area's reputation for civil discourse and multicultural tolerance. The reality is that, in urban areas where racial/ethnic minorities are expanding their presence and asserting their rights, we observe ongoing tensions over the future direction of these cities and their populations. Latinos are increasingly a player in these dynamics.

The central inquiry of this book is this: How is the Latino community influencing New England's socioeconomic, political, and cultural life, and, reciprocally, how is the community being shaped in its interaction with the region's peoples, traditions and institutions?

An underlying premise of this inquiry is that the Latino community, though multiethnic and multiracial, generally acts as a collective identity when interacting with the larger society. Yet, under specific circumstances, each national origin group ("sub-Latino" identity) may simultaneously express its political agency, cultural identity, and economic activity differently from other national groups. Latino social action takes place along a spectrum that ranges from unified collectivity (Pan-Latinismo) to nationalistic individuality (ethnic nationalism).

There are corollary themes addressed in the chapters that comprise this volume. The contributors each deal with one or more of the following questions:

- What is the extent and what are the sources of population growth in the recent past, and what are the socioeconomic trends and conditions at the regional, state, and local level?
- What are some key racial/ethnic and class dimensions of Latino socio-economic trends and Latino life?
- What are some examples of the host society's response to the incursion of Latino newcomers? And the subsequent impact on Latino identity and political and social projects?
- How do the various ethnic groups in the Latino community relate to each other?
- What can we say about the relationship of ethnic identity (either country-specific or pan-Latino) to political participation and representation, social movements, and community institutions? What does the New England experience tell us about the ongoing debate concerning the viability of a pan-Latino identity?

This volume disaggregates data and information by national origin sectors, describing discrete instances of Latino community formation and conditions. It assumes that variations within the population are just as instructive as differences between Latinos and the rest of the population. Studying the Latino condition through the lens of region, state, and sub-Latino ethnicity is a major goal of this collection. Hopefully, the accumulation of several case studies—each homing in on a specific nexus of geographic and ethnic contexts—will improve our understanding of the Latino experience, in its variations and multiple expressions.

Our methodology is multidisciplinary. The chapters include an eclectic array of approaches: oral histories, case studies, ethnographic inquiries, focus group research, statistical and regression analyses, and surveys.[4]

## Demographic Trends, Socioeconomic Issues

Only three decades ago few people took notice of Hispanic demographics. Today the subject has permeated every aspect of American life. By now everyone recognizes three characteristics of the Latino population: its explosive growth, its geographic dispersion, and its ethnic diversity. The New England scene is no exception to these trends.

Will the long winters deter the massive influx we have seen in other parts of the country? Perhaps. Most Latin American immigrants come from regions within and contiguous to our hemisphere's tropical zone. Nevertheless, according to the 2000 census, there were close to a million Latinas and Latinos residing in the six states that make up New England.[5] Cold weather or not, the numbers will only grow. These immigrants, their children, and the descendants of the core Latino communities that have already been living in the region for decades will ensure a vibrant presence well into the future.

Between 1990 and 2000, the Latino population in New England grew 60 percent, from about 545,000 to over 871,000. They comprised 6.3 percent of the total New England population. The number of Latino residents (and share of population) for each state was 427,340 (6.7) for Massachusetts, 318,947 (9.4) for Connecticut, 90,452 (8.6), for Rhode Island, 19,910 (1.6) for New Hampshire, 9,226 (0.7) for Maine, and 5,316 (0.9) for Vermont.[6] Ninety-five percent of New England's Latinos live in southern New England: Massachusetts, Connecticut, and Rhode Island.

As elsewhere in the country, growth is accompanied by significant geographic dispersion. Cities such as Boston and Hartford, the classic hubs of Latino New England, are no longer the dominant centers of Latino population growth. For example, the Latino growth rate during 1990–2000 for these cities was 37 percent (increasing from roughly 62,000 to 85,000) and 12 percent (increasing from roughly 44,000 to 49,000), respectively.

Other cities are now taking their place alongside these. Among cities where we find fairly substantial Latino populations—say, of at least 20,000—there are a number in which Latino growth rates greatly exceed that of Boston. These include Providence (whose Latino population grew from 25,000 to 52,000, or by 108 percent), Springfield (growing from 26,500 to 41,300, or by 56 percent), and Waterbury (growing from 14,600 to 23,400, or by 60 percent). Other cities in this category are Lawrence (47 percent), New Haven (53 percent), and New Britain, (56 percent). There are also a good number of Latino concentrations in smaller towns of less than ten thousand inhabitants; some of these may appear to outsiders as having cropped up out of nowhere. To name some, whose population at least doubled during the 1990s: East Hartford, Danbury, and Willimantic (in Connecticut), Central Falls and Pawtucket (in Rhode Island), Haverhill (in Massachusetts), and Manchester (in New Hampshire).

Another new wrinkle in the Hispanic "demographic" is the increasing variety of national origins. Latinos of Puerto Rican heritage were always the largest single component in New England, and they continue to be so. But their share has declined steadily, even as their tenure in the region continues as the longest. In 1990, 55.7 percent of all Hispanic New England originated from Puerto Rico, a U.S. territory. By 2000 that figure was 49.4 percent (about 430,000 of the 871,000 Latinos in New England). The Dominican share has doubled, officially, to almost 10 percent. This number represents a significant undercount, perhaps by as much as a quarter or a third. Postcensus examination has shown that many Latinos misconstrued the wording on the census forms. The confusion had the greatest impact on all groups that fell outside the traditional "Hispanic/ Latino" identifiers of Mexican, Puerto Rican, and Cuban. The result, in the case of New England, was an estimate of 15.4 percent of Latinos (some 134,000 respondents) who identified themselves as "other Hispanic/Latino," making this anomalous group the second largest population after Puerto Ricans. Researchers, including census officials, have recalculated the counts using other personal data on census forms to arrive at new, unofficial estimates. The result is that the "Other" category is much smaller, and the count for groups such as Dominicans, Salvadorans, Guatemalans, Colombians, and Ecuadorians is much higher.[7] There is no reason to expect a change in the growing ethnic diversity among Latinos.

In their population and economic profile of Latino New England, Marcelli and Granberry accentuate the positive (Chapter 1). Rapid growth of unfamiliar newcomers has always been a source of alarm for Americans, as it has been for people throughout history. Yet without these infusions this country would never have attained economic affluence. The authors demonstrate that present-day Latino demographics are of the sort that have propelled economic growth in the past, because Latinos are more likely to form families, have children and spend. A further economic advantage that they offer is their relatively low elderly population: "the Latino population is important not only because without them New England's population would have stagnated between 1990 and 2000, but also because of an age profile that intimates future contributions to regional consumption and productivity."

Still, the authors are cognizant that the economic position of Latinos is problematic. They show the statistical gaps between Latinos and other New Englanders in variables such as education, labor force participation, earnings and employment, and job types. Also identified are the differences among the various Latino groups. The persistent inequalities faced by such groups as Puerto Ricans, Dominicans, Salvadorans, Guatemalans, and Mexicans, is disconcerting. It is not coincidental that many of the chapters in this volume dwell on aspects of this divergent reality.

Of the Hispanics in the region, some 30 percent were identified as foreign born by the 2000 census. A third of these are naturalized U.S. citizens, meaning that 20 percent of New England's Latino population was classified as nonnaturalized immigrants.[8] Compared to national levels, New England's Latinos have a lower foreign-born population and a higher rate of citizenship among its immigrant population.

Uriarte, Granberry, and Halloran examine recent immigration policies, and find them adversely affecting Massachusetts' foreign-born (Chapter 2). Groups such as Salvadorans, Guatemalans, Hondurans, and Colombians have been caught in a severe policy squeeze. The erosion of sympathy for newcomers dates back to the mid-1990s and is reflected in policy changes that have lead to a "vision of immigration that ignores the social dynamics of population flows and the fundamental interaction between the origin and destination of the flow. This blind spot continues to pull policy in the direction of ever stronger border controls and punitive measures for those who succeed in entering the country nevertheless." The authors remind us that after September 11, worsening attitudes towards immigrants make it only more difficult to appreciate their contributions, and what they need to achieve success in this society.

Tightening controls and financial hardship have made it more difficult for people to see kin in their homeland, or to receive visitors from abroad. Budgetary cuts at the state level, where responsibility for immigrant benefits and services is now situated, have reduced access to basic needs, such as health care and housing. The intertwining of immigration and social policies has meant only trouble for this most vulnerable of Latino groups, according to these authors.

Looking specifically at housing and homeownership issues, Michael Stone (Chapter 3) uncovers some alarming trends. Latinos seeking housing are having an especially difficult time. The majority of Latino renters, and a quarter of Latino homeowners, lives in a state of "shelter poverty." By this he means that their rental or mortgage costs are so great that they are left with insufficient funds to cover all the other basic household needs. During the 1990s the rise in shelter poverty was greater for Hispanics, especially Latina-headed households, than for any other major ethnic group in Massachusetts. As a result, Latinos have the lowest rate of homeownership. Further compounding the problem is the existence of programs and policies that entice low-income renters into premature homeownership.

## Migration and Community

Several authors offer insights into the process of community formation in New England.[9] Three case studies of medium-sized cities are described: Waterbury, Connecticut; Providence, Rhode Island; and Cambridge, Massachusetts.

Ruth Glasser's portrait of Waterbury depicts an interesting case of Latino ethnic interaction outside the major urban centers (Chapter 4). The original Puerto Rican population, dating back to the 1950s, has been joined by a growing Dominican settlement. Like their predecessors from the Caribbean, Dominicans have relied on kinship and social networks to identify residential and economic niches within which to pursue a new life. Affordable rents, the relative ease of home ownership, and plentiful work in the lower occupational echelons of this old industrial town: these are the appeals of Waterbury to Dominicans, whether they be former New Yorkers seeking a more sedate environment or islanders ready to abandon the tropical warmth for a chance at economic opportunity.

Glasser situates the Dominican experience in the context of the prior history of Puerto Ricans. As the original Latino group, Puerto Ricans were instrumental in laying the groundwork for Latino community formation in Waterbury. The two groups are not quite co-ethnics (that is, they are not of the same country of origin), but anyone familiar with Caribbean history and with post-1960s migration patterns will attest to the long-standing relations and interactions between the two. It is not coincidental that Puerto Rico is a primary site for immigrants from the Dominican Republic, and that in many places where Dominicans have settled, there is a contiguous Puerto Rican barrio. Waterbury is another locale in which the Boricua-Quisqueyano nexus is being played out.

Rhode Island, the smallest state in the country, is home to another thriving Latino community. And though there are other sites of Latino settlement in the state, the capital city of Providence is the center of Latino activity. Providence seems to be unlike other New England cities in that there was not really a substantial Puerto Rican population base out of which a subsequent Latino community is forged. From the beginning, in the 1950s and 1960s (not to speak of earlier decades in which a smattering of Spanish-speaking immigrants had settled in Providence and other Rhode Island towns), the Hispanic presence had been comprised of a variety of Latin Americans and Caribbeans, as Miren Uriarte points out (Chapter 5).

Tracking the community's development over time, Uriarte posits that the Latino experience here varies from standard expectations about the immigrant incorporation process. Neither Gordon's "assimilationist" model nor the "ethnic resiliency" approach, advocated by Portes and others, quite captures what is going on in the Providence scene. She argues that political activism has taken root quite early in the community's evolution, that it has occurred despite significant exclusion from the political and economic structures, and, finally, that it is not exclusively focused on local struggles. Latino diversity, a constant feature of the community's history from its incipient stages, has a lot to do with this trajectory of political activism.

It is fair to say that Waterbury (exemplifying Latino succession) and Providence (exemplifying Latino diversity) both represent case studies of promising futures, notwithstanding the authors' concerns regarding Latino social and economic conditions. The city of Cambridge, on the other hand, symbolizes the case of a mature Latino community in the throes of stagnation and exclusion. In the words of a long-time community leader, Latino Cambridge is in the midst of a "quiet crisis" (Chapter 6).

Cambridge too has experienced intense Latino political activism and ethnic succession. There was an initial period of ascendancy during the 1960s and 1970s, centering on movements for civil rights and socio-economic advancement. Later in the 1980s a complex process of Latino succession occurred in which Central Americans augmented the early base of Puerto Ricans and Dominicans. The Central Americans, mostly Salvadorans, caught the brunt of America's rightward turn in social and immigrant policy. Most recently a third cohort of newcomers has made its presence felt, a group dominated by professionals: highly educated, affluent, and including many South Americans. While this later group has made inroads in the city's social and political elite, their success has not lifted the standing of other Latinos who arrived previously.

Deborah Pacini's inquiry into the causes of this decline includes an assessment of changing social welfare policy, the variability of ethnic and class relations among Latinos, and the "power of place." She reminds us that models of immigrant incorporation can hardly be expected to account for locales such as Cambridge, with an "elite economic environment" that is inhospitable to low-skill, low-wage workers. The specialized nature of Cambridge's key industries and excessive housing costs (the city ended rent control in the mid-1990s) leave little maneuverability for Latinos and other groups on the margin of society. The story of the Puerto Ricans, Dominicans, and Salvadorans of Cambridge is not a happy one. It is the story of a community with questionable prospects for stable growth and vigorous participation in the city's future.

Latino community formation is anything but uniform, as the chapters in this book demonstrate. The sources of immigration are multiple and varying, heavily dependent on what is occurring in the home country, or in U.S. territories such as Puerto Rico. Internal migration leads to the emergence of new U.S. communities as older Latino populations relocate and establish newer settings: from Hartford to West Hartford, New York City to Danbury, Boston to Framingham. Settlement patterns are further consolidated as the second-generation sinks roots in the same locale pioneered by their parents. Community formation ideally leads to the successful incorporation of the second and subsequent generations. (Im)migration, settlement, incorporation: the desired scenario. Various chapters in this collection show how this idealized process is at variance with reality, often with problematic outcomes.

Camayd, Karush, and Lejter (Chapter 7) argue persuasively that in places such as Manchester, New Hampshire, Latinos are on an upwardly mobile track. They make a useful distinction between Latino enclaves and Latino diasporas, the latter representing "Latino settlement characterized by branching regional dispersal from traditional areas of concentration into new enclaves in nontraditional states and cities." Furthermore, in less urbanized states such as New Hampshire, there is a secondary diasporic pattern of movement to suburban areas. Latino growth in Hillsborough county (where Manchester is located) was appreciable during the 1990s, and featured individuals with characteristics untypical of Latinos in the traditional settlement areas.

Compared to the rest of the region, New Hampshire's Latinos have a higher ratio of U.S.-born status, and more of them trace their national origin to South America (as opposed to Central America or the Caribbean). Along most demographic and human capital dimensions, New Hampshire's Latinos approximate the characteristics of the mainstream population. Their levels of income, earnings, and asset ownership are higher than for Latinos elsewhere in New England. These are signs of an "emerging middle class" and present opportunities for economic and political contributions to the region.

Up to now we have described several contributions to this volume that have depicted communities of place. Hosffman Ospino (Chapter 9) looks at an important religious community within the Latino experience. His study analyzes the terrain of encounter between the European and Latin American traditions within Catholicism in New England. Latinos are the bearers of "gifts" to the regional church. But often they face resistance to their forms of spirituality, echoing some of the tensions Latinos experience in the political and economic realms. If there is a breach separating the two traditions in the Church, it is not entirely due to mainstream resistance. Ospino suggests that Latin American Catholics may be accustomed to a different way of dealing with the hierarchy, because of "their experience with the clericalist and paternalistic structures of the church in Latin America." They are often surprised to find that in many U.S. congregations, lay members are encouraged to be involved in the internal decision-making process.

Latinos comprise 12 percent of the Catholic Church's following, which is double their share of the region's overall population. Their membership in key urban dioceses, such as Boston and Hartford, is much greater. As in other parts of the country, they embody much of the Church's future. The manner in which this institution adapts to internal demographic change will determine how successfully it retains this important group. In a sense, the Latino Catholic experience serves as a microcosm of the larger society's handling of newcomer "incorporation." Will religious commonalities overcome cultural differences? The culturally sensitive practices of other Christian denominations continue to attract Latinos away from mainstream Catholicism. How will the political and theological fissures in the Church play out for Latinos? What will be the impact on Latino congregants of the controversies over reproductive rights and gay unions? Ospino's study opens the door to consideration of these questions.

The idea that Latin American immigrants continue to maintain ties with the home country, well after they settle in the United States, has been thoroughly documented.[10] The New England experience offers plenty of evidence that transnational linkages are an important element in Latino community formation.

Dominican migration to Waterbury is incentivized not only by the availability of work and housing, but also by the opportunity to accumulate capital for home building back in *La Republica*. Glasser notes this pattern, described by some of her informants. Since migration from the Dominican Republic is more costly than it is from Puerto Rico, Dominicans who come to Waterbury tend to come from a higher economic stratum than Puerto Rican newcomers to the city. They tend to hail from the families of business proprietors, farmers, and ranchers. This is less the case for Puerto Ricans, who (when they arrived in large numbers during the 1960s and 1970s) generally were agricultural laborers recruited to work the fields of New England.

The selectivity of Dominican immigrants, however, did not lead them to seek housing outside of the Latino working class barrios. They preferred to live in the same areas populated by Puerto Ricans, with whom they were culturally familiar, where affordable housing could be attained. Dominicans of relatively upper-class background could stow away resources for a longer-term goal: building their retirement homes back in the Caribbean. Each year these individuals visit their homeland and, with the funds economized, augment their property: home building on the installment plan.

Transnational activity of this sort differs qualitatively from the pattern of sojourner laborers, who work seasonally in a region and often don't return to the same locale. The *bodeguero* in Waterbury is a vital member of the community, residing here throughout the year and often involved in social and political efforts. Compared to his homeland status, this individual has dropped a notch or two in class standing, but these immigrants will accept some downward mobility as part of a rational strategy for security and comfort in later years, when they return to their birthplace.

Connections with their homelands can also draw immigrant communities into the political realm. Several examples of such transnational linkages are described in this collection. During the 1980s, the Salvadoran community in Cambridge and elsewhere was at the center of solidarity movements protesting U.S. intervention in Central America. In Connecticut and Massachusetts, since the 1970s, Puerto Ricans were galvanized by the controversy over the use of Vieques island as a site for bombing practices by the U.S. Navy. In 2004 Waterbury's Dominicans mobilized compatriots to vote, using absentee ballots, in the Dominican national elections. Many Latin American countries—including Brazil—have increased the profile of their consulates in New England, offering immigration counseling and community development assistance. Countries south of the U.S. border are increasingly recognizing that the nationals who live in New England need to be attended to.

## Identity and Politics

Judging by several chapters in this volume, Latino ethnic awareness owes as much to negative experiences in the host society as it does to pride in one's cultural heritage. The idea that society's hostility toward immigrants can foment nationalistic sentiments among newcomers has a long tradition. More recently scholars have shown how this process applies equally to the Hispanic experience in America. New England provides it own examples of this process of "reactive ethnicity."[11]

When Massachusetts's citizens voted overwhelmingly in 2003 to vote in favor of "Question 2," a proposal to eliminate the state's bilingual education programs, Latinos and other linguistic minorities were stunned. They were shocked not so much by the outcome but by the margin of defeat. Was the chasm between Latinos (along with other linguistic minorities) and the mainstream *that* large? Outside of a few cities and towns of liberal leaning, a virtually unanimous sentiment was rendered by the state's majority-white population: it was time to end targeted educational programs for non-English speakers. In the future, after a year of transition, foreign students would be channeled into "immersion" classrooms, where they would be expected to learn the language of the land. The fact that Massachusetts was home to the first publicly supported bilingual education program, established thirty years earlier, was not lost on supporters of English-only initiatives across the country.

Jorge Capetillo and Robert Kramer's assessment of the referendum—based on exit polls, focus group discussions, and media analysis—examines several aspects of this contentious issue (Chapter 13). In their view, English-only proponents exploited mainstream fears of immigrants, and held out the hope that "by ending bilingual education voters might begin to mend the fractures of present day America." Central to the defeat of the program was the expertly organized and well-financed campaign conducted by bilingual education's critics and national figures such as Ron Unz.

It is true that bilingual education's demise was speeded along by an effective campaign drive. Nevertheless, Capetillo and Kramer say, there was a deeper basis for the defeat: an underlying shift in the cultural mood of the majority Massachusetts population. Sympathetic attitudes towards racial/ethnic diversity have been displaced by a concern with large-scale immigration. Today, residents of the Bay State seem to be insisting that newcomers make a commitment to rapid assimilation.

Despite this policy setback, Latinos gained immeasurable experience in the political process. Voter participation increased significantly and their ethnic consciousness appears to have intensified, not waned. Latinos interpreted the vote as a rebuke to their cultural identity, not merely a desire by mainstream voters to rid the state of a costly social program.

For Amílcar Barreto, the dispute over Question 2 illustrates the dangers of mainstream myopia regarding language policy (Chapter 14). New Englanders should look northward, not southward, if they want a glimpse at the problems created by a forced monoculturalism. For decades the French-speaking Quebecois were deemed outsiders in their Canada. They responded by affirming their differences to the point, almost, of formal succession.

"Latino political activism in the northeast developed, for the most part, outside the formal party structure," Barreto argues. The resounding defeat of bilingual education is another instance in which cultural and political obstinacy may encourage minorities to seek redress through unconventional approaches. Much will hinge on the dominant society's attitude toward diversity. "The various forms of future Latino political participation may depend as much on the reactions of the area's majority as on the actions of Latinos themselves."

In his intergenerational study of Dominicans in Rhode Island, José Itzigsohn finds that Spanish-language retention among Latino youth reflects a desire to assert cultural pride in the face of discrimination (Chapter 12). In a departure from the practices of earlier European immigrants, Itzigsohn's interviewees even declare their intention to raise *their* children (the third generation) to be bilingual in Spanish. For the children of immigrants, the Spanish language—and ethnic music, food and celebrations—are used as a "marker of identity." In the U.S. context of discrimination, "maintaining identity symbols like language is in part a form of reactive ethnicity and in part a way of asserting their uniqueness in a plural society where a strong group identity is important for many to forge a strong individual identity."

Dominicans of different generations seem to share a similar worldview: they want to have their children be bilingual, they are critical of U.S. society, and they exhibit "transnational attachments" to the Dominican Republic. Yet the daily practices emanating from this common outlook differ across the generations. For the U.S.-born cohort, Spanish-language maintenance and fondness for their island are symbolic expressions. These practices are less ingrained in concrete living than they are for the first generation. The original immigrants rely on Spanish as their language of birth and speak it daily, and they connect to the homeland through political and economic activities.

For the second generation, "the attachment to Spanish and to a transnational identity are part of asserting their place and identity in the United States." The United States, which to them "feels like home," is the main context for their daily practices, even if its values seem to be at variance with their worldview. Itzigsohn concludes that the path of second-generation Dominican incorporation "combines strong critical views of mainstream society, strong pan-ethnic and transnational attachments, and middle-class aspirations."

Once again, we see how Latino ethnic formation emerges from both negative and affirmative forces.

Pantojas' study of Latino political opinion and behavior in Connecticut is premised on the notion that racial/ethnic minorities are aware of their politically disadvantaged status (Chapter 10). They therefore tend to be alienated regarding formal governmental structures. He draws on the "political empowerment" thesis to test the argument that, only through the election of Latinos and Latinas to public office (that is, the increase in "ascriptive representation"), will mainstream political institutions gain the community's trust and participation.

There is plenty of evidence that Connecticut's Latinos feel separated from the political system, according to Pantojas' analysis of survey data. The results reveal cynicism toward political officials and political parties, whether in their home state or in Washington, DC. "These are troubling findings, since these orientations are often associated with political apathy or participation in other antidemocratic behaviors."

There are two interesting additional results of this study. First, that among the state's second-generation Latinos there is even greater distrust of government than among immigrant Latinos. Second, that cynicism toward certain political institutions is greater among those with higher levels of education. It appears that increased exposure to the system undermines confidence in it.

José Cruz provides another perspective on Latino participation in the arena of formal politics (Chapter 11). The author reports on his interviews of a dozen Latino political leaders in Connecticut. The bulk of Latino leadership is Puerto Rican, reflecting the fact that Connecticut is the state with the highest share of Puerto Rican population. In the few instances of elected officials of other Latino origins, even these were dependent on the Puerto Rican electorate, which combines citizenship status with longest residency in the area. Cruz goes so far as to say that, in the case of Connecticut, "the pan-ethnic category (of Latinos) is not much more than an artificial label for what are essentially Puerto Rican politics."

One might assume a certain convenience in connection with this virtual dominance of a single group within the Latino polity. There would be no need for constant negotiation among the Latino partners as they try to forge pan-Latino collaboration. Cruz argues, however, that the Puerto Rican–dominated leadership has not succeeded in building an effective statewide presence. For example, the majority of his informants (all are elected officials) do not view coalition building as a requirement for political success. And he finds that there is no "systematic effort...to coordinate and share resources, ideas, and strategies among themselves."

In the end, the author says, there is not much of a basis for optimism. Despite the achievements at the local level, where a number of cities and towns have elected Latinos into government, there has not emerged a coherent policy agenda or strategy for action at a broader level. This would require a deliberate and focused approach on unifying Latinos internally, and reaching out to natural allies. In the meantime, Cruz is concerned that "Latinos achieve political representation but are not able to address the basic needs of the community.... [They] seem unable to impact the socioeconomic status of Latinos as a whole."

## Inter-Latino Relations

In their daily lives Hispanic New Englanders of varying nationalities are interacting actively with each other. Recent demographic trends have assured that there will be no single group exercising political and cultural hegemony, as was the case of Puerto Ricans during the 1960s and 1970s. The future development of the community, including the manner of its incorporation or participation in society, is likely to be shaped by the forms of inter-Latino relations. We can reasonably posit that the stronger and more cooperative are these relations, the less likely Latinos will pursue the traditional assimilationist path. There are a number of examples of Latino interconnectivity identified in this collection.

As community-based organizations were formed in the context of the War on Poverty during the 1960s and 1970s, Puerto Ricans were the primary actors. Agencies like Concilio Hispano, based in Cambridge, were a leading force for social change and a center of Puerto Rican and Dominican activity (Chapter 6). By the 1980s, Concilio's clientele increasingly mirrored the shift toward Central Americans that was taking place in Cambridge. Reagan-era politics frowned on advocacy and forced a transformation in Concilio's original mission, from grass roots organizing to direct social service. The capacity to implement even this latter role was reduced by budgetary cuts, and with each passing year the organization faced tighter constraints.

Within the context of a single organization, the process of Latino succession was occurring. Yet it would be erroneous to imagine a sharp break between the two phases (Puerto Rican–Dominican to Central American). As long as Concilio was a "player" in city politics and could wield at least some resources, the earlier group of Latinos continued to relate to it. Until the early 2000s, for example, the board chairwoman was a Puerto Rican.

Waterbury's Puerto Ricans had established church and social clubs in the early years of the community (Chapter 4). In time Dominicans and other Latinos arrived, joining them and participating in congregations such as of St. Cecilia's. Religious celebrations gradually took on a more diverse flavor, with observation of non–Puerto Rican symbols and dates. Hosffman Ospino's discussion of Catholics in New England (Chapter 9) also illustrates the multi-Latino character of religious communities.[12]

As with community based organizations and churches, businesses also serve as settings for inter-Latino relations. For evidence of this claim, we can again look to the studies on Waterbury and Cambridge in this collection. In the Waterbury case, Glasser shows that as Dominicans took over Puerto Rican businesses, they astutely marketed themselves with a generic identity. For example, El Utuadeño and Borinquen Grocery were replaced by Hispano and Las Colinas. Bodegas were decorated with an array of national flags. To capture a broader, more variegated Latino demographic, businesses need to cast a wider net.

In Cambridge the Dominican owners of a travel agency and a moving company used a reverse strategy. During the 1970s, when Puerto Ricans were the largest Latino group, they opted to give their businesses a Puerto Rican name (La Borincana).

Because they share certain affinities with Spanish-speaking immigrants, Brazilians are often included within the designation of Hispanic or Latino. Is this appropriate? Are these newcomers, who have come to populate areas of New England in significant numbers, to be considered an integral part of the Latino community? Siqueira and Laurenço review these and other questions in their assessment of the Brazilian immigration to Massachusetts (Chapter 8).

According to the authors' interviews with students and workers, Brazilians do not view themselves as "Latino" or "Hispanic." Like many, if not most Latinos, their primary reference point as to ethnicity is their nationality: Brazilians. However, they are unlike Salvadorans, Dominicans, Mexicans, and Puerto Ricans who are adopting the Latino rubric as a second-level identifier. And even though the Portuguese-speaking Brazilians find themselves working side by side with other Latinos in service and light manufacturing jobs, they tend not to enter into social relations with them.

There are several possible reasons for this cultural breach. First, and most obvious, is language. Secondly, it appears that Brazilians may want to distance themselves socially from Hispanics, whom they perceive as targets of hostility and discrimination by the dominant society. They even manifest some of the same stereotypes about Latinos that are held by the majority population. Siqueira and Laurenço also examine the Brazilians' perplexity concerning U.S. racial identification and note their resistance to accepting the "white" versus "black" dichotomy. Might it be that this resistance to being pigeonholed into U.S. racial categories is linked to avoidance of membership in the "Latino" group? After all, the logic and provenance of the latter label are likely more ambiguous to new arrivals on the U.S. scene. The authors acknowledge Brazilians wariness about accepting the Latino label, but regard this an open question that will only be resolved as the community figures out its place in U.S. society.

## Pan-Latinismo

There has been a virtual cottage industry generating studies on the question of Latino identity formation. Several scholars argue that movement toward a pan-Latino identity has taken hold during the last decades, inspired by a complex of political and commercial forces.[13] Others dismiss this trend as artificially imposed from external sources and as lacking substantive meaning at the community level.[14] Resistance to an umbrella term grouping Latinos is independent of political ideology. On the right or the left can be found writers who doubt the veracity or utility of the notion.[15]

Skepticism is based on several arguments. The sheer diversity in nationality, ethnic/racial traits, and linguistic characteristics preclude a "Latino/a label." Differences in class background among the various groups are too severe to allow for a common Latino identity. Variations in citizenship status are prevalent (from undocumented to legal resident to citizen), undermining a coherent political vision. Political differences among the three major subgroups (Mexican, Puerto Rican, and Cuban)—originating in differences in origin of immigration—invalidate the notion of a Hispanic voting bloc at the national level. Inter-Latino relations can be problematic in settings of intense competition for resources and power: for example, in higher education institutions, in the domains of immigration and language policy, and in local politics. In the case of Puerto Ricans, submersion into a Hispanic identity threatens a perceived historical unity with African Americans, and also implies a diminution, even elimination, of blackness from their identity.[16]

Despite these doubts the idea of a pan-Latino identity seems here to stay. Explanations abound. (1) Notwithstanding their internal differences, Latinos continue to embrace the "Latino" or "Hispanic" label when speaking generally of their condition and aspirations within U.S. society. Although ethnic-specific terminology (e.g., Mexican American, Chicano, Puerto Rican, Dominican) is preferred, "Latino/Hispanic" is accepted as an additional identifier. (2) The structure of North American thinking about racial identity compels Hispanic-origin peoples to define themselves in a pan-Latino sense or be dissolved ultimately into the black-white racial order. (3) Racial categorization systems used by government agencies give Latino political activists a practical reason to assert a pan-ethnic identity when making claims for a greater share of resources and representation.[17]

Additional explanations have been advanced in defense of the generic terminology. (4) In large metropolitan settings some groups (e.g., Puerto Ricans in New York City) have adopted an "instrumentalist use" of Hispanic identity to strengthen their political standing. (5) This phenomenon gives credence to the idea that identity formation can be fluid and situational; that it is no longer remarkable to observe Latinos living comfortably with multiple identities, since such identities are formed and transformed in dynamic engagement with America's evolving cultural debates and with changing official definitions of race. (6) Finally, the growth of Latino diversity in an increasing number of urban settings creates the demographic basis for the forging of pan-Latino identity.[18]

The chapters in this book offer evidence, historically and contemporaneously, of pan-Latinismo as a vibrant force in New England. In their daily lives—and in their social, economic, and political activities—Latinas and Latinos transcend the bounds of ethnicity and interact vigorously with each other. In their engagement with the larger society and institutions, they are forging an autonomous identity that stands intermediate between their native nationalities and the dominant U.S. culture. In their encounter with the U.S. racial order, they are staking out a territory that blurs and complicates the color line.

The sources of this pan-Latino identity are various:

- the diversity of Latino ethnicities and the lack of a clearly hegemonic group within the Latino population;
- the history of extensive inter-Latino relations and practices, strengthened and channeled by organizations and institutions which are reproduced over time;
- the dominant society's resistance to the inclusion of Latinos in the region's social and economic structures.

As mentioned above, studies have identified a number of potential obstacles to a Pan Latino identity. For the time being, however, none of these countervailing forces—class fractures, racial background, ethnic heritage, political orientation, citizenship status, differential incorporation into society—appear to threaten its continued development. These factors surely undermine any notion of Latinas and Latinos operating as a monolithic block within U.S. society. Yet cultural identity and political pragmatism seems to be overriding the centrifugal forces.

## Conclusion

Perhaps it is more useful to think of pan-Latinismo as a transitional identity, occupying a unique and temporary space within the U.S. social and racial order. It is a powerful idea, adopted by millions of people as they define and pursue collective aspirations.

And what might those aspirations be? Winning the race for socio-economic achievement, perhaps with "model minority" status? Incorporation into a vaguely defined "mainstream"? Acceptance by the mainstream society of Latino cultural symbols and political representation, even at the cost of continued class inequality and racial exclusion?

I believe the underlying assumption of most contributors to this volume is that none of these aforementioned aspirations is satisfactory. They would say, I think, that the truly distinctive achievement would be one in which Latinas and Latinos help nudge America in the direction of a society that is more egalitarian and more respectful of multicultural values. Today the people of this country, in New England and elsewhere, are asked to choose between an "ownership society" and a "fairness" society. The forms of community life, the expressions of cultural identity, and the strategies of political action that Latinos adopt must ultimately address these competing visions of the future.

This introductory overview has discussed some of the central themes running through this volume, but not all. In the interests of brevity, I have neglected several topics that are covered in greater depth by the contributors, such as socioeconomic trends at the state and local level, social and economic policy debates and recommendations, and proposals for community development and political action. For an appreciation of these themes, and to gain a fuller sense of what is happening in New England, the reader is invited to proceed on to the next pages.

## Notes

1. Robert Miller, *Shamrock and Sword: The St. Patrick's Battalion in the U.S.-Mexican War* (University Press of Oklahoma, 1989); George Winston Smith and Charles Judah, *Chronicles of the Gringos: The U.S. Army in the Mexican War, 1846–1848* (Albuquerque: University of New Mexico Press, 1968); Peter F. Stevens, *The Rogue's March: John Riley and the St. Patrick's Battalion, 1846–1848* (Dulles, Virginia: Potomac Books, 1999). Thanks to Mary Jo Marion for bringing my attention to the story of the San Patricios.

2. Lawrence Buell, *Emerson* (Cambridge, Harvard University Press, 2003), 137, 243, and 249; José Martí, *Selected Writings*, ed. Ester Allen (New York: Penguin, 2002), 116–129; Philip S. Foner, ed., *Inside the Monster by José Martí* (New York: Monthly Review Press, 1975), 30.

3. My thanks to Anthony de Jesús for providing a copy of Albizu Campos's student records, which Harvard University recently made available to the public. The letter cited, "Puerto Rico and the War," appeared in the *Harvard Crimson*, April 14, 1917; 2, 7. For more on the life and politics of Albizu Campos see Juan Manuel Carrión, Teresa C. Gracia Ruiz, and Carlos Rodríguez Fraticelli, eds., *La nación puertorriqueña: ensayos en torno a Pedro Albizu Campos* (San Juan: Editorial de la Universidad de Puerto Rico, 1993); Ronald Fernandez, *The Disenchanted Island: Puerto Rico and the United States in the Twentieth Century* (Westport, CN: Praeger, 1996).

4. Some readers will be justifiably surprised to find that there is no chapter dedicated to Boston. On the one hand, the Boston Latino experience is inevitably addressed in the several chapters dealing with Massachusetts. On the other hand, there is a significant body of scholarship about Boston over the years, and the contributor response to the editor's original call for papers was heavily skewed toward non-Bostonian contexts. Yet there certainly is room for more work on Boston, and the editor is happily aware of new scholarship in the pipeline. Recent political developments, such as Felix Arroyo's historic victory in 2003 as the first Latino elected to the Boston City Council, call for scholarly analysis. Arroyo surprised most pundits by winning an at-large seat, essentially by tapping into a broad and progressive multiracial constituency. In so doing, he became the biggest Latino vote-getter in Massachusetts history. Michael Jonas, "Arroyo Singing a Song of Reelection," *Boston Globe*,

January 16, 2005. In the same year, Jeffrey Sánchez's election as a State Representative meant that Boston's Latinos would have a voice in the State House for the first time since Nelson Merced's term in the late 1980s. Sánchez's strategy, also dependent on coalition politics, offers another case study of how Latinos can gain electoral power. Despite differences in political orientation, Arroyo and Sánchez each demonstrated that success depends on a creative relationship between ethnicity, pan-Latino identity, and multiracial politics. How each approached class aspects in their program was also an important factor. Finally, it should be noted that State Senator Jarrett Barrios, the most influential Latino politician in Massachusetts, receives considerable support from Boston's Latinos. Though his electoral district is based in Cambridge and Chelsea, he is a significant figure in Boston's Latino politics. As this book goes to press, Senator Barrios is running for District Attorney of Middleset County, often a steppingstone to a statewide office.

5. As of this writing (2006) there is no doubt that the one million mark has been passed, even if the 60 percent growth rate of the 1990s is not replicated. Projections of the national Latino population during the early 2000s estimate that the growth rate continues unabated. Roberto Ramírez, *U.S. Hispanic Population 2002* (U.S. Census Bureau, Population Division, Ethnicity and Ancestry Branch, 2003). Daniel Vásquez prepared the census profiles that give Latino population counts for the region, the six states, and some fifty cities and towns in New England. The sources for these counts are U.S. Census, 1990 and 2000, SF-3 Data. Unless otherwise noted, the discussion in this section is based on these tables, which can be consulted at http://www.gaston.umb.edu/resactiv/index.html.

6. Population figures for the region and states that are cited in other chapters of this book may vary slightly from these, since they may have been based on different sources within the series of the census 2000 releases.

7. The Lewis Mumford Center for Comparative Urban and Regional Research reported that the wording of the Census's "Hispanic Origin" question led to "a highly inflated number of uncategorized 'other Hispanics.'" http://mumford1.dydndns.org/cen2000/HispanicPop/HspPopData.htm (accessed February 16, 2005). For another estimate of the "Other" population, Roberto Suro, "Counting the 'Other Hispanics': How Many Colombians, Dominicans, Ecuadorians, Guatemalans and Salvadorans Are There in the United States?" (Washington DC: Pew Hispanic Center, May 2002).

8. Daniel Vásquez, "Latinos in New England," unpublished paper, Mauricio Gastón Institute, University of Massachusetts Boston (February, 2004).

9. This introduction uses the term *community formation* in a generic sense, to refer simply to the evolution and consolidation of U.S. Latino communities over time. This definition ignores the controversies over the contested interpretations of this and related concepts such as "community development" and "community empowerment." Useful discussions of this literature include William V. Flores and Rina Benmayor, eds., *Latino Cultural Citizenship: Claiming Identity, Space and Rights* (Beacon Press, 1997), 72–76; Carol Hardy-Fanta, *Latina Politics, Latino Politics* (Temple University Press, 1993), 99–102; Michael Jones-Correa, *Between Two Nations: The Political Predicament of Latinos in New York City* (Cornell University Press, 1998), 20–21; and George Yúdice, "Community," in *New Keywords: A Revised Vocabulary of Culture and Society*, ed. Tony Bennett, Lawrence Grossberg, and Meaghan Morris (Oxford: Blackwell Publishing, 2005), 51–54.

10. Robert C. Smith, "Mexicans in New York: Membership and Incorporation in a New Immigrant Community," in *Latinos in New York: Communities in Transition*,

ed. Gabriel Haslip-Viera and Sherrie L. Baver (Notre Dame: Notre Dame University Press, 1996); Ramona Hernández and Glenn Jacobs, "Beyond Homeland Politics: Dominicans in Massachusetts," in *Latino Politics in Massachusetts: Struggles, Strategies, and Prospects*, ed. Carol Hardy-Fanta and Jeffrey Gerson (New York: Routledge, 2002); Peggy Levitt, *The Transnational Villagers* (Berkeley: University of California Press, 2001). For an explanation of why the new immigrants are likely to retain transnational attachments more so than earlier (European) immigrants to the United States, see Peggy Levitt, "Migrants Participate across Borders: Toward an Understanding of Forms and Consequences," in *Immigration Research for a New Century*, ed. Nancy Foner, Rubén G. Rumbaut, and Steven J. Gold (New York: Russell Sage Foundation, 2000).

11. "This process of forging reactive ethnicity in the face of perceived threats, persecution, and exclusion is not uncommon. . . . it is one mode of ethnic identity formation, highlighting the role of a hostile context of reception in accounting for the rise rather than erosion of ethnicity." Alejandro Portes and Rubén G. Rumbaut, *Legacies: The Story of the Immigrant Second Generation* (Berkeley: University of California Press, 2001), 148. Also see Alejandro Portes and Ruben G. Rumbaut, *Immigrant America: A Portrait* (Berkeley, University of California Press, 1996), 95.

12. For a case study of a Catholic church in Willimantic, Connecticut, see X. A. Reyes, *Language and Culture as Critical Elements in Qualitative Research* (Lewiston, NY: Mellen Press, forthcoming 2006). Based in Boston, La Congregación León de Judah is one of the largest evangelical Latino churches in New England and features "a very diverse sector of the Hispanic community . . . Practically all the countries of Hispanic America are represented in its congregation, and the leadership includes a broad range of nationalities and cultures . . . ." http://leondejuda.org. For an account of how Puerto Ricans and Colombians found themselves pitted against each other in different local Catholic churches (in Lowell, Massachusetts), see Jeffrey N. Gerson, "Latino Migration, the Catholic Church and Political Division" in Hardy-Fanta and Gerson, *Latino Politics in Massachusetts*, 2002.

13. Antonia Darder and Rodolfo D. Torres, "Latinos and Society: Culture, Politics and Class," in *The Latino Studies Reader: Culture, Economy and Society*, ed. Antonia Darder and Rodolfo D. Torres (Oxford: Blackwell, 1998); Richard Delgado and Jean Stefancic, *The Latino/a Condition: A Critical Reader* (New York: New York University Press, 1998).

14. Arlene Dávila, *Latinos, Inc.: The Marketing and Making of a People* (Berkeley: University of California Press, 2001); Vilma Santiago-Irizarry, *Medicalizing Ethnicity: The Construction of Latino Ethnicity in a Psychiatric Setting* (Ithaca: Cornell University Press, 2001).

15. On the right, Linda Chavez, *Out of the Barrio* (New York: Basic Books, 1991); on the left, Juan Flores, "Pan-Latino/Trans-Latino: Puerto Ricans in the 'New Nueva York,'" *CENTRO Journal* 8, nos. 1–2 (1996); in between, Harry Pachon and Louis DeSipio, *New Americans by Choice: Political Perspectives of Latino Immigrants* (Boulder, CO: Westview Press, 1994).

16. On diversity: Suzanne Oboler, *Ethnic Labels, Latino Lives* (Minneapolis: University of Minnesota Press, 1995). On class: Chavez, *Out of the Barrio*, Chapter 8, and Martha Giménez, "Latino Politics—Class Struggles: Reflections on the Future of Latino Politics," in *Latino Social Movements*, ed. R. Torres and G. Katsiaficas (New York: Routledge, 1999). On citizenship status: Harry Pachon and Louis DeSipio, *New Americans by Choice: Political Perspectives of Latino Immigrants* (Bolder: Westview

Press, 1994). On political differences: Rodolfo De la Garza, Louis DeSipio, F. Chris García, John García, and Angelo Falcón, *Latino Voices: Mexican, Puerto Rican and Cuban Perspectives on American Politics* (Boulder: Westview Press, 1992); and José Cruz, "In Search of Latino Politics," review of Rodney Hero, *Latinos in the U.S. Political System*, in *Latino Review of Books* 1, no. 1 (1995). On inter-Latino relations in immigration and language policy: R. De La Garza et al., *Latino Voices*. On local politics: Jones-Correa, *Between Two Nations*, Chapter 6. On Puerto Ricans and African Americans: Juan Flores, "Pan-Latino/Trans-Latino: Puerto Ricans in the 'New Nueva York,'" *CENTRO Journal* 8, nos. 1–2 (1996). On blackness in the Puerto Rican identity: Raquel Z. Rivera, *New York Ricans From the Hip Hop Zone* (New York: Palgrave MacMillan, 2003), 32–33.

17. On the openness to multiple identities: Jones-Correa, *Between Two Nations*, 117–119. On Latino identity and the U.S. racial order: Gerald Torres, "The Legacy of Conquest and Discovery: Meditations on Ethnicity, Race and American Politics," in *Borderless Borders: U.S. Latinos, Latin Americans, and the Paradox of Interdependence*, ed. Frank Bonilla, Edwin Meléndez, Rebecca Morales, and María de los Angeles Torres (Philadelphia, Temple University Press, 1998). On racial categorization systems: John García, *Latino Politics in America: Community, Culture and Interests* (Lanham, MD: Rowman & Littlefield, 2003).

18. On "instrumentalist use": Jones-Correa, *Between Two Nations*, Chapter 6. On the fluidity of identity formation: Clara Rodríguez, *Changing Race: Latinos, the Census and the History of Ethnicity in the United States* (New York: New York University Press, 2000), 7 and following. On Latino urban diversity and social practice: Milagros Ricourt and Ruby Danta, *Hispanas de Queens: Latino Pan Ethnicity in a New York City Neighborhood* (Ithaca: Cornell University Press, 2003); Augustín Lao-Montes and Arlene Dávila, eds., *Mambo Montage: The Latinization of New York* (New York: Columbia University Press, 2001); and José Itzigsohn, "The Formation of Latino and Latina Pan ethnic Identities," in *Not Just Black and White*, ed. Nancy Foner and George M. Frederickson (New York: Russell Sage Foundation, 2004), 197–216.

# Part I

# Demographic Trends, Socioeconomic Issues

# 1 Latino New England: An Emerging Demographic and Economic Portrait

Enrico A. Marcelli and Phillip J. Granberry

## Introduction

Three recent demographic developments have generated concerns about the likelihood of continued historic immigrant socioeconomic integration, and more generally, of future ethno-racial relations in the United States.[1] First, approximately 30 million new foreign-born residents (immigrants) settled in the United States during the past three decades—a flow figure that is almost identical to the number who arrived during the last great wave of immigration between 1880 and 1930.[2] In terms of the total stock of immigrants residing in the country, however, the 31.1 million immigrants enumerated in the 2000 U.S. Census represented a smaller proportion (11.1 percent) of the total population than the approximately ten million (or 13.6 percent) in 1900.[3] Second, whereas most immigrants a century ago came from southern and eastern Europe, since the 1960s most have come from Asia, Mexico, and other Latin American countries. Correspondingly, while the racially self-identified black population rose only slightly between 1970 and 2000 (from 11.1 percent to 12.3 percent of the total U.S. population), the white population declined from 87.4 percent to 75.1 percent, and those in the residual "Other" category, which includes many Latinos, increased from 1.4 percent to 12.5 percent.[4] Third, in addition to immigrants' rising numbers and greater national ethno-racial diversity, during the 1990s newcomers increasingly settled in nontraditional immigrant destination states (i.e., outside of California, Texas, New York, Illinois, New Jersey, and Florida) in both nonestablished Latino immigrant metropolitan areas such as Providence, Rhode Island, and Charlotte, North Carolina, and in the suburbs of traditional Latino immigrant receiving areas, such as southern California, and of nontraditional Latino immigrant receiving areas, such as the Boston metropolitan area.[5] For instance, although the percent of foreign-born Latinos in the six New England states grew only moderately (32 percent) compared to most states during the past decade, the proportion grew equally or almost as fast as two of the six leading destination states (i.e., Texas and New York). As of 2000 fully one-third (Maine) to one-half (Connecticut, Massachusetts, New Hampshire, Rhode Island) of all Latino foreign-born residents had lived in the United States for less than a decade; and the foreign-born constituted from 15 percent (Maine) to 46 (Rhode Island) percent of all Latino residents.[6]

At a time when a number of states—most notably Massachusetts and Connecticut in New England—are threatened by overall population decline, public opinion about how these three emerging demographic patterns will affect economic growth, community well-being, and ethno-racial relations is conflicted. Some fear that the rising proportion of Latino and other non-Anglo residents in New England will present formidable fiscal and complicated cultural challenges; others emphasize that minorities (especially foreign-born workers) are playing an important economic role in regional production and in serving an increasingly aging non-Latino white population. Although immigrants constitute less than 30 percent of the Massachusetts population, for instance, they were responsible for more than 80 percent of the state's labor force growth during the past decade.[7]

This does not suggest that all foreign-born workers fare well in their host community's labor market. It has been argued, for example, that more than labor market opportunities stimulates Dominican immigration to New York City and that immigrants do not always succeed as predicted by conventional rational choice or structural theoretical frameworks.[8] Whatever the threat of population aging and decline in New England on perceptions of how Latinos are likely to impact the region and regardless of whether these newcomers conform to conventional modes of scholarly thought concerning socioeconomic integration—increases in the absolute number of newcomers, rising ethno-racial heterogeneity, and a greater residential dispersion among immigrants—these are the three broad demographic changes that are having, and will continue to have, cultural, economic, and political effects in New England and throughout the nation.

The discussion that follows is divided into five sections. The first part gives a brief historical overview of the importance of immigration for population growth throughout the United States by major geographic region. In the subsequent section we estimate the contribution of Latino immigrants to population growth in New England compared to the state of New York from 1850 to 2000, and the changing representation of particular Latino populations in New England and New York between 1990 and 2000.[9] Then, demographic patterns among the principal Latino groups are identified for the 1990–2000 period. Section four is an economic portrait, depicting various outcomes among the main Latino subpopulations in New England relative to non-Latino ethno-racial groups. We conclude with policy and social implications of these changing demographic and economic patterns, and suggest several directions for future research.

## Historical and Recent Contribution of Immigration to U.S. and Regional Population Growth

Over the long term, a complex set of forces has attenuated U.S. population expansion. Although the shape of the declining population growth rate curve in the United States (down from 25 per 1,000 in 1870–1875 to 10 per 1,000 in 1985–1990) tracked the net immigration rate (which bounced between 10 and less than one per 1,000 from decade to decade prior to World War II), the overall decline in the population growth rate was driven primarily by the fact that the birth rate fell faster (from 40 to 16 per 1,000) than the net immigration rate (from 7 to 3 per 1,000)—and fast enough to offset rising life expectancy. This last pattern of rising life expectancy was reflected in a declining death rate from 22 to 9 per 1,000.[10] The post-World War II population boom that peaked in the late 1950s also mainly followed the up-and-down swing in the birth rate rather than changes in either the net immigration or death rate, both of which have remained relatively flat since the 1940s.[11]

One may still reasonably contend that immigration profoundly augmented U.S. population growth historically—and does so today—even if the foreign-born represent a relatively small proportion of the total U.S. population. Indeed, by 1920 immigrants who entered the United States during the nineteenth century and their descendents had doubled the size of the U.S. population that would have obtained from the colonial stock of 1790 alone. More recently (e.g., between 1980 and 2000) new immigrants (seventeen million)—excluding their U.S.-born children—constituted approximately 31 percent of the total increase of fifty-five million in U.S. population.[12]

This contemporary contribution to U.S. population growth resulted from a comparatively low but slowly climbing net immigration rate moving in the opposite direction of somewhat higher birth and death rates. Two patterns are worth highlighting in this regard. First, just following the 1848 conclusion of the U.S. war with Mexico, New England already had a smaller population than all other major regions in the nation except the West. Second, in addition to contributing significantly to overall U.S. population growth, immigration contributed differently across regions. In other words, varying initial regional population concentrations in 1850 and subsequent net international migration flows

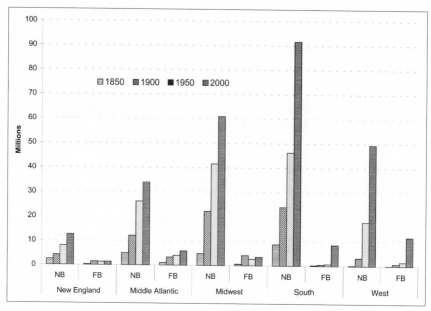

FIGURE 1.1. U.S. population by major region and nativity, 1850–2000.
*Source:* 1850–2000 U.S. Censuses. NB, native born; FB, foreign born.

combined such that population growth in the four other U.S. regions outpaced that of New England. Only New England and the Midwest had fewer foreign-born residents at the end of the twentieth century than at its inception.

Immigration has thus contributed considerably to U.S. population growth since the colonial period—albeit proportionately less in New England compared to other major regions since the mid-nineteenth century. Importantly, Figure 1.1 reminds us that relative to U.S.-born residents, the foreign-born represent a minority population across all major regions in the United States—not only in New England.

## Comparative Population Trends: New England and New York

Demographers and economists in the United States, often at odds with general opinion, have sometimes been concerned more with the insalubrious economic effects of low fertility and population decline than with "overpopulation." This was true especially as the infant nation was attempting to establish its political economic independence as the period of industrialization intensified following the Civil War and leading up to World War II.[13] But this real or perceived expert-lay difference of opinion is no longer as apparent. The public, or at least the media and policy-makers, are beginning to acknowledge that population decline is not ne-cessarily desirable, and conversely, that population stabilization or growth is potentially advantageous economically and politically.

During a recent period of economic expansion (1995–2000), for in-stance, Massachusetts lost almost fifty-five thousand U.S.-born residents of whom more than one-third had graduated from college. Were it not for the influx of about two hundred thousand immigrants, of whom almost thirty-four thousand were college graduates, the state would have experi-enced population decline and a net outflow of college-educated workers.[14]

Immigrants—regardless of their cultural, educational, or linguistic background—have historically added to New England's overall population and have therefore augmented demand for goods and services produced by others. But because of differences in labor force participation, some im-migrant flows are likely to have a greater economic impact than others.

Below we provide a demographic sketch of the characteristics of the ten largest Latino subpopulations in New England. Two notes regarding the following discussion are warranted. First, we conduct a New York–New England comparison for illustrative purposes, cognizant that a state-level perspective has its limits. It may be that metropolitan-area comparisons more accurately reflect interregional similarities and differences. In the following pages New England Latino patterns are compared with those of New York to provide a benchmark against which to assess how Latinos may be influencing New England, or are likely to in the near future.

Secondly, our coverage of the Latino subgroups focuses on the ten lar-gest populations. This means that the data we describe reflect the char-acteristics of the large majority (88 percent), but not *all* Latinos. For example, the 2000 U.S. Census we employ suggests that the total New England Latino population was 875,377, and that the number of Latinos in the top subpopulation groups we analyze separately was 770,000.

In absolute numbers, Latinos grew more than other ethno-racial groups in New York and New England between 1990 and 2000. Whereas ap-proximately three hundred thousand new Latino residents were counted in the 2000 versus the 1990 U. S. Census in New England among the ten largest Latino subgroups (Figure 1.2), there were approximately 225,000 new non-Latino blacks and Asians, and about ninety-seven thousand fewer non-Latino whites in the region. Overall, and as noted above, the Latino population (largest ten subgroups) grew to almost 770,000 by 2000 in New England.

In New York (Figure 1.3) the story is somewhat different partly because of larger initial population group sizes. The approximately 613,000 new Latino residents constituted fully 58 percent of all 1990–2000 population

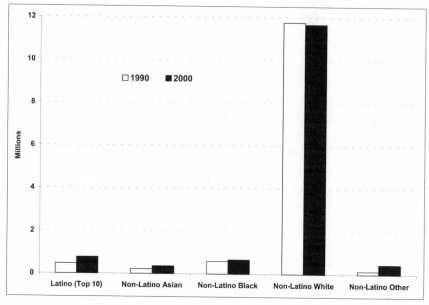

FIGURE 1.2. Population in New England by ethno-racial group, 1990–2000.
*Source:* 1990 and 2000 Census of Population and Housing: 5 percent PUMS.

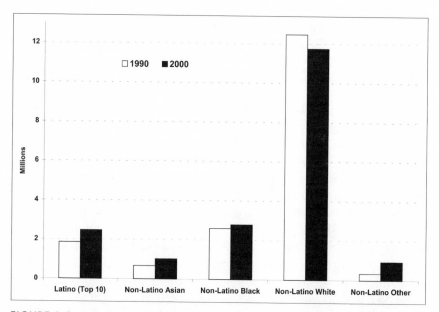

FIGURE 1.3. Population in New York by ethno-racial group, 1990–2000.
*Source:* 1990 and 2000 Census of Population and Housing: 5 percent PUMS.

growth in New York, compared to the 34 percent contribution of non-Latino Asians, the 19 percent contribution of non-Latino blacks, and the 57 percent contribution of non-Latino Other residents who did not self-identify with a racial category. The number of non-Latino whites—as in New England—actually fell by 715,000 and thus negatively impacted population growth by 68 percent. In conclusion, Latinos drove population growth in both New England and New York, and in New England more than offset the decline in the non-Latino white population.

As a first step toward assessing the current and potential socioeconomic integration of Latinos in New England, we distinguish by country of birth, state of residence, age, gender composition, and marital status. Each of these demographic characteristics may be associated with the likelihood of success in the formal labor market.

Two observations are worth noting at the outset. First, although persons included in the top ten Latino subgroups in New England represented a relatively small fraction (5.5 percent) of the total population (ranging from less than 1 percent in Maine and Vermont to 8.5 percent in Connecticut) in 2000, growth in the number of persons within this group during the 1990s was actually higher (65 percent) than in New York (33 percent)—home to the nation's second leading immigrant gateway city. Second, although the proportion of Latinos in New York rose by 2.7 (from 10.3 to 13.0) percent during the decade and the percent in New England increased by 2.0 (from 3.5 to 5.5), southern New England (Connecticut, Rhode Island, and Massachusetts) experienced a 3.0 percent rise—0.3 percent higher than New York. Conversely, the Latino population in the three northern states of New England (Vermont, New Hampshire, and Maine) rose by only 0.2 percent. The three southern states are similar to New York in terms of how Latinos are influencing population growth, and the three northern states are quite different. In other words, when we think about how Latinos are transforming, and being transformed, in New England we are essentially intimating processes mainly occurring in Connecticut, Rhode Island, and Massachusetts.

To repeat, although a gain of approximately 3 percentage points in terms of their proportion of the total New England population from 1990 to 2000 may seem small, it is useful to remember that New England has a population of some fourteen million and that Latinos constituted more than half of all population growth during the 1990s. Those interested in understanding how New England is changing, therefore, would be remiss to overlook the characteristics and experiences of this emerging population.

Puerto Ricans are the dominant Latino population subgroup in New England and New York, and Dominicans and Mexicans rank second and third in both locations (Figure 1.4). Furthermore, whereas the

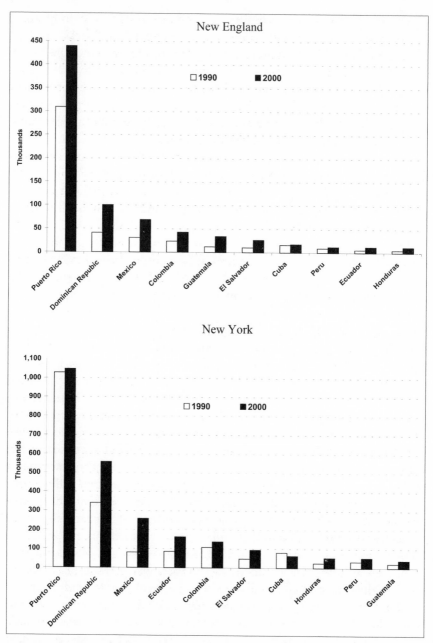

FIGURE 1.4. Top 10 Latino subpopulations, New England and New York, 1990–2000.
*Source:* 1990 and 2000 Census of Population and Housing: 5 percent PUMS.

Puerto Rican population increase was seven times larger in New England than in New York during the 1990s, that of Dominicans was almost four times and that of Mexicans was almost five times greater in New York than in New England. Members of these three national-origin groups constitute approximately two-thirds of the total Latino populations in New England and New York. Finally, New England and New York both had the same top-10 Latino subgroups, and Cubans in New York are the only group having experienced depopulation during the 1990s.

Among the top three Latino populations in New England and New York, Figure 1.5 shows that the proportion born abroad (not in the continental United States) has fallen for those of Puerto Rican ancestry and risen among Dominicans and Mexicans. In New England, furthermore, whereas a minority of Mexicans (43 percent) and Puerto Ricans (48 percent) were born abroad as of 2000, a substantially higher proportion of Dominicans (70 percent) were foreign born. Thus, many more Puerto Ricans and Mexicans are being born in the United States compared to the remaining top ten Latino subpopulations.

## Demographic Patterns: Age, Gender, and Marital Status

An early argument that an increasing population triggers economic growth in developed countries such as the United States was premised on the notion that a larger population places greater demands on resources and thus provides the incentive and capacity for technological advancement. Thus, population growth can create the conditions for ensuring the current standard of living for those longer-term residents accustomed to it and for providing economic opportunities for newcomers.[15] But population growth (either through fertility or migration) has historically been influenced by prior economic conditions as well. The most important conclusion from this literature on the economic-demographic relationship is that it is bidirectional, with the impact of population growth on economic growth determined mainly by the propensity for increased household formation and consumption. In the early 1960s, for instance, although the U.S. economy was growing and those born during or soon after World War II began entering the labor market, socioeconomic conditions had a dissuasive effect on marriage and fertility, aggregate demand, and consequently continued economic growth. This was mainly, according to the Easterlin or "relative income" hypothesis, due to an upsurge in the supply of young adult workers that led to deteriorating earnings opportunities (compared to the previous generation), and a higher average age of marriage and family formation.[16] Alternatively,

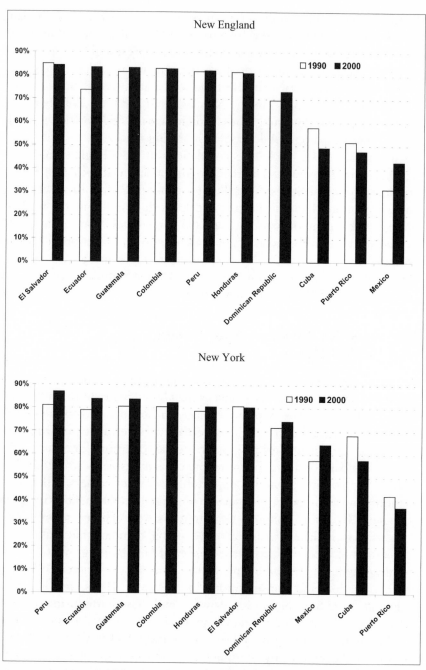

FIGURE 1.5. Percentage of Latinos born outside the continental United States, New England and New York, 1990–2000.
*Source:* 1990 and 2000 Census of Population and Housing: 5 percent PUMS.

before the 1940s, because the international and domestic migrant workers who moved in response to urban labor market opportunities were able to earn more than their parents a generation earlier—and thus had an incentive to marry, have children and spend at a younger age—the demographic feedback effect on longer-term economic growth was positive.

Expressed alternatively, this simply suggests that economic growth is likely to be positively related to the availability of labor force participants who are more likely to form families, have children and spend—those characterized by relatively low elderly dependency ratios—and negatively associated with populations that are comparatively old.

The graphs constituting Figure 1.6 describe child and elderly dependency ratios by ethno-racial group in New England from 1990 to 2000. The child dependency ratio is defined as the number of persons who are less than eighteen years of age divided by the total population of a particular ethno-racial group, and the elderly dependency ratio is the number of persons who are older than sixty-four years of age divided by the total population of a particular ethno-racial group. Latinos among our top ten subgroups collectively had a slightly lower proportion of children (22 percent) than the entire population of New England (24 percent) but a much lower proportion of those older than age sixty-four (3.4 versus 13 percent) in 2000. But there is considerable variation across Latino groups. The three largest Latino groups have relatively high child and low elderly dependency rates, for instance. And whereas those of Puerto Rican descent had the highest child dependency ratios, several Latino groups (e.g., Cubans, Guatemalans, Peruvians, Ecuadorians) and non-Latino whites had significantly lower rates.

Although the population-wide rise in child dependency between 1990 and 2000 was slightly below one percent (0.8) there was considerable variation by ethno-racial group. Asians (−4.1 percent) and the top 10 Latino subgroups (−3.7 percent), for instance, saw their child dependency ratios decline; and non-Latino Caribbean (+11.3), black (+0.7), white (+0.3), and other (+6.0) ethno-racial groups saw theirs rise. The ratio fell by 2.9 percent among the three largest Latino subgroups (Puerto Rico, Dominican Republic, and Mexico).

When one considers the elderly dependency ratio, only Cubans (10.8 percent) come close to the population-wide average of 13 percent in 2000. This average is driven primarily by non-Latino whites, 14.6 percent of whom were above age sixty-four in 2000. All non-Cuban ethno-racial groups have much lower elderly dependency ratios.

Age structure viewed by ethno-racial-group–specific dependency ratios offers only one window into the possible labor market contributions residents of New England are currently making and will make in the

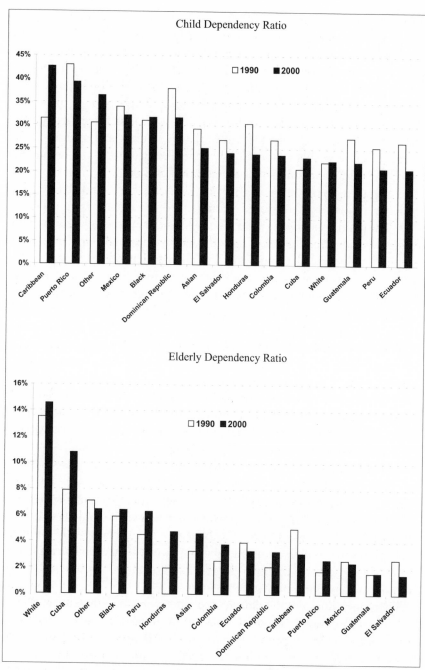

FIGURE 1.6. Dependency ratios by ethno-racial group, New England,
1990–2000.
*Source:* 1990 and 2000 Census of Population and Housing: 5 percent PUMS.

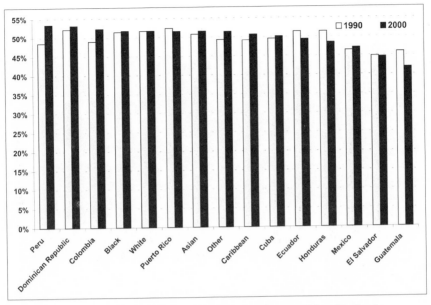

FIGURE 1.7.  Percentage of women by ethno-racial group, New England,
        1990–2000.
*Source:* 1990 and 2000 Census of Population and Housing: 5 percent PUMS.

foreseeable future. We should also consider the likelihood that they will form families, bear children, and contribute to the regional economy in the longer term through their productive activities and consumption patterns.

Gender is another demographic variable that may differentially influence the probability of family formation and labor market participation by ethno-racial group. Compared to age structure, however, Figure 1.7 shows that there is very little change during the 1990s and much less intergroup variation in the proportion of women. The average in both 1990 and 2000 was 53 percent, and the only groups that appear to diverge significantly are Mexicans, Guatemalans, and Salvadorans—each of which has smaller proportions of women on average.

Figure 1.8 suggests that among adults only three ethno-racial groups had above-average rates of marriage—Peruvians and non-Latino Asians and whites. All other group rates were below the 56.2 percent average, and non-Latino blacks and those of Dominican or Puerto Rican background had the lowest rates of marriage.

The relatively low rates among Latinos partly reflect the gender composition differences presented above, but also group-specific age structures. Had we inspected the entire age distribution above we would have seen that although Latinos have relatively more adults of working age

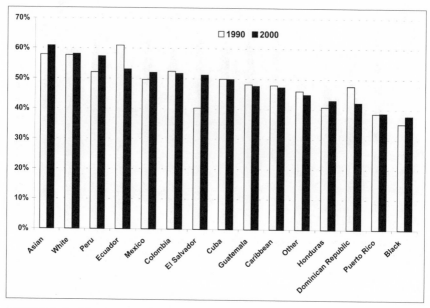

FIGURE 1.8. Marriage rate by ethno-racial group, New England, 1990–2000.
*Source:* 1990 and 2000 Census of Population and Housing: 5 percent PUMS.

(sixteen to sixty-four years), much higher proportions of adults in their ethno-racial groups are under age twenty-four.

Mean age of the entire New England population, for example, was thirty-seven years in 2000. And whereas non-Latino whites (thirty-nine years) had an above-average mean age, all other groups had lower-than-average mean ages. The top ten Latino groups (twenty-seven years) had the lowest mean ages.

If marriage and family formation tend to lag entry into adulthood and the formal labor market as noted earlier, then this represents one potential explanation of why all Latino groups have lower mean marriage rates.

## An Economic Portrait: Education, Labor Participation, Employment, Occupation, Earnings, and Home Ownership

In this section we investigate the economic position of Latinos in New England by analyzing their educational attainment and various employment and occupational patterns. The analytical separation of individual characteristics into demographic and economic categories is somewhat arbitrary, but education, labor force participation, employment status, occupation, earnings, and home ownership are six that researchers often associate more with labor market and overall economic outcomes. We therefore consider these in the current rather than in the previous section, but lay no claim that variables in these two categories are in reality unconnected.

Figure 1.9 illustrates that Cubans, Peruvians, and non-Latino Asians and whites have above-average educational attainment. All remaining ethno-racial groups have high school completion rates that are lower than the population average of 37.6 percent. And among the three largest Latino groups in New England, those of Dominican and Puerto Rican origin had very low proportions having a high school education as of 2000.

Although much attention is given by the media and scholars to the undesirable aspects of increasing numbers of less educated residents, labor economists are soundly ambiguous regarding the impact such persons will have in particular labor markets. While less-educated newcomers may compete with less-educated longer-term residents, this is not necessarily the case, and the fact that the former may complement the education and skills of most working-age residents in New England may override any detrimental wage or employment effects in the aggregate. This, of course, is a topic of considerable debate and of little unemotional research and discussion.[17] For now, we simply highlight the intergroup educational differences as of the last U.S. Census and subsequently consider several important labor market outcomes.

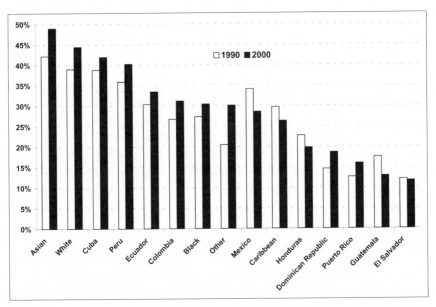

FIGURE 1.9. High school or more education by ethno-racial group, New England, 1990–2000.
*Source:* 1990 and 2000 Census of Population and Housing: 5 percent PUMS.

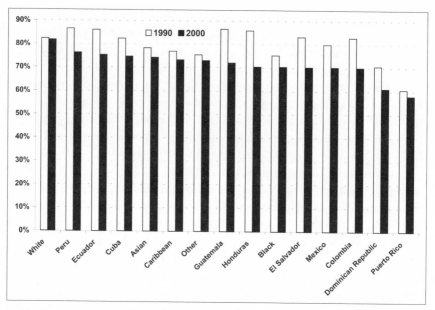

FIGURE 1.10. Labor force participation by ethno-racial group, New England, 1990–2000.
*Source:* 1990 and 2000 Census of Population and Housing: 5 percent PUMS.

As depicted in Figure 1.10, all ethno-racial groups had lower labor force participation rates compared to non-Latino whites in 2000. On average, fully 82 percent of non-Latino whites and 80 percent of all New Englanders aged sixteen to sixty-four who were not in school were either employed or unemployed (but not characterized as outside the labor force due to giving up the search or other reasons). Puerto Ricans and Dominicans, however, had the lowest labor force participation rates among all New Englanders with 58 and 61 percent respectively. These relatively low rates are likely to be related to the comparatively high child dependency (Figure 1.6) and female-to-population (Figure 1.7) percentages reported earlier. Analysis of employment rather than labor force participation by ethno-racial group, however, may offer a different story.

One may reasonably argue that a better metric for understanding a group's expected contribution to New England's formal labor markets is the employment rate. This is because the labor force participation ratio incorporates those who may be less likely to work formally due to parenting or home care responsibilities in the denominator (which will have a deflationary effect). The employment ratio, alternatively, excludes from the denominator those who may reasonably be expected to be less likely to work formally.[18] For example, an ethno-racial group with more children to take care of (and therefore with a higher child dependency ratio) is likely to have a lower labor force participation rate simply because of parenting responsibilities. This may also, however, reflect stronger traditional family values or structures.

What is striking about Figure 1.11 is how similar employment rates are across ethno-racial groups and over time. Despite the fact that Dominicans and Puerto Ricans, for instance, remain at the low end of the distribution, fully 90 percent of those one would expect to be employed in a perfect labor market actually were employed. This figure, furthermore, was only slightly lower than all other ethno-racial groups.

The increase in the number of jobs between 1990 and 2000 of 24 percent was unevenly distributed by occupational category. The number of service sector jobs, for instance, more than doubled (rose by 108 percent) and the number of manufacturing sector (blue-collar) jobs declined (by 29 percent).[19] White-collar employment meanwhile increased by 16 percent during the decade.

Partly because of initial (1990) representation in particular job categories, members of various ethno-racial groups were affected differently by this overall reorganization of work away from blue-collar work in New England (Figure 1.12). For instance, except for Cubans, the proportion of

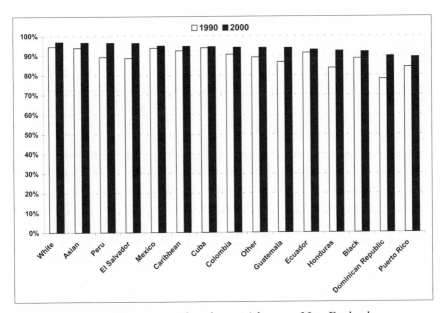

FIGURE 1.11. Employment rate by ethno-racial group, New England, 1990–2000.
*Source:* 1990 and 2000 Census of Population and Housing: 5 percent PUMS.

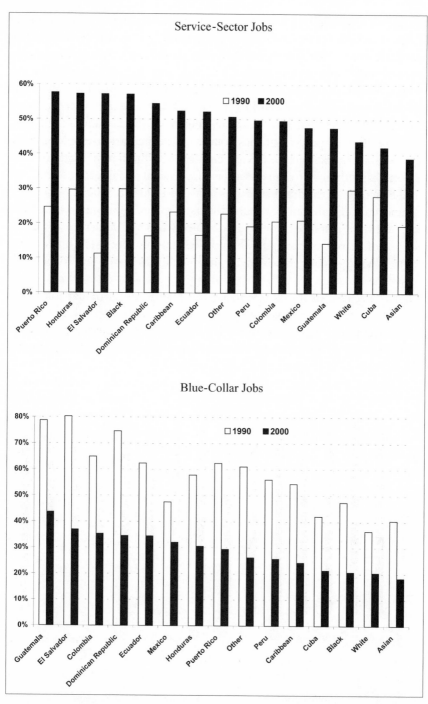

FIGURE 1.12. Occupation by ethno-racial group, New England, 1990–2000.
*Source:* 1990 and 2000 Census of Population and Housing: 5 percent PUMS.

all Latino workers who were employed in service-sector jobs rose faster during the past decade than it did for non-Latino Asians and whites and was higher as of 2000. Conversely, the proportion employed in blue-collar jobs fell faster for almost all Latino groups than it did for non-Latino Asians, blacks, or whites. Finally, non-Latino Asians and whites as well as those of Cuban origin were over-represented in the occupational category not observed here in 2000 ("white collar" jobs).

The different maximum dollar values on the vertical axes of the three graphs constituting Figure 1.13 indicate that those working in white-collar jobs earned considerably higher wages than those in either service-sector or blue-collar jobs regardless of ethno-racial group affiliation.

A second outcome worth highlighting is that with few exceptions Latino workers earned less than other New Englanders across the three categories of employment, in both 1990 and 2000. Only Columbians and Cubans employed in white-collar jobs in 2000 had average hourly earnings that exceeded the mean of this occupational category ($28), only Dominicans and Salvadorians employed in service-sector jobs had average hourly earnings that were higher than the mean in this category ($17), and no Latino group workers earned above the average hourly pay in blue-collar jobs ($17). The only group that had above-average earnings in this last occupational category was non-Latino whites.

Although it is beyond the scope of this chapter to assess their usefulness for Latinos in New England, there are several hypotheses commonly offered to explain differential earnings outcomes. Among these are human capital (e.g., educational attainment, work experience), ability or attitudinal disposition, employer discrimination, preferences, how far one resides from employment centers ("spatial mismatch"), the character of one's job or social networks, and whether a group's skill set matches those needed in the regional labor market. To this list of factors that may influence labor market outcomes might be added relatively precarious residency statuses such as unauthorized immigrant or legal permanent resident.[20]

## Home Ownership

One of the most important uses of earned income and components of the so-called American dream is home ownership. The proportion of all New England residents (e.g., rather than only working age adults who are not in school) who resided in a home they owned or was owned by a family member rose only slightly between 1990 and 2000—from 67 to 68 percent.

Consistent with our finding that Latino workers earned less than others in New England on average during the 1990s is that they were less likely

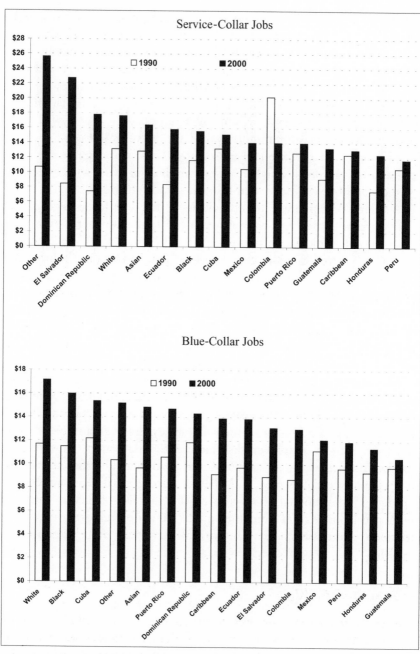

FIGURE 1.13a. Hourly earnings by ethno-racial group, New England, 1990–2000.

*Source:* 1990 and 2000 Census of Population and Housing: 5 percent PUMS.

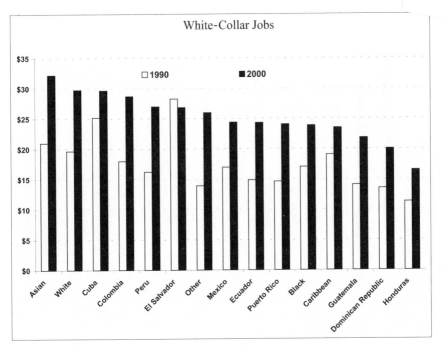

FIGURE 1.13b. (Continued).

to have owned the home in which they resided (Figure 1.14). Those with the smallest proportion owning a home in 2000 were Dominicans (22 percent), Salvadorans (24 percent), and Puerto Ricans (25 percent). Home ownership rates, however, were below average among all groups other than non-Latino whites—74 percent of whom owned their home in 2000.

## Conclusion

We have presented descriptive population and economic statistics for New England by major ethno-racial group (Latino, and non-Latino Asian, black, white, and other) as a first step toward trying to understand the role persons of diverse national-origin backgrounds have played in New England demographically and economically, and how well Latino populations are integrating socioeconomically.

The unprecedented rise in the number of foreign-born residents entering the United States during the past three decades (similar to the number who arrived between 1880 and 1930) has been characterized by a wider geographic dispersion that has helped stabilize New England's population, but also by more ethno-racial heterogeneity—a development which has led some to question the region's ability to integrate newcomers.

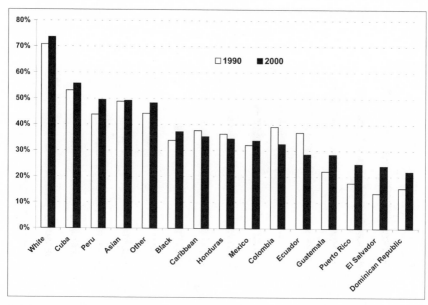

FIGURE 1.14. Homeownership rate by ethno-racial group, New England, 1990–2000.
*Source:* 1990 and 2000 Census of Population and Housing: 5 percent PUMS.

Placing our analysis in the context of how demographer-economists, such as Gunnar Myrdal and Richard Easterlin, have traditionally estimated the effect of population growth on economic well being suggests that populations with relatively young age profiles are more likely to benefit a regional or national economy in both the near and far term. This is because (on the demand side) first marriage and household formation are highly correlated with higher levels of consumption, and (on the supply side) younger adults are likely to be employed and therefore contribute to production.

Employing 1990 and 2000 U.S. Census data, we find that the increase in Latinos was important for reasons other than their proportional contribution to population growth. First, their age profile is more conducive to family formation, child bearing, and spending in the near term. The three largest Latino groups (Puerto Ricans, Dominicans, and Mexicans), for instance, have very low elderly dependency ratios and relatively high but declining child dependency ratios. And although Latino marriage rates are somewhat lower than other groups, this reflects their younger age profile and recent entry into New England's labor markets. In other words, the Latino population is important not only because without them New England's population would have stagnated between

1990 and 2000 but also because of an age profile that intimates future contributions to regional consumption and productivity.

The Latino contribution to regional productivity through employment is another factor that speaks to Latinos' current and possible future benefit. Although having less education, lower labor force participation rates, lower earnings, and lower home ownership rates compared to members of other ethno-racial groups, Latino workers had only slightly lower employment rates in 2000 and educationally complemented the rest of the region's workforce. For example, in the context of the ongoing blue-to-other collar occupational shift during the 1990s in New England, Latinos were over-represented in blue-collar and service-sector jobs and under-represented in white-collar jobs. Latino workers are thus an important component of a regional economy that is continually being restructured. Contributions to a region's economy, unfortunately, are not necessarily reflected by pay. Across all occupational sectors in 2000 (including white-collar work), Latino workers earned less on average than those of other ethno-racial groups.

Arguably there are several factors that may negate our suggestion that Latinos have benefited New England's economy during the past decade and are likely to do so in the future. First, our optimistic interpretations are based solely on descriptive analysis rather than a sophisticated statistical approach that would directly estimate how an influx of Latino immigrants influenced the employment and earnings of other workers in the region or Latinos' occupational and earnings outcomes. Such an effort might uncover certain relatively less educated New Englanders who were harmed by the growth of the Latino population.[21] Second, we have offered no estimates of public assistance use or costs associated with educating children of Latino origin, nor have we considered additional medical expenses borne by taxpayers in general. Third, the greater the proportion of earnings remitted to one's community of origin, the lower the contribution to the regional economy an ethno-racial group may make. But this dichotomous interpretation, although apparently logical, may not hold in every circumstance. Recent evidence among foreign-born Mexicans in Los Angeles County suggests, contrary to conventional wisdom, that whether remittances are sent to one's home community may be positively related to purchasing a home in the United States and negatively related to receiving public assistance such as Medicaid.[22] In short, although less than a handful of studies in the United States and elsewhere exist (none in New England as far as we are aware), remitting may not diminish the likelihood of Latino immigrants investing in the host communities to which they have migrated, and remitters do not appear to subsidize their remittances with public assistance funded by U.S. taxpayers.

We have only begun to assess the likely direction Latino integration will take in New England. But convincing reasons for studying the Latino population as a whole *and* by its subnational components exist. Politically—as illustrated by the increasing import of the Latino vote—the ethno-racial category of Hispanic or Latino has taken on national importance; theoretically, how the timing of an ethno-racial group's population increase and its cultural and geographic proximity to the home country influence integration in the host country may be better understood by comparing the Dominican to the Puerto Rican and Mexican experiences; and historically, the shared experiences of immigration, U.S.–Latin American relations, and racialization in the United States may have lasting effects that resonate across all Latino groups.[23]

Contemporary New England offers a unique opportunity for researchers to study Latino integration and its theoretical, political, and economic implications. The size of Dominican and Mexican ethno-racial groups, for instance, have only recently become sufficient to make useful statistical comparisons between groups within New England and with those residing in other metropolitan areas such as New York, Chicago and Los Angeles.

Still, census and other public data include very little on such important topics as neighborhood, work and school environment, social networks, access to medical care, health, remittances, et cetera. And these data tell us little of how immigrant legal residency status or generational status influences any of these or the few economic outcomes analyzed above. Collecting both ethnographic and random household and workplace data on Latino residents throughout New England should be a top priority among scholars and community groups already interested in or serving Latino groups, and equally important, among private and public funding agencies.

## Notes

1. On integration concerns, see A. L. Fairchild, "Policies of Inclusion: Immigrants, Disease, Dependency, and American Immigration Policy at the Dawn and Dusk of the 20th Century," *American Journal of Public Health*, 94, no. 4 (2004): 528–539. On ethno-racial relations see S. P. Huntington, "The Hispanic Challenge," *Foreign Policy* (March/April 2004), 30–45. The term *integration* is preferred over *assimilation, incorporation,* or *Americanization* among immigration scholars because it recognizes that both immigrants and host communities change to accommodate one another. Each of the other three words emphasizes change among immigrants *or* communities. Historically, one may distinguish two types of effort in the United States aimed at incorporating immigrants. Charity organizing societies, for instance, attempted to mold immigrant behavior in the 1860s by volunteers visiting immigrant households to teach

them mainstream values and encourage them to alter their behavior accordingly, and alternatively, some contend that the settlement movement of the Progressive Era was less concerned with social control than with working with immigrants in particular neighborhoods to prepare them for socioeconomic opportunity. On this see J. Addams, *Twenty Years at Hull-House* (New York: Macmillan, 1910) and M. Hargraves and R. W. Thomas, "Infant Mortality: Its History and Social Construction," *American Journal of Preventive Medicine*, 9 (Suppl.), (1993): 17–26.

2. J. M. Lindsay and A. Singer, "Changing Faces: Immigrants and Diversity in the Twenty-First Century," in *Agenda for the Nation*, ed. H. J. Aaron, J.M. Lindsay, and P.S. Nivola (Washington, DC: Brookings Institution Press, 2003).

3. A. Singer, *The Rise of New Immigrant Gateways* (Washington, DC: The Brookings Institution, 2004).

4. Lindsay and Singer, "Changing Faces."

5. W. H. Frey, *Melting Pot Suburbs: A Census 2000 Study of Suburban Diversity*, unpublished manuscript, Washington, DC, 2001; E. L. Glaeser and J. M. Shapiro, *City Growth and the 2000 Census: Which Places Grew, and Why*, unpublished manuscript, Washington, DC, 2001; E. A. Marcelli, "From the Barrio to the 'Burbs? Immigration and Suburbanization in Southern California," in *Up Against the Sprawl: Public Policy and the Remaking of Southern California*, ed. J. Wolch, J. Pastor, Manuel, and P. Dreier (Minneapolis: University of Minnesota Press, 2004); A. Singer, *The Rise of New Immigrant Gateways* (Washington, DC: Brookings Institution, 2004); A. Sum, I. Khatiwada, N. Pond, and J. Motroni, *The New Great Wave: Foreign Immigration in Massachusetts and the U.S. During the Decade of the 1990's*, unpublished manuscript, Boston, MA, 2002; R. Suro, and A. Singer, *Latino Growth in Metropolitan America: Changing Patterns, New Locations*, unpublished manuscript, Washington, DC, 2002; M. Uriarte, *Rhode Island Latinos: A Scan of Issues Affecting the Latino Population of Rhode Island* (Boston: Mauricio Gaston Institute, 2002).

6. B. L. Lowell and M. Bump, *New Settlers in the Heartland: Characteristics of Immigrant Minority Population Growth in the Nineties*, unpublished manuscript, Washington, DC, 2004.

7. M. M. Lassen and A. S. Garfunkel, "Investing in Mass. Immigrants," *Boston Globe*, November 30, 2002, A15.

8. R. Hernández, *The Mobility of Workers Under Advanced Capitalism: Dominican Migration to the United States* (New York: Columbia University Press, 2002).

9. Although we do not distinguish Latino from other immigrants in our historical overview, it will be useful to note that Asians and Latinos did not begin to dominate the immigration flow into the United States until the 1960s. See J. P. Smith and B. Edmonston, eds., *The New Americans: Economic, Demographic, and Fiscal Effects of Immigration* (Washington, DC: National Academy Press, 1997).

10. In other words, the rate of population growth ($P$) equals the birth rate ($B$) plus the net international migration rate ($M$) minus the death rate ($D$). Essentially, $D$ and $M$ have been relatively flat compared to $B$, which has been falling and hence is the only possible explanation for declining $P$. See R. A. Easterlin, "Twentieth-Century American Population Growth," in *The Cambridge Economic History of the United States*, vol. 3, ed. S. L. Engerman and R. E. Gallman (New York: Cambridge University Press, 2000), 505–548.

11. The recent brief rise in fertility rates since 1987 is, according to the so-called relative income hypothesis, the result of a growing scarcity of young workers emanating from the baby bust of the 1960s and strong aggregate demand. Three alternative

theories of fertility change (rising value of female labor, easier contraceptive use, and new female work-family values) predict only continued declines in the fertility rate. See Easterlin, "Twentieth-Century American Population Growth."

12. On 1920 levels, see R. A. Easterlin, "Immigration: Economic and Social Characteristics," in *The Harvard Encyclopedia of American Ethnic Groups*, ed. S. Thernstrom and O. E. Handlin (Cambridge, MA: Belknap Press, 1980). On recent trends, see D. M. Heer, *Immigration in America's Future: Social Science Findings and the Policy Debate* (Boulder, CO: Westview Press, 1996). See U.S. Census Bureau Web site (http://factfinder.census.gov/home/saff/) for 2000 updates to Heer, *Immigration in America's Future*, 28.

13. On the concern with population decline, see G. Myrdal, *Population: A Problem for Democracy* (Gloucester, MA: Harvard University Press, 1962 [1940]) and S. H. Preston, "The Decline of Fertility in Non-European Industrialized Countries," in *Below-Replacement Fertility in Industrialized Societies*, ed. K. Davis, M. S. Bernstam, and R. Ricardo-Campbell (New York: Cambridge University Press, 1987), 26–47. On the postcolonial period, see M. L. Hansen, *The Atlantic Migration, 1607–1860: A History of the Continuing Settlement of the United States* (Safety Harbor, FL: Simon Publications, 2001 [1940]); on the post–Civil-War period, see J. Higham, *Strangers in the Land: Patterns of American Nativism, 1860–1925* (New Brunswick, NJ: Rutgers University Press, 1994 [1955]); on pre–World War II, see R. A. Easterlin, "Immigration."

14. D. E. Lewis, "As Domestic Residents Leave Mass., Immigrants Move In," *Boston Globe*, August 10, 2003, B3.

15. E. Boserup, *The Conditions of Agricultural Growth* (Chicago: Aldine, 1965); E. Boserup, *Population and Technological Change: A Study of Long-Term Trends* (Chicago: Chicago University Press, 1981); C. Clark, *Population Growth and Land Use* (New York: St. Martin's Press, 1967); A. Fishlow, *American Railroads and the Transformation of the Antebellum Economy* (Cambridge, MA: Harvard University Press, 1965); A. Hirschman, *The Strategy of Economic Development* (New Haven, CT: Yale University Press, 1958); J. Simon, "On Aggregate Empirical Studies Relating Population Variables to Economic Development," *Population and Development Review* 15, no. 2 (1989): 323–332.

16. R. A. Easterlin, *Population, Labor Force, and Long Swings in Economic Growth* (New York: National Bureau of Economic Research, 1968).

17. J. Pastor, Manuel, and E. A. Marcelli, "Somewhere over the Rainbow?: African Americans, Unauthorized Mexican Immigration, and Coalition Building," *Review of Black Political Economy* 31, no. 1–2 (2003): 125–155; S. Shulman, ed. *The Impact of Immigration on African Americans* (New Brunswick, NJ: Transaction Publishers, 2004).

18. See Enrico A. Marcelli and Colin C. Williams, *Informal Work in Developed Nations* (Ann Arbor: University of Michigan Press, 2006).

19. Service-sector jobs include (1) sales, (2) administrative support and clerical, and (3) protective and other service occupations; "blue-collar" jobs include (1) farming, forestry, and fishing, (2) precision, craft, and repair, (3) transportation and material-moving occupations, and (4) machine operators, assemblers, and inspectors and (5) handlers, equipment cleaners, and general helpers and laborers; "white-collar" jobs refer to (1) executive, administrative, and managerial, (2) professional specialty, and (3) technicians and related support occupations.

20. R. G. Ehrenberg and R. S. Smith, *Modern Labor Economics: Theory and Public Policy* (Boston: Addison-Wesley, 2003); M. Pastor Jr. and E. A. Marcelli, "Men N the Hood: Skill, Spatial, and Social Network Mismatch among Male Workers in

Los Angeles County," *Urban Geography* 21, no. 6 (2000): 474–496; E. A. Marcelli, "The Institution of Unauthorized Residency Status, Neighborhood Context, and Mexican Immigrant Earnings in Los Angeles County," in *The Institutionalist Tradition in Labor Economics*, ed. D. P. Champlin and J. T. Knoedler (Armonk, NY: M. E. Sharpe, 2004), 206–228.

21. E. A. Marcelli, J. Pastor, Manuel, and P. M. Joassart, "Estimating the Effects of Informal Economic Activity: Evidence from Los Angeles County," *Journal of Economic Issues* 33, no. 3 (1999): 579–607; Pastor, Manuel, and Marcelli, "Somewhere over the Rainbow?" 125–155.

22. E. A. Marcelli and B. L. Lowell, "Transnational Twist: Pecuniary Remittances and Socioeconomic Integration among Authorized and Unauthorized Mexican Immigrants in Los Angeles County," *International Migration Review* 39, no. 1 (2005): 69–102.

23. M. M. Suárez-Orozco and M. M. Páez, "Introduction: The Research Agenda," in *Latinos: Remaking America*, ed. M. M. Suárez-Orozco and M. M. Páez (Berkeley: University of California Press, 2002), 1–37.

# 2 Immigration Status, Employment, and Eligibility for Public Benefits among Latin American Immigrants in Massachusetts

Miren Uriarte, Phillip J. Granberry, and Megan Halloran

The movement of people—and their adaptation and integration to a new society—remains a topic as timely and as fascinating as the first time that historians and sociologists began to document it. In the case of Massachusetts, long an area of concentration for new immigrants, newcomers have historically been a major contributor to economic and social development.[1] In the last decades, immigration has been a particularly salient aspect of the state's population growth, adding significantly to the expansion of its workforce. The 2000 census reported a growth of 35 percent in the immigrant population of the state;[2] without the flow of immigrants the state would have suffered a decline in population.[3] The region's workforce has also expanded due to the increase of immigrant workers. Immigrants account for one out of every six workers in Massachusetts, the seventh highest ratio in the nation and one that exceeds that of states with traditionally high numbers of immigrants such as Texas and Illinois.[4] Sum and others show that Massachusetts would have experienced a significant decline in its workforce were it not for the entry of immigrant workers, who accounted for 409 percent of the new increase in the civilian labor force of the state during the 1990s.[5]

The growth in the foreign born population is being driven primarily by the increase in the immigration of Latin American and Caribbean people, of Asians and, to a lesser extent, of Africans. European immigrants have traditionally been the strongest of the national cohorts among the foreign born in Massachusetts, and they still account for about 32 percent of all foreign born in the state.[6] Today, Latin Americans alone account for 30 percent of the immigrant population, a significant increase from 18 percent in 1990.[7]

Among the Latin American population in Boston, 31 percent are foreign born, but the rate of foreign born is not distributed evenly among all national groups. Among Puerto Ricans, for example, all persons are American citizens at birth and, although those that migrate from Puerto Rico experience a change in culture and language, they are not exposed to the vagaries of immigration policy and its limitations. On the other hand, among Dominicans, Salvadorans, Colombians, and Guatemalans the majority of the population are immigrants; the percent of immigrants among these nationalities ranges, for example, from a low of 35 percent among Mexicans to a high of 79 percent among Salvadorans. Taking into account that many of the U.S. born in these groups are the children of the newcomers makes the immigrant experience the prevalent one among these groups.

What is the Latin American immigrant experience in Massachusetts? How are these groups faring? What are the major challenges in their incorporation and adaptation? Research on these groups residing in other areas of the country underscores the weight of labor migration among Dominicans, the violence and trauma of the migration and the desire for family reunification after wars and natural disasters as a factor in the immigration of Central Americans, the overrepresentation of undocumented immigrants in all the groups, the importance of entrepreneurship among the economic activity of Colombians, the strong organizational capacity of Salvadorans, and the political activism of the Dominicans.[8] Studies of these immigrant groups in the Boston area highlight these findings as well as the fact that immigrants from these groups are relatively recent arrivals to the Boston area and thus are immersed fully in the process of adaptation.[9]

Prevalent thinking points to the characteristics of immigrants as the determining factor in their adaptation; education, language, and work skills are seen as critical variables in the ability of immigrants to incorporate into the labor market. The usual story is that immigrants are largely poor and uneducated and that therefore they begin at the bottom of the labor scale and rise only as they attain better work skills, language, and knowledge. Although there is partial truth to this story, it fails to explain differences between groups of immigrants with similar characteristics. For example, compare the social and economic experience of an engineer from Chile, who immigrates to the United States under the sponsorship of a corporation, to that of a similarly trained engineer from Colombia who leaves his country because of the violence, overstays his tourist visa and remains in the United States undocumented. One can live openly in the United States, applying his or her professional skills and earning a livable income, while the other lives in fear of deportation and will likely be earning a marginal wage since he or she is unable to benefit from his or her professional skills. The individual characteristics of immigrants tell only a partial, albeit important, story.

Less attention is given to the contextual factors that interact with the assets immigrants bring (education, skills, and language ability) and that result in differential outcomes.[10] Portes and Rumbaut, for example, describe three critical contextual factors that shape the ultimate experience of immigrants: the policies of the receiving government; the attitudes of the host society toward the racial, class, cultural, and religious background of the immigrants; and, finally, the characteristics of the co-ethnic community that receives the immigrant.[11] The more welcoming the policies, the more closely immigrants resemble the race, class, and culture of the majority, and the stronger the ethnic community to which they arrive, the more successful is the outcome not only of the newcomers, but also of their children. Differences then can manifest themselves between groups—and even within groups—as different waves of immigrants exhibit different assets, are greeted by different policies, and are embraced by different types of communities once they arrive.

An important story of the Latin American immigrant experience in the region refers to the effect of policies on their lives and their possibilities. Among Latin American groups, there is significant layering of nationalities and immigrant flows, each with differences in the method and the time of entry and therefore differences in the type of policy that has greeted the newcomers. This is most evidenced in differences in immigration statuses between and within the groups—including persons that are naturalized citizens, lawful permanent residents (LPRs), refugees, persons on temporary permits, and persons who are undocumented. At any time these groups contain U.S.-born persons interspersed among several generations of immigrants and among the newer arrivals, persons who are just settling in as well as some already incorporated at different levels in the local labor market and in the local institutional environment.

U.S. policy toward immigrants has focused most closely on controlling their entry. In spite of the liberalizing policies of the 1960s, guarding against the unauthorized entry of immigrants has been a top priority. The Office of Immigration Statistics of the U.S. Department of Homeland Security estimated that there were 7 million undocumented immigrants in the United States in January 2000, which amounts to about 22 percent of the foreign-born population in the country. Mexico is by far the largest source of undocumented immigration; it is followed by El Salvador, Guatemala, Colombia, Honduras, and China. It is estimated that there were eighty-seven thousand undocumented persons in Massachusetts in 2004.[12]

These immigrants may have overstayed a tourist, student, or work visa or may have crossed or been smuggled through the Mexico-U.S. border. Family reunification is a common motivator for unauthorized entry due to the very long waits for visas, especially for extended family members. Escape from political turmoil and violence, as was the case among Central Americans in the 1980s and is among Colombians at the present time, is another cause. But the vast majority comes to work and improve the opportunities for themselves and their families. There is evidence that lack of documentation and other issues related to immigration status are a critical factor in the experience of new Latin American immigrants to Massachusetts, thus setting the boundaries for the opportunities and the choices available for these individuals. Work, access to public services, and education are affected by the status of the immigrant. As a Colombian activist working on immigration issues in Boston expressed, "the issue of immigration is the root of every problem."[13]

In contrast to the sharp focus on immigration policy, attention to the policies and conditions that support the incorporation of immigrants has been sporadic and unfocused. Historically, initiatives have originated at the federal level and have focused primarily on alleviating the local costs of refugee resettlement, and the cost of educating the children of new-comers, and on providing limited support for literacy and English language instruction for adults.[14] States and localities have also funded immigrant-specific programs, mostly in reaction to the demands placed on local services by newcomers, including nonrefugee populations. But in general, the assumption has been that immigrants would integrate into localities essentially on their own, using existing benefit programs funded by the federal government and the states as needed. Although cultural and language barriers have affected access to benefits and services on the part of newcomers, access was not generally barred by legal or institutional constraints.

This was to change in 1996 with the passage of both the Personal Responsibility and Work Opportunity Reconciliation Act (PRWORA), better known as welfare reform, and the Illegal Immigration Reform and Immigrant Responsibility Act (IIRIRA). The intertwining of immigration and social policy—done with the express goal of curtailing unauthorized immigration—made immigration status a key point of differentiation in access to social and public services, including health services and higher education, housing and assistance to families in need. Federal policy denied access to federal programs to legal immigrants who arrived after August of 1996. These included programs such as Supplemental Security Income (SSI), food stamps, Temporary Aid for Needy Families (TANF), housing benefits, and Medicaid. In 1997 and in 1998, under pressure from states with large immigrant populations, Congress reversed some of the harsher measures for "qualified aliens," a new category of immigrant that includes permanent residents, asylum seekers, parolees, Cuban/Haitian entrants, veterans, battered persons, and those who had worked in the United States for ten years, among others.[15] Congress also restored access to benefits such as SSI for legal immigrants and to food stamps for legal immigrant children and elderly. But these were limited to immigrants who had been in the country legally by August 1996.

For Latin American immigrants in Massachusetts, both their recent arrival and the diversity of their immigrant statuses make them especially vulnerable to these new restrictive policies. The current link between IIRIRA and PRWORA and the limiting of access to basic food, health, and housing services for legal immigrants provides no federal "safety net" for these groups. Massachusetts initially maintained eligibility for some services, including emergency cash assistance, the state portion of the Medicaid program (MassHealth), and food stamps for lawful permanent residents and for newly arrived legal immigrants. These eligibility requirements were maintained until the state's budget crisis in 2003 and 2004, when the state cut all state-funded MassHealth coverage and food stamps for immigrants, affecting ten thousand legal immigrant adults, including the elderly and the disabled.[16] The result is that new immigrants who institutional supports at a critical time in their adjustment.

This chapter reviews the situation of new Latin American immigrants in Massachusetts, focusing on the effect of policy changes in the last decade. We look at the effect of immigration status on employment outcomes and on access to basic federal and state benefits and services. Our study relies on several sources: findings from an analysis of census data; and secondly, results from interviews and focus groups with Latin American immigrants and with persons who provide services to them.[17]

## Immigration Statuses among Latin Americans in Massachusetts

Although there are Latin Americans from every country in the hemisphere residing in the state, Dominicans, Mexicans, Salvadorans, Colombians, and Guatemalans are the largest Latin American immigrant groups in Massachusetts (Table 2.1).[18] These groups are characterized by the large percentage of foreign born in their midst, ranging from a low of 35 percent among Mexicans to a high of 79 percent among Salvadorans. They are also characterized by their relatively recent arrival in the state. Over 50 percent of Colombians, Guatemalans, Hondurans, Mexicans, and Salvadorans have been in the United States for less than ten years. The figure for Dominicans is 46 percent. Substantial proportions of these populations—ranging from 20 percent among Dominicans to 42 percent of Colombians—arrived after 1995.[19] This was just ahead of the August 1996

TABLE 2.1. Population and foreign born as share of population, Latino population and selected Latin American immigrant groups,[a,b] Massachusetts, 2000

|  | Population | Percentage foreign born in population |
|---|---|---|
| Hispanic or Latino | 427,340 | 31.16 |
| Dominican | 53,350 | 67.57 |
| Mexican | 21,201 | 34.93 |
| Salvadoran | 17,235 | 78.88 |
| Colombian | 14,157 | 78.12 |
| Guatemalan | 12,020 | 75.66 |

*Source*: U.S. Census Bureau, 2000 Census, Summary File 4, sample data

[a]Puerto Ricans are not "foreign born"; they are U.S. citizens by birth, and therefore they are not included in this listing.

[b]The five groups listed are the national groups with the largest representation among Latinos in Massachusetts.

implementation of the more exclusionary federal immigrant and welfare reform legislation. The method of entry varies greatly depending on the time and the circumstance of the migration of these groups and of cohorts within national groups. This leads to great diversity in the types of immigration status that immigrants in these groups possess.

For all groups, the majority of the immigrant population enters the United States as LPRs after qualifying for one of the preferences available in immigration law (Table 2.2). These preferences include family reunification, employment, international adoptions, beneficiaries of the diversity lottery, and those designated refugees or asylum seekers who have been in the United States for at least a year, among others. These persons usually arrive with full capacity to work. Sponsors of immigrants applying for residency under this rubric must be U.S. citizens or permanent residents themselves and, after 1996, prove that they can support their relative at 125 percent above the federal poverty level. Many of these persons cross the U.S. border legally after traveling in an airplane or a car, without great undue hardships. Persons in this category, after five years, can become U.S. citizens.

A second group of immigrants from all these groups lives in the United States without legal authorization (referred to as unauthorized, illegal, or undocumented immigrants). These are immigrants who may enter legally and later overstay a tourist, student, or work visa; others cross or are smuggled through the U.S. border. The demand for visas from each of these Latin American countries far outweighs the annual limits imposed by the United States, due both to the economic pressure to migrate from these lands as well as the demand for family reunification. Therefore, there is a continued entry of undocumented immigrants from Mexico, the Dominican Republic, Guatemala, and El Salvador. In the case of the recent immigration from Colombia, violence in their homeland drives these nationals to overstay their visas in the United States. All these immigrants are vulnerable because of the constant possibility of deportation and separation from their families. Fear of discovery affects every aspect of life—from where and how one works, to the level of interaction one has with community institutions, including schools and health care and human service programs, the relationships one establishes with neighbors and coworkers or with landlords and others in authority.

In the case of the Central Americans, advocacy efforts and the support of their native countries have led to special immigration programs. Temporary protected status (TPS) and the Nicaraguan and Central American Relief Act (NACARA) provide avenues for legalization or for obtaining permits to work in the United States legally. Similar relief is not available for undocumented Dominicans, Mexicans, or Colombians.

Salvadorans who arrived in the United States undocumented may qualify for TPS. Persons in this situation are not considered immigrants by the U.S. Government, and are authorized to be in the United States because the U.S. Congress has granted them temporary protection. This status is awarded to groups when the attorney general finds that conditions in a particular country pose a danger to personal safety due to armed

TABLE 2.2. Immigration statuses common among Colombian, Dominican, Guatemalan, Mexican, and Salvadoran immigrants

| Status | To which group does this status apply? |
| --- | --- |
| Lawful permanent resident<br>*Permission to permanently live and work in the United States* | All |
| Undocumented immigrant<br>*In the United States without the authorization of the USCIS* | All |
| Temporary protected status (TPS)<br>*Temporary immigration status granted to eligible nationals of designated countries* | Salvadorans |
| NACARA/Asylum applicant<br>*Persons benefited by the NACARA law and waiting determination of asylum application* | Salvadorans and Guatemalans |

*Source*: M. Uriarte, P. Granberry, M. Halloran, R. Kramer, and S. Winkler, *Salvadorans, Guatemalans, Hondurans and Colombians: A Scan of Needs of Recent Latin American Immigrants to the Boston Area* (Boston: Mauricio Gastón Institute for Latino Community Development and Public Policy, University of Massachusetts, 2003). http://www.gaston.umb.edu/publications/pubs/sghc/salv-guat-hond-colo.pdf.

conflict or an environmental disaster.[20] Grants of TPS are initially made for periods of six to eighteen months and may be extended depending on the situation in the country of origin. Obtaining a designation of temporary protection does not lead to the award of permanent residency; it only provides protection from deportation and a work permit. When the Attorney General terminates a country's TPS designation, beneficiaries return to the same immigration status they had prior to TPS or to any status that they may have acquired while registered for TPS. Therefore immigrants with this type of status live with uncertainty and constant legal and bureaucratic maneuvers that expose them to abuse and exploitation.

Guatemalans and Salvadorans who may have arrived in the United States undocumented may qualify for country specific adjustments under the American Baptist Church (ABC) Settlement and NACARA. The ABC settlement arises from a legal suit brought against the Immigration and Naturalization Service (now the U.S. Citizenship and Immigration Services or USCIS) and the United States Department of State by a group of religious and refugee organizations that claimed that these government agencies were discriminating against Salvadorans and Guatemalans.[21] The government agreed to a settlement that provided: (a) an initial or a new asylum interview and adjudication under the more lenient asylum regulations, (b) a suspension of deportation, and (c) an authorization to work. This benefit applies to a very specific group of persons, for example, Salvadorans present in the United States on or before September 19, 1990, who applied for TPS or ABC by October 31, 1991, and had not been apprehended at the time of entry after December 19, 1990. For Guatemalans the same conditions apply with the date for entry being October 1, 1990, and December 31, 1991, for application to ABC.

NACARA, in 1997 and again in 1999, extended the limits for application and included authorization for similar relief to spouses and unmarried children. Qualifying to apply for NACARA means that a person can go about his or her life with the expectation of eventually becoming a legal resident of the United States. But the process is long, often five to seven years, longer if one takes into account the time the applicants usually spend under TPS.[22]

One great concern of undocumented immigrants in applying for TPS and NACARA is that they must provide personal information about themselves—such as addresses and places of employment—to the immigration authorities before they are assured of coverage by these programs. In both cases, nonrenewal or denial of an application means immediate return to undocumented status and/or deportation. Therefore some do not apply even when eligible because they feel that it places them at great risk in the event that their application is denied. The uncertainty in the case of the TPS is even higher because it depends on yearly agreements between the U.S. government and the government of the country of origin.[23]

A variety of immigration statuses coexist within these groups and even within families. For persons other than U.S. permanent residents, immigration is a reality that must be managed on a daily basis. The immigrant with TPS, for example, must be vigilant when it comes to the bewildering paperwork that is involved, as one small error can mean the difference between staying in the United States and being deported. But by far the most vulnerable status is that of the undocumented immigrant. Being undocumented affects where immigrants can work and their working conditions, their access to drivers' licenses, and their ability to qualify for federal and state benefits. In the next two sections we explore the interaction of immigration status and these critical issues in immigrants' lives.

## Immigration Status and Employment

Improving their economic condition is a principal goal for immigrants. Among immigrants from groups like those highlighted here, who initially came to the United States to escape war and violence in their countries of origin, socioeconomic progress is important for survival in their new setting, and often is critical to those left behind.[24] Analysis of the 2000 census indicates that these groups are active in the labor market, with high rates of labor force participation. For example, participation rates of Colombians, Guatemalans, Mexicans, and Salvadorans exceed those of the total population (66 percent). In 2000, these groups also showed high unemployment rates, meaning that, even in the positive economic climate at the end of the 1990s, their success in obtaining jobs was much less than that of the general population. Analyses of occupational distribution show that across all groups, the largest percentage work in the service sector followed by industrial and managerial work. Only Mexicans show a sizeable cohort of workers (35 percent) holding professional and managerial jobs.

As is true for many groups that concentrate in the lower occupational levels of the service and manufacturing sectors, earnings tend to be low among these groups. Median earnings for all groups are comparable and well below those of the general population ($28,420). In the case of Colombians, Dominicans, and Salvadorans, theirs are below the already low earnings of the overall Latino population of the state ($18,125). Although still low across the board when compared to the general population, there is more variability among family incomes for the groups.

The fact that more members of the family work among some groups seems to be a factor. Although all groups have a higher percent of families with three or more workers than the general population (14 percent), the rates among Salvadorans and Guatemalans, at 28 percent and 31 percent respectively, are noteworthy.

## Status and the Economic Experiences of the Groups

The experience of these groups of Massachusetts immigrants offers a window into the interaction between individual characteristics (such as education and English language ability), the contextual factors (such as time of arrival and immigration status, etc.) and the resulting differences in outcome. Each group, and in some cases cohorts within groups, has its own story.

Mexicans exhibit the best economic outcomes when compared to the other four groups. Although trailing that of the general population, they have the highest percent of the working population in professional and managerial occupations (35 percent), the highest individual earnings ($19,537), and the highest family income ($45,669) of all the groups. A relatively high percentage of Mexicans living today in Massachusetts are native born (65 percent), speak English (86 percent), and have a high level of education (66 percent with a high school degree and 24 percent with a college degree), when compared to the other groups. In general, their position in the labor market is strong in comparison with other groups considered here.

But there is another group of Mexicans whose experience is quite different. Mexican immigrants have lower incomes and higher levels of poverty than native-born Mexican Americans, a similar pattern to that of the general population. Just over one-third of Mexicans in Massachusetts are foreign born and, of these, 38 percent have been in the United States only since 1995. It is likely that among them there is a large segment of undocumented persons without any relief for legalization, and it is these who probably work in the low-wage sectors of the economy. The contrast in experience (e.g., time in the United States and immigration status) between the more established Mexican Americans and the new Mexican immigrants is important in understanding the outcomes for the group.

Colombians exhibit a similarly polarized economic experience and for similar reasons. Compared to Mexicans, outcomes are more depressed, probably because of the larger representation of recent immigrants (42 percent in the country since 1995) many of who are also undocumented and without relief for legalization. About a quarter of the Colombian population are long-term residents in Massachusetts who came in the 1970s and early 1980s. Most of these cohorts were legal immigrants and those that were not, benefited from the IRCA legalizations in 1986. Many were professionals with a good education who were able to attain professional and managerial jobs. But Colombians also have a very high percent of newly arrived immigrants: 42 percent of Colombians who were living in Massachusetts in 2000 had been in the United States for less than five years. Many of the new immigrants are here undocumented.[25] The new Colombian immigrants also have high levels of education, but the recency and the conditions of their migration contribute to a labor market placement well below their education and skills. Of all the groups considered here, Colombians have the highest percent of their population affected by the restrictions on benefits for immigrants.

A Colombian immigrant expressed it succinctly: "There are two barriers for . . . Colombians: the documents and the language."[26] Lack of English proficiency is clearly an important factor (34 percent speak English not well or not at all), but legal status is also a formidable barrier to work in professions in which they have experience and expertise. Explained a Colombian activist working on labor issues:

> Most Colombians arrive with a good package of knowledge and education. They are self-starters and because of their legal status their opportunities are limited or stop them from advancing. So you are going to find many Colombians working in building and facility maintenance or in other areas that don't require any specific skill or ability.[27]

Many newly arrived Colombians work in low-paying jobs because these are available without work permits. Although language barriers and low level of education characterize some of the Colombian experience, these factors are overwhelmed by the salience of their undocumented status.

The story of the Central Americans—the Guatemalans and Salvadorans—is somewhat different. These are groups with large cohorts of immigrants, 76 percent and 79 percent, respectively; the native born among these are primarily children. Although there has been a tiny settlement of Guatemalans and Salvadorans in Boston since the 1960s, most of these immigrants came in the 1980s as a result of the war in Central America. Many came as refugees and many more of the early cohorts benefited from the IRCA legalizations in 1986. Those that came before 1990 can also benefit from the relief of special legislation such as NACARA, and the Salvadorans that arrived before February 2001 are also eligible for TPS. This protection does not cover everyone, is precarious, and has to be constantly attended to. Nevertheless, TPS and NACARA make obtaining a legal work permit possible, providing some relief from the fundamental barrier that undocumented status represents in relationship to employment. This does not mean that immigration status is no longer a major concern for these groups; many are ineligible for these programs and any mistake in making renewals makes an immigrant on TPS deportable. But the fact is that TPS and NACARA blunt the impact of undocumented status. For Central Americans, low levels of educational attainment and English proficiency inhibit success in the labor market. Advancement even within the service or manufacturing sectors usually requires more education. The challenge is that only about 33 percent of Salvadorans and 48 percent of Guatemalans over the age of eighteen have completed high school and 46 percent and 39 percent, respectively, speak little or no English. A Central American immigrant leader put it this way:

> Sometimes they do not have the education required to qualify for courses, for example for a carpentry course, in which you have to read diagrams. Training to either be a carpenter or a painter is designed for people with at least a high school diploma.[28]

Low levels of educational attainment will likely keep Central Americans in marginal jobs, even if their immigration status is adjusted. In 2000, these groups had the largest percentages of workers in the low wage service and production jobs and the low representations among managers and professionals (Guatemalans have a stronger representation in the latter). Working in favor of these groups is the intensity with which they work. Salvadorans and Guatemalans have the highest levels of labor force participation, the highest percentages of persons working more than thirty-five hours a week (86 percent and 83 percent respectively compared to 72 percent for the general population) and by far the largest percentages of families with more than three workers (28 percent and 31 percent, respectively, compared to 14 percent for the general population).

Dominicans are the largest Latin American immigrant group in Massachusetts and the one with the longest tenure in the area: 29 percent arrived before 1985, according to 2000 census figures. The makeup of the migrant stream, although heterogeneous in terms of class and education, is weighted toward unskilled workers, typical of the labor migrations from the region.[29] Dominicans have slightly better education and language profile than the typical Central American, but with 45 percent of their population over sixteen with less than a high school degree and 30 percent of their adults of working age unable to speak English, their labor market placement is concentrated in the low-wage production and service occupations. Most Dominicans are immigrants (68 percent), with a significant group that came after the legalizations of 1986 (70 percent of the immigrants) and a small cohort of recent immigrants (only 20 percent have come after 1995). Nevertheless, they have a sizable undocumented population without relief from legalization.

Dominicans have the lowest individual earnings and family income of the groups considered here. Poverty among Dominicans is higher among native born (34 percent) than among immigrants (28 percent), but it is higher in both cohorts in comparison to the other groups. As a group, Dominicans do not benefit from a cohort with considerable levels of education, whether attained in their country of origin (as is the case of most of the Colombians) or after generations in the United States (as is the case of the Mexicans). Neither do they have the relief from the impact of undocumented status available to some groups of undocumented among the Central Americans. Their story—and their economic outcomes—shows the effects of the absence of either of these advantages.

Although the characteristics of immigrants are important in understanding their experience in the labor market, contextual variables, such as time of entry and immigration status, are critical as well. For these groups, time of entry, immigration status, and education seem to interact with each other, and each with the specific characteristics of the local labor market. The result is an array of differential outcomes that offer advantageous positions to some and less advantageous niches to others. Being foreign born does not necessarily lead to lower outcomes. In most cases it is the opposite: poverty is lower among immigrants than among the native born for Dominicans, Salvadorans, and Guatemalans. Being undocumented is a critical variable. As is evident in the case of the Colombians, the barriers of undocumented status are not overcome easily, even with the high levels of education present in this population. Finding solutions to the immigration status of undocumented workers is crucial to creating access to better jobs and to protecting workers from employer abuse. But as the experience of the Central American groups demonstrates, relief in the area of legalization does not completely address the disadvantages of low educational status. Improving educational opportunities for adults can improve the outcomes of immigrant workers, be it through adult basic education, English as a second language classes, or workforce development programs.

## Immigration Status and Barriers to Services

Immigration is fraught with the trauma of the process of departure and arrival and the tensions of the adaptation. Some Central America immigrants came, first escaping war and later in the aftermath of great natural disasters and economic upheavals in their countries of origin. New Colombian immigrants escape today the violence in their country. A few arrive as permanent residents and their travel is largely uneventful. Others arrive legally as tourists and later stay undocumented. Still others arrive undocumented, making their way through the Mexican border and experiencing significant hardships in the process of migrating to the United States. For example, in a survey of 150 Salvadoran immigrants in San Francisco, 33 percent had been assaulted once, and 70 percent felt their life had been placed in danger at some time during the trip.[30] Media accounts point to the increasing danger inherent in the crossing of the U.S.-Mexican border in recent years, as the security after September 11 leaves fewer options for safe entries. "Coyotes," those who bring undocumented immigrants into the United States for a fee, are now about the only option for making it across the border, and these crossings are now taking place more and more frequently as dangerous passages across the desert.[31]

Most, regardless of how they arrive, experience the trauma of leaving family and friends behind. Separation from loved ones in the country of origin is a common experience and many do not see their families for years, either because they cannot afford to return or because they may not have the necessary immigrant status that would allow them to go back for a visit and return to the United States to work. As a provider working in East Boston explained, "This is a very big issue for people in terms of the sadness, leaving their families, or their families not being all together. That's very difficult emotionally."[32]

Lack of English proficiency impacts immigrants' efforts to find work and to access services. Financial problems are common as are disorientation and the problems that arise "not understanding how things work here and being treated very differently," explained a social worker dealing with new Salvadoran and Colombian immigrants.[33] This can be specially challenging when immigrants find themselves devalued in the U.S. context—be it because of a lack of English proficiency, or being undocumented, or being the victims of racism. This can be a traumatic situation for those who once held places of respect in their communities of origin but for whom immigration has meant downward mobility—either social or economic.

Historically immigrant policy in the United States has been scattered and unfocused, particularly that affecting immigrant groups like the ones considered here. Refugees received a modicum of support, but this is not a status common among the groups we have focused upon. More common is the arrival, unannounced, to local communities. In these cases, families and friends usually provide the first line of support, orienting new immigrants and providing them support. Families are usually large and extended, and households often include friends and family members. Religious communities and groups made up of conationals extend family networks even more. Community organizations are a source of support to the adaptation of immigrants. They offer legal assistance, language classes, connections to work, and basic supportive services. The strength of the connections between families and community organizations differs between groups, depending on the development of these resources within the immigrant community.[34] Even in the best of times, most immigrants were left to their own devices—and those of their communities—to deal with the stresses of separation (or reunification) and the process of adaptation to the new environment.

The 1996 federal welfare reform initiative (PRWORA) changed policies for immigrants in two important ways. The first is that the time of entry of the immigrant and immigration status became a key point of differentiation in determining access to social and public services. In addition to age, income, disability, or other specific program eligibility requirements, the designation of an immigrant as a "qualified alien" is key to the determination of eligibility. "Qualified aliens" are: (1) LPRs, (2) refugees, asylum seekers, and persons granted withholding of deportation, or conditional entry (in effect prior to April 1, 1980); (3) Cuban/Haitian entrants; and (4) certain cases involving battered spouses and children. Not-qualified immigrants include all noncitizens who do not fit within the "qualified" immigrant categories. In general, the cut-off date determining immigrant eligibility, even for "qualified" immigrants, is August 22, 1996. An immigrant needs to be a "qualified" immigrant *and* have been residing legally in the United States before the cut-off date of August 22, 1996, to qualify for most federal benefits; qualified immigrants who arrived after that date must wait five years from the time of entry to be eligible for any federal public benefits. In the case of NACARA applicants who successfully gain asylum and permanent residency, the wait is usually five years from the time asylum is granted. Eligibility for federal public benefits for those on TPS is minimal, and there is no eligibility for public federal benefits for the undocumented.

The second way in which policies changed in 1996 is the devolution of authority to the states regarding the provision of benefits for immigrants. Up to this time, most initiatives of services toward immigrants were federal and focused on services to specific groups, such as refugees. This new authority allowed the states flexibility in the provisions of services, especially those funded by the states. Under this authority, Massachusetts initially maintained eligibility for emergency cash assistance, the state portion of the Medicaid program (MassHealth) and food stamps for lawful permanent residents, for newly arrived legal immigrants during their first five years in the United States In addition, persons protected under NACARA and TPS are considered to have Permanent Residence Under

Color of Law (PRUCOL) in Massachusetts. This allowed for access to state benefits that federal programs do not allow. In reaction to the state budget crises of the early 2000s, Massachusetts has severely curtailed access to services on the part of immigrants, including legal immigrants.

The link articulated in recent times between immigration and social policies—between IIRIRA and PRWORA—and the limitations it introduced in terms of access to basic services for legal immigrants, makes an already difficult situation even more problematic. On the one hand, immigrants became ineligible for federal programs such as health services (including mental health services), income support, or emergency services. On the other, services for immigrants at the local level now compete for ever-decreasing public funding for benefits and services. This has led to less eligibility for immigrants for local services and a weakened capacity on the part of community based organizations to address their needs. In addition, because immigration status varies widely between and within the groups, the eligibility restrictions also vary widely, at times even within families. Eligibility requirements have evolved into a confusing patchwork of benefits that leaves families and providers with the task of figuring who is eligible for what, under what conditions and for how long. The result is confusion and limiting of access: in many ways new immigrants are more on their own than ever before.

The curtailment of services to immigrants affects all immigrant groups in Massachusetts, but particularly those with large number of recent immigrants. Among the groups considered here are large percentages of immigrants who arrived after the cut-off date of August 1996. This is particularly so among Colombians, Mexicans, Guatemalans, and Salvadorans. The changes in policy also have great impact among those groups in which there are large numbers of immigrants on temporary status or undocumented. All the groups considered here are in this situation.

Public health insurance programs, perhaps among the most generous in Massachusetts, provide a case in point for both the federal and the local effects. Table 2.3 provides a list of federal and state health insurance programs and the eligibility of persons with different statuses for each of the programs. Of federal programs, Medicare Part B provides the least eligibility. While all categories of immigrants (except undocumented) are eligible for Medicare Part A, a five-year waiting period is required for Lawful Permanent Residents to qualify for Medicare Part B, and those with NACARA and TPS status are ineligible for this type of Medicare benefit. The undocumented are ineligible for both Medicare programs.

MassHealth is the state Medicaid program for individuals whose income is below 200 percent of the poverty level. It integrates the State Children's Health Insurance Program and Healthy Start. The MassHealth

TABLE 2.3. Eligibility for public health insurance programs (federal and state) in 2004 by immigrants with immigration statuses common among Latin American immigrants in Massachusetts

| 2004 | Benefit | Lawful permanent resident | | ABC/NACARA | Temporary protective status | Undocumented |
|---|---|---|---|---|---|---|
| | | Entered United States before 8/22/1996 | Entered United States after 8/22/1996 | | | |
| | | Applies to all groups | | Applies to Salvadorans and Guatemalans only | Applies to Salvadorans only | Applies to all groups |
| Health | Medicare Part A[a] | Eligible | Eligible | Eligible | Eligible | Not eligible |
| | Medicare Part B[a] | Eligible after 5 years in the United States | Eligible after 5 years in the United States | Not eligible | Not eligible | Not eligible |
| | MassHealth Standard[b] | Eligible | Eligible after 5 years in the United States[g] | Not eligible[g] | Not eligible[g] | Not eligible[g] |
| | MassHealth Basic[b] | Eligible | Eligible after 5 years in the United States[g] | Not eligible[g] | Not eligible[g] | Not eligible[g] |
| | MassHealth CommonHealth[b] | Eligible | Eligible after 5 years in the United States | Not eligible[g] | Not eligible[g] | Not eligible[g] |
| | MassHealth Buy In | Eligible | Eligible after 5 years in the United States | Not eligible[g] | Not eligible[g] | Not eligible[g] |
| | MassHealth Family Assistance (S-CHIP)[b] | Eligible | Eligible after 5 years in the United States | Not eligible[g] | Not eligible[g] | Not eligible[g] |
| | MassHealth Essential | Eligible | Eligible after 5 years in the United States | Not eligible[g] | Not eligible[g] | Not eligible[g] |
| | MassHealth Prenatal | Eligible | Eligible | Eligible[g] | Eligible[g] | Eligible[g] |

(continued)

TABLE 2.3. Continued

| 2004 Benefit | Lawful permanent resident | | ABC/NACARA | Temporary protective status | Undocumented |
| | Entered United States before 8/22/1996 | Entered United States after 8/22/1996 | | | |
| | Applies to all groups | | Applies to Salvadorans and Guatemalans only | Applies to Salvadorans only | Applies to all groups |
| MassHealth Limited[b] | Eligible | Eligible | Eligible | Eligible | Eligible[c] |
| Children Medical Security Plan[d] | Eligible | Eligible | Eligible | Eligible | Eligible |
| Free Care Pool[e] | Eligible | Eligible | Eligible | Eligible | Able to apply[c] |
| Healthy Start | Eligible | Eligible | Eligible | Eligible | Able to apply[c] |
| Mass Women, Infants and Children Supplemental Nutrition Program (WIC)[f] | Eligible | Eligible | Eligible | Eligible | Eligible |

[a]National Immigration Law Center, *A Guide to Immigrant Eligibility for Federal Programs 2003*, http://www.nilc.org/immspbs/special/Ovrvw_Imm_Elig_Fed_Pgms_4.03.pdf.

[b]Massachusetts Department of Medical Assistance, *MassHealth. Information for Members: Other Things You Need to Know*, http://www.state.ma.us/dma/masshealthinfo/otherthings12.htm.

[c]Neighborhood Legal Services, *Health Resources for People Regardless of Immigration Status* http://www.neighborhoodlaw.org/page/159460;cat_id=.

[d]Boston Public Health Commission, Children's Medical Security Plan. www.bphc.org/howto/ins_cmsp.asp.

[e]Boston Public Health Commission, Massachusetts Uncompensated Free Care Pool. http://www.bphc.org/howto/ins_mucp.asp.

[f]Mass Department of Public Health, Women, Infants, and Children Program (WIC) (Boston: Massachusetts Department of Public Health, Bureau of Family and Community Health, Nutrition Division), http://www.state.ma.us/dph/fch/wic.htm.

[g]People who were on MassHealth on June 30, 1997, continue to get benefits regardless of immigration status if otherwise eligible.

programs (in light gray) in Table 2.3 are state-run programs funded in part with federal funds. Eligibility for these mirrors the more restrictive standards of Medicare Part B, with the exception that immigrants who arrived before 1996 are eligible for all programs. The current eligibility (2004) represents a change from 1997, when, even in the face of federal restrictions, Massachusetts maintained eligibility for most of these programs (MassHealth Basic, MassHealth CommonHealth, and MassHealth Family Assistance). The eligibility on the part of persons in the United States for less than five years, for persons under NACARA, and for persons on TPS were restricted as part of the state budget cuts in FY2003 and FY2004, and they have not been restored to date.

Immigrants in these categories are eligible for MassHealth programs that serve uninsured persons in cases of emergency. As indicated in Table 2.3, these are all funded solely by the state (and appear in white).[35] Eligibility requirements are generally broader: MassHealth Limited, for example, is available to anyone in the Commonwealth meeting income guidelines, including undocumented immigrants. This program provides inpatient and outpatient emergency care and labor and delivery. Other medical programs available are the Department of Public Health's Children's Medical Security Plan, paid from the state's cigarette tax fund, which provides medical care for children under age nineteen with no health insurance. Finally, the Free Care Pool administered by individual health institutions offers emergency health care for families with incomes under 200 percent of the Federal Poverty Guidelines regardless of immigration status. Those with family incomes between 200 percent and 400 percent are eligible for partial free care.

Institutional barriers to benefits and services for immigrants are now the law of the land. They exist in health care, in Social Security and SSI and they exist in regards to TANF (welfare), food stamps, and emergency assistance for families. These limitations apply to housing programs and even to after-school services for children.

One area in which institutional barriers to access have received significant attention is in higher education. Massachusetts has no specific legal barriers for immigrants to attend colleges and universities, both public and private; but administrative requirements and cost act as actual barriers for students with temporary or undocumented status who reside in the state. These students are classified as international students and must, first of all, present valid student visas or other legal documentation for registration in institutions of higher education, a clear barrier to the undocumented. In public institutions, they must pay out-of-state tuition, which can more than double the cost of college. Temporary and undocumented immigrants are also ineligible for federal financial aid grants, which are the basis of most need-based financial aid decisions in both public and private colleges and universities. Unless an immigrant can obtain federal financial aid, acceptance to a school may not be sufficient for the individual to continue to pursue one's education. U.S.-born children of temporary and undocumented immigrants are also affected by administrative rules governing the application for federal financial aid, since their parents must fill out financial aid applications. These young people are affected by the financial aid limitations that the status of their parents imposes, although once independent from their parents they may apply for financial aid. This situation leaves many promising young adults who have excelled in high school with no chance of betterment. These are usually students who, after being educated in the public school system, face a closed door when it comes to higher education. The impediment is not limited to the graduating student. As a Salvadoran community leader pointed out, "when you have an older brother or sister who is the brightest in the class...the valedictorian, but that because of the papers is not allowed to go to college, the younger kids see that and say 'why should I start?'"

There is considerable support for federal and state efforts to remedy this problem. A proposal to allow students who have been in the United States for five years, have graduated from high school, and do not have a criminal record, to apply for a green card was introduced in Congress. In 2004 the Development, Relief, and Education for Alien Minors (DREAM) Act (S-1291, 107th Congress), as this initiative is called, was making its way through Congressional Committees sponsored in the U.S. Senate by Utah Republican Orrin Hatch and Illinois Democrat Richard Durbin. The DREAM act would allow these students to apply for financial aid and in-state tuition rates, as well as provide all the benefits accorded an authorized immigrant. In Massachusetts, a bill seeking to make students eligible to qualify as residents regardless of status (as long as they graduated from a Massachusetts high school after attending for three years) was successful in the legislature in 2004, but was vetoed by the governor.

## Other Barriers of Access to Public Services

As the previous discussion evidences, legal restrictions are an institutional barrier to access to benefits brought about by the inter-twining of immigration and social policy that took place under PROWORA and IIRIRA. But there are other kinds of restrictions that prevent services from reaching those who are eligible. Studies have identified a significant decline in the use of cash transfers, health services, and other services by eligible immigrants who need them.[36]

One factor is the confusion families demonstrate regarding eligibility. With the patchwork shown above, it is clear that deciphering eligibility for benefits is not an easy process, particularly for newcomers and for those for whom language is a barrier.

The fear of discovery that accompanies the interactions between undocumented immigrants and institutions is another factor. Immigration status causes the stress of "living in the shadows... not being seen, not being acknowledged, not being respected, and not being there," explained a provider in East Boston.[37] The undocumented fear discovery of their situation as they apply for services for their children or other members of the family who may qualify for them. This affects access to services for American-born children in mixed-status families, who have very low participation in benefit programs for which they are eligible.[38]

Legal immigrants may also resist using services due to the regulations inherent in their immigrant status. Since 1996, in order to obtain legal residency permits, immigrants' sponsors have had to commit to pay for all medical needs for at least five years. So it is common for immigrants to abstain from using public services for that period of time. Immigrants with other statuses such as TPS and NACARA are also reluctant to use services to which they and/or their children are entitled for fear that they will be perceived as in danger of becoming a public charge, which would prevent them from obtaining permanent residency in the United States.

## Conclusion

A critical factor in immigrant adaptation is the array of public policies that apply to the newcomers. Latino immigrant communities, because of the differences in time of arrival and in the experiences of migration, are thickly and differentially layered in terms of immigrant status. There are differences between groups, within groups and even within families. Census information provides evidence that within the groups considered here—Dominicans, Mexicans, Colombians, Guatemalans, and Salvadorans—there are persons at every stage of the process of adjustment. They include new arrivals, persons settling, and some with already established routines that incorporate them at different levels into U.S. society. Some who immigrated long ago may have stable situations, while others who have also been in the United States for many years still struggle to attain stability. Others are here on temporary status or undocumented. In the case of recent immigrants, the stresses due to the process of immigration feed into problems related to the immigrants' status and the difficulties they encounter due to language and cultural differences. For this reason it is critical to understand the timing and the situations that brought these groups to the United States.

Immigration status influences all aspects of an immigrant's life. Here we have focused on two: employment and access to benefits and services. In employment, status interacts with the characteristics of immigrants and of the labor market to fix immigrants in different experiences. For some, the barriers of status trumped strong human capital, as was the case of the Colombians. In others, relief from the worst effects of undocumented status was not sufficient to overcome the effects of low educational standing.

We also examined the effects of policy-driven institutional barriers, such as status, in determining access to services for immigrants. There is evidence that providing a range of services can be supportive of optimal adjustment. Such services include cash transfers and food support at the start, small business loan programs, English classes for adults, bilingual education programs for children, higher education loans, and the means for professionals to validate their credentials.[39] Today, the lack of a coherent set of policies related to immigrants leaves their future subject to the vagaries of local budgets and political maneuvering. In 1996, for example, social policy was used to buttress a failing immigration system.

What often gets lost in this discussion is the immigrant perspective. Policies that make sense for lawmakers, because they reinforce international objectives or domestic economic needs, often seem inconsistent and arbitrary to immigrants. This is especially true with respect to policies that limit the ability to work or the eligibility for health care or education. The fact that groups with similar histories and situations have different standing in relationship to immigration law seems arbitrary and preferential. An example is the case of TPS, for which Salvadorans are eligible and Guatemalans ineligible. Similarly confusing is the emphasis on nationality in some contexts and in pan-national identities (such as Latino) in others. For most immigrants, people in the United States do not appear to be aware of the differences among Latin American nationalities and assume a broad identity as "Latino" or "Hispanic." But this changes quickly when it comes to immigration or eligibility for public benefits. Then, nationality and time of arrival is paramount. The lack of awareness that these differences exist confuses immigrants and alienates them from their surroundings.

Policy changes in the last years have favored a vision of immigration that ignores the social dynamics of population flows and the fundamental interaction between the origin and the destination of the flow. This blind spot continues to pull policy in the direction of ever stronger border controls and punitive measures for those who succeed in entering the country nevertheless. Of late, those punitive measures have been accompanied by an increasingly negative vision of immigrants, particularly immigrants from poor countries, that is mostly unfounded but that now is even more confounded in the environment created by the aftermath of the events of September 11, 2001. Together, they obscure what immigrants contribute to their new country and what immigrants and their children require to have a successful adjustment.

## Notes

1. A. Sum and N. Fogg, *The Changing Workforce: Immigrants and the New Economy of Massachusetts* (Boston: MassINC and Citizens Bank, 1999).
2. U.S. Bureau of the Census, Census 2000, Summary File 4 (SF4), Sample Data, and 1990 (STF3).
3. A. Sum, I. Khatiwada, J. Motroni, and N. Pond, *Moving Out and Moving In: Out-Migration and Foreign Immigration in the Northeast Region and New England During the 1990s* (Boston: Center for Labor Market Studies, Northeastern University, 2002), 22.
4. Ibid, 9.
5. A. Sum, S. Palma, M. Trubb'sky, and I. Khatiwada, *Foreign Immigration and Its Contributions to Population and Labor Force Growth in Massachusetts and the U.S.: A Recent Assessment of 2000 Census and CPS Survey Findings* (Boston: Center for Labor Market Studies, Northeastern University, 2001), 8.
6. Sum and Fogg, *The Changing Workforce*, 36, and U.S. Bureau of the Census, Census 2000 Summary File 4 (SF4), Sample Data.
7. Ibid. In both years, the numbers of Caribbean and Latin Americans do not include Puerto Ricans. Immigrants from Africa had an insignificant representation in 1990 but today account for 8 percent of the foreign born in Massachusetts.
8. See for example, O. Cadaval, *Creating a Latino Identity in the Nation's Capital* (Garland Publishing, 1998); D. W. Hart, *Undocumented in LA: An Immigrant's Story* (Wilmington, DE: Scholarly Resources Inc, 1997); C. Menjivar, *Fragmented Ties: Salvadoran Immigrant Networks in America* (Los Angeles: University of California Press, 2000); C. Redden, *A Comparative Study of Colombian and Costa Rican Emigrants to the United States* (New York: Arno Press, 1980).
9. S. Baker, B. Lykes, E. Mishler, and V. Steinitz, "Threatened Lives: Undocumented Central American Refugees," unpublished paper, Boston College, Mental Health Committee, Department of Psychology, March 1989; H. Hayes, "The Impact of Immigration Status on the Social and Economic Needs of Undocumented Immigrants in the Boston Area," PhD dissertation, Boston College, Graduate School of Social Work, May 1993; M. Uriarte, *"Contra Viento y Marea* (Against All Odds): Latinos Build Community in Boston," in *Latinos in Boston: Confronting Poverty, Building Community*, ed. Miren Uriarte, Paul Osterman and Edwin Melendez (Boston: Boston Foundation, 1993); S. Torres-Saillant and R. Hernandez, *The Dominican Americans* (Westport, CN: Greenwood Press, 1998); Sum and Fogg, Th*e Changing Workforce*; R. Hernandez and G. Jacobs, "Beyond Homeland Politics: Dominicans in Massachusetts," in *Latino Political Representation: Struggles, Strategies, and Prospects*, ed. C. Hardy-Fanta and J. Gerson (New York: Garland Publishing, 2001); Sum, et al., *Moving Out and Moving In*; M. Uriarte, P. Granberry, M. Halloran, R. Kramer, and S. Winkler, *Salvadorans, Guatemalans, Hondurans and Colombians: A Scan of Needs of Recent Latin American Immigrants to the Boston Area* (Boston: Mauricio Gastón Institute for Latino Community Development and Public Policy, University of Massachusetts, 2003);

D. Sussman, *The Impact of Remitting Upon the Self-Sufficiency of Immigrants in Boston*, MALD thesis, Fletcher School of Law and Diplomacy, May 2004.

10. See for example, S. Pedraza-Bailey, *Political and Economic Migrants in America: Cubans and Mexicans* (Austin: University of Texas Press, 1985); A. Portes and R. Bach, *Latin Journey* (Berkeley: University of California Press, 1985); A. Portes and A. Stepick, "Unwelcome Immigrants: The Labor Market Experience of 1980 (Mariel) Cuban and Haitian Refugees," *American Sociological Review* 50 (August 1995): 493–514; Redden, *A Comparative Study*.

11. A. Portes and R. Rumbaut, *Immigrant America* (Berkeley: University of California Press, 1996), 46–48.

12. Office of Immigration Statistics, Department of Homeland Security, *Yearbook of Immigration Statistics* (Washington DC: U.S. Government Printing Office, 2003), 213; J. S. Passel, R. Capps, and M. Fix, *Undocumented Immigrants: Facts And Figures* (Washington DC: Urban Institute Immigration Studies Program, January 12, 2004), 1; estimate a total of 9.3 million unauthorized immigrants in the United States, amounting to 26 percent of the total foreign-born population.

13. Interview with 04mull. All interviewees were promised full confidentiality at the time of the interviews. Therefore, throughout this study interviewees are identified with a notation that protects the identity.

14. M. Fix, W. Zimmerman, and J. S. Passel, *The Integration Of Immigrant Families In The United States* (Washington DC: Urban Institute, 2001), 43.

15. T. MaCurdy and M. O'Brien, *Reform Reversed? The restoration of welfare benefits to immigrants in California* (San Francisco: Policy Institute of California, 1998), 7–9; R. Daniels, *Guarding the Golden Door: American Immigration Policy and Immigrants since 1882* (New York: Hill and Wang, 2004), 247.

16. Massachusetts Immigrant and Refugee Coalition, "10,000 Legal Immigrant Adults Lost State MassHealth on August 1, 2003," www.miracoalition.org/masshealth_alert_7–24–03.htm, September 9, 2004.

17. Unless otherwise indicated, all quotations in this chapter are from the original research study reported in Uriarte et al., *Salvadorans, Guatemalans, Hondurans and Colombians*. The study was conducted as part of the Applied Research Practicum in the PhD program in public policy, John W. McCormack School of Policy Studies at the University of Massachusetts Boston in collaboration with Centro Presente in Cambridge, Massachusetts. We thank Susan Kelly, Rob Kramer, Sandra Winkler, Jennifer Murillo, Udaya Wagle, Randall Wilson, Elena Letona and the staff of Centro Presente, all of whom contributed to that report, as well as the Mauricio Gastón Institute for Latino Community Development and Public Policy and the public policy PhD program, both of which supported the research financially and logistically.

18. The Lewis Mumford Center for Comparative Urban and Regional Research estimates a slightly higher total population of Latinos in Massachusetts at 428,739 and different representation of the populations of Latino groups: Dominicans, 73,646, Mexican 23,656, Salvadoran, 23,707, Colombian 19,847, and Guatemalan 17,003; http://mumford1.dyndns.org/cen2000/HispanicPop/HspPopData/25st.htm.

19. U.S. Census Bureau, 2000 Census Summary File 4, Sample Data, reported in M. Uriarte et al., 2003, 5, Figure 1.

20. U.S. Immigration and Naturalization Service, *Statistical Yearbook of the Immigration and Naturalization Service, 2000* (Washington DC: U.S. Government Printing Office, 2002), A2–13.

21. U.S. Citizenship and Immigration Services, The American Baptist Churches vs. Thornburgh Settlement Agreement, 2003, http://uscis.gov/graphics/services/residency/abc.htm.

22. U.S. Citizenship and Immigration Services, Immigration through the Nicaraguan Adjustment and Central American Relief Act, Section 203, http://uscis.gov/graphics/services/residency/nacara203_main.htm, November 7, 2003.

23. This is a situation that is imbued with politics as governments that request TPS for their citizens in the United States are vulnerable to foreign policy pressures.

24. In this section discussing the link between immigration status and employment, all empirical statements are based on analysis of U.S. Census Bureau, 2000 Census, Summary File 4, Sample Data.

25. M. W. Collier and E. Gamarra, *The Colombian Diaspora in South Florida* (Miami: Florida International University, Latin American and Caribbean Center, WPS #1, 2001), http://lacc.fiu.edu/publications_resources/working_papers/working_paper_01.htm; Uriarte et al., *Salvadorans, Guatemalans, Hondurans and Colombians.*

26. Group interview 2, interviewee 6.

27. Interview 04mull.

28. Interview 02mull.

29. Torres-Saillant and Hernández, *The Dominican Americans,* 34–35.

30. Menjivar, *Fragmented Ties.*

31. Hadden, "The Trail of Latino Migration: A Desert Crossing," National Public Radio, October 1, 2003, http://www.npr.org/features/feature.php?wfId=1451521.

32. Interview 16swpnl.

33. Interview 19swpl.

34. Uriarte et al., *Salvadorans, Guatemalans, Hondurans and Colombians.*

35. National Immigration Law Center, *A Guide to Immigrant Eligibility for Federal Programs* 2003, http://www.nilc.org/immspbs/special/Ovrvw_Imm_Elig_Fed_Pgms_4.03.pdf; Massachusetts Department of Medical Assistance, *MassHealth. Information for Members: Other Things You Need to Know,* http://www.state.ma.us/dma/masshealthinfo/otherthings12.htm; Massachusetts Department of Transitional Assistance, *Noncitizen Desk Guide* (Boston: Executive Office of Health and Human Services, 2003), 02-275-1003-05 NCDG, 10/03, http://www.mass.gov/Eeohhs2/docs/dta/noncitizenguide/status.pdf; Neighborhood Legal Services, *Health Resources for People Regardless of Immigration Status* http://www.neighborhoodlaw.org/page/159460;cat_id=; Boston Public Health Commission Children's Medical Security Plan. www.bphc.org/howto/ins_cmsp.asp and Massachusetts Uncompensated Free Care Pool, http://www.bphc.org/howto/ins_mucp.asp; Massachusetts Department of Public Health, Women, Infants, and Children Program (Boston: Massachusetts Department of Public Health, Bureau of Family and Community Health, Nutrition Division), http://www.state.ma.us/dph/fch/wic.htm.

36. There is now a large body of evidence pointing in this direction. See for example: P. A. Holcomb, K. Tumlin, R. Koralek, R. Capps, and A. Zuberi, "The Application Process for TANF, food stamps, Medicaid, and SCHIP: Issues for Agencies and Applicants, Including Immigrants and Limited English Speakers," http://aspe.os.dhhs.gov/hsp/app-process03/index.htm; Randy Capps, Leighton Ku, Michael Fix, Chris Furgiuele, Jeffrey Passel, Rajeev Ramchand, Scott McNiven, Dan Perez-Lopez, Eve Fielder, Michael Greenwell, and Tonya Hays, *How Are Immigrants Faring after Welfare Reform? Preliminary Evidence from Los Angeles and New York City* (Washington, DC: Urban Institute, 2002), http://aspe.os.dhhs.gov/hsp/immigrants-faring02/report.pdf;

M. Wang and J. Hollahan, *The Decline in Medicaid Use by Noncitizens since Welfare Reform* (Washington DC: Urban Institute, 2003); M. Fix and J. S. Passel, *Lessons of Welfare Reform for Immigrant Integration* (Washington DC: Urban Institute, 2002) and *Trends in Citizens' Use of Public Benefits Following Welfare Reform: 1994–1997* (Washington DC: Urban Institute, 1999).

37. Interview 18swpnl.

38. M. Fix and W. Zimmerman, *All Under One Roof: Mixed Status Families in an Era of Reform* (Washington DC: Urban Institute, 1999); R. Capps, *Hardship among Children of Immigrants: Findings from the 1999 National Survey of America's Families* (Washington DC: Urban Institute, 2001).

39. S. Pedraza Bailey, *Political and Economic Migrants in America.*

# 3 Latino Shelter Poverty in Massachusetts

Michael E. Stone

## Introduction

Latinos experience the greatest incidence of housing affordability problems of any of the 4 largest racial/ethnic groups in Massachusetts.[1] Over three out of five Latino renters and nearly one out of three Latino home owners are "shelter poor"—experiencing so great a squeeze between their incomes and housing costs that they are unable to meet their nonshelter needs at even a minimal level of adequacy. Between 1990 and 2000 the number of shelter-poor Latino households in Massachusetts increased by more than 60 percent.[2]

There were about 121,000 Latino-headed households in Massachusetts in 2000, an increase of over 54 percent from 1990. In 1990 Latino-headed households were 3.5 percent of all households in the state; by 2000 they were nearly 5 percent of all households. The number of Latino home owners increased by 95 percent over the decade, while the number of Latino renters increased by 46 percent. Latinos had a home ownership rate of slightly less than 22 percent in 2000, an increase from just over 17 percent in 1990, yet still the lowest rate of any major ethnic group in the state.

The low rate of home ownership among Massachusetts Latinos is undoubtedly due in part to persistent discrimination in housing and mortgage markets and lack of equal access to information about home ownership opportunities. But it is also a consequence of profound socio-economic differences between most Latino home owners and renters. Massachusetts Latino home owners have a median income of nearly $60,000 (only a little less than that of white non-Latino home owners), which is nearly three times that of Latino renters. They are more likely to be married couples and have higher average levels of education and longer durations of residence on the U.S. mainland than do Latino renters. Nonetheless, nearly a third of Latino home owners are shelter poor, which is defined as the inability of a household to meet its nonhousing needs at some minimal level of adequacy. Latino shelter poverty is much higher than for whites and slightly higher than for blacks and Asian Americans. The relatively high rates of affordability stress among Latino (as well as black and Asian American) home owners suggests the wisdom of caution against overselling home ownership to lower-income renters, as well as the need for appropriate policies to aid lower-income home owners in maintaining their homes and dealing with the risk of mortgage default and foreclosure.

For the most part, though, in both number and severity, very-low-income Latino renters have the most serious housing problems. Half of Latino renters in Massachusetts have incomes of less than $20,000 a year. More than 60 percent (almost 58,000 households) were shelter poor in 2000. With a median income of just $12,700 and a median size of 3.2 persons, shelter-poor Latino renters are disproportionately Latina single parents. While access to education, job training, and child care are essential elements for this population to begin to deal with the income side of the affordability crisis, without provision of deep housing subsidies, secure tenure, and supportive residential environments—that can only be assured through social housing—it is unrealistic to expect much decline in their shelter poverty.

This study seeks to extend and deepen the understanding of housing affordability problems experienced by Latinos in Massachusetts. To do so, I address the following questions:

- What is the extent of housing affordability problems among Latinos as measured by the conventional percent of income standards and the more realistic shelter-poverty standard?
- How do housing affordability problems of Latinos compare with those of black, Asian American, and white non-Latinos?
- How did the housing affordability problems of Latinos change from 1990 to 2000?
- What are some implications of the findings for policy and strategy?

The "long form" decennial Census of Population and Housing (the Census) generates the most detailed data on housing costs, incomes, and household characteristics at all geographical scales for Latinos and other groups from the largest samples of households. However, published Census data available through the Census do not provide the detail necessary for precise 5-dimensional analysis of housing affordability by race/ethnicity, tenure, income, household size, and housing cost. This study therefore utilizes data from the 1990 and 2000 Census public use microdata samples (PUMS) for Massachusetts. Basic cross tabs have been generated by the Massachusetts State Data Center according to my specifications. The data have then been analyzed for housing affordability according to the conventional standards (exceeding 30 percent and 50 percent of income) and the alternative "shelter poverty" standard I have developed.

## The Shelter Poverty Concept of Affordability

The conventional definition of housing affordability uses a cut-off of 30 percent of income as the maximum amount a household ostensibly can pay for housing without hardship. In the early 1980s this standard replaced the traditional 25 percent of income rule of thumb that had been widely used since the nineteenth century; and in recent years, 50 percent of income has been used as a measure of "worst case housing needs." In the early 1970s, I formulated a more realistic sliding scale called shelter poverty, which recognizes that relatively larger and lower-income families cannot realistically afford 30 percent, or even 25 percent, of their incomes for housing without compromising their other needs, and that households of relatively smaller size and higher income can afford more than 30 percent without hardship.[3]

The shelter poverty sliding scale arises from recognition that housing costs are by far the largest after-tax expense for most households and the expense they usually pay for first; nonhousing expenditures are limited by how much income is left after paying for housing. This means that a household is shelter poor if it cannot meet its nonhousing needs at some minimum level of adequacy after paying for housing. Since the nonhousing expenses of small households are, on average, less than those of large households (to achieve a comparable basic standard of living), smaller households can reasonably devote a higher percentage of income to housing than can larger households with the same income. Since low- and higher-income households of the same size and type require about the same amount of money to meet their nonhousing needs at a comparable basic standard of living, those with lower incomes can afford to devote a smaller percentage of income for housing than otherwise similar, higher-income households can afford.[4]

The shelter-poverty scale uses a conservative minimum standard of adequacy for nonhousing necessities, scaled for differences in household size and type, somewhat like the federal poverty standard. Unlike the official poverty standard, though, it takes into account the actual cost of a standardized, basic "market basket" of nonhousing necessities, plus federal and state taxes, in determining the maximum amount of money that households can afford to spend for housing and still have enough left to pay for this basic market basket of nonshelter necessities.[5] In this way, the shelter-poverty scale emerges as a sliding scale of housing affordability—varying with household size, type, and income—that is more realistic than any fixed percentage of income. For example, in Massachusetts in 2000:

- An employed single parent with one child, working full time at a minimum-wage job ($6 an hour in Massachusetts at that time) could afford $115 a month for housing (11 percent of her income) on the shelter-poverty standard—if she also had health insurance and subsidized child care; without these benefits she could afford even less. She would need a job paying $9 an hour (plus health care and child care) to be able to afford a rent of $470 a month (30 percent of her income), which was the HUD "fair market rent" (FMR) for unsubsidized one-bedroom apartments in Berkshire and Worcester counties, the least expensive parts of the state. In order to be able to afford the $750 a month FMR for one-bedroom apartments in metropolitan Boston, she would need an income of at least $26,000 a year (plus child care). To be able to afford the $940 a month FMR for two-bedroom apartments in metro Boston she would need an income of at least $29,500 (plus child care). And for each additional child she would need about $7,000 a year more in after-tax income to be able to afford the same level of housing cost and still meet her family's nonshelter needs at a very basic level.
- A married couple with two children, with both parents working full time at minimum-wage jobs ($25,000 a year) could afford *nothing* for housing if they were to pay their taxes and meet their family's nonshelter needs at a basic level. To be able to afford a rent of $560 a month, which was the FMR for two-bedroom apartments in Pittsfield in 2000, in the least expensive part of the state, they would need an income of $36,500 a year (and would be paying 18 percent of their income, all they could afford). To be able to afford the $940 FMR (in 2000) for two-bedroom apartments in metro Boston, they would need an income of nearly $43,000 (and be paying 26 percent, all they could afford).
- A senior citizen living alone and depending entirely upon Social Security survivor's benefits of $500 a month could have afforded *nothing* for housing and still meet her other needs. If she received Social Security payments of $900 a month (and no medical costs beyond Medicare premiums), she could have afforded just $380 a month, which is barely above the FMR for studio apartments in the cheapest parts of the state, Berkshire and Worcester counties in 2000. To be able to afford the nearly $670 a month that is the FMR for studio apartments in metro Boston, she would need an income of over $1,200 a month ($14,400 a year).

This study examines who is paying more than they can afford for housing based on the shelter-poverty standard, as well as the 30 percent and 50 percent of income standards. The focus of this report presents affordability problems in terms of the shelter-poverty standard, but there are included some comparisons with the conventional 30 percent and 50 percent standards of affordability. For the most part, when viewed through the shelter-poverty lens, the scope of the affordability problem is found to be *comparable* to the 30 percent of income standard but *more* extensive than on the 50 percent of income standard. Beyond these aggregate patterns, though, the shelter poverty approach reveals significantly different distributions of the problem, properly focusing attention on those lower-income and larger Latino households who are experiencing the most painful squeeze between high housing costs and inadequate incomes—a squeeze that leaves them unable to meet their nonhousing needs at even a minimal level of adequacy.

## Latino Shelter Poverty in Massachusetts: 2000

According to 2000 Census data, there were 121,000 Latino households in the Massachusetts, 4.9 percent of all households in the state. They had a median income of $27,600. Nearly a third had incomes of less than $15,000, a third had incomes from $15,000 to $40,000, and about a third had incomes of $40,000 or more. Their median household size was three persons. A little over one in six Latino households contained just a single person, while a little over one-fifth had two persons, about one-fifth had three persons, about one-fifth had four persons, and about a fifth had five or more persons.

The home ownership rate of Massachusetts Latinos was a little under 22 percent in 2000. This compares with about 32 percent among black non-Latinos, 41 percent among Asian Americans, and 67 percent among white non-Latinos. Even among Latino households with incomes of $40,000 or more the home ownership rate was only 43 percent in 2000, compared with 75 percent for all Massachusetts households with incomes of $40,000 or more.

The differences between Latino renters and home owners are so great that housing affordability is best considered by tenure rather than for Latinos in the aggregate. Specifically, Latino renters had a median income of $21,000 in 2000 and a median size of 2.9 persons, while Latino home owners had a median income of $57,000 and a median size of 3.6 persons. Thus, in the following sections the housing situations of Latino renters and home owners are examined separately.

## Latino Renters: Households, Incomes, and Shelter Poverty

In 2000 there were nearly 95,000 Latino renter households in Massachusetts. These households had a median size of 2.9 persons. Nearly 40 percent contained four persons or more, while a fifth had three persons, a little over a fifth had two persons, and a little less than a fifth one person in the household. Latinos were about 10 percent of all renter households in the state in 2000, but they differed significantly from other groups of renters: over 40 percent of all renter households had just one person, and nearly 70 percent contained two or fewer.

The median income of Latino renter households in Massachusetts was $21,000 in 2000. About 26 percent had incomes of less than $10,000, and 12 percent had incomes of $10,000 to $15,000. By contrast, the median income of all renter households was $30,000. Nonetheless, just over a quarter of Latino renters had incomes of $40,000 or more in 2000. Many of these higher-income households probably have multiple wage earners and, unless they have many children, are unlikely to have serious housing affordability problems. Many members of this latter group of Latino renters may therefore be potential candidates for home ownership.

There are substantial differences among Latino renters by household size. The relatively small group of one-person Latino renters had median income of only $9,800 in 2000. This very low-income group probably consists mostly of nonelderly, single, recent immigrants with barriers to adequate employment as well as some elderly.

The median income of two-person and three-person Latino renter households was about $20,000, with about a quarter having incomes of less than $15,000. Most of these extremely low-income households are probably single mothers with children. Among households with four or more persons the median income was nearly $30,000, but over a quarter had incomes of under $15,000. Some of these larger very-low-income households may have two adults but probably just one wage earner.

As a group, there are over 24,000 Latino renter households with incomes of less than $15,000 a year and containing at least two persons; they account for over a quarter of all Latino renters in Massachusetts. The very low incomes and relatively large size of so many Latino renters' households in comparison with other renters point toward high rates of housing affordability problems as well as stress in meeting their nonshelter needs.

Focusing on renter households dealing with shelter poverty provides another perspective on the issue of affordability.

In 2000, nearly 58,000 (61 percent) of all Latino renter households in Massachusetts were shelter poor (see top panel of Table 3.1). They had a median income of only $12,700, an amount less than 60 percent of the median income of all Latino renters ($21,000). The median size of shelter-poor Latino renter households was 3.2 persons (see Table 3.1). This is slightly greater than the median size of *all* Latino renter households (note: the numbers and household composition of all Latino renter

TABLE 3.1. Latino renter households with affordability problems, Massachusetts, 2000

| | Total households with income below $10,000 | Total households with income below $15,000 | Total households all incomes | Median income | Persons in household |
|---|---|---|---|---|---|
| **Household size** | | | | | |
| Shelter poor | | | | | |
| 1-Person household | 8,376 | 9,237 | 9,378 | 6,200 | 9,378 |
| 2-Person household | 5,051 | 7,986 | 10,882 | 10,700 | 21,764 |
| 3-Person household | 5,013 | 7,579 | 12,742 | 25,300 | 38,227 |
| 4-Person household | 2,897 | 4,712 | 11,656 | 18,600 | 46,626 |
| 5-Person household | 1,466 | 2,360 | 7,279 | 21,200 | 36,397 |
| 6+ Person household | 949 | 1,695 | 5,979 | 25,300 | 40,296 |
| TOTAL | 23,752 | 33,569 | 57,916 | 12,700 | 192,687 |
| Median size | | | 3.2 | | |
| Paying 50% or more of income for housing | | | | | |
| 1-Person household | 4,513 | 5,282 | 5,739 | 5,800 | 5,739 |
| 2-Person household | 3,331 | 4,393 | 5,087 | 6,900 | 10,175 |
| 3-Person household | 3,453 | 4,571 | 5,401 | 7,300 | 16,202 |
| 4-Person household | 2,067 | 2,902 | 3,731 | 9,100 | 14,924 |
| 5-Person household | 1,091 | 1,508 | 2,120 | 9,700 | 10,600 |
| 6+ Person household | 716 | 1,087 | 1,538 | 10,700 | 10,365 |
| TOTAL | 15,171 | 19,742 | 23,616 | 7,400 | 68,004 |
| Median size | | | 2.7 | | |

(*continued*)

TABLE 3.1. Continued

| | Total households with income below $10,000 | Total households with income below $15,000 | Total households all incomes | Median income | Persons in household |
|---|---|---|---|---|---|
| | | | Paying 30% or more of income for housing | | |
| 1-Person household | 6,503 | 8,054 | 10,304 | 8,000 | 10,304 |
| 2-Person household | 4,141 | 6,053 | 9,495 | 11,600 | 18,990 |
| 3-Person household | 4,236 | 5,921 | 9,334 | 11,300 | 28,002 |
| 4-Person household | 2,499 | 3,733 | 7,106 | 14,300 | 28,424 |
| 5-Person household | 1,287 | 1,889 | 4,079 | 16,100 | 20,394 |
| 6+ Person household | 841 | 1,362 | 3,060 | 18,300 | 20,625 |
| TOTAL | 19,507 | 27,011 | 43,377 | 11,500 | 126,738 |
| Median size | | | 2.7 | | |

*Source:* 1990 and 2000 public use micro data samples.

households and home owner households are not shown in the tables of this study).

Shelter-poverty problems vary considerably by household size. Among one-person and two-person renters, 20,260 households (comprising a little over 50 percent of all Latino renter households of this size) were shelter poor in 2000. Shelter poverty for this group is concentrated almost entirely among households under $15,000. Among three-person and four-person Latino renter households, 24,400 households (comprising over 67 percent of such households) were shelter poor in 2000. For households with five or more persons, the shelter-poverty rate was 71 percent. The reach of shelter poverty up the income distribution for larger households reflects not only higher housing costs for larger apartments but also the greater cost of meeting nonshelter needs in households with more people.

Looking at conventional affordability burdens, about 45.9 percent of Latino renters (equivalent to the 43,377 households that appear in the third panel of Table 3.1) paid over 30 percent of their incomes for housing in 2000. This proportion is considerably lower than the 61 percent that are shelter poor (see the "Latino" panel under "Rental households" in Table 3.2). Households paying over 30 percent of their income in housing had a median income of $11,500. Separate data (not reported here) show the differential patterns by household size. Among one- and two-person households, the rates of shelter poverty are comparable to the rates paying over 30 percent of income; by contrast, among larger households, shelter-poverty rates are much higher than the rates paying over 30 percent of income. The household-size differences exist because the conventional standard reflects incomes only, rather than taking into account the household-size effects of nonshelter necessities, as does the shelter-poverty approach. That is, the shelter-poverty standard provides a much more sensitive measure of affordability burden by household size.

About 25 percent of Latino renters paid over 50 percent of income for housing, with a median income of just $7,400 (Table 3.1). For small households shelter-poverty rates are about twice the rates of 50 percent or more of income. However, for large households shelter-poverty rates are three to four times as great. On both of the conventional standards, three-person households have by far the most severe problem, unlike shelter poverty, which is strongly correlated with household size.

Let us now compare Latino renters with other renters. In 2000 Latino renters accounted for about 10 percent of all renter households in Massachusetts. Their median income of $21,000 was lower than that of all non-Latino groups of renters: blacks ($25,000), Asian Americans ($32,000), and whites ($32,000).

TABLE 3.2. Households with affordability problems, Massachusetts, 1990–2000

| | Renter households | | | | | | Homeowner households | | | | | |
|---|---|---|---|---|---|---|---|---|---|---|---|---|
| | Number of households (thousands) | | Percentage of households | | Change 1990–2000 | | Number of households (thousands) | | Percentage of households | | Change 1990–2000 | |
| | 1990 | 2000 | 1990 | 2000 | Number | % | 1990 | 2000 | 1990 | 2000 | Number | % |
| **All** | | | | | | | | | | | | |
| Shelter poor | 289.8 | 340.3 | 31.7% | 36.4% | 50.5 | 17.4% | 169.9 | 310.2 | 12.8% | 20.6% | 140.3 | 82.6% |
| Paying 50%+ | 191.3 | 185.4 | 20.9% | 19.8% | −5.9 | −3.1% | 104.6 | 143.9 | 7.9% | 9.5% | 39.3 | 37.6% |
| Paying 30%+ | 380.7 | 376.2 | 41.6% | 40.2% | −4.5 | −1.2% | 304.7 | 398.6 | 22.9% | 26.4% | 93.9 | 30.8% |
| **Latino** | | | | | | | | | | | | |
| Shelter poor | 38.3 | 57.9 | 59.1% | 61.2% | 19.6 | 51.2% | 2.3 | 8.6 | 16.8% | 32.9% | 6.4 | 280.7% |
| Paying 50%+ | 21.2 | 23.6 | 32.8% | 25.0% | 2.4 | 11.4% | 1.3 | 4.0 | 9.4% | 15.4% | 2.7 | 211.0% |
| Paying 30%+ | 34.9 | 43.4 | 53.9% | 45.9% | 8.5 | 24.2% | 3.4 | 8.9 | 25.1% | 33.7% | 5.5 | 161.4% |
| **Black** | | | | | | | | | | | | |
| Shelter poor | 27.6 | 39.0 | 41.8% | 48.2% | 11.4 | 41.2% | 3.9 | 11.9 | 15.6% | 30.7% | 7.9 | 201.3% |
| Paying 50%+ | 16.8 | 19.2 | 25.4% | 23.8% | 2.4 | 14.5% | 2.4 | 6.4 | 9.5% | 16.5% | 4.0 | 165.8% |
| Paying 30%+ | 30.6 | 36.8 | 46.5% | 45.5% | 6.1 | 19.9% | 5.9 | 13.5 | 23.4% | 34.9% | 7.6 | 129.3% |
| **Asian American** | | | | | | | | | | | | |
| Shelter poor | 10.8 | 21.0 | 48.9% | 45.3% | 10.2 | 94.6% | 2.4 | 9.1 | 15.9% | 28.8% | 6.8 | 285.7% |
| Paying 50%+ | 7.3 | 12.0 | 32.9% | 26.0% | 4.7 | 64.8% | 1.5 | 3.6 | 10.1% | 11.4% | 2.1 | 140.7% |
| Paying 30%+ | 11.7 | 21.1 | 53.1% | 45.6% | 9.4 | 80.1% | 4.3 | 9.6 | 28.9% | 30.2% | 5.3 | 122.1% |
| **White** | | | | | | | | | | | | |
| Shelter poor | 213.1 | 222.4 | 28.0% | 31.4% | 9.4 | 4.4% | 161.3 | 280.5 | 12.6% | 19.9% | 119.2 | 73.9% |
| Paying 50%+ | 146.0 | 130.5 | 19.2% | 18.5% | −15.5 | −10.6% | 99.4 | 129.9 | 7.8% | 9.2% | 30.5 | 30.7% |
| Paying 30%+ | 303.4 | 274.9 | 39.8% | 38.8% | −28.5 | −9.4% | 291.1 | 366.6 | 22.8% | 26.0% | 75.5 | 25.9% |

*Source:* 1990 and 2000 public use micro data samples.

Table 3.2 shows that the rate of shelter poverty among Latino renters (61 percent) was much higher than that of non-Latino black (48 percent), Asian American (45 percent), and white renters (31 percent). These differential rates reflect differences in household size as well as income. For example, even though Latino renters had higher median income than black renters did, the median size of shelter-poor Latino households was 3.2 persons compared with 2.1 persons among shelter-poor black households and 2.5 among Asian Americans.

By contrast, on the conventional affordability standards, Latino renters showed rates very similar to those of non-Latino blacks and Asian Americans: about 46 percent on the 30-percent standard and 25 percent on the 50-percent standard. All three populations of color had considerably higher rates, though, than did non-Latino white renters (about 39 percent and 19 percent, respectively, on the two conventional standards).

## Latino Home Owners: Households, Incomes, and Shelter Poverty

In 2000 there were about 26,000 Latino home owner households in Massachusetts, according to Census data. The median size of these households was 3.6 persons, considerably greater than the median size of renter households (2.9 persons). Over 70 percent of Latino home owner households had three persons or more; 21 percent had two persons; less than nine percent had one person.

Economically, Latino home owners differ very substantially from Latino renters. The median income of all Latino home owners in 2000 was about $57,000, compared with just $21,000 for all Latino renters. Fewer than 10 percent had incomes of under $20,000, while fewer than 20 percent had incomes of less than $30,000. By household size, home owners with three, four, and five persons had medians incomes of about $60,000, while those households with six or more persons in the household had median income of over $73,000.

Examining shelter poverty among home owners brings out other interesting trends. Nearly 33 percent (8,649 households) of Latino home owners in Massachusetts were shelter poor in 2000. Their median income was $31,600, equal to about 55 percent of the median income of all Latino home owners (see top panel of Table 3.3). Their median size was 3.8 persons, slightly higher than the median size of all Latino home owner households. Data not reported here show that the incidence of shelter poverty is correlated—albeit imperfectly—with household size: among one- and two-person households the rate was 23 to 24 percent, ranging up to 41 percent of five-person and 49 percent of six-or-more person

TABLE 3.3. Latino homeowner households with affordability problems, Massachusetts, 2000

| | Total households with income below $10,000 | Total households with income below $15,000 | Total households, all incomes | Median income | Persons in household |
|---|---|---|---|---|---|
| Household size | | | | | |
| **Shelter poor** | | | | | |
| 1-Person household | 341 | 444 | 544 | 8,600 | 544 |
| 2-Person household | 178 | 387 | 1,255 | 23,100 | 2,510 |
| 3-Person household | 99 | 177 | 1,942 | 34,700 | 5,827 |
| 4-Person household | 184 | 250 | 1,725 | 31,800 | 6,901 |
| 5-Person household | 138 | 190 | 1,722 | 34,100 | 8,611 |
| 6+Person household | 86 | 137 | 1,460 | 39,300 | 9,725 |
| Total | 1,026 | 1,585 | 8,649 | 31,600 | 34,119 |
| Median size | | | 3.8 | | |
| **Paying 50% or more for housing** | | | | | |
| 1-Person household | 257 | 356 | 612 | 13,600 | 612 |
| 2-Person household | 157 | 296 | 817 | 22,000 | 1,634 |
| 3-Person household | 91 | 154 | 716 | 26,000 | 2,147 |
| 4-Person household | 176 | 237 | 771 | 23,200 | 3,085 |
| 5-Person household | 135 | 179 | 663 | 23,400 | 3,314 |
| 6+Person household | 82 | 128 | 464 | 23,900 | 3,094 |
| Total | 899 | 1,350 | 4,043 | 22,400 | 13,885 |
| Median size | | | 3.3 | | |
| **Paying 30% or more for housing** | | | | | |
| 1-Person household | 341 | 478 | 1,113 | 18,900 | 1,113 |
| 2-Person household | 176 | 350 | 1,773 | 32,400 | 3,545 |
| 3-Person household | 98 | 169 | 1,770 | 34,600 | 5,309 |
| 4-Person household | 183 | 247 | 1,800 | 35,700 | 7,202 |
| 5-Person household | 138 | 187 | 1,389 | 33,000 | 6,945 |
| 6+Person household | 86 | 135 | 1,021 | 34,400 | 6,802 |
| Total | 1,022 | 1,566 | 8,866 | 32,700 | 30,917 |
| Median size | | | 3.4 | | |

Source: 1990 and 2000 public use micro data samples.

households, but with the order inverted among three-person (37 percent) and four-person (28 percent) households.

On the conventional standards of affordability, about 34 percent of Latino home owners in Massachusetts were paying over 30 percent of income for housing—slightly higher than the shelter-poverty rate—while 15 percent were paying over 50 percent of income (see the "Latino" panel under "Home owner Households" in Table 3.2). Those who are paying over 50 percent of income are spending much more than specified by conventional mortgage underwriting standards. In some cases, these costs may reflect ownership of multifamily houses, in which some of the costs are offset by rental income. In other cases, though, their income may have declined after purchase, or income may have been exaggerated to qualify for a mortgage.

Comparisons of Latino home owners with non-Latino home own-ers merit our attention. Latino home owners in Massachusetts had a median income ($57,000) nearly the same as non-Latino black home owners ($56,000) in 2000 but much lower than Asian American home owners (nearly $77,000) and non-Latino whites (almost $65,000). Latino home owners had slightly higher rates of shelter poverty than black home owners did: 32.9 percent versus 30.7 percent. This differential is con-sistent with the slightly larger median size of shelter-poor Latino home owners: 3.6 persons vs. 3.2. Asian American home owners had only slightly lower rate of shelter poverty—28.8 percent—reflecting the con-centration among large Asian American home owner households (median size of 3.7 persons among the shelter poor). By contrast, non-Latino white home owners had a much lower rate of shelter poverty: 19.9 percent (see Table 3.2).

Using the conventional percent of income standards, non-Latino black home owners have 1 percentage point higher rates of affordability prob-lems than Latinos do. Both Latinos and blacks have higher rates than do Asian Americans and non-Latino whites, although the differentials are smaller than on the shelter poverty standard (see Table 3.2).

## Trends in Housing Affordability Problems: 1990 To 2000

As might be expected renters confronted the most serious challenges in the previous decade. The number of all Latino renter households in Massachusetts increased from 64,800 in 1990 to about 94,600 in 2000. This is a growth of more than 45 percent over the ten-year period, as Latino renters increased from 7.1 percent of all renters in 1990 to 10.1 percent in 2000.

The median income of all Latino renters in 1990 was $18,000, increasing to $21,000 in 2000. However, adjusted for inflation, the median income of Latino renters in 2000 was 10 percent lower than it had been in 1990. This reflects both the influx of lower-income Latinos into the state during the period as well as the failure of the economic boom of the 1990s to provide much of an economic boost to many Latinos.

Consequently, from 1990 to 2000 the number of shelter-poor Latino renter households rose from 38,300 to 57,900—an increase of 51 percent. Shelter poverty grew slightly faster than the overall growth of Latino renters, resulting in a rise in the incidence from 59.1 percent in 1990 to 61.2 percent in 2000 (see Table 3.2).

Throughout the 1990s Latino renters experienced by far the highest rates of shelter poverty of any group. In 1990 the incidence of shelter poverty was 10 percentage points higher than that of Asian American renters, 17 percentage points higher than that of non-Latino blacks and more than 30 points higher than non-Latino white renters. By 2000 the gap between Latino rate of shelter poverty and that of Asian American renters grew to 16 percentage points; the gap with non-Latino blacks narrowed a little to 13 percentage points; while the gap with non-Latino whites remained 30 percentage points (see Table 3.2).

Latino home owners faced different issues during the 1990s, than those confronted by renters. In 1990 there were about 13,500 Latino home owners in Massachusetts, barely 1 percent of all home owners in the state. By 2000 the number had nearly doubled to 26,300, 1.7 percent of all home owners. The median income of Latino home owners rose from $48,600 in 1990 to $57,000 in 2000. Since there was a very large increase in the number of Latino home owners during this particular period, the income increase reflects more than just improved conditions for those who were home owners already in 1990; it is also a consequence of many middle-income Latino renters taking advantage of home ownership opportunities provided by the economic growth and first-time home buyer programs.

In 1990 about 17 percent of Latino home owners were shelter poor. By 2000 the rate had increased to nearly 33 percent (see Table 3.2), despite the booming economy. The explanation for this apparent anomaly is that in the mid- and late 1990s many Latino households were taking on substantial debt burdens in order to become home owners. Since the standards for both conventional and first-time home buyer loans do not take into account household size, many households were able to qualify for loans even though their home ownership costs left them squeezed in relation to their nonshelter needs (i.e., they were shelter poor). Indeed, the growth in the rate of Latino home owners paying more than 30 percent of income, from 25 percent in 1990 to 34 percent in 2000, is consistent with this interpretation, as underwriting standards typically use ratios somewhat in excess of 30 percent of income. In some cases households may have stretched or exaggerated their incomes to qualify for loans, but ended up with severe cost burdens in excess of 50 percent of income; this rate grew from a little under 10 percent of Latino home owners in 1990 to over 15 percent in 2000. Those in this latter group have probably disproportionately faced foreclosure in the years after 2000.

In 1990 Latino home owners had a rate of shelter poverty about 1 percentage point higher than both non-Latino black and Asian American home owners—an insignificant difference—and about 4 percentage points higher than that of non-Latino white home owners (see Table 3.2). Between 1990 and 2000 shelter poverty increased significantly for all groups, with Latinos still having a slightly higher rate than both and blacks and Asian Americans, but all home owners of color still were rather higher than whites. During this period non-Latino black home ownership surged even more than Latino home ownership in response to first-time home buyer programs and advocacy around mortgage lending, with financial risks at least comparable to those faced by new Latino home owners.

## Approaches to Addressing Latino Shelter Poverty

This section looks at approaches for addressing Latino shelter poverty for three groups: shelter-poor renters, moderate-income renters, and shelter-poor home owners.

### Shelter-Poor Latino Renters

By far the most extensive and serious housing needs of Massachusetts Latinos are among the very low-income renter families with children. Statewide, 58,000 Latino renter households are shelter poor, with median income of just $12,700, median size of 3.2 persons; over half are female-headed.

This profile points to the need for extensive and comprehensive strategies that combine income development with housing support, focused primarily in the cities and neighborhoods with concentrations of very low-income Latino renters. For, on the one hand, unless these households are able to increase their incomes quite substantially, most will remain shelter poor. Even under the best of circumstances, it is unlikely that housing subsidies will be sufficient in quantity and depth to reach all who currently are deeply shelter poor. On the other hand, without secure tenure and manageable housing costs, the daily struggle for survival makes it exceedingly difficult, if not impossible, for many Latina mothers to obtain basic education, skills, and access to jobs.

The recent experience of Inquilinos Boricuas en Acción (IBA) in Boston's South End, one of the oldest and best-known community development corporations (CDCs) in the country, is illustrative of the dilemmas and some of the possibilities. Of the approximately 450 families living in IBA's Villa Victoria, 75 percent are femaleheaded, and 92 percent are below the federal poverty level. Because of the extremely low incomes of most residents, many are shelter poor even with housing subsidies because the subsidies are based on the 30 percent of income standard. As has been occurring with many CDCs, IBA has increasingly been providing services aimed at income development and not just traditional social services. Through refinancing of the development, IBA has wired Villa Victoria for the Internet. With foundation grants, IBA is providing every household with a computer and printer, as well as offering personalized training and support and a community technology center. As their Villa Tech flyer says: "The goal is to facilitate opportunities for self-directed educational and employment-related achievement."

Given the Villa Victoria resident population, Latina single moms are certainly a major part of IBA's Villa Tech initiative. Nonetheless, there remain major challenges for young Latinas with young children. Having a computer and Internet access within the apartment, and training and technical assistance in the development, provide terrific learning opportunities. Translating this into employment is severely constrained, though, by the insufficiency of subsidized child care. IBA has a long waiting list, and whenever they are able to obtain more child care slots, they are filled immediately.

Holyoke's Nueva Esperanza and Lawrence's Community Works are two examples of CDCs in other parts of Massachusetts that also primarily serve very-low-income Latinos, have a substantial number of units, and increasingly are linking income development and other projects with their housing efforts. Nonetheless, the minuscule amounts of federal and state funding for new subsidized housing as well as the enormous complexity of doing development in the current environment mean that most shelter-poor Latino renters do not and will not have access to the security of tenure and support services provided by the most creative CDCs.

A quite different strategic approach is offered by City Life/Vida Urbana, based in the Jamaica Plain neighborhood of Boston but with a history of also working in Roxbury and more recently in other Boston neighborhoods as well. For thirty years City Life/Vida Urbana has focused on tenant organizing, political education, and advocacy for social housing permanently outside of the speculative market. Their constituency has been predominantly Latino, but they actively pursue multiracial, multicultural coalition building and leadership development bringing together African Americans and Haitians with Latinos.

City Life/Vida Urbana has four major elements to their work. The largest component has always been tenant organizing, with their recent efforts returning primarily to their historical focus on building-level organizing, providing assistance to low-income renters in subsidized and unsubsidized private rental housing. As of mid-2002, they were working with tenants in 25 buildings—with over five hundred tenant families, mostly Latino and African American. In this work, practical assistance with housing problems is always coupled with leadership development and political education about housing and the economy. The grassroots organizing also provides a base for coalition work on housing policies with organizations such as the Boston Tenant Coalition.

The Healthy Homes/Healthy Families initiative of City Life/Vida Urbana works out of local community health centers, providing advocacy and tenants' rights training to help people stay in their apartments and get housing conditions improved. An effort that has been running for about twelve years, Healthy Homes/Healthy Families has reached about five hundred to a thousand families a year, most of which are headed by Latina mothers.

In addition, City Life/Vida Urbana has been providing home buyer education for about six years. Their approach has evolved from conventional home buyer education programs toward more emphasis on issues of predatory lending, foreclosure risks, and nonspeculative home ownership alternatives, such as limited-equity cooperatives.

Finally, for about five years City Life/Vida Urbana has had a Latino Leadership Development Program that is part of tenant organizing. Consisting of intensive workshops for about 20 to 25 people and ongoing involvement through the Latino Committee, this endeavor focused on parent organizing around educational issues and voter registration and mobilization.

For low-income Latino communities outside of Boston, City Life/Vida Urbana offers an important and appealing complement or alternative to the more standard models of housing development and conventional home ownership.

## Moderate-Income Latino Renters

Given the hard reality of shelter poverty among Massachusetts Latinos, it should be apparent that the almost singular focus of national and state policy makers on expanding conventional home ownership among

Latinos is misplaced and indeed unfair to those with the greatest need. Despite the understandable emotional and symbolic significance attached to home ownership, and the apparent potential for housing security and asset accumulation, it is politically and morally essential to avoid false promises about the possibilities and benefits of conventional home ownership for lower-income households. It is important to recognize that adequate and secure income is the necessary foundation for the dream of home ownership not to become a nightmare. As this study has shown, a third of all Latino home owners in Massachusetts are shelter poor; more than 80 percent of Latino home owners with yearly incomes of less than $40,000 are shelter poor; and almost 14 percent of those with incomes of $40,000 or more are shelter poor.

Mortgage qualification does not consider the costs of utilities, maintenance, and repairs, which are sizable and often unanticipated burdens in older houses. Lower-income home owners are disproportionately victimized by financial scams, as has again become apparent recently. Those who buy multifamily houses with the expectation that rental income will make their housing affordable face the challenges and contradictions of being a landlord, not just a home owner; the owner's limited income creates a strong incentive to seek tenants with the highest and most secure incomes. And emotional and financial stress is high, with mortgage defaults and foreclosures not unusual, resulting in loss of home, savings, and even self-esteem.

To be sure, those Latinos who have a sufficient level and stability of income must be assured of full and nondiscriminatory access to housing markets, mortgage credit, and home owner insurance. But given the evidence of shelter poverty among Latino home owners and the other risks of conventional ownership, home ownership opportunity programs should be targeted to Latino renters with stable incomes of at least $40,000 a year and sufficient savings to be able to cover unanticipated repairs. The data used for this study suggest that about twenty-four thousand Latino renter households had incomes of $40,000 or more in 2000. It is essential that Latino leaders and housing advocates act responsibly to determine for whom home ownership is and is not appropriate.

For lower-income Latinos, especially those with incomes from about $20,000 to $40,000, one important component of a strategy would be to work on increasing their incomes and savings, on the one hand. On the housing side, complementary strategies should promote models of community and resident-controlled nonspeculative ownership—such as limited-equity cooperatives and mutual housing associations—which can provide greater security of tenure and affordability than conventional home ownership, as well as providing experience in resident control and community building.[6]

### Shelter-Poor Latino Home Owners

What might be done to assist those Latinos who are already home owners but are shelter poor and, for the most part, have incomes of less than $40,000? The most obvious answer is that they need more income, since the squeeze between their incomes and housing costs is leaving them unable to meet their nonshelter needs at a minimum level of adequacy. Since income strategies are beyond the scope of this chapter, but more importantly, since such households may not achieve sufficient income to sustain their housing payments despite squeezing their families' other needs, the intriguing question is whether there are housing strategies that might help them avoid losing their homes to foreclosure.

For shelter-poor Latino and other home owners who cannot afford to pay their mortgages, there is a need for a public program to provide permanent mortgage relief. Such a program would complement and go beyond current attempts of advocacy groups and public officials to encourage private lending institutions to exercise forbearance and refinance on more favorable terms. One form of direct financial assistance could be a monthly subsidy in the form of a deferred-payment, low-interest loan—a type of "soft" second mortgage—that would be repaid either over time when the owner's income increases, or at the time of eventual sale. A variation, which could ensure affordability not only for the current owner but future owners as well, would provide the monthly subsidy as a grant that would not have to be repaid. In return for this grant, a permanent affordability restriction would be recorded, limiting the resale price in order to keep the home affordable to eligible lower-income buyers in the future. The legal mechanisms for both of these models are well established. To implement them would require financing and capable enforcing agencies.

## Conclusion

The great majority of Latinos in Massachusetts are renters, and the great majority of Massachusetts Latino renters are shelter poor. Latino leaders and housing advocates should make conscious and deliberate efforts and seek resources to organize Latino renters so that they can act on their own behalf to resist rent increases, improve their living conditions, defend their rights, and build confidence, skills, and solidarity.

At the same time, other types of organizing efforts are also needed to begin to address Latino shelter poverty in an effective way. Apart from the organizations mentioned above and a handful of others, Latino organizations and leaders in Massachusetts have focused their efforts primarily on improvements in employment, education, and social services, rather than housing. Given the critical importance of housing for social and economic well-being, it is apparent that Latino organizations ought to give higher priority to housing in their own work and enter into coalitions with housing advocacy organizations at both the local and state levels.

Latino workers are also a growing part of the constituency of trade unions and trade union organizing in Massachusetts. As Latinos participate in organizing drives and collective bargaining, and move into leadership positions, it is to be hoped that they will help push the labor movement to give greater attention to housing issues.

Latinos are the largest population of color in Massachusetts and one of the fastest growing. They face some of the most severe housing challenges that deserve the attention of all responsible policy makers and citizens. Yet Latinos themselves also have the opportunity and responsibility to exert leadership in confronting not only Latino shelter poverty, but also shelter poverty in general as a fundamental failure of the institutions of our society and economy.

## Notes

1. This study originated from discussions with Andrés Torres and MaryJo Marion, director and associate director of the Gaston Institute; their encouragement and support have been much appreciated. Robert Lacey and Roy Williams of the Massachusetts State Data Center generated basic cross tabs of household data from the Census public use microdata samples (PUMS) for 1990 and 2000. The discussion of strategies and policies benefited greatly from discussions with Luis Aponte-Parés, David Cortiella, Juan Leyton, and Andrea Luquetta.

2. This study is based on an analysis of 1990 and 2000 Census public use microdata samples (PUMS) for Massachusetts. The 4 largest nonoverlapping racial/ethnic categories are Latino, black non-Hispanic, Asian non-Hispanic, and white non-Hispanic.

3. See Michael E. Stone, *Shelter Poverty: New Ideas on Housing Affordability* (Philadelphia: Temple University Press, 1993) for detailed discussion; also see Michael E. Stone, "Housing Affordability," in *Housing: Foundation for a New Social Agenda*, ed. Rachel Bratt, Michael E. Stone, and Chester Hartman (Philadelphia: Temple University Press, 2005), for further discussion of the logic of affordability.

4. Household size is the most decisive element of household composition in distinguishing affordability. Other elements, particularly age and relationships, are also significant, though somewhat less so than household size. The fully developed sliding scale, as presented in this chapter, has been derived for nonelderly married-couple

households, nonelderly single-adult households, and elderly households in order to take into account elements other than just household size.

5. To be sure, the official poverty level is based not on housing costs but instead on a food standard. However, the poverty level suffers from a number of conceptual weaknesses as a measure of overall income adequacy (see Stone, *Shelter Poverty*, 1993), and its food-driven approach is not the only reason why it is especially inappropriate as the starting point for constructing a housing affordability standard.

6. For further discussion of housing alternatives see Michael E. Stone, "Social Ownership," in *Housing: Foundation for a New Social Agenda*, ed. Rachel Bratt, Michael E. Stone, and Chester Hartman (Philadelphia: Temple University Press, 2005).

# Part II

# Migration and Community Formation

# 4 Mofongo Meets Mangú: Dominicans Reconfigure Latino Waterbury

Ruth Glasser

onnecticut is experiencing a cultural reconfiguration, and Waterbury is literally and figuratively in its middle.[1] The state with the highest proportion of Puerto Ricans among its Latinos, the highest per capita Puerto Rican city in the United States (Hartford), the first capital city with a Puerto Rican mayor (also Hartford) is becoming more nuanced, as newcomers from a variety of Spanish-speaking countries arrive daily to make their homes here.[2]

Dominicans are the most prominent group of newcomers reshaping Waterbury's social, cultural, and economic landscape: Dominican-owned grocery stores abound. Dominican children form the core of a group dancing Colombian *cumbia* in Waterbury's schools. Local funeral homes now advertise that they can send bodies to Santo Domingo as well as San Juan.

Unlike most northeastern states, Connecticut's urban life takes place in small cities—its largest, Bridgeport, has only 139,529 people. These are cities with heavily industrial economies in steady decline since World War II, when their factories began to shut down.[3] Waterbury was in the most industrialized corridor of the state, the center of the brass industry and related manufacturing, and was among the hardest hit.[4]

This study is a preliminary investigation of two questions: (1) how has the arrival of a new group of Latino immigrants affected the nature of Latino Waterbury and Waterbury as a whole, and (2) what does the addition of new Latino groups have to tell us about interethnic interaction in general and the reshaping of U.S. Latino identities in particular? Since World War II, Puerto Ricans have been the dominant Latino group in Connecticut. However, in the last twenty years, Connecticut's Latino communities have become more multiethnic, as illustrated in the story of Waterbury. Waterbury is also emblematic of the kind of small city to which Puerto Ricans, Dominicans, and other Latino groups have increasingly migrated during the last several decades. This trend is a departure from the traditional pattern of migration to New York City, still the main focus of studies about Puerto Rican migrants and Dominican immigrants.

This chapter intends to bring such smaller but increasingly popular destinations into the historical literature on Latinos in the United States. The history of Dominicans in Waterbury is a still-unfinished story of immigration and community development, and this chapter will, hopefully, begin to portray their community in the making. It represents a continuation of the author's research on Latino community history in Connecticut, a project that was begun with the Puerto Rican experience.[5]

The author's approach here is eclectic: statistics from the U.S. Census are supplemented with evidence of the physical and cultural geography of ethnic changeover. "Geography" refers both to the configurations of ethnic space and the meanings and attachments with which people endow them. As Lewis Holloway and Phil Hubbard suggest, we need to look beyond numbers to a humanistic geography that takes into account how people change places and endow them with personal meaning.[6] The author uses her personal observations of the changes in businesses, clubs, and other neighborhood institutions, and has asked her interviewees about them. Shows, advertisements, and announcements aired over local radio stations also provide clues to this cultural realignment.

This geography, in turn, is shaped with information culled from oral history interviews with Puerto Ricans and Dominicans who have settled in this central-western Connecticut city. Information for this chapter is in large part drawn from interviews with more than fifty Puerto Ricans conducted throughout the course of the 1990s. Twelve Waterbury Dominicans as well as five from other parts of the state were interviewed formally by the author and her students in two urban and community studies classes taught at the University of Connecticut Waterbury Campus. Informal conversations also took place over a period of a year with dozens of Dominicans in a variety of settings, including a local Dominican restaurant, a C-Town supermarket, a Dominican-owned party shop, a Dominican-owned beauty salon, and at Hispanic child care provider meetings. Context was also provided by interviews done by students and the author with immigrants to Waterbury from Peru, Colombia, Ecuador, Mexico, Guatemala, and El Salvador.

## Waterbury's New Dominican Immigrants

In small cities, even a few hundred or thousand migrants or immigrants from one country have a significant impact. Waterbury's population has long hovered between 100,000 and 110,000.

Waterbury's Dominican arrivals came to a multiethnic city colonized over time by thousands from Europe, Lebanon, Cape Verde, and French Canada and by African American migrants from the U.S. South. The city was already "Latinized" by Puerto Ricans. From the 1940s onward Puerto Ricans arrived in significant numbers to work in area factories. Most came from small towns in the south-central mountains and southern coast of the island. Boricuas usually spent only a brief period in New York City—sometimes only long enough to board the railroad to Waterbury. Others came directly, through agricultural contracts arranged by the Puerto Rican Department of Labor. After working on vegetable farms, in orchards, and nurseries in nearby towns, they arrived in Waterbury, where factories offered better pay and more independent lifestyles.[7]

Most early Puerto Rican migrants were young men who got established, then sent for loved ones. They settled in apartments and boarding houses near downtown, most particularly the city's South End. The community grew through chain migration, secondary migration from New York, and through generations born here.

With relatively well-paying factory jobs, many Puerto Rican *pioneros* were able to buy homes and educate their children. Scores of these children became professionals, many social service workers and teachers who ministered to the newer Puerto Rican migrants and the growing population of Spanish-speaking immigrants. This generation typically moved away from the increasingly devastated inner-city neighborhoods to the outlying areas of Waterbury and nearby suburbs.

Like previous immigrant groups, Puerto Rican pioneros and their children achieved upward mobility with a base of good factory jobs and created small businesses, churches, and clubs. Such achievements were short-lived, for the physical havoc of highway building and urban renewal starting in the 1960s, along with the closing of the "Big Three" brass mills and other factories not only destroyed many of these institutions but also made it difficult for ensuing migrants to scale similar social and economic ladders.

Context is everything, however. Both sending country conditions and those of New York City made smaller cities like Waterbury still an attractive choice for Latin American immigrants. Within the new "hourglass" economy, immigrants from countries where the dollar stretches far are able to sustain lives at home and here with jobs at the bottom, especially in a city where rents are relatively cheap.[8]

Census figures reflect these new, multicultural migration trends. In 1980, out of a total of 6,912 of "Spanish Origin" in Waterbury, 5,819 (84 percent) were Puerto Rican. By 2000, the Puerto Rican population rose to 18,146. This actually represented a decline in the share of the overall Hispanic population (to 77.7 percent). By the turn of the century there were 23,354 Hispanics, representing 22 percent of Waterbury's residents. These numbers included Mexicans, Ecuadorians, Colombians, and Cubans.

Particularly prominent were Dominicans, who now numbered 1,336, a more than threefold increase since 1990.[9]

Dominican immigration differed from Puerto Rican migration in ways that fed into the economy. The industrial jobs that remained in Waterbury were mostly in smaller factories that paid relatively low wages and mostly employed women. And it was women who were coming in significant numbers from the Dominican Republic, in contrast to the young male Puerto Rican migrants.

There were other differences between the two groups. Immigrants from the Dominican Republic were more urbanized, with stronger serial migration patterns.[10] Whereas many of the earlier Puerto Rican migrants had come from smaller towns, Dominicans came from larger cities such as Santo Domingo and Santiago. Many had been born and raised in smaller settlements but had migrated to ever-larger, urbanized areas in search of education and jobs. Moreover, many Dominican immigrants spent several years in New York City before coming to Waterbury.

Perhaps because immigration from the Dominican Republic was more difficult and expensive than migrating from Puerto Rico, many Quisqueyans came from higher economic positions than most Boricua migrants. Whereas the latter were often struggling small farmers, farm laborers, or fishermen, Dominican immigrants interviewed were more typically children of small business proprietors or farmers or ranchers with sizable landholdings or themselves had operated businesses thwarted by a teetering economy. Francisco Hernández, for example, was born in the town of Guaranico, where his family had a farm. He later moved to the capital to pursue his education. Hernández had trouble finding work in Santo Domingo, so he moved to Bonao, where he worked in a bank and then started a restaurant. Finally, economic difficulties forced him to close up shop and migrate to the United States.

According to interviewees, the first Dominicans came to Waterbury in the late 1960s. They had started off in New York City with no plans to move anywhere else. Apparently, close ties between New York City and Waterbury area manufacturers made the smaller city part of immigrants' mental geography. Gladys Maldonado explained:

> I came [to New York] in 1966. First my brother-in-law came looking to improve his life as a barber. A friend who had a barbershop helped him to come legally. Then after some time passed, he put in a request for my mother. My mother was a seamstress and seamstresses had a lot of work in New York in the 1960s.[11]

Maldonado's cousin's tailor husband moved with his company from New York to Waterbury. Maldonado joined her relatives there after seven years in New York. Similarly, Judith Mariñez recounted how she, a talented designer working in a garment factory in New York, was asked by a Waterbury area couple to work in their factory.[12]

Those immigrants established a beachhead in Waterbury and now "sold" it as a place with a better *ambiente* for the children. Maldonado recalled:

> In the year '73 my nieces and nephews were in the elementary grades. We were worried because [they] were very shy, and the public school in New York, well, it was a bit of a problem. So my cousin Carmen said, "Why don't you move to Waterbury?" Carmen told us it was a very peaceful city.[13]

Others found the city through community connections. Adelaida Garcia, who had lived in Puerto Rico and then New York, discovered Waterbury through a friend in her Pentecostal church. She left her troubled marriage behind and came north with several children:

> I lived in the Bronx, a dangerous place where if a woman went out alone at such and such an hour something could happen to her. The "sisters" in New York visited the "sisters" in Waterbury. I began to explore the place, and then I decided to take the step to come and live here. There were about five Christian families who helped me to move.[14]

Once single mothers such as Garcia had come to Waterbury, they urged others to migrate. Looking back, they believed that they had had a historical role in creating a community made up of their families and friends. As Felicia Díaz said:

> First my sister came, she brought my mother, my mother brought her children— we were seven—and their spouses. Those spouses could then bring their mothers, their siblings; those siblings could bring their spouses. There was always someone having a hard time in Santo Domingo to whom one could lend a hand. If you stop to think about the connections you've made to bring people, you almost believe you've created a complete Waterbury, with all the families that have come here.[15]

Within such a small city that they had helped shape, Dominican pioneras felt effective as recruiters and ultimately, as we shall see, as community leaders. Dominicans sacrificed time and space to build this community. On top of multiple jobs, they spent many hours getting immigrants acclimated. Felicia Díaz remembered:

> If someone didn't have a car and needed to get to work, the other person went to pick him up. If he needed to go to the hospital, we would get him an interpreter. We would tell the person who came from Santo Domingo or New York where there was work, where they sold the cheapest clothes, where he could find Hispanic food.[16]

They also routinely shared their homes. Felicia's only son, Victor, recalled that he almost never had a room to himself. As his mother explained: "People always came who had nowhere to live. And if you're humanitarian you say, 'Stay with me until you get a job.' When they got a job, the person left, but by [that] time another one had arrived. So since [Victor] always took the biggest room, he had to share."[17]

## Dominican Residence Patterns

Perhaps because of the long, arduous process of acquiring visas, it has taken many years for this Dominican chain migration to yield a sizable community. Only in the 1980s and the 1990s has Dominican Waterbury become visible to outsiders. But the early settlers established some patterns that continue to this day.

In the late 1960s and early 1970s, a few Dominicans lived among Puerto Ricans in the South End, but the majority settled in the North End of town. Dominicans found housing close to North End factories, allowing them to walk to jobs and be accessible to their children. Another factor in residential choices has been long-term plans. Workers' Compensation Commissioner Amado Vargas, a Dominican attorney with close ties to Waterbury's community, explained why many of his compatriots stayed in inner-ring neighborhoods such as the North End:

> I think Dominicans would rather live a life in a working-class neighborhood even though they're making middle-class income, because for those who are in their 40s, 50s, 60s and who emigrated here in the 70s, 80s, their goal is to go back to the island. They'd rather not invest money in a nicer home [here]. They start a home in the Dominican Republic, buy their property and then once or twice a year when they have the money they'll start adding to it. So by the time they're ready to retire, they have a house to go to.[18]

The low cost of living in the Dominican Republic compared to New York made life easier for both those who planned to go back to the island and those who stayed. One immigrant, Mercedes Sánchez, described her family's decision to come to Waterbury from New Jersey:

> A sister of my husband that lived here from 1982 was always pushing all her brothers, sisters, and her mother to move to Waterbury because it's too crowded in New York, the jobs don't pay enough and here [would] be much better for the children. Me and my husband were tired of paying one thousand dollars' rent for a two-bedroom apartment a lot smaller than this one and only my husband was working. I was tired [of being] at home with the kids and I couldn't find a job. So, we came one weekend to stay at his sister's home. We decided to come. He started [working] right away.

We came here paying five seventy-five [a month for rent]. We have to pay for heat but it was cheap, cheap, cheap. We park right here, in New Jersey forget it. We were paying for a parking lot. One hundred dollars every month.[19]

Family position has affected how Dominicans feel about the move. While parents looking for affordable housing and relatively crime-free neighborhoods liked Waterbury, their children and young adults were less enthusiastic. For newcomers from the Dominican Republic, iconic images of New York as *the* immigrant destination were very strong and alluring. There were no pictures of such a place as Waterbury on the television or in the mental geographies from home. Grismilda Pérez, a teenaged migrant, explained: "I didn't have any ideas because what they show you on TV is New York. You think you're going to see a lot of people and a lot of buildings and when I came it was really lonely and there were not many people."[20] Those who came directly to Waterbury sometimes had comical misconceptions of what the city might be like. Felicia Díaz was told she was moving to "the country." She envisioned raising her own chickens, and told her small daughter that now she'd be able to have the horse that she coveted.[21]

To adult female caretakers, Waterbury seemed quiet, uncrowded, a city but not too urban, on the edge of the country. Its hills were comforting, reminding many of the landscapes of home. For young men or teenagers accustomed to life in a Dominican city or in New York, though, Waterbury seemed like the end of the world. Enrique Familia came to Waterbury so that his U.S.-born wife, pregnant with triplets, could be near her family, but not without misgivings:

> The great majority of the Dominicans, if they say that they're going to the United States, it means New York where there are a lot of people, a lot of Dominicans. But we came here. Some friends helped me move. A cousin of mine, we got here to Waterbury and he saw all this, said, "Oh my God! Later, don't be calling me to come get you." And I thought, I have to get used to this.[22]

One can well imagine how Waterbury would look to an adventurous adolescent expecting New York City. Miles of ramshackle triple-decker houses canted on hills; shopping strips bearing big-box retail stores; low-lying, mostly abandoned brick factories or the rubble they leave behind as the city avidly demolishes signs of its industrial past. There are few New York-style commercial districts with dense blocks of storefronts pushed close to the street. Waterbury's public transportation is spotty, consisting of a few buses running infrequently during (narrowly defined) working hours. It is a city of drivers where pedestrians en masse are virtually nonexistent. It rolls up its sidewalks at night and looks abandoned.

Waterbury is typical of the kinds of U.S. cities many immigrants are moving to—most do not have the physical and social configurations of visibly busy communities. Often, as in Waterbury, their dense districts of locally owned stores have been urban-renewed out of existence. There is no New York-style "Sabana Church" nor "Quisqueya Heights" in Waterbury—the community that does exist is scattered and sparse, based in people's homes or in individual businesses. The isolation and lack of old-country neighborliness that immigrants complain of is compounded in a small city where there is little public ethnic life. Deindustrialization, the attendant erosion of the tax base, and federal and state disinvestment in cities have taken away some of the amenities earlier groups had, such as recreation programs for children and well-tended parks. Earlier migrant groups, including Puerto Rican pionero children, had gone to neighborhood schools. Today, most travel by bus to faraway schools, further eroding a sense of the neighborhood as a social unit.

Teenagers without drivers' licenses or cars, especially girls with strict old-world guardians, could feel like prisoners in their homes. For Grismilda Pérez, Waterbury was desolate when she first came:

> My neighborhood was so quiet. In my country you sit on the balcony, see people walking up and down, hear people talking and people wave at you. But I was sitting at a window and I had no friends and nobody to talk to and I was just so sad I started crying. I was like, "This is the most ugly place in the whole world."[23]

## Dominicans in Factories and Businesses

While the large brass factories were declining into nonexistence, a cluster of small garment and metal-parts factories in Waterbury's North End provided jobs for Dominican newcomers. Leather jackets, pocketbooks, gloves, and cosmetics cases were manufactured in small workshops on North Main Street and Cherry and Maple Avenues. Immigrants particularly recall cutting, stitching, and packing for "La Correa" and "La Chalina," local belt and tie manufacturers. As more immigrants arrived and factories shut down, Dominicans could be found on construction sites, as certified nurses' aides, and in restaurants. In most cases, they worked alongside Puerto Ricans as well as members of other immigrant groups with a growing presence in Waterbury.

Puerto Ricans who came to Waterbury after World War II talk about a city without stores to service their needs. The closest they could come to their products was at Italian grocery stores, where they could get espresso coffee and short grain rice. Otherwise, Boricuas had to make special trips to New York. From the mid-1950s, however, a vibrant Puerto Rican business community began to form in Waterbury's South End neighborhood. People who worked in factories got loans from relatives and friends to start furniture stores, record and jewelry stores, and groceries with Caribbean products.

When Dominicans first arrived in Waterbury some ten or fifteen years later, they found a few bodegas run by Puerto Rican pioneros where they could get most of what they needed. However, they still longed for specific products from home, as Felicia Díaz recalled: "Upon arriving here one found nothing from Santo Domingo. All the seasonings from Santo Domingo people brought from over there, the mints, the candies, until a short time ago. It was difficult because [those things are] part of one's culture."[24]

Dominicans were eventually served by compatriots looking for alternative livelihoods to the increasingly insecure factory jobs. As in New York, one of the most popular niches was the bodega. Juan Laras felt that the time was right to start his own business as the job market in the Waterbury area declined: "I lasted for eight or nine years working in several factories because before it was easy, people would move from one place to another for a dollar. Now the level of unemployment in Connecticut is too high."

Interviewees have described an explosion of Dominican-owned bodegas in Waterbury and throughout Connecticut during the last five to ten years. Some saw it as natural ethnic succession. Just as Puerto Ricans had previously taken over stores from Italian and Jewish merchants, now Dominicans were replacing Puerto Ricans. These Boricuas were aging. Their children had climbed the occupational ladder and had livelihoods that did not include grueling shopkeepers' hours. As Juan Laras put it:

> I have to be in here for fourteen hours, seven days a week. It looks easy. That man is a bodeguero and in five years he has X amount of money, yes, but in those five years he's there 150 hours a week, 362 days a year. On New Year's, when you're in your house unwrapping your gifts, I have to open up the bodega.
>
> The Puerto Ricans were the ones who began the bodega business. It's not easy. Probably that's why those who made their money got tired and they retired to enjoy what they earned. So they've passed the baton to the Dominicans. That's the future here.[25]

As with the factories, New York City connections played a role in the development of Waterbury bodegas. Dominicans who had started in New York began to expand into Connecticut in order to find new markets and investment opportunities—bolstered by credit from New York bodegueros.

Libio Rosado was one of these enterprising bodegueros. His photocopy center in Santiago foundered in the wake of a bank crisis, and he reluctantly moved to New York in 1989. Rosado worked in the produce and grocery business in Brooklyn until the opportunity arose to invest in Waterbury's C-Town supermarket. With credit offered by a co-ethnic from New York, Rosado happily moved his family to Connecticut and since 1994 has been a co-owner of the local C-Town. He has also opened a wholesale food warehouse and invested in other local bodegas or helped compatriots to open them.[26]

As in New York, a small percentage of Dominicans in Waterbury become bodegueros. But their number is belied by the visual strength of their presence—all over Waterbury are groceries that have been opened or bought out by Dominicans. Support by co-ethnics has helped. Juan Lara, for example, is buying his bodega gradually from his brother-in-law. Family support is often compounded by economic and social capital. Libio Rosado's mother owned a bodega in Santiago where he worked from a young age. Amado Vargas describes one family of bodegueros, close friends from his hometown of La Boca:

> They were like my family, well-known cattle people, upper middle class. When they came here, the first thing they did was open up a business. There must be at least six or seven brothers and sisters. [The] first little bodega was on Bank Street. And then from there they opened up a second bodega on Cherry Street, and then from there another brother opened one up on Congress [Avenue]. The sister also was an entrepreneur; she had a restaurant on East Main Street, one of my favorite places to eat.

Even with little or no English, these kinds of people had the material resources and the savvy to deal with the city bureaucracy. As Vargas observed: "It takes someone with skills to come here and open up a business."[27]

## Dominican Women in Business

After many years spent working in clothing and metal parts factories, Sonia Rosario decided she wanted her own business. Long-standing, close ties with Puerto Ricans enabled her to do so. She had met Joaquín and Hilda Batista in local factories. The couple had a daughter who owned a party shop, which Sonia admired:

> I decided it was nice work, entertaining, not too hard. We were all good friends and finally she said to me, "You've always wanted to work here. I'll sell it to you!"[28]

Sonia wanted to give the shop a Dominican feel and so she renamed it Merengue Party Shop: "I was looking for a name that was more Dominican. Sonia, there are twenty thousand Sonias. So I said to myself, everyone knows 'merengue.' Now as I walk around that's how everyone knows me. 'Look, there's Sonia Merengue!' "

Through the accretion of such small actions, Dominican women have helped to alter Waterbury's Latino landscape, as they become bodegueras, clothing shop owners, and beauty salon operators. Some make "Dominican cakes," prepare and sell food from their homes, or clean houses. Single mothers like Felicia Díaz have always cultivated more than one income stream, looking for jobs that allowed them the flexibility to be with their children:

> I always had a full-time and a part-time job. I did jobs at home, like those where you pack things and send them back by mail, manicures and pedicures on the weekends. People said, "I'm cleaning houses" and I said, "Do you need a helper?" There were days when [my children] went with me to work.[29]

But the most unusual niche among Dominican women in Waterbury is the child care business, becoming as ubiquitous and organized as any bodegueros' association. As with bodegas, opportunity and changing economic circumstances combined to create this niche. Dominican women earning their living in a variety of ways began to see the writing on the wall.

Adelaida Garcia, for example, had brought clothes and knickknacks up from New York City and sold them from her home, where she also worked as a beautician. But then came welfare reform: "The majority of my customers were people who lived on welfare. When they began to take away welfare, I began to prepare myself, because my customers were going! So I began to take day care classes."[30]

It was that very welfare-to-work transition that inspired the formation of the Waterbury Hispanic Professionals Day Care Association, in which Adelaida Garcia, Felicia Díaz, and dozens of other Waterbury Dominicanas are active members. In 1996, Luz Lebrón, a Puerto Rican single mother, formed a group of women transitioning off welfare. They brainstormed about their skills and how they could deploy them to earn a living. The most important skill that emerged was child rearing. It seemed the perfect solution—form a group of women who could provide affordable, culturally appropriate day care in a city with few Spanish-speaking providers. Women with limited English and relatively low levels of formal education would train to have their own businesses, providing needed services to other mothers returning to the workforce.[31]

The first ten women began classes to get their state-approved day care certifications. Felicia Díaz was one of them:

> I always wanted to have my own business. And I was always interested in children. One day I read in the newspaper that Luz Lebrón was giving a training class to open a day care. I got my first training there, I never missed a class. I got my license. We were very united; this was a support group. If something happened in my day care I would call another [provider]; we lent each other toys.

For Díaz and the other women, the association offered leadership opportunities as well:

> At the beginning we sat down at the table and said, you can be president because you're always speaking on behalf of others, you can be treasurer because you're good with money. Now the association is eight years old, and it's one of the biggest in Connecticut. We have about fifty-five women, but with those who've come and gone it's a hundred and something.

Although the association is multicultural, Dominicans such as Díaz and Garcia have been instrumental in making licensed, home-based day cares an attractive economic niche for their female compatriots. Felicia Díaz assiduously works her ethnic networks, making day care a counterpart to the chain-like opening of bodegas among men:

> I go to see my Dominican *compañeras* and I say to them, "Look, things are going well for me, why don't you come with me?" So I get them into the association. In fact today a Dominican called and asked me about it. I told her, "This is a great business, what area do you live in? There? Magnificent, we don't have providers in that area." It's a way for them to be able to work while staying in their homes. The majority of Dominican women love children.[32]

Membership in the association provides educational opportunities, licensing in different areas, leadership positions. Members believe they provide educational and cultural services to their young charges and beyond. As Felicia Díaz explained: "The association gets together once a month, we bring in news of what's happening in our community. We also go to visit convalescent homes, we do street cleanings. We do different community activities for Christmas or for Halloween.[33]

The variety of local Dominican business enterprises, be they bodegas or day care centers, become jumping-off points for larger activities along the continuum between community work and politics.

## The Evolution of Dominican Collective Activities

> Before it was wonderful because the Dominicans who were here were very close. On the weekends, it was always the same group, "Tomorrow we'll go to church," and everyone got together at Mass. From Mass, "let's go to the

flea market, to the house of Fulano, who's making a *sancocho.*" We danced but in the house, among family, not like now where everyone goes to the discotheque.[34]

From the 1960s, Dominican immigrants in Waterbury gathered informally at each other's houses to celebrate birthday parties, independence days, and other festivities. At first, Dominicans got their social and recreational needs met informally among compatriots or with Puerto Ricans. As time passed they began transforming already existing institutions as well as forming their own.

Many early Puerto Rican migrants had gathered in the basement of Immaculate Conception Roman Catholic Church in downtown Waterbury, later working with a local priest to form a Hispanic parish in the late 1950s in the formerly German St. Cecilia's.[35] Sports teams, Boy Scouts, political and social clubs grew up among the Puerto Ricans of the late 1950s and early 1960s.

The building of the interstate highway and urban renewal devastated many of early Puerto Rican attempts at community-building, flattening houses, storefronts, and clubhouses in the fragile, still-forming community. Even St. Cecilia's Church was not spared by the bulldozer. After the original church was demolished, members of the embattled congregation relocated to a much smaller building on one of the blighted streets adjacent to the "renewed" area.[36]

Puerto Ricans had struggled in the 1950s to form cultural beachheads, only to see them destroyed and rebuild them. Dominicans and other Latinos slowly began to enter these painfully constructed institutions and to make them more multicultural. After a long time of participating side by side with Puerto Ricans in church, several Qusiqueyanas decided they wanted a Dominican festivity. In the late 1980s, St. Cecilia's began celebrating the festival of the patron saint of the Dominican Republic. As Gladys Maldonado explained:

> We have a group of Puerto Ricans, Dominicans, but we are all Hispanics. And each group celebrates the festival of its country's patron. The Puerto Ricans have a very big parade. But the Dominicans in this little town, no.
>   I started it and others helped me, a Mass in honor of the Virgin of Altagracia. As time went on and we kept doing it, people were invited by mail or through the [church] bulletins. Now the church fills up with many more Dominicans than the ones I know.[37]

In Dominican Waterbury, women have been instrumental in starting ethnic celebrations and institutions. The idea to start a Dominican club, for example, emerged a few years ago among patrons of Sabor Latino restaurant and its owner, Ycelsa Díaz.[38] After a few months, the group rented the former Cape Verdean Club, near the small North End factories where many Dominicans had worked.

The Dominican club is an important community symbol, a modest location at a major intersection that displays the Dominican flag to passing motorists. It has become an important point of contact for Dominican clubs and organizations that have developed in other cities in Connecticut, most notably Hartford, Danbury, Bridgeport, and New Britain. It sponsors domino tournaments and baseball games where Dominican teams from Waterbury compete against those in other cities, strengthening intercity Dominican ties.

Perhaps because Dominicans are additions to an already-formed Latino community, even their club reflects a multicultural outlook, with members from a multitude of Spanish-speaking groups, none of which currently have a formal recreational center. Puerto Ricans, Peruvians, Costa Ricans, and others participate in informal socializing and formal social activities at the club.

## Dominican-Puerto Rican Relations

Within a multiethnic world increasingly populated by immigrants from Central and South America, Dominicans appear to feel especially close to Puerto Ricans. Both cultural affinities and proximity have fostered these relationships. Puerto Ricans often attend the same churches and work in the same factories. Puerto Ricans were among the first to orient Dominicans and provide them with basic services. The two groups have intermarried and become *compadres* and *padres de crianza* for each other's children.

There are, however, important differences that sometimes create hard feelings or awkwardness, as Felicia Díaz observed: "They can come here just by buying a plane ticket. For us it's more difficult. They are Americans but we have to fill out a lot of papers in order to immigrate to the United States." On one occasion, Díaz and her conationals in the day care association had to take tuberculosis shots, while the Puerto Rican members didn't.[39]

Stereotypes lurk around the edges of relationships between Dominicans and Puerto Ricans, reflecting mutual awareness of cultural differences and the tensions between their respective political and economic positions. Sometimes children become the barometers for these feelings. Felicia Díaz's son Victor, who grew up in Waterbury among Dominicans and Puerto Ricans, remembered that he and his playmates would exchange insults. "You eat plantains," Puerto Rican children would say to their Dominican peers. "Yes, but you don't have a flag," the Dominican children would answer. Many Puerto Ricans and Dominicans affirm that they believe that Dominicans are naturally superior at business. When Delmaliz Medina's half-Dominican, half-Puerto Rican niece began to sell cosmetics at school, for example, her elders nodded sagely and commented that her "Dominican side" was emerging.[40]

## Visible Identities

As Dominicans have opened up groceries, restaurants, hair salons, and clothing stores, the landscape of Hispanic mercantile activity has changed. Bodegas that formerly had Puerto Rican hometown or national names such as El Utuadeño or Borinquen Grocery have now been rechristened more generically as Hispano, pluralistically as Quisquella [sic]-Borinquen, or with names that evoke everyone's Caribbean homeland, such as Las Colinas (The Hills). The sign above the Dominican-owned La Cazuela restaurant on the corner of Willow and West Main proudly proclaims that it serves "Dominican, Puerto Rican, and Cuban Cuisine." Davis Record Shop and Botanica, owned by a Boricua pionero, now displays a Dominican flag alongside its Puerto Rican one.

One exception is the Peñuelas Barbershop, now a beauty salon owned by Edil Gómez. An immigrant from Santo Domingo, Gómez had worked for several years at the shop until its Puerto Rican owner sold it to her. "The owner was such an incredibly good person," Gomez said, that she hated to change the name. Peñuelas is also a powerful symbol for local Puerto Ricans—perhaps the major town of origin for local Puerto Ricans, it has become a kind of sister city with baseball team exchanges and other shared activities. Apparently, local Dominicans don't need to have this business specifically signposted, for it is a popular and well-known gathering place. It is only newcomers who may have problems, and they are quickly initiated.

The development of scattered but recognizable Dominican landmarks in recent years—most notably stores and the club—means that newcomers don't have to search very hard to find compatriots. While this configuration at first baffles some who come expecting the dense Dominican districts of New York City, newcomers quickly learn to negotiate this more elusive territory. When Enrique Familia came to Waterbury in 2000, he says:

> The first thing I did was to go to Los Chicos Alegres, a *colmado*. I asked, "Are there many Dominicans here?" And [someone] said to me, "Yes," and he took me to C-Town. That's where I began to get to know people and to realize that there were a lot of Dominicans here. I had thought that if there were ten it would be a lot.[41]

As these visible institutions have attracted newcomers, they have provided meeting places and catalysts for larger community-based and political activities.

## Dominican Activism and Politics

Increased organization and visibility among local Dominicans have drawn them into leadership roles, some of which reflect immigrants' homeland experiences. Enrique Familia was a leader in his Santo Domingo neighborhood. As a teenager in Santiago, Felicia Díaz worked with President Joaquin Balaguer's sister to organize community activities. In Waterbury, her roles as informal community emissary and child care provider enable her to work for broader community changes:

> I was always interested in seeing that children from Santo Domingo were enrolled in school as quickly as possible, that they were properly evaluated and not put in grades that were too low. I was the vice president of the Migratory Program and the Bilingual Program [of the Waterbury Department of Education].[42]

Dominicans who have attained their citizenship and are deeply concerned about local affairs also work to make sure that people who represent community interests are elected. Díaz speaks about her organizations' political potency:

> We are independent, we don't belong to anybody. What we say [to politicians] is, "What are you going to offer us?" If they're going to improve education or health care. We have the Dominican Club and the [day care] association. I don't tell them that we're fifty people, I tell them that we're 150. The majority are married, the majority of us are citizens, take into account husbands and children older than 18 who can vote. That's how [the association] got a van for the School Readiness program. Those politicians who I see are going to offer the most, I bring them to the bodegas, and I say, "Vote for this one." Both sides are always looking for me, because they know that I get around.[43]

Bodegas are important sites for political discussion. By the very nature of what they do, bodegueros, like the day care providers, must be intensely aware of politics as it plays out around them. Libio Rosado of C-Town and other Dominicans, for example, are active in Waterbury's new Hispanic Chamber of Commerce. Rosado supported the current mayor, Mike Jarjura, with whose family he has close business ties, for Jarjura and Sons is a produce company that supplies grocery stores:

> Here in the United States and locally in Waterbury, I've participated with Jarjura. We've known each other for ten years. We've given financial support

to his campaign and we've allowed his people to distribute their campaign literature, and to register people in the front [of the store]. We thought he could do a good job in Waterbury. [Jarjura] works with everyone, he doesn't have a favored group.[44]

Of course, homeland politics remain important, and often there is a continuum between local and homeland concerns. In 1996, the Dominican government had approved dual citizenship for Quisqueyanos living abroad. The following year, these expatriates gained the right to vote in presidential elections. Since no polling places were set up abroad during the 2000 elections, thousands of Dominicans took flights home to vote, including Waterbury Quisqueyans. Dominicans abroad—who send billions of dollars yearly to people back home—used their influence to ensure that they would be able to vote from their adopted countries during the next elections. On May 16, 2004, Dominican nationals living overseas were for the first time able to vote in the presidential elections from their adopted homeland.

This election had more than symbolic importance, as current economic conditions in the Dominican Republic affected these remittance-sending immigrants. The collapse of several major banks in 2003 and attendant spiraling inflation sent shock waves through the country, burdening an already precarious economy. Immigrants felt compelled to drastically increase the amount of money they sent home to compensate for tripling or quadrupling prices. As Libio Rosado remarked, "Although I'm here I have to help [my] family there. My parents take medications, they go to doctors, gasoline is expensive there, electricity is expensive."[45]

It was difficult for Dominican immigrants to send home food and money especially when they already worked multiple low-wage jobs to make ends meet in a declining Connecticut economy. The delicate arrangement only worked if the large differential between prices here and there stayed the same. Thus, many Dominicans living here felt an urgency about the 2004 presidential elections back home. Many felt that if former president Leonel Fernández reassumed power, the Dominican economy would improve.

From the fall of 2003, Waterbury's Dominicans became politically active. Discussions in Edil Gómez's Peñuelas Barbershop produced a local committee affiliated with the Partido de la Liberación Dominicana [PLD] and its presidential candidate, Leonel Fernández. Guarín Contreras, a construction worker, walked door to door to find hundreds of local Dominicans eligible to vote.[46] Enrique Familia had a show on the local Dominican-owned Radio Galaxia, bought time in the name of the PLD, and exhorted Dominican listeners to register for the election.

Local organizers worked in tandem with Dominican clubs and organizations in Bridgeport, Hartford, Danbury, and New Britain. Gómez, Contreras, Familia, and other activists were trained in voter registration by New York's Dominican Board of Elections. Organizers registered locals in several fall sessions at key community spots, including the Dominican club, local bodegas, and restaurants.

Leonel Fernández visited Danbury, while other members of his party held fundraisers in Hartford and Waterbury. A few weeks before the election, activists set up a PLD headquarters in a compatriot's storefront and worked to secure a local voting site for the election.[47] At the last minute, Dominicans in Connecticut were told to go to Yonkers, New York to vote.

As they stood in the parking lot of C-Town that Sunday morning waiting for the school bus they had chartered for the trip to Yonkers, organizers expressed disappointment. The Dominican Board of Elections had said that it was the multiparty activity that had invalidated Waterbury as a polling place. However, organizers believed that the Board of Elections, controlled by President Hipólito Mejía's government, had put up obstacles, threatened by so many overseas voters supporting the opposition.[48]

Some organizers believed that Dominicans in Connecticut were still rather invisible, sandwiched as they were between the larger, more vocal Dominican communities of New York City, Boston, and Providence. However, hundreds of Connecticut's Dominicans still turned out to vote, helping to reelect Leonel Fernández.

## Conclusion

Dominicans are an increasingly integral part of Waterbury, and their presence is subtly altering the city's Latino community. As the children and grandchildren of Puerto Rican pioneers forsake shopkeeping careers and inner-city neighborhoods, Dominicans have filled the gaps. Their presence as the second major Spanish-speaking group has influenced their settlement strategies. Dominicans have integrated already-formed institutions, such as St. Cecilia's Church, injecting bits of their own culture through special celebrations such as the Fiesta de la Virgen de la Altagracia. When Dominicans found their own stores and social clubs, they are careful to balance Dominicanidad with a broader pan-Latino perspective, offering everything from grocery products to social activities to an increasingly multicultural Hispanic community. Thus, their presence enriches the Spanish-speaking community overall.

Dominicans have come to Waterbury during an era of shrinking economic opportunities, but the strength of the dollar in their homeland, their social capital, and their somewhat elevated class position have allowed many to make a better place for themselves than current Puerto Rican migrants to Waterbury. Nevertheless, many local Latinos believe that Dominicans are "naturally" better at business and have innate cultural traits that have allowed them to succeed in the local climate.

Connections between New York City and Connecticut churches, bodegas, and factories have been an important catalyst for the growth of Waterbury's Dominican community. Waterbury is relatively far from New York and extremely different. However, Waterbury may be more typical of the small, deindustrialized cities of the Northeast where Dominicans and other Latino immigrants are settling in growing numbers. The physical configurations of such cities are more elusive than New York's, consisting of scattered pockets rather than dense districts.

Dominicans in Waterbury have established institutions such as the Dominican Club that allow them to provide social and political activities for members and link up with similar institutions in other cities. Thus, local Dominicans and those in Danbury, Hartford, Bridgeport, and other cities used preexisting connections to organize voters for the 2004 election. While Dominicans in Connecticut cities could not muster the political clout to obtain a local polling place, their growing level of political organization presages a future in which Dominican communities such as Waterbury's will be increasingly visible to politicos from home as well as to non-Latino locals accustomed to thinking of all Spanish-speakers as Puerto Ricans.

## Notes

1. Special thanks to Delmaliz Medina, who conducted interviews, transcribed, and translated for this project, and to Luis Pomales, who visually documented Waterbury's Dominican presence, and thanks to all the individuals who agreed to be interviewed. Regarding the title of this chapter: *Mofongo* and *mangú* are Puerto Rican and Dominican dishes, respectively. Each uses plantains as its main ingredient, but different methods of preparation and other ingredients make them quite distinct from each other in taste and texture.

2. In the 1990 census, 69 percent of all of Connecticut's Hispanics were Puerto Ricans, as compared to 49 percent in New York. In the 2000 census, 60.7 percent of Connecticut's Hispanics were Puerto Ricans, as compared to 36 percent in New York.

3. See, for example, Jeremy Brecher, Jerry Lombardi, and Jan Stackhouse, comps. and eds., *Brass Valley* (Philadelphia: Temple University Press, 1982).

4. Brecher, Lombardi, and Stackhouse, *Brass Valley*, passim.

5. Ruth Glasser, *Aquí Me Quedo: Puerto Ricans in Connecticut* (Middletown: Connecticut Humanities Council, 1997).

6. Lewis Holloway and Phil Hubbard, *People and Place: The Extraordinary Geographies of Everyday Life* (Essex, England: Pearson Education, 2001), 13.

7. Glasser, *Aquí Me Quedo*, 63.

8. See, for example, Sarah J. Mahler, *American Dreaming* (Princeton: Princeton University Press, 1995), 7–10. Other sources that were consulted in the writing of this chapter are Sherri Grasmuck and Patricia Pessar, *Between Two Islands: Dominican International Migration* (Berkeley: University of California Press, 1991); Ramona Hernández and Francisco L. Rivera-Batíz, *Dominicans in the United States: A Socioeconomic Profile, 2000* (New York: CUNY Dominican Studies Institute, 2003); Michael Jones-Correa, *Between Two Nations: The Political Predicament of Latinos in New York City* (Ithaca: Cornell University Press, 1998); and Peggy Levitt, *The Transnational Villagers* (Berkeley: University of California Press, 2001).

9. U.S. Department of Commerce, Bureau of the Census, *1980 Census of Population and Housing*, Census Tracts Waterbury, Connecticut SMSA (July 1983) Table P-7; Data Set: 1990 Summary Tape File 3 Sample Data, Table PO11: Hispanic Origin: Persons, Waterbury, Connecticut; Data Set: Census 2000 Summary File 1 100 Percent Data, QT-P9: Hispanic or Latino by Type: Waterbury, Connecticut, http://factfinder.census.gov.

10. A later generation of Puerto Rican migrants to Waterbury would share this serial migration pattern but not the class advantages.

11. Gladys Maldonado, interview by Ruth Glasser, August 28, 2003.

12. Carmen Judith Mariñez, telephone interview by Ruth Glasser, May 24, 2004.

13. Gladys Maldonado, interview by Ruth Glasser, August 28, 2003.

14. Adelaida Garcia, interview by Delmaliz Medina, April 10, 2003.

15. Felicia Díaz, interview by Ruth Glasser, August 13, 2003.

16. Ibid.

17. Ibid.

18. Amado Vargas, interview by Ruth Glasser, August 27, 2003.

19. Mercedes Sanchez, interview by Kevin Fitzpatrick, April, 2003.

20. Grismilda Perez, interview by Jayra Quiles, April 22, 2003.

21. Felicia Díaz, conversation with Ruth Glasser, May 30, 2003.

22. Enrique Familia, interview by Delmaliz Medina, May 13, 2004.

23. Grismilda Perez, interview by Jayra Quiles, April 22, 2003.

24. Felicia Díaz, interview by Ruth Glasser, August 13, 2003.

25. Juan Laras, interview by Delmaliz Medina, May 13, 2004.

26. Libio Rosado, interview by Delmaliz Medina, March 10, 2004.

27. Amado Vargas, interview by Ruth Glasser, August 27, 2003.

28. Sonia Rosario, interview by Ruth Glasser, March 22, 2004.

29. Felicia Díaz, interview by Ruth Glasser, August 13, 2003.

30. Adelaida Garcia, interview by Delmaliz Medina, April 10, 2003.

31. Luz Lebrón, interview by Delmaliz Medina, August 28, 2003.

32. Felicia Díaz, interview by Ruth Glasser, August 13, 2003.

33. Felicia Díaz, interview by Ruth Glasser, August 13, 2003.

34. Sonia Rosario, interview by Ruth Glasser, March 22, 2004.

35. Glasser, *Aquí Me Quedo*, 109.

36. Glasser, *Aquí Me Quedo*, passim.

37. Maldonado, August 28, 2003.

38. Díaz, August 13, 2003.

39. Díaz, August 13, 2003.

40. Delmaliz Medina, conversation with author, May 24, 2004. See also Yanet Baldares, "Variations of Culture, Class, and Political Consciousness Among Latin

Residents in a Small Eastern City" (PhD diss., Rutgers, the State University of New Jersey, 1987).

41. Enrique Familia, interview by Delmaliz Medina, May 13, 2004.

42. Felicia Díaz, interview by Ruth Glasser, August 13, 2003.

43. Felicia Díaz, interview by Ruth Glasser, August 13, 2003.

44. Libio Rosado, interviews by Delmaliz Medina, March 10, 2004, and April 18, 2004.

45. Libio Rosado, interview by Delmaliz Medina, March 10, 2004.

46. Guarín Contreras, conversation with author, May 16, 2004. Voting requirements for the 2004 election were strict, effectively whittling down the number of Dominicans abroad who were able to participate in the elections. As Ernesto Sagas points out in "The 2004 Presidential Election in the Dominican Republic," *Electoral Studies*, forthcoming, only 52,000 Dominicans overseas were registered to vote, and slightly more than half actually did so.

47. There does not seem to have been local activity by other Dominican parties in Waterbury. Rather, people seem to have gathered around the PLD. Conversations with some Dominican Waterburians going to Yonkers to vote on May 16 indicated that some were normally PRD (Partido Revolucionario Dominicano) members who were disenchanted with the current president. Dominican Waterbury's ad hoc approach to home country politics may be the sign of a still-forming community, and its political life may eventually become more variegated as in Boston and New York.

48. Miguel Melenciano, Junta Central Electoral, New York City, conversation with author, May 27, 2004. Ernesto Sagas suggests that Connecticut may not have had the minimum number of registered voters or the required representative from each of the three major political parties to supervise the election. However, in places such as Orlando, there were fewer than three hundred registered voters and yet that city had a polling place (e-mail communication, May 26, 2004). Connecticut organizers claim that there were at least four hundred registered state residents. This is hard to verify, since Connecticut residents were folded into the 24,333 registered in New York (Junta Central Electoral at www.jce.do/exterior/contactovotoext.asp).

# 5 Growing into Power in Rhode Island

Miren Uriarte

lthough present in the state since the 1960s, Rhode Island Latinos erupted into the consciousness of the region in the late 1990s with two critical facts. The first is that the growth of the Latino population in the state had been explosive.[1] Since 1990, Latinos quadrupled their share of the population, and today, with 90,820 persons, they account for 8.7 percent of the total population and for 48 percent of the racial/ethnic minority population of the state. Without the influx of Latinos, Rhode Island would have experienced negative population growth in the 1990s.[2] In Providence and Central Falls, Latinos account for a significant percent of the populations of those cities, 30 percent and 47.8 percent, respectively. In those cities, the presence of Latinos can no longer be ignored.

Even as the numbers climbed, there appeared to have been little acknowledgement of the meaning of the demographic change to the institutions and politics of the state. Through the 1990s there had been some appointments to the boards of nonprofit organizations and the presence of Latinos grew in key areas, such as health care delivery. But in general, there was scant attention to the supports that this large influx of newcomers would require.[3] At the end of that decade, Latinos faced serious barriers of access to services of all types and were caught between mainstream public and private systems of service delivery unable to serve them well and policies that strongly restricted Latinos' capacity for building service organizations of their own. The avenues used by Latinos in New York, Hartford, and Boston to meeting the communities' needs for services to support their adjustment and incorporation (such as for example, community-based service organizations) have been largely out of reach to Latinos in Rhode Island, as the growth of the Latino population largely coincided with the cuts in federal funding for the urban programs that had made those services possible in other areas of the region.

In Rhode Island, meeting the community's needs has meant obtaining access to decision making at the state and city levels. And that brings us to the second fact that brought Latinos in Rhode Island to the attention of observers in the region. In Rhode Island, Latinos were running for office and getting elected. Anastasia Williams, a Panamanian woman, had represented Providence's District 9 in the State Legislature since 1992. Luis Aponte, a Puerto Rican, had been elected city councilor for Providence's Ward 10 in 1998 on his second try. Victor Capellán and Miguel Luna, both Dominicans, had run campaigns for state representative in 1996 and 1998, which resulted in very narrow losses; Luna would be successful in 2002 in his run for the Providence City Council. León Tejada became state representative in Providence's District 11 in 2000, and Juan Pichardo, in his second try, was elected state senator in Providence's District 2 in 2002 (both Tejada and Pichardo are Dominicans). In Central Falls, Ricardo Patiño, a Colombian, was elected to the city council in 2000. From the perspective of Latinos in other areas of New England, this was a rise to electoral success the swiftness of which was unparalleled in the region.

The ideal process of immigrant assimilation described by classic American sociology is still the prevalent thinking about the factors that lead to political participation among immigrants. The assimilation model places "civic assimilation," or the active participation in civic society, at the pinnacle of the process of "Americanization," a tale that evolves over several generations.[4] New immigrants first struggle to acculturate and incorporate themselves into the economy and social institutions, facing discrimination. As they make themselves familiar with and familiar to others already here, this discrimination diminishes, opening the door to the increased participation by the second generation of immigrants in the social institutions of the broader society. This broad, unimpeded interaction promotes social relations that lead to intermarriage and, with that, a sense of identity in the third generation that is based less in the ethnic identity of yore and more in the common identity as "Americans." This sense of common future as Americans is, according to the model, the basis for the political participation of newcomers.

In spite of the power of this paradigm to shape the American perspective as well as policies toward immigrants, the experience of immigrant groups—both old and new—points in a somewhat different direction.[5] On the one hand, the pull of the countries of origin proved stronger than anticipated, particularly in the first generation. The growing ease of transportation and communication has only underscored further this natural connection, often extending it into later generations. On the other, residential segregation, the sharing of similar workplaces, and the discrimination and exclusion that immigrants have faced once in the United States have served to reinforce ethnic identity and bonds well into the second and third generations.[6] But although the focus of later generations may be on issues related to their lives in the United States, their political expression has taken a decidedly ethnic route, whether they are Irish in Boston, Mexicans in Los Angeles, or Dominicans in New York.

Scholarship on Latino communities in this region indicates that political activism has been shaped by the polarization along racial lines and the intensity of urban struggles of the 1960s and 70s, which coincided with the growth of Latin American immigration to the northeast and specifically New England.[7] Many Latinos were moved by the struggles against displacement from urban neighborhoods, their exclusion from social institutions, and the efforts to develop resources within their communities. These processes underscored the racial/ethnic content of political mobilization and provided vehicles for disenfranchised groups to gain a slight leverage in the policy arena. This activism has been characteristic of Latino groups in the region and has provided the training ground for a generation of Latino leaders and professionals.

The fact is that the experience of Latinos in Rhode Island does not fit easily into either set of explanations. On the one hand, the political activism of Latinos in Rhode Island is taking place among a relatively recent immigration and does not reflect the generations-long process of incorporation described by the assimilationists. It is also taking place in the midst of a rather pervasive exclusion of Latinos from the economic and social fabric of the state and not as a result of its resolution. But on the other hand, the activism of Latinos in Rhode Island is far from being exclusively focused on social issues and community building. Theirs is a process that, although maybe not unique among immigrants, departs significantly from the activism experienced by other Latino communities in the region.

This chapter focuses on three issues that frame the process of Latino political development in Rhode Island. The first is the way in which Latinos in Rhode Island have addressed the great diversity of its population in terms of national groups and immigration statuses, resulting from the characteristics of the migration and settlement of the groups. I argue that how Latinos in Rhode Island have addressed this diversity has been an important component of their political success. The second is the hardship and poverty that Latinos faced as they sought entry into the local economy. Until recently neither the swiftness of the settlement nor the high rates of poverty had attracted much institutional attention, which brings us to the third and final context discussed here: the social and political environment that greeted Latinos and the strategies that they devised in response. This chapter relies on data from the 2000 U.S. Census and interviews conducted with Latino leaders to Latinos in Rhode Island in 2001 and 2003.[8]

## The Challenge of Diversity

As is the case of most Latino communities, Rhode Island's is far from homogeneous. In fact we can safely say that this is one of the most diverse Latino communities in the region. Although there is a range of sizes of national groups, no one group completely dominates numerically. There is also a layering of migration and immigration cohorts that results in many different statuses and, therefore, experiences of incorporation and adaptation to Rhode Island, of relationships with its institutions and even of relationships within the community itself.

As far as national groups go, Puerto Ricans, Dominicans, Guatemalans, Colombians, and Mexicans have the largest national representations (see Table 5.1) among Latinos in Rhode Island. Puerto Ricans began to arrive in the 1920s as migrant farm workers, staying in the south Providence area only for the harvest. As the process of deindustrialization accelerated in the region, Puerto Rican migrants began to stay to work in jobs in the naval yard and later the dwindling manufacturing sector;[9] the community grew as Puerto Ricans began to migrate from New York and Connecticut. Experienced Colombian textile workers were also recruited to work in manufacturing; this time it was the textile mills in Central Falls, where in the 1960s Colombians breathed some life to these fading industries.[10] Since then, several waves of Colombians have migrated to the United States and made their way to this settlement as their own country was racked with violence.[11]

This industrial niche also attracted Dominicans, who began arriving in the 1970s. Most Dominicans made their way first to New York, then moved north to Providence and Lawrence, Massachusetts where they worked in

TABLE 5.1. Largest Latino national groups, Rhode Island, 2000

| Group | Population | Percentage of Latino population |
|---|---|---|
| All Latinos or Hispanics | 90,820 | |
| Puerto Rican | 25,422 | 27.9 |
| Dominican | 17,894 | 19.7 |
| Guatemalan | 8,949 | 9.8 |
| Colombian | 5,706 | 6.3 |
| Mexican | 5,881 | 6.5 |
| Others[a] | 26,968 | 29.8 |

*Source:* U.S. Bureau of the Census, Census 2000, Summary File 1, 100% Data
     (http://actfinder.census.gov/).
     [a]These include persons from other Latin American nationalities and those that identify
     themselves as Hispanic or Latino or as Spanish or Spaniards.

the disappearing textile shops.[12] Providence and Central Falls also became a stopover for Guatemalans on the way to Canada to seek asylum and refuge from the war that ravaged Central America in that decade.[13] Guatemalans have benefited from federal legislation that allows them to seek asylum while in the United States, and many have remained here. Regardless of the road taken to Rhode Island, what is clear is that by the 1980s, the basis for Latino population growth was set by both the economic needs of the region and the realities of U.S. policy in Latin America.

Today, as is the case in most Latino communities across the United States, many Latinos arrive pulled by Latinos already settled here. Many make their way to Rhode Island after experiences in other cities and choose it because of its safety and tranquility in comparison with other U.S. cities. "I came from Hartford," says a Puerto Rican man now living in Providence, "and saw that (here) the environment was calmer. I have children and here my children are fine, it has gone well for me raising them here."[14] But most continue to arrive pulled by the availability of entry-level service and manufacturing jobs as well as the presence of family and friends already in the area. This is particularly the case among Guatemalans and Colombians, who often migrate directly to Rhode Island.

Another aspect of the layering of the community is the blending of native-born persons and immigrants and of different immigrant cohorts. The different experiences that result from the timing of the migration and the policies that greet the immigrants—often out of the control of the immigrants themselves—have lasting implications for the future incorporation of the different Latino groups, as well as for relations within the Latino community itself.

According to the U.S. census, most Latinos in Rhode Island, 55.8 percent, are U.S. born.[15] But this figure confounds the impact of immigration, incorporation, and adjustment in the community. First of all, this figure includes the large Puerto Rican population, all of whom are citizens at birth, whether born in Puerto Rico or in the mainland United States But although for this reason Puerto Ricans are not considered immigrants, Puerto Ricans coming to the United States from Puerto Rico migrate to a place with a different culture and language and therefore are exposed to many of the same problems of adjustment that immigrants face. When Puerto Ricans in Rhode Island were asked where they lived in 1995, 13.1 percent indicated that they were living in Puerto Rico signaling that significant numbers in this population are of recent arrival.[16] Secondly, among the native-born Latinos, the majority (58.1 percent) are children under eighteen (Table 5.2). Among some groups, notably Colombians and Guatemalans, an overwhelming majority of the native born are children, most of them likely the U.S.-born children of the immigrants.

TABLE 5.2. Nativity of selected Latino national groups, Rhode Island, 2000

|  | All Latinos | Colombians | Dominicans | Guatemalans | Mexicans | Puerto Ricans |
|---|---|---|---|---|---|---|
| Native born (born in the United States, including Puerto Rico) | 55.2% | 23.29% | 33.52% | 23.78% | 57.71% | 98.8% |
| Native born who are children under 18 | 58.1% | 74.0% | 47.3% | 81.6% | 43.9% | 44.8% |

*Source:* U.S. Bureau of the Census, Census 2000, Summary File 4 (SF4), Sample Data (http://factfinder.census.gov/).
[a]of persons 5 years old and over.

The share of immigrants among the other national groups varies greatly (Table 5.2). For example, among Mexicans, the majority are native-born persons. But among Colombians, Dominicans, and Guatemalans the weight of immigration and the presence of immigrants is very significant. The vast majority among them are foreign-born or first-generation immigrants; this is the case for more than 75 percent of the populations of Colombians and Guatemalans. Another aspect of the layering within the community is the immigrant cohorts that coexist in the settlement. These cohorts are determined by their time of arrival in the United States (Table 5.3). Across all groups, there is a core of long-standing immigrant residents who have lived in the United States since before 1980. Among Colombians and Dominicans these "experienced immigrants" account for

TABLE 5.3. Time in the United States for selected Latino immigrant groups,[a] Rhode Island, 2000

|  | All Latinos | Colombians | Dominicans | Guatemalans | Mexicans |
|---|---|---|---|---|---|
| Immigrants in the United States before 1980[a] | 16.6% | 19.0% | 18.5 | 7.7% | 9.63% |
| Immigrants in the United States between 1980 and 1989[a] | 31.6% | 31.8% | 32.7% | 29.5% | 27.0% |
| Immigrants in the United States between 1990 and 2000[a] | 51.9% | 49.2% | 48.8% | 62.8% | 63.4% |

*Source:* U.S. Bureau of the Census, Census 2000, Summary File 4 (SF4), Sample Data (http://factfinder.census.gov/).
[a]The census reports time of arrival in the United States only for foreign-born persons; Puerto Ricans are considered native born.

almost 20 percent of their newcomers. They are an important resource for newcomers, since they often house them and provide them with guidance as they start their process of adaptation. But across all groups, the majority of the immigrants are of much more recent tenure in the city. The largest cohort is that which arrived between 1990 and 2000, especially among Mexican and Guatemalan immigrants. The recency of the migration and the large share of the newcomers denote that the immigrant experience—with the trauma of separation and its process of adjustment and adaptation—is a very strong one in this population.

Groups have come to Rhode Island from a variety of situations that include the labor migration of Dominicans and Mexicans and the escape from violence of Guatemalans and Colombians. Each group—and even different cohorts within groups—arrives under different policies that give different legal coloring to their experience. Among Latino immigrants, the majority are lawful permanent residents, who have obtained this status after qualifying for one of the preferences available in immigration law. These include family reunification, employment, and those designated refugees or asylum seekers. Lawful permanent residents arrive with full capacity to work.

Others arrive without legal authorization and reside undocumented in the United States. Most Latino groups have persons in this category as well. This happens primarily because immigration policies limit the number of persons that can migrate to work or to join family already here, often forcing waits of several years. Many persons choose to remain in the United States after overstaying a tourist or student visa or by crossing the U.S. border illegally. In the case of Colombians, for example, those recruited to work in Central Fall factories were joined later by persons escaping the many waves of violence that have swept the country over the last decades. Many of them did so with legal entry visas or obtained legalization—as have others—through programs offered periodically by the U.S. government. But most recent immigrants from Colombia, under great pressure to leave due to the violence in their country, are frequently arriving undocumented. By contrast, Central American groups, after years of advocacy, have obtained some relief to the harshest effects of unauthorized immigration. Guatemalans and Salvadorans for example, are eligible for a more lenient process of asylum application as a result of the Nicaraguan Adjustment and Central American Relief Act (NACARA).[17] Salvadorans and Hondurans are also eligible to apply for Temporary Protected Status (TPS), a status awarded to groups when the attorney general finds that conditions in a particular country pose a danger to personal safety due to armed struggle or an environmental disaster.[18] TPS does not lead to permanent residency as does NACARA, but it provides protection from deportation and a work permit.

Different immigration policies and the resulting immigration status often result in very different treatment of these groups. This has been particularly salient since 1996, when immigration status became a critical factor in eligibility for all types of public benefits, following the passage of both the Personal Responsibility and Work Opportunity Reconciliation Act, known as welfare reform, and the Illegal Immigration Reform and Immigrant Responsibility Act. Under the new laws, lawful permanent residents must wait five years after entering the United States to be eligible for most federal benefits; asylum seekers and those under temporary protection have severe limitations in their eligibility.[19] Undocumented persons are shut out of most federal benefits as well as many state services.

The differences in opportunity that accompany different types of statuses have lasting implications for the economic and social outcomes of immigrants. These differences also often affect the social relations within the Latino community itself. Many relate instances of solidarity and support of the most vulnerable, often taking risks to do so. But there was also evidence of negative attitudes toward unauthorized immigrants, on the one hand, and toward the privilege that policy provides some groups, on the other.

## Channeling Diversity

Although language and common historical experience as Latin Americans provide bonds for Latinos regardless of where they come from, the great diversity in nationality, immigrant status, tenure in the United States, and cultural characteristics represents both a strength and challenge to the community. "We put ourselves under this neat umbrella," says a Latino leader in Rhode Island, "but we are so diverse.... We have different cultures, we come with different levels of education, and we are here for very different reasons."[20]

These differences have represented an important barrier to pan-Latino unity and organization, often splintering political efforts and diluting political strengths. In Rhode Island, Latinos have made significant efforts to bridge these differences. One example is the shape that social organization has taken in these communities.[21]

Community leaders explain that, initially, social organization was dominated by organizations focused on national groups; "Puerto Ricans had their organization, Colombians had their own organization and Dominicans had their own organization and nobody accomplished anything," explained Puerto Rican community leader Pablo Rodriguez.[22]

Efforts at a more collective process also began early, emerging first in 1976 with the formation of the Latin American Community Center. But at that time, there was significant conflict between those that sought to organize along national lines and those that took a pan-Latino approach. This conflict led to the demise of the first pan-Latino organization when funders, used to dealing with minorities as a block, were disturbed by the lack of consensus among the different Latino groups. But, in time, other organizations followed this pattern: a focus on community-wide issues and a focus on bringing together and providing services to persons from all groups. These included pioneer small service organizations, such as the Club Juvenil, Orientación Hispana, Acción Hispana (later Progreso Latino) Proyecto Persona, and La Comunidad en Acción, which provided a range of supportive services. Later, service coordination and advocacy organizations formed, such as the Coalition of Hispanic Organizations (founded in 1976) and the Hispanic Social Services Committee (1979), the precursor of the present Center for Hispanic Policy and Advocacy (CHisPA). Outsiders made many efforts, some of them successful, to co-opt and control these processes.[23] But over time, a consensus arose that this form of organization afforded benefits to the community. It has been hard road to efficacy, as both leaders and organizations have undergone development and growth, but this experience seems to have prepared the ground for the entry into the political arena.

By 1985, pan-Latino efforts had taken a decidedly electoral bent with the creation of the first Hispanic Political Action Committee. Over the next years, several Latinos would run for office, but only one would be successful: Anastasia Williams, who won largely with the support of her African American constituency. In 1998, a pan-Latino group of seasoned leaders founded the Rhode Island Latino Political Action Committee (RILPAC) with the purpose of raising funds to support the races of Latinos and non-Latinos that advance a platform compatible with Latino interests. Here Latino interests are defined broadly and include education, immigration policy, employment, and small business and economic development, bridging the common gap between the interests of immigrants and those with longer tenure in the United States.

"RILPAC is like an umbrella.... it united so that we can come to an agreement on the issues," says Juan Pichardo, a Dominican and founder of RILPAC and now Rhode Island's first Latino state senator, but individual organizations "could be separate and do things on their own."[24] And that is how Puertorriqueños Unidos, Quisqueya en Acción, the Asociación Cultural Mexicana, and Guatemaltecos Unidos coexist with the broader efforts. Pablo Rodriguez, a Puerto Rican leader, puts it this way:

> I have seen in the last 16 years a coming together of Colombians, Dominicans, Puerto Ricans, Guatemalans. We have a very diverse Latino community here that does not seem to have the same degree of animosity that other cities have

shown to each other. It's hard to find a meeting, it's hard to find a demon-stration, (and) it's hard to find a gathering of Latinos that involves only one particular group.[25]

To a significant degree, Latinos in Rhode Island mastered the interplay between the two faces of immigrant organization: the internal processes that keep the community organized and the face that the community has to present to the outside world in order to be understandable and to be taken seriously. Along the way, they have demonstrated a model for Latinos to bring their strong national group organizations into a broader Latino-wide strategy for power.

The model represented by the Rhode Island experience relies on a strong base of small organizations, clearly identified nationally, that come together into pan-Latino structures for action directed at the broader, non-Latino political environment. This interplay is most evident during elections, when groups are mobilized through their national or community networks to participate in discussion of candidates and positions within RILPAC. RILPAC is a nonpartisan, pan-Latino group. It promotes discussion and facilitates consensus among members, leading to endorsements of both Latino can-didates and other politicians willing to address the Latino agenda. It raises funds and contributes to the candidates they endorse. Mobilization takes place through networks: "We communicate with that one person and he or she communicates with everyone else," in their group, explained Pablo Rodriguez in 2003. Kurland describes the process on election day:

> At . . . the city's most heavily Latino polling place, lines reached down a flight of stairs and out to the street, while Dominican-owned taxi shuttle services dropped off vanloads of voters in 15-minute intervals, and dozens of campaign volunteers swarmed the sidewalks. *Poder 1110*, the city's most popular Latino radio station, pounded the airwaves all day, broadcasting live from the polls and exhorting listeners to get out and vote Latino.[26]

It has been the ability to harness the diversity of the community into common political projects that has made a great difference in the electoral arena. "We need to continue . . . talking about our issues. . . . every na-tionality has their own issues, each country is different," says Juan Pichardo, "but one thing that is not different is the issues that we got to deal with here in the United States."[27]

## An Uneasy Economic Fit

Issues related to the economic well-being of the Latino community have been high among the priorities of leaders and organizations. And this attention is well warranted. Labor market disadvantage has brought high rates of poverty for Latinos in Rhode Island. This is true among Latinos of all ages, but particularly so among Latino children. Comparing the percentages of all Latinos, Latino children under eighteen, Latino workers, and Latino elderly who live below the federal poverty rate nationally, in New England, and in Rhode Island, in all instances, the Rhode Island rates are higher than those found elsewhere. In addition, the rate of Latino poverty in Rhode Island continued to increase even when Latino poverty receded nationally in the 1990s.[28]

The most frequent explanations for the high rates of poverty among Latinos[29] include some of the common themes of poverty research, such as the structure of families and issues specific to the Latino experience as immigrants. Others focus on the position of Latinos in the labor force and on the determinants of their low earnings. The individual characteristics of the workers (e.g., level of education, English proficiency, and work skills) as well as factors related to the structure of the labor market and discrimination toward workers are some of the factors considered here. A clear conclusion is that no factor in isolation can explain Latino poverty. It results from a complex set of social and economic factors that create labor market disadvantage, such as industrial restructuring, ethnic and racial discrimination, inadequate schooling, and low educational attainment, compounded by the social adaptation and the problems in language proficiency that are the consequences of immigration.[30]

The overrepresentation of immigrants is often mentioned as a factor for the high rates of Latino poverty.[31] In Rhode Island the picture is not that simple. Rates of poverty are higher among newly arrived immigrants (less than five years in the United States), but immigrants who have been in the United States for ten years have rates of poverty similar to those that have been in the United States much longer. This signals that the effects of immigration may be temporary, with immigrants attaining higher levels of income in a reasonably short time. The highest poverty rates are found among Puerto Ricans, which reach 50 percent.[32] A comparison of poverty rates among U.S. born, those born in Puerto Rico, and foreign born (first-generation immigrants) shows, again, that poverty rates are highest among those born in Puerto Rico (51.3 percent) followed by U.S.-born Latinos (39.7 percent), while those of the foreign born show rates of 28 percent.[33] Immigrants had the lowest poverty rates of the three groups.

Lack of jobs and low wages seem to be at the heart of the problem. Latinos appear to be concentrated in the declining sectors and in those areas of the growing service industry where salaries are low. The largest group of Latino workers (36.3 percent) works in manufacturing, which has declined significantly, at a rate of 33.5 percent between 1988 and 1998.[34]

Trade, both retail and wholesale, also declining sectors, had the second-highest representation of Latinos at 13.8 percent. Latino representation in the government sector is quite low, reaching only 1.6 percent.[35] In general, Latinos have experienced higher levels of unemployment than the general population of the state (6.9 percent versus 5.6 percent in 1999), according to the U.S. census. This is particularly the case among Puerto Ricans and Dominicans, whose unemployment rates surpass not only those of the general population but also those of the overall Latino population.[36] But in spite of this, commitment to the labor force was strong, particularly among Colombians, Guatemalans, and Mexicans for whom labor force participation surpassed that of the general population.[37] In spite of this, earnings for Latinos were only 28 percent of those of the general population.[38]

The outcomes of Latinos' engagement in the labor force are mediated by factors such as education and lack of English-language proficiency. For example, half of all Latinos (49.6 percent) have less than a high school education.[39] Educational attainment varies greatly by group; among Colombians, 36 percent have less than high school while this rate is 66.8 percent for Guatemalans. Curiously, earnings for Guatemalans were higher than for most Latino groups, including Colombians. Higher earnings in this group may be related to the number of jobs that immigrants hold[40] or the protection NACARA offers undocumented workers, usually those with the lowest wages. This protection is not available to Dominican, Colombian, or Mexican unauthorized immigrants.

The level and persistence of poverty among Latinos in Rhode Island remained relatively hidden until analyses of the 2000 U.S. census came to light.[41] Within the community, economic hardship was explained as the result of the large influx of new immigrants, which is, as was described above, only part of the story since the most significant poverty is found among the native born and a population that are U.S. citizens. But leaders also pointed to the lack of jobs with wages above poverty for persons with low levels of education as the heart of the problem.[42] With the flight of good-paying industrial jobs, the possibilities for persons with lower levels of education to earn wages above the poverty rate have almost disappeared in Rhode Island. Yet many come to this region precisely because there is an expansion of low-wage jobs in the service and personal care sectors that require lesser levels of education.[43] Leaders focused on improvements in education, availability of workforce development opportunities, support for small businesses, and support for families as key for the advancement of Latinos.[44]

And clearly, these were the key issues. By the year 2000, the outcomes for Latino children in public schools were dismal. Latinos had the highest drop-out rates and the lowest NAEP scores in most areas (except science) and across of all grades of any group in the state.[45] The demand for employment and training programs and GED and ESL classes for adults greatly outstripped supply.[46] Programs directed to small business development were largely inaccessible for Latino small businesses because of language barriers and lack of information.[47] And perhaps the most salient gaps were found among those services that supported families in need. Latino leaders classified the systems of care as linguistically and culturally inaccessible to Latinos, "in denial" about the needs of this growing population in order to avert the changes that the demographic transformation would require of their structure and functioning.[48] Latino community activist Victor Capellán summarized it this way: "The institutions fail to understand that Rhode Island has undergone a demographic shift."[49]

## Taking Care of the Community's Business

Institutional resistance to demographic change is not new in urban areas. Perhaps the most salient historic example was the profound resistance of white urban institutions to address the needs of blacks that migrated to northern cities after World War II. By the 1960s urban inequalities were so profound that they prompted federal intervention, through the "War on Poverty" programs. This came first through the Community Action Program of the Office of Equal Economic Opportunity, created in 1964, which sought to impact both the economic and the institutional exclusion of the poor. The economic initiatives included training through the Job Corps, Neighborhood Youth Corps, educational support through programs such as Head Start, Upward Bound, and Title I of the Elementary and Secondary Education Act and supports for families in need such as Emergency Food Aid, Food Stamps, the school lunch programs, neighborhood health centers, and Medicaid.[50] Institutional barriers were addressed less successfully since the programs sought to involve the same local governments and institutions that had systematically disenfranchised large sectors of the urban populations. The problem was so pervasive that funding for legal services was provided to assist the disenfranchised in obtaining needed services. This was a time in which the federal government was taking leadership on issues of equality, and so the second round of programs directed to address urban inequalities, the Model Cities programs, sought to bypass entrenched local bureaucracies and provide funding directly to the neighborhoods and communities in need. Model Cities funding was comprehensive, including funds for local development, housing, and social services.[51]

There is significant debate about the efficacy of these programs in addressing urban poverty, a debate that will not be repeated here. The point relevant here is that, regardless of their ultimate efficacy, these programs provided vehicles for disenfranchised groups to gain a sem-blance of leverage in the policy arena. This slightly opened door was often contested by local governments and institutions and was the source of great rivalry between disenfranchised groups. But nevertheless, it was the door that brought African Americans and Latinos to the policy table across the region, from Massachusetts, to Connecticut, and to New York.[52] These programs and the organizations that emerged from them made black and Latino communities visible in the urban areas of New England and provided the training ground for a generation of black and Latino leaders and professionals.

The early history of Latinos in Providence reflects some of these struggles: in the emphasis on services of the early community organiza-tions, in the struggles to obtain funding from local sources, and in the efforts of local government and bureaucracies to co-opt and control emerging Latino leadership through the politics of brokered representa-tion.[53] But the fact is that by the time Latinos organized in Rhode Island, the "War on Poverty" programs were essentially over.

Latinos have come of age in Rhode Island during a radically different era. In 1980, with the election of Ronald Reagan and the rise of the "New Federalism," began a process of federal government retreat from the type of interventions that the War on Poverty represented. Reagan's programs devolved authority for the distribution of federal dollars to the state and localities through categorical block grants, but left disbursement decisions up to the states, which quickly directed them to local priorities. Federal devolution involves policies and funding in the areas of urban develop-ment, social services, and education.

The process of devolution seems to have had critical impact on the capacity to address the needs of new populations in New England. This happens for several reasons. First, attention to the needs of new groups is hampered by the lack of ability and willingness of local bureaucracies to adapt services to their needs. Up to this point, with the exception of relatively small concentrations of African Americans and Latinos in the larger cities, most of New England remained homogeneously white as did their state and local governments and bureaucracies. There was little experience dealing with newcomers or minorities and decisions at the local level were often the result of internal negotiations between white ethnic groups, which controlled both the governments and the bureau-cracies at the time of devolution. With the federal government and its demand for "maximum feasible participation" and equity out of the pic-ture, it was "business as usual" at the state and local levels. Devolution permitted local bureaucracies to resist the adoption of new priorities, the transformation of public workforces, and the alteration of processes of decision-making in order to reflect the new demographic realities.[54] The temptation has proven to be most irresistible in localities controlled by political machines, as was the case of Providence until very recently.[55] Part of the local resistance is related to the fact that government jobs in cities with strong local political machines, as is the case of Providence, are a source of employment and part of the system of reward used by the political machines to hold onto power.[56]

Second, the capacity to respond to new populations is hampered by the increasing weakness of the public sector. The same political forces that supported the process of devolution at the federal level propelled "no tax" revolutions at the state and local levels. Reduced state funding for programs, added to the net loss in federal funding that the block grants represented, placed significant pressure on local bureaucracies. They had to manage the dwindling resources while at the same time uncovering new sources of revenue and competing effectively for funding. Some states and cities have coped better than others with these challenges, but in most cases, it has promoted the privatization of public services. In many instances it is a "soft" privatization, that is, public agencies contracting with private nonprofits for the delivery of services while retaining public accountability for services. In these contracts, the state usually favors established agencies, which are often not culturally or linguistically accessible, and does not specify the requirements to provide culturally competent services to new groups.

In Rhode Island, publicly funded services are delivered by established human services agencies. These agencies present significant barriers to Latino clients due, first, to the lack of linguistically accessible information about availability of services, second, to the lack of bilingual, culturally competent personnel who can deliver services, and finally to the lack of trained, culturally competent professionals who can design and implement culturally appropriate services.[57] Latino leaders expressed that the attitude of the human services system in Rhode Island has been very close to "benign neglect."[58]

Finally, another effect of devolution—and the accompanying funding reductions—has been the curtailed availability of specialized services, which in many areas of the country has meant services directed at specific groups. Historically, there have been two types of "ethnic social services": those established by the groups themselves—such as the Scott's Charitable Society, founded in Boston in 1657, the Mexican *mutualista* societies, the Chinese Benevolent Associations, and the like[59]—and those services developed to help or transform the newcomers or minorities—such as the Native American schools and the settlement houses, established in cities of the Northeast and Midwest in response to the great influx of immigrants. During the first part of the twentieth century, most "ethnic" communities were left largely to their own devices. Those that had means developed an extensive network of supports, and we can see this in the plethora of religious (Catholic, Jewish) and ethnic-based (Irish, Italian, etc.) institutions in the cities of the region. But those without resources sunk into ever-deeper poverty.

It was this poverty that the War on Poverty sought to ameliorate by placing resources in the hands of the poor and disenfranchised so that they too could develop resources for their communities. And many did. A number of Latino community-based service organizations in the New England region have their roots if not directly in the programs of the War on Poverty, at least indirectly through the values that it promoted within the human service structure: the equitable distribution of services and the participation of its recipients in the design and implementation of the services. Community-based service organizations are rarely supported solely from community resources. They represent a partnership: the Latino community provides the organizational capacity, which, combined with support from public and private sources, provides the basis for a network of services to the community. Without a doubt, the survival of community-based organizations has been difficult because of funding and leadership challenges. But, particularly in the New England area, these organizations have been a strong element of the organizational environment in Latino communities and frequent vehicles for capacity building and community empowerment.[60]

At the time that Latinos gathered strength in Providence and Central Falls, the national policies that sustained community-based, racial/ethnic-oriented, and racial/ethnic-controlled service agencies were gone. With the advent of devolution, the funding of these specialized services was left to state and local bureaucracies, which were limited in their flexibility to respond because of their own budget shortfalls as well as their lack of experience in developing appropriate supports for the new populations. Changes in federal policy, on the one hand, limited the responsiveness of established service bureaucracies and, on the other, limited the capacity of poor, newcomer groups to develop their own service system with public dollars. This has been reflected in the experience of Latinos in Rhode Island as they have sought to build an autochthonous structure of community based services and a platform from which to participate in policy development.

Different factors have conspired to reduce the number of community-based service organizations in Rhode Island to two agencies: Progreso Latino in Central Falls, founded twenty-five years ago, and the Center for Hispanic Policy and Advocacy (CHisPA) in Providence, founded fifteen years ago.[61] Many organizations have come and gone due to internal problems related to administrative and leadership skills. But there is also evidence that there has been resistance in establishing a complementary system of services for Latinos. Organizational leaders point to the lack of consistent funding of services through state contracts and the lack of availability of United Way or similar funding to strengthen organizational capacity. At this point, for example, only Progreso Latino is a United Way agency. They also point to the absence of funding for services provided by community-based organizations because of the large number of persons settling in the area: orientation and information; case management and referral to appropriate services; information about immigration, housing, public assistance and public utilities; translations; and advocacy.[62] Undoubtedly, Latino community-based service organizations have been confronted with administrative and leadership problems. But the changes in the policies and the practices related to the funding of services for minorities and newcomers have also represented a critical barrier to the development of an autochthonous structure of community-based services. The result is the relatively thin representation of this type of organization in the community compared to their strong presence in other Latino communities of the region.

According to Victor Capellán, community-based organizations have played a leadership role, a political role: "these agencies have kept the Latino agenda on the table in Rhode Island."[63] But the fact is that community based organizations—whether ethnic, racially or geographically identified—are struggling to survive.[64] In this new environment, new community-based organizations could develop healthily only with a very strong public and private commitment to this type of service. In its absence, new immigrant communities are left not only without supportive services but also without the vehicles for the participation in the design and implementation of policies to meet their needs. Communities coming of age in the era of devolution must look for other windows into the political system and other avenues to political power.

By the mid-1980s Latino Rhode Islanders had come to understand that options to "take care of the community's business" available to Latino communities in other areas would not be available to them. They continued to work toward building community institutions and expanding access to services and benefits, but they were slowly but surely transiting from what Jennings and King would label "the politics of access" to the "politics of power."[65] That route would take them from the brokered representation by Latinos working for the powerful, through the struggle with the machine politics of the Cianci administration and the naming of Latinos to appointed positions. But the thrust was moving surely toward an electoral strategy. "We have been involved in voter registration since 1996, year round," said Juan Pichardo, who became state senator in 2002. "We have to make sure that people are informed of the process and that every day they are being effective."[66] Between 1987 and 1997, eight Latinos ran for office. Only one was successful, but the margins between the winner and loser were very close in several elections. In 1998, RILPAC was formed. By 2002, they were on their way to electoral success. In 2004 three Latinos were elected to statewide public office in Rhode Island.

For Latinos in Providence, the height of electoral activism coincided with the time that the city's political machine began to lose its absolute hold as a result of federal investigations and the eventual indictment and jailing of the major. Latinos participated actively in the election of the new mayor and made a critical difference in his campaign's success. Some argue that growing Latino power in Providence and Rhode Island is a result of being in the right place at the right time, of slipping through the cracks of the crumbling political machine. But Latino activists explain that the process of political development had been taking place over a long period of time, as the population grew, with the constant advocacy for inclusion, by becoming ever more organized.[67]

## Conclusions

Latino political organization in Rhode Island has emerged with force in the first generation and in the midst of exclusion from almost every other area of social activity in the state. It is not the product of a slow process of incorporation, decreased discrimination, and broad political acceptance, as traditional sociological theory would predict. Also, unlike the processes documented in other Latino communities of the region, Latino activism is not exclusively focused on the development of resources for the im/migrant community in the shape of the service programs that trained leaders and professionals for decades across the region.

I have argued that the particular shape of political participation in Rhode Island has to be examined in the light of three critical factors. The first is the urgency of the economic and social conditions facing Latinos in the state. Rhode Island Latinos have the worst economic outcomes of Latinos in the region. Institutional resistance to change, affecting the process of Latino incorporation throughout the region, has been very strong in Rhode Island: up to very recently Latinos in Rhode Island suffered an almost complete exclusion from social institutions in the state.

The second factor has been the impact of public policy on the capacity of the public sector and of the community itself to address these burgeoning community needs. The process of devolution affected the capacity of the state and local bureaucracies to address the needs of new populations. Devolution represented a net loss in resources from the federal government at a time when the state was also involved in cutting its own costs of government. As Latinos began to arrive in Rhode Island, state government was being pressured to do more with less. In some instances, the quality of public services has severely declined, just as the newcomers arrived. In others, the state was forced to "softly" privatize services, favoring established service organizations without experience in addressing the needs of the newcomers. At the same time, devolution undermined the capacity of poor urban communities to develop services directed to their specific needs. By the time Latinos gathered in the state, the policies and structures which engaged a whole generation of Latinos in the region in the process of building the infrastructure of community support was largely unavailable for Latinos in Rhode Island.

In the search for new vehicles to power, Latinos in Rhode Island directed themselves to the electoral arena, finding ways to address the problems presented by the great diversity within Latino groups in the state. This third critical factor involves nurturing the internal organizing process that helps mobilize the community from the inside and developing an organizational face that the community presents to the outside world. The strategy behind the Rhode Island experience relies on a principal feature of the Latino community—the myriad nationality- and community-based groups that characterize its organizational environment, in combination with the power of collective action through pan-Latino organizations. RILPAC, founded in 1998, has been the focus of the latter. RILPAC has built consensus around candidates and raised money to support those whose program best fit the interest of the community. It has established structured and transparent ways of participation and decision-making.

Gaining an understanding of the environment, harnessing this community's organizational strength, and managing the forces of divisiveness have been critical ingredients in the electoral success for Latinos in Rhode Island. But many challenges remain. One is maintaining unity as electoral activism grows and matures. A critical issue, for example, will be how the consensus-building process within RILPAC addresses the sponsorship of competing Latino candidates and the growing pressure to support non-Latino contenders.[68] Another challenge will surely be commitment to maintain the community's needs at the center of the electoral process. But perhaps most important is the question which Rhode Island Latinos will inevitably face about the efficacy of electoral politics as a strategy for development and empowerment. Policies have left few other options for Latinos to address "the business of the community," aside from the electoral process. Rhode Island's Latinos are committed to an electoral approach to Latino empowerment and well-being. Only time will tell whether this strategy will result in an improvement in Latino social and economic conditions.

## Notes

1. Support for research reflected in this paper has been provided by the Rhode Island Foundation (1991) and the Mauricio Gastón Institute for Latino Community Development and Public Policy, University of Massachusetts Boston (2004). I would like to thank Charles Jones, Carlos Maynard, and Daniel Vasquez for their work on the census data and Maria Estela Carrion for her work on interviews of Rhode Island leaders.

2. In fact, in 1999, the U.S. Bureau of the Census estimated that Rhode Island would have a population loss of 1.3 percent. See http://www.dlt.state.ri.us/lmi/TrendsinRI percent20Ecomony/popCESLAUS.htm.

3. M. Uriarte and N. Carithers, "Access to Services for Latinos in Rhode Island," in *Rhode Island Latinos: A Scan of Issues Affecting the Latino Community of Rhode Island*, ed. M. Uriarte, with M.E. Carrion, C. Jones, N. Carithers, J.C. Gorlier, and J.F. Garcia, 122–134 (Providence: The Rhode Island Foundation, 2002), www.rifoundation.org/popup_latino.htm.

4. M. Gordon, *Assimilation in American Life*, (New York: Oxford University Press, 1964).

5. For a review of these sociological theories see A. Portes and R. Bach, Introduction, in *Latin Journey* (Berkeley: University of California Press, 1985) and A. Portes and R. Rumbaut *Immigrant America* (Berkeley: University of California Press, 1996), 93–140. For a more recent review from the perspective of political science see R. Schmidt, R. Hero, A. Aoki, and I. Alex-Assensoh, "Political Science, The New Immigration and Racial Politics in the United States: What Do We Know? What Do We Need to Know?" presentation at the 2002 Annual Meeting of APSA, Boston, August 31, 2002.

6. Traditional theories of immigrant social organization postulate that common nationality and culture—ties of blood, faith and land—provide the basis for the development of organizations that maintain ties to nations of origin and to concentrate social relations within the group. Other explanations focus on spatial concentration, on the sharing of similar workplaces, and on the commonalities that arise from those proximities as the basis for ethnic organization. See, for example, W. L. Yancey, E. P. Ericksen, and R. N. Juliani, "Emergent Ethnicity: A Review and Reformulation," *American Sociological Review* 41, no. 3: 391–403. Rather than a "lag from the past" and a barrier to social incorporation, newer thinking focuses on these factors as the formal expression of the dense networks characteristic of immigrant communities as well as the vehicles for social support and political activism among these groups.

7. See J. Jennings, "Puerto Rican Politics in Two Cities: New York and Boston," in *Puerto Rican Politics in Urban America*, ed. James Jennings and Monte Rivera (Westport, CN: Greenwood Press, 1984); M. Uriarte and N. Merced, "Social Service Agencies in Boston's Latino Community," *Catalyst* 5: 17–18; J. Jennings and M. King, *From Access to Power: Black Politics in Boston* (Cambridge, MA: Schenkman Books, 1986); C. Hardy Fanta, *Latina Politics, Latino Politics* (Philadelphia: Temple University Press, 1993); R. Borges-Mendez, "Migration, Social Networks, Poverty and the

Regionalization of Puerto Rican Settlements: Barrio Formation in Lowell, Lawrence and Holyoke, Mass," *Latino Studies Journal* (May 1993): 3–21; M. Uriarte, "Contra Viento y Marea (Against All Odds): Latinos Build Community in Boston," in Uriarte et al., *Latinos in Boston*; J. Cruz, *Identity and Power* (Philadelphia: Temple University Press, 1998); K. Bergantz, P. Kim, A. Lelyveld, M. Lucero, I. Stewart, and E. Tierney, "Bridges and Barriers: The Evolution of Latino Political Empowerment in Providence, RI," report from Brown University's Urban Borderland (Providence: Rhode Island Historical Society, 2000); R. Hernandez and G. Jacobs, "*Beyond Homeland Politics: Dominicans in Massachusetts*," in *Latino Political Representation: Struggles, Strategies, and Prospects*, ed. C. Hardy-Fanta and J. Gerson (New York: Garland Publishing, 2001); M. Martinez "Latinos of Rhode Island," in *Rhode Island Latinos*, ed. Uriarte et al., www.rifoundation.org/popup_latino.htm; R. Borges-Mendez and M. Uriarte, "Tales of Latinos in Three Small Cities: Latino Settlement and Incorporation in Lawrence and Holyoke, Massachusetts, and Providence, Rhode Island," paper delivered at the Color Line Conference: Segregation & Integration in America's Present and Future, Harvard University, August, 2003.

8. The results of this research are reported in Uriarte et al., *Rhode Island Latinos*, and Borges-Mendez and Uriarte, "Tales of Latinos." This chapter also includes secondary analysis of interviews conducted by Bergantz et al., "Bridges and Barriers," the complete transcriptions of which are included in their report.

9. Bergantz et al., "Bridges and Barriers," and Martinez, "Latinos of Rhode Island," 35–37.

10. Martinez, "Latinos of Rhode Island," 41.

11. M. W. Collier and E. Gamarra, "The Colombian Diaspora in South Florida" (Miami: Florida International University, Latin American and Caribbean Center, WPS #1, 2001), http://lacc.fiu.edu/publications_resources/working_papers/working _paper_01.htm.

12. Martinez, "Latinos of Rhode Island," 38–39, and Borges-Mendez and Uriarte, "Tales of Latinos."

13. Martinez, "Latinos of Rhode Island," 44, and Borges-Mendez and Uriarte, "Tales of Latinos."

14. Focus group 4, November 6, 2001.

15. U.S. Bureau of the Census, Census 2000, Summary File 4 (SF4), Sample Data (http://factfinder.census.gov/).

16. Ibid.

17. U.S. Citizenship and Immigration Services, Immigration through the Nicaraguan Adjustment and Central American Relief Act, Section 203, 2003 (http:// uscis.gov/graphics/services/residency/nacara203_main.htm).

18. U.S. Citizenship and Immigration Services, Temporary Protected Status, 2003 (http://uscis.gov/graphics/services/tps_inter.htm, March 11, 2004).

19. See National Immigration Law Center, A Guide to Immigrant Eligibility for Federal Programs, 2003 (http://www.nilc.org/immspbs/special/Ovrvw_Imm_ Elig_Fed_Pgms_4.03.pdf), and Chapter 2 of this volume.

20. Interview with Roberto Gonzalez, September 2001.

21. Yancey, Erickson, and Juliani, "Emergent Ethnicity: A Review and Reformulation," 391–403.

22. Quoted in Bergantz et al., "Bridges and Barriers," 63.

23. Ibid., 32.

24. Ibid., 46.

25. Interview with Pablo Rodriguez, September 2001.

26. S. Kurland, "Brown Power vs. Black Power," in *Color Lines/ Race, Culture, Action* 4, no. 1 (Spring 2001).

27. Quoted in Bergantz et al., "Bridges and Barriers," 46.

28. For comparative Latino poverty rates by age cohorts see U.S. Bureau of the Census, Census 2000, Summary File 4 (SF4), Sample Data (http://factfinder. census.gov/). Also, while national poverty rates among Latinos decreased from 25.3 percent in 1990 to 22.6 percent in 2000, those among Latinos in Rhode Island increased from 30.4 percent to 36.1 percent in the same period, according to the U.S. Bureau of the Census, 1990 Census of Population and Housing, Summary Tape File 1, 100% Data (http://factfinder.census.gov/); 2000 Census, Summary File 4 (SF4), Sample Data (http://factfinder.census.gov/).

29. For a succinct analysis of the research on Latino poverty, see E. Melendez, "Competing Explanations of Latino Poverty," in Uriarte et al., *Latinos in Boston* (Boston: Boston Foundation, 1993).

30. Ibid., 5

31. Ibid.

32. U.S. Bureau of the Census, 2000 Census, Summary File 4 (SF4), Sample Data (http://factfinder.census.gov/). Figures for other groups are 20 percent for Mexicans, 24 percent for Guatemalans, 39.4 percent for Dominicans, and 23.1 percent for Colombians.

33. Ibid.

34. U.S. Bureau of the Census, 2000 Census, Summary File 4 (SF4), Sample Data, and Rhode Island Economic Development Corporation, The Rhode Island Economy, (March 1999), 12, http://www.riedc.com/aboutri/economy/econframe.html

35. U.S. Bureau of the Census, 2000 Census, Summary File 4 (SF4), Sample Data.

36. Ibid.

37. Ibid.

38. Ibid.

39. Ibid.

40. See Chapter 2 in this volume.

41. See Uriarte et al., *Rhode Island Latinos*, and Rhode Island Kids Count, *Child Poverty in Rhode Island* (Providence: Rhode Island Kids Count, 2002), http://www. rikidscount.org/matriarch/d.asp?PageID=231&PageName2=issuebriefpoverty&p= &PageName=childpoverty%2Epdf.

42. Discussion with community leaders on findings of Uriarte et al., *Rhode Island Latinos*, CHisPA, February 8, 2002.

43. K. Blanton, "Losing Ground: High-Paying Jobs Shrinking, Lower-Wage Ones Grow in State," *Boston Globe*, September 8, 2004, C1.

44. Uriarte et al., *Rhode Island Latinos*.

45. Ibid., 84–87.

46. Ibid., 97.

47. Ibid., 101.

48. Ibid., 112.

49. Interview with Victor Capellán, September 2001.

50. G. Galster, "Poverty," in *Reality and Research: Social Science and U.S. Urban Policy since 1960*, ed. G. Galster (Washington DC: Urban Institute, 1996), 45.

51. C. Walker and P. Boxall, "Economic Development," in Galster, *Reality and Research*, 20.

52. For accounts of Boston and Hartford, see M. King, *Chain of Change* (Boston: South End Press, 1981); Jennings, "Puerto Rican Politics"; Uriarte and Merced, "Social Service Agencies"; Jennings and King, *From Access to Power*; Cruz, *Identity and Power*; and Hardy Fanta and Gerson, *Latino Political Representation*.

53. Bergantz et al., "Bridges and Barriers," 31–33.

54. Borges-Mendez and Uriarte, *Tales of Latinos*, 17.

55. Ibid., 15–22.

56. Ibid., 18.

57. M. Uriarte and N. Carithers, "Access to Services for Latinos in Rhode Island," in Uriarte et al., *Rhode Island Latinos*, 125, www.rifoundation.org/popup_latino.htm.

58. Interview with Vidal Perez, October 2001.

59. According to A. P. Iglehart and R.M. Becerra, *Social Services and the Ethnic Community* (Prospect Heights, IL: Waveland Press, 1995), Mexican *mutualista* societies and Chinese benevolent associations, established in the early 1800s, were another early precursor of "ethnic services."

60. See Uriarte and Merced, "Social Service Agencies"; Uriarte, 1993; Cruz, *Identity and Power*; R. Borges-Mendez, "Industrial Change, Immigration, and Community Development: An Overview of Europeans and Latinos," *New England Journal of Public Policy* 11 (Spring/Summer 1995): 43–58; and M. E. Letona, *State Government Provision of HIV/AIDS Prevention Programs: Towards a Partnership Model of the Contractual Relationship Between State Governments and Community Agencies* (Boston: Taylor & Francis, December 1999).

61. Interviews with Luisa Murillo, September 21, 2001; Victor Capellán, September 21, 2001; and Patricia Martinez, September 24, 2001. For an account of the barriers faced in developing community organizations see Bergantz et al., "Bridges and Barriers"; for an analysis of the challenges facing the Latino agencies in the mid-eighties see K. Castagna, "Hispanic Identity in Rhode Island: Some Recent Immigrants," senior project submitted in partial fulfillment for a bachelor of arts degree in the concentration of Latin American Studies at Brown University, April 18, 1986, and R. Michaelson, (1986) *Report on the Hispanic, Portuguese and Cape Verdean Populations in Rhode Island*, unpublished paper, The Rhode Island Foundation, 1986; and for an analysis of the situation at the end of the 1990s see Uriarte and Carithers, "Access to Services."

62. Interviews with Luisa Murillo, September 21, 2001, and Patricia Martinez, September 24, 2001. See also Uriarte and Carithers, "Access to Services."

63. Interview with Victor Campellán, September 26, 2001.

64. See J. Jennings, *Welfare Reform and the Revitalization of Inner City Neighborhoods* (East Lansing, Michigan: Michigan State University Press, 2003), 46–49, for a description of the effect of welfare reform policies on community based service organizations. See Uriarte and Carithers, "Access to Services," for the situation of Latino service agencies in Rhode Island.

65. Jennings and King, *Chain of Change*.

66. Oral history interview quoted in Bergantz et al., "Bridges and Barriers."

67. Interviews with Pablo Rodriguez, September 2001 and July 2003, and Luisa Murillo, September 2001.

68. This had already become an issue in 2004 when RILPAC endorsed only one Latino candidate out of the five running for state slots when none of the other candidates obtained consensus within RILPAC. This included the critical primary race between Rep. Luis Tejada and newcomer Grace Díaz. T. Pina, "Latino PAC Takes Heat for Backing Only 1 Latino Candidate in 5 Races," *Providence Journal*, September 7, 2004.

# 6  Quiet Crisis: A Community History of Latinos in Cambridge, Massachusetts

Deborah Pacini Hernandez

While the foundational work characterizing the earliest stages of the field of Latino studies focused on particular ethnic groups—primarily Mexican Americans/Chicanos and Puerto Ricans, the newer subfield of comparative Latino studies has focused instead on places—mostly cities with large Latino populations such as New York, Los Angeles, and Miami but more recently in newer receiving areas such as New England—where multiple ethnic groups, Latinos and non-Latinos alike, share space and influence each other's development.[1] This approach has encouraged viewing Latino communities in relation to other ethnic groups inhabiting these spaces—other Latino ethnic groups and non-Latinos alike. This work has gone a long way toward bringing into relief the profound heterogeneity of the urban Latino experience in the various parts of the United States.

Many of the authors of such place-focused studies have been sociologists, economists, and political scientists who have typically relied heavily on quantitative data such as census figures because these are clearly the best ways of identifying broad patterns and historical trends—for example, labor force participation, education levels, and residential patterns—characterizing specific communities and how these have changed over time. Seeking to add to this rich body of knowledge, cultural anthropologists and public historians, acknowledging Sidney Mintz's observation that "people are at once products and makers of the social and cultural systems in which they are lodged,"[2] have employed ethnographic research—oral history and in-depth interviews—in order to reveal the individual stories and perspectives of those whose daily lives and struggles have collectively constituted these systems.

Equally valuable, from a different theoretical perspective, is that such studies can serve to assess whether models developed from research in other regions and from other data sources can be generalized. It is common knowledge, for example, that today's U.S. Latino population is the consequence of decades of successive migratory waves from diverse Latin American sending regions. Typically, the earlier arrivals—Puerto Ricans on the East Coast and Mexican Americans in the Southwest—provided a base that facilitated the later arrival of relatives and friends (as well as pioneers from other ethnic groups such as Dominicans), who themselves subsequently become links in the rapidly extending *cadenas* (migration chains). The earliest immigrants to urban East Coast cities were drawn by the region's manufacturing sector, while later arrivals have generally been incorporated into less remunerative and secure service-sector jobs. Unlike their European predecessors, however, who were eventually accepted by the majority society, Latinos have been unable to overcome the barriers of racism, segregation, and exclusion. Indeed, with the exception of the first wave of Cubans in the 1960s and 1970s, Latino immigration patterns have subverted the optimistic theories positing that all immigrants would eventually assimilate into the great "American melting pot" by shedding their ethnicity. As Andres Torres has pointed out, "Instead of dissolving into a single entity, they compete intensely, and ethnic identity and language continue to figure in their political, social and economic activities"[3]—a pattern which stimulated "mosaic" models of incorporation. In other cases, especially among Spanish Caribbeans, some assimilation did occur, but laterally into African American rather than white Eurocentric society.[4] As Latinos continue to increase steadily in numbers, their political and economic visibility within the host society has also been increasing, generating newer theoretical models suggesting that ethnic political and economic succession become inevitable when an immigrant minority community grows large enough relative to the host society. Hardy-Fanta and Gerson's work, for example, demonstrated such progressions in two Massachusetts cities, Lawrence and Chelsea, as the percentage of the Latino population in these cities increased dramatically.[5]

Latinos in the city of Cambridge, Massachusetts, are another story. The city's economy is heavily dependent on high-skilled, private, service-sector employment; these include jobs in education—Harvard and MIT are Cambridge's two largest employers—and health-related services—six of the city's eleven top employers are companies such as Genzyme and Biogen.[6] Such an elite economic environment dramatically raises the bar for immigrants and minorities, making their incorporation even more difficult. Moreover, Cambridge is extremely expensive: it has a greater concentration of million-dollar homes than any other major U.S. city. In spite of these inauspicious characteristics, Cambridge's Latino population has increased steadily, from 4,536 in 1980 to 7,455 in 2000.[7] But behind the census data showing increasing numbers that elsewhere might imply a community growing in strength and visibility lies a more dismal story:

a once tightly knit Latino community is deeply fractured and disintegrating. The cleavages run primarily along lines of socioeconomic class, but they also correlate strongly with ethnicity. The oldest group, comprised of working-class Spanish Caribbeans, was established in the 1960s. The culturally distinct but even poorer and more vulnerable Central Americans began arriving as refugees in the 1980s. The newest group is comprised of highly educated, affluent professionals (many of whom are South American) attracted to Cambridge because of its cultural resources. The newcomers appear to be moving toward greater economic, political, and cultural influence, but the children of working-class Spanish Caribbeans and Central Americans are generating the sad litany of dismal statistics: the lowest high school enrollment and graduation rates and the highest representation in the lowest-paid and most-unskilled jobs. Thus, in spite of growing numbers, long-term residence, and years of social and political activism, this group has slipped backward into what community activist Dennis Benzan has called "a quiet crisis."

The essay that follows, then, describes an exception to the patterns of immigrant incorporation predicted by existing models. Based on oral histories (correlated with census and other statistical data), it traces the major contours of an interrupted trajectory leading to the present crisis of community among working-class Latinos in Cambridge. Oral history is particularly valuable for the task of understanding the development of marginalized social groups, such as working-class Latino communities, because their history, considered too insignificant to merit systematic study, is, as Alessandro Portelli has noted, "either missing or distorted."[8] Undergraduate students and I, in a community-based research seminar I teach at Tufts University, collected the oral histories cited below. They provide a much-needed venue for ordinary individuals, who rarely have access to the domain of public discourse, to voice their recollections and perspectives.[9]

## Puerto Ricans and Dominicans: Cambridge's Pioneer Latino Community

Individuals of Latin American descent who today would be called Latinos have lived in Cambridge for decades. Some of the earliest were students from families wealthy enough to send their children to Harvard or MIT, although most did not remain in Cambridge once their studies were completed; an illustrious example is the Puerto Rican nationalist Pedro Albizu Campos, who attended Harvard in 1913. A handful of working-class women from various Latin American nations also arrived as domestic servants to work in the homes of affluent Cambridge residents and ended up staying. Latinos did not begin settling in Cambridge in substantial numbers, however, until the 1960s. The pioneers were Puerto Ricans, mostly from the towns of Coamo and Jayuya, who arrived in Massachusetts as migrant farm workers in the 1950s, laboring in the agricultural areas around Boston. Cambridge had been New England's third-largest manufacturing center since the nineteenth century, and its Cambridgeport neighborhood, where many of its factories were located, had been a primary port of entry for generations of European immigrants because it provided not only employment but also ample affordable housing within walking distance. When Puerto Rican migrants found that manufacturing jobs were easy to get, some ended up staying, establishing themselves in Cambridge.

As the relatives and friends of these pioneering families—the Santiagos, Colons, Pagans, Maldonados, and Ortizes—heard about the advantages of Cambridge, the rate of migration from Puerto Rico picked up; city telephone books from the early 1960s, for example, reveal that one Santiago family resided in Cambridge in 1961, but by 1972 there were eleven. The adults were well employed, mostly in the older factories such as NECCO and Polaroid—although a few, such as Luis Colon, were working as laborers in electronics-oriented firms such as the KLH Research and Development Corporation. Telephone books also reveal that many apartments located in Cambridgeport were vacant;[10] in this regard, Cambridge resembled other urban areas from the time, including downtown Boston, that were losing an earlier generation of immigrant laborers to deindustrialization and suburbanization. These changes were initially beneficial to the new arrivals because spacious and affordable apartments were easy to find. A 1967 architectural survey of Cambridge's housing stock also confirms that most of the buildings in Cambridgeport, while by no means luxury apartments, were in relatively good condition and large enough to accommodate large families.

Except for their choice of destination—a New England city lacking a tradition of receiving immigrants from Latin America—these Puerto Ricans were no different from the thousands of their largely unskilled, working-class compatriots fleeing rural poverty and unemployment in Puerto Rico by migrating to the New York City. Since so many of them came from Coamo and Jayuya, the social connections so useful in finding jobs, housing, and otherwise assisting with the adaptation process emerged and solidified quickly. While it was not easy relocating to Cambridge—unlike New York City, the city did not have a comparably well-established Latino community—conditions were favorable enough that family members continued to join the *cadena*. Within a decade, the number of Puerto Rican immigrants had grown exponentially, from approximately fifty in the mid-1960s to several thousand in the 1970s. Thus, within little more than a decade they had reached sufficient numbers to create an extended network of relatives and friends willing and able to work together toward common goals, from organizing tenants' councils and pressuring the city to address its housing and education needs to organizing softball leagues and cultural events—in other words, to constitute a viable community.

A handful of Dominicans also arrived in the early 1960s, among them the Benzan and Acevedo families, who had come to escape the turmoil ensuing the death of the dictator Rafael Trujillo and the subsequent U.S. invasion of the Dominican Republic. Unlike the Puerto Ricans, who, as U.S. citizens, were spared problems with visas, had access to social services, and could vote, the Dominicans were less able to easily recruit as many family members from home, so they attached themselves to the Puerto Rican community and its networks. Relations between Dominicans and Puerto Ricans were not entirely devoid of the tensions that have long existed between these two national groups elsewhere, but in Cambridge, given their shared experiences as Spanish Caribbean immigrants in a city with little understanding or respect for their cultures, they seem to have cooperated successfully. Rafael Benzan and Ramon Acevedo, for example, named both their co-owned travel agency and moving company, which catered primarily to Puerto Ricans, *La Borincana* rather than a name invoking their own national homeland.

While the first Puerto Rican families to arrive in the early 1960s had been scattered throughout the socioeconomically diverse Cambridgeport neighborhoods both north and south of Massachusetts Avenue (the city's main thoroughfare), those arriving later in the decade settled in a subsection just north of Massachusetts Avenue, which contained a larger percentage of low-income housing, including numerous multifamily apartment buildings. One of these, Columbia Terrace, became the epicenter of the Spanish-Caribbean community. The Terrace's particular architectural configuration encouraged social interactions among its residents: its units, large enough to accommodate sizable families (and their newly arrived relatives), were constructed around an enclosed courtyard where everyone's children could play under the watchful eyes of the adults. The Columbia Street neighborhood also had two of the city's oldest government housing projects, Newtowne Court and Washington Elms. The residents of these apartment complexes had historically been racially and socioeconomically diverse, but after 1969, when income guidelines were changed and rents began to be subsidized, they became increasingly black and Latino.[11] The neighborhood had a reputation for being tough, and unlike other Cambridge neighborhoods, which were

l by appealing names such as Old Cambridge or North Cam-
was referred to by city officials and nonresidents by its police
ᴅᴇsɪɢɴᴀᴛɪᴏn: Area 4. To its residents, however, it was known as "the Port,"
reflecting their awareness that the area was in fact the northernmost extension of Cambridgeport.

The concentration of working-class Puerto Ricans and Dominicans in
the Port was a crucial factor in fostering the development of a cohesive
community, and confirms Miren Uriarte's observations regarding

> the importance of a stable physical 'place' in the building of formal and in-
> formal social networks and organizations that allow for the development of a
> community's functions of production, socialization, control, participation, and
> support.[12]

It also brings into relief the relationship between place and ethnic
identity: as Dolores Hayden has noted:

> Identity is intimately tied to memory: both our personal memories (where we
> have come from and where we have dwelt) and the collective or social mem-
> ories interconnected with the histories of our families, neighbors, fellow
> workers, and ethnic communities. Urban landscapes are storehouses for these
> social memories.[13]

Resident José Ortiz's recollections resonate with Uriarte and Hayden's
observations on the importance of place:

> When I came here, there were many Latinos on Columbia Street. They called
> it *el pueblo*, they called it the Puerto Rican *pueblo*, because they were all from
> Puerto Rico, from my town. And we used to get together in a park, and we'd
> start talking.... And it was a beautiful time, very beautiful when we got
> together.

The ever-widening circle of family and friends who constituted the later
links in this chain migration—those arriving in the 1970s—unfortunately
came as Cambridge's manufacturing base was being replaced by a more
high-tech electronics-, engineering-, and research-oriented economy,
which was heavily dependent on the brainpower harnessed by MIT and
Harvard but offered fewer well-paying employment opportunities to unskilled workers. These institutions also began to impact the availability of
affordable housing that had made the neighborhood attractive to immigrants. In the late 1960s and early 1970s, MIT, Harvard, and a growing
number of high-tech enterprises sprouting up near them began to purchase the factories they were replacing in order to add new offices and
laboratories. MIT, for example, purchased the Kraft Cheese Company
building, a library furniture factory, and a candy factory and conver-
ted these buildings into a nuclear-engineering center. They also began

expanding into the surrounding residential neighborhood—the Port; the construction of Technology Square, for example, required the clearing of an entire block of affordable multifamily houses. The demand for real estate coupled with the decline in the housing stock would have caused the neighborhood's housing costs to become prohibitively expensive, but fortunately for the continually arriving Puerto Ricans and Dominicans, progressive sectors in Cambridge—long a political force and the reason behind the city's nickname, "The People's Republic of Cambridge"— succeeded in their goal of preserving the city's economically and ethnically diverse character by instituting rent control, first in 1968–1970, and again from 1972 to 1994. Thus, until 1994, low-income neighborhoods such as the Port managed to retain their ethnic, working-class character.

Rent control kept housing affordable for working-class Latinos, but the blue-collar jobs they had depended on were becoming harder to find: between 1950 and 1980, the percentage of manufacturing jobs in Cambridge fell from almost 30 percent to under 14 percent.[14] As economic conditions for the newer arrivals worsened, the community began experiencing conflict with the city when it failed to respond to their plight, which included obstacles in obtaining housing assistance to which they were entitled, difficulties in voting because they were considered aliens, lack of (and later substandard) bilingual education, and hospitals that would not offer translation services.

As their numbers burgeoned, Latinos were increasingly perceived by some city officials and white residents as unwanted foreigners; or they were simply lumped in with the city's other subordinated group, African Americans. Community leader Roberto Santiago recalled the tensions in the neighborhood:

> It became very unstable, because the Anglo kids, they were ganging together to try to stop us from using the park.... and then the police came.... We had to move [but] the other group could stay there in the park.

Latinos were also caught up in the busing conflicts of the 1970s. María Bermúdez recalls the racial climate:

> We weren't accepted there by the other students, by the white kids, you might say. They didn't want us there. [The bus was] met with kids with rocks and bottles. A lot of times the bus driver had to drive away. It took a while just to get us into the building safely.... When we moved, my mother found an apartment, very close to the school. The white kids in the neighborhood threw stuff at our windows and said, "You Spics!" and "go back home!"

These difficulties, however, served to galvanize the growing, socially interconnected community; as Santiago noted, "It was many, many problems ... [and] ... we were forced to unite." The Puerto Ricans, aware of their rights as citizens and familiar with the strategies being used by other Puerto Rican communities in Boston and elsewhere to challenge official indifference, began to organize. The epicenter of political activity was the Columbia Terrace apartment complex, which housed the largest number of Puerto Rican families. Santiago recalled that in the late 1960s, Puerto Ricans began pressuring city officials for better access to public services and demanding full civil rights. An early victory came in 1969, following an initially unsuccessful appeal to the Cambridge Economic Opportunities Commission (CEOC) to direct a share of the city's federal antipoverty funds to assist the city's Spanish-speaking population, which at that time was estimated at three thousand. When the CEOC refused, the group rented a U-Haul truck and parked it in front of the CEOC; from this makeshift "office" they organized picket lines and engaged pedestrians in dialogues about the city's funding disparities. Bowing to pressure, the CEOC provided the group with an $18,000 grant to pay for a permanent office and a secretary and the right to select two members to serve on the CEOC's board.

Once the group was officially recognized, the activists established a civic association called the Cambridge Spanish Council, *Concilio Hispano*, with Roberto Santiago as president, and a thirteen-member board of directors, five of whom were women.[15] For the next two decades, Concilio Hispano continued to function as an organization run primarily by and for the Puerto Rican community. Some of the group's accomplishments included pressuring the legislature to require recording of court proceedings so that abuses could be challenged, demanding the Elections Commission guarantee Puerto Ricans the right to vote, exposing police harassment, and lobbying local universities—Harvard, MIT, and Tufts—to provide the community with more jobs at better pay. Indeed, the degree to which members of Concilio Hispano took advantage of these elite institutions differentiated them from their activist counterparts elsewhere. Because Cambridge's universities attracted students from wealthy Puerto Rican and Latin American families studying law and other prestigious professions, activists recognized the students' potential value as allies and advocates. As Santiago recalls:

> Our committee people said, "I think we have to talk to the students. They speak the language very well, they are inside universities, and I don't think the police are going to attack them when presented with issues in the city." ... I met some students in Central Square, from Harvard, and I spoke to them. I said, "listen, this is what is happening here in this community." So they said, "why don't we meet." ... so we invited people from Tufts University, Brandeis, Boston University, Harvard, MIT ... and got the students together.... We were very happy to have them, and they were very happy to be involved in community issues.... Sometimes we had two hundred students.

The students assisted Concilio Hispano with translating letters and petitions into English, advised them on legal rights, represented them in meetings with community agencies, and pressured their institutions to cooperate more with the community; MIT, for example, hosted social and fundraising events in the university's Puerto Rico Room, and Harvard established a Latino Board to deal with employment issues. In some cases the students received credit for their work in the community—early examples of what today might be called engaged citizenship and service learning—which brought community's issues to the attention of professors and university administrators.

One of Concilio Hispano's most intensive struggles involved bilingual education: first pressuring the city to establish a bilingual program and subsequently ensuring that it adequately served its students. Bilingual education had been established in Cambridge in 1970, primarily for children of the city's growing Portuguese population. Concilio Hispano forged a coalition with the Cambridge Organization for Portuguese Americans (COPA) and in 1972 began pressuring the School Committee to increase the woefully inadequate number of bilingual classrooms (only forty-five spaces for four hundred eligible students).[16] While separate bilingual programs were subsequently established for both Portuguese and Spanish speakers, the city never committed adequate funds to bilingual education, so in 1975 a broader coalition of parents, the Master Parents Advisory Council (PAC)—which now included parents of Greek-, French-, and Chinese-speaking children as well—complained to the city about the lack of space and resources—including fundamental materials such as books.[17] Additionally, a number of children who spoke English were being improperly assigned, on the basis of their ethnicity alone, to the substandard bilingual classrooms in which subjects needed for graduation, such as science, were not being taught. PAC complained to the federal Department of Health, Education, and Welfare's Office for Civil Rights, which in 1979 charged the Cambridge school system with failing to protect the civil rights of its bilingual students.[18]

In addition to their political work, the members of Concilio Hispano also recognized the importance of culture in maintaining community cohesion. Roberto Santiago organized a baseball league (which still exists and bears his name) that played other Latino teams from Massachusetts as well as New York, and there was a softball team for girls, Las Chicas. Wives and other family members participated by providing food and helping with fundraisers such as raffles and monthly dances held at the VFW. Thus, organized sports simultaneously strengthened neighborhood-based identity and created connections with Latinos elsewhere in the state. Another important form of cultural work was organizing the annual

Hispanic Festival, inaugurated in the early 1980s. The festival, which took place across the street from the Terrace, in what then was the parking lot for the Polaroid factory, offered Puerto Rican food, music, and games— including a traditional greased-pole climbing competition—the *palo encebado*. The festival's highlight was a parade featuring elegantly dressed queens seated atop floats decorated by neighborhood residents. These displays of ethnic culture and pride and the months of planning meetings and fundraisers that made them possible greatly solidified the community and gave it a public presence: when the parade traveled down Columbia Street, it traced the main axis of the community, but when it entered Massachusetts Avenue and proceeded to City Hall, it publicly inscribed Latinos onto the map of mainstream Cambridge's cultural geography. At its height in 1990, the festival attracted up to four thousand people, including attendees from other Boston-area Latino communities.

If the community was thriving socially and was relatively successful in political terms, economically it continued to struggle. Blue-collar jobs were becoming scarcer and the community's economic base weakened: by the end of the 1980s, only 10.4 percent of Cambridge's residents as a whole were still engaged as "operatives and laborers."[19] There were, of course, a handful of entrepreneurs who had established successful businesses offering ethnically specific goods and services, such as bodegas, hair salons, and restaurants serving Spanish-Caribbean food, and these provided family and community members with employment opportunities. But as Peggy Levitt noted in her study of Cambridge's small Latino businesses, "the same dense grid of social expectations and reciprocal obligations that engenders and sustains Latino businesses also constrains them," not only because their businesses' growth was limited by the economic possibilities of their customers but also because their owners' cultural emphasis on community ties and stability was more important than individual accumulation.[20]

A noteworthy exception was the partnership between Rafael Benzan and Ramon Acevedo, who successfully capitalized on the demographic changes characterizing the larger Boston metro area in the 1960s and 1970s by expanding their Latino-oriented businesses well beyond the Columbia Street community in Cambridge. These entrepreneurial Dominicans began modestly in the early 1960s with one of Cambridge's first bodegas, which they named Wild World Foods. Subsequently they purchased a travel agency on Massachusetts Avenue from its previous African American owner and renamed it *La Borincana*, and then they established a moving company, also named *La Borincana*. The moving company, which at first functioned only on weekends and evenings when Benzan and Acevedo were not working at their day jobs (Acevedo was a dishwasher at MIT, Benzan did factory work), soon grew to be, according to Acevedo's son Ray Jr., Boston's largest Latino moving company and the largest Latino-oriented business in the Northeast. Acevedo and Benzan also began buying apartment buildings in declining urban Boston neighborhoods such as Dorchester, Jamaica Plain, and Roxbury, that were, like Cambridge, experiencing deindustrialization and being vacated by their former white working classes moving to the suburbs; these apartments were then rented to the steadily increasing stream of Puerto Ricans and Dominicans arriving into the Boston area—many of whom also found employment in Benzan and Acevedo's various businesses. In addition to providing their co-ethnics with assistance with travel, moving, housing, and employment, they offered them cultural services as well. They began by producing dances with top Latin bands, first in local hotel ballrooms, but later they purchased a large Loew's theatre in Boston's South End, which they renamed *Teatro Las Americas*. The theatre played (mostly) Mexican films during the week, but on weekends, they produced concerts by major salsa and merengue stars, such as Celia Cruz and Johnny Ventura.

Unlike the small Cambridge Latino business owners interviewed by Levitt, who tended to remain in the community they worked in, both Benzan and Acevedo purchased homes outside of Cambridge as soon as they could afford to, in order to remove their children from a neighborhood they perceived was becoming a ghetto. This does not imply that the Dominicans were indifferent to the political or social activities of their Puerto Rican cohorts: indeed, Rafael Benzan recalls that in 1962, a year after he arrived in Cambridge, he joined with his Puerto Ricans friends in establishing *La Confraternidad Hispana*, a social organization founded years before the more politically oriented Concilio Hispano became active. All the people I interviewed, Puerto Rican and Dominican alike, spoke of close and cordial relationships between the two groups. But the Dominicans, because of their reduced numbers in Cambridge, were not similarly embedded in the deep social networks described by Levitt, making it easier for them to disassociate themselves from the Cambridge community and expand their businesses to other neighborhoods.

Benzan and Acevedo were correct in their perceptions that the neighborhood was becoming a less favorable place to raise children: in the 1980s, the Latino community, already subject to the effects of poverty and racial discrimination, was also experiencing the scourge of drugs and associated crime that was similarly afflicting urban areas throughout the nation. Indeed, while the people I interviewed remembered the 1960s and 1970s with great nostalgia, as a period when the community was vital, family-oriented, and cohesive, they all mention that in the early 1980s drugs entered the neighborhood and degraded the quality of life. Moreover, as drug activity and crime attracted more police presence, conflicts between the community and the authorities intensified. Dennis Benzan reported that many of his childhood friends ended up in jail, and noted the corrosive changes in the once tightly knit neighborhood:

> [Earlier], if your mom passed by, they would be like, "Buenos días, Señora, como está?" There was a certain level of respect. It's kind of ironic that the community was still somewhat secure in its own way. That is so absent right now.

Indeed, Cambridge's school system had failed to prevent the catastrophic impact of drugs on its Latino youth. In the early 1980s, as the drug crisis began to hit the Latino community, the dropout rate of Latino students in Cambridge was an astounding 67 percent—a reflection of the abysmal treatment many of them were receiving in the substandard bilingual programs many of them had been corralled into. Making matters worse, unlike in other urban areas devastated by deindustrialization, Cambridge's land values continued to rise precipitously. Landlords, once happy to have immigrant renters, chafed when rent control prevented them from profiting from rising real estate prices, and they began neglecting their buildings. Even the Port's housing projects, one of which, Newtowne Court, had once been the pride of the neighborhood, turned into blighted slums in the wake of public and private disinvestment characterizing the Reagan years. With the Port's crime rates rising, the neighborhood's physical space declining, jobs close to home difficult to find, its children being poorly educated and increasingly susceptible to drugs and police harassment, many Latino families began moving out, some to more affordable nearby cities such as Revere and Lynn, many back to Puerto Rico. Indeed, the neighborhood had gotten so bad that when the Port's housing projects, Washington Elms and Newtowne Court, were redeveloped between 1982 and 1985, most of the Latino residents who were relocated did not return once the renovations were completed, even though their rents would have been subsidized.[21]

In 1994, the state of Massachusetts—over the objections of many of Cambridge's progressive residents—outlawed rent control. This provided the proverbial last straw to the community's viability, since those Latinos who did not already own their own homes or businesses or who were not in public housing were forced to move. As one long-time resident noted (in 2000):

> In the 1970s you could find a three-bedroom for $160 to $180 a month. We bought our four-family home for $21,000 in 1978. Now the real estate market has gone crazy, I could never afford to live in Cambridge today. The house

question about where you're coming from, and you used to say everybody was Puerto Rican, because the Puerto Ricans had the immigration status. [Its] the same way people are doing with Mexicans. Rather than say "I'm from El Salvador," [they say] "I'm Mexican," because of all of the immigration stuff…so your numbers might show a lot of Mexicans, but they might not be Mexican.

Whether or not this interpretation—that many of the "Mexicans" may in fact be Salvadorans—is correct, the fact remains that the perilous legal and economic circumstances of the Salvadorans' entry into Cambridge and the difficulties of surviving in an inordinately expensive city has not favored the creation of a visible community active in the public domain— where the struggle for political voice must eventually occur. Instead, most Salvadorans have been forced to seek incorporation in the private do-main—primarily within churches, and networks of families, friends, and coworkers. This is not to say that Salvadorans are lacking in the ability to organize economically and politically—Centro Presente certainly tes-tifies to their abilities in this regard—but rather that most Salvadorans, like their Puerto Rican and Dominican antecedents in the earliest years of their settlement in Cambridge, have been more active in informal forms of social interaction and cohesion such as soccer leagues and church services—the sort of "associations for religious and fraternal solidarity" described by Hardy-Fanta and Gerson as the first stage of ethnic suc-cession, that precede the more visible and public stages of organizing for economic success, followed by organizing for political power.[25] It is sig-nificant to note, however, that the social communities fostered by chur-ches and soccer leagues are more likely to be pan-Latino rather than ethnically specific, so they could, in principle, serve as a medium for the creation of pan-ethnic collective action in the political realm. One church member, for example, expressed confidence in the effectiveness of pan-Latinidad, saying, "To be positive influences in the community, we need to work hard as Hispanics, as Latinos." Interestingly, this development seems to confirm Andrés Torres' observation that:

Ironically, it is in minority communities that the idea of the "gorgeous mosaic" has been embraced most enthusiastically: the least powerful are advancing the most encompassing and egalitarian notion of social relations.[26]

## The "Professionals"

Statistics from the Gaston Institute reported to the *Cambridge Chronicle* in 1999 note that Cambridge Latinos, as a group, were over-represented in lower-paid, service-sector jobs, and only 11 percent of Latino adults held

down the street sold for over $300,000 and it's not even close to the size of ours.

Thus, beginning in the late 1980s, Cambridge's working-class Puerto Rican community began to shrink, both in numbers—from a high of 1,875 in 1990 to 1,637 in 2000.[22] With the displacement of so many of the older families, the once cohesive and active community simply began to unravel.

## Salvadorans: Cambridge's Underground Latino Community

It would be logical to imagine that with manufacturing jobs virtually gone by the 1980s and affordable housing increasingly scare, Cambridge would become a less attractive destination for impoverished working-class im-migrants from Latin America. But in fact the opposite occurred: the city became a magnet for Salvadorans and other Central Americans. The first arrivals came in the early 1980s as refugees from the U.S.-sponsored wars in their home countries. These established the first links for the later chain migration of relatives and friends who continued to leave El Salvador after the wars ended to escape the economic devastation left in the wars' wake. By then the city's economy was highly dependent on high-tech businesses and a well-educated managerial class, but a plentiful and cheap supply of low-skilled service workers were also required to serve them. The Sal-vadorans were thus able to find low-paying, benefit-poor jobs as custo-dians, food-service workers, house cleaners, and nannies. Because the pay for these positions is so low, most had to work multiple jobs to support themselves and send remittances to family members at home.

The Salvadorans, many of whom were poorly educated *campesinos*, had considerably more legal, language, and educational obstacles to adapting to life in Cambridge than their Puerto Rican predecessors. In 1981, in the earliest stages of this new wave of immigration, an organization called *Centro Presente* was created to meet the legal and other needs of the growing numbers desperately poor Salvadorans, most of whom were undocumented. At the time, Salvadorans had the benefit of considerable support from a groundswell of activism, generically referred to as the Solidarity Movement, which had emerged throughout the nation to oppose the U.S.-supported wars in Central America. The Solidarity Movement was particularly active in historically progressive Cambridge, where a number of local organizations were founded to help the refugees, such as Cambridge and Somerville Legal Services, the *Comité de Solidaridad con El Salvador*, and the Cambridge Sanctuary movement, all of which (like Centro Presente) were collabora-tions between non-Latino and immigrant activists committed to helping

Central American refugees. In 1984, for example, members of the Old Cambridge Baptist Church voted to declare the church a sanctuary for undocumented immigrants, which subsequently spearheaded a broader movement to designate the entire city of Cambridge a Sanctuary City. On April 8, 1985, with support coming from various sectors of the political spectrum, the city council declared Cambridge a Sanctuary City. While it would be problematic to ascribe a direct cause and effect between the city's decision to declare itself as Sanctuary City and the influx of Salvadoran immigrants (who settled in other areas of Boston that were not sanctuary cities), Cambridge was clearly attractive as a safe haven, where they could work, send their children to school, and receive health care without fear of being reported to the Immigration and Naturalization Service.

Salvadorans who arrived in the 1990s, however, received far less public attention. The Solidarity Movement waned after the wars in Central America ended, and many of the non-Central American activists diverted their energies to other causes. Salvadoran activists continued their struggle to assist their continually arriving and still extremely vulnerable compatriots, but they did so without the advantages of advocacy on their behalf by the non-Latino progressive political community. The concurrent departure of so many of the Puerto Rican activists, who could have helped them navigate the city's sometimes Byzantine political structures, deprived the newcomers of potentially valuable allies and their accumulated social capital. Moreover, as noncitizens, most Salvadorans were ineligible to vote, and the substantial percentage of them who were undocumented were afraid to rock the boat by taking their troubles to the public.

The Salvadorans benefited from Cambridge's rent control policies until 1994, but affordable housing in Cambridge was increasingly hard to find, so many of them managed to stay in the city only by doubling up wherever an apartment could be found large and cheap enough to do so—but these were not necessarily located in a geographically contiguous neighborhood. Furthermore, high rents prevented them from establishing the sort of small businesses catering to their ethnic cohorts that helped Salvadorans elsewhere Boston incorporate into their host communities. Scattered throughout Cambridge and with little time to spare (given their double shifts) for political and cultural organizing, they could not create the sort of spatially and socially coherent community the Puerto Ricans and Dominicans living in the Port had enjoyed in the 1960s and 1970s, which had been so conducive to collective action.

As for Concilio Hispano, by the time the Central Americans began to arrive in Cambridge in the 1980s, it had become a well-established agency whose (always precarious) funding came from both private and public grants and contracts. While having access to such resources made it

possible for Concilio Hispano to offer desperately needed assist the newcomers, obtaining the funding had required Concilio His transform itself from a grassroots organization run by com members into a professional multiservice agency whose staff m were selected on the basis of their credentials as social workers rath their ties to the community: they did not necessarily live in the borhood, nor were they necessarily Puerto Rican or Dominica more of the Puerto Rican and Dominican families who had been C Hispano's constituents left the city, Concilio's staff made the log cision to change its orientation to meet the needs of its now pr Central American clients. For Cambridge's remaining Puerto Ric Dominican residents, the changes at Concilio Hispano were sympt the decline of their once-cohesive community; by 1990, only 28 per the city's Latinos were Puerto Rican (compared to 53 percent wide).[24] These changes were most painfully symbolized by C Hispano's decision to discontinue the Hispanic Festival in 1992.

Because of their legally and economically precarious lives, the dorans, unlike their Puerto Rican antecedents, existed largely bel city's radar screen. Reliable demographic data on the early Salva community is hard to obtain because data such as school statist gregated individuals of Latin American ancestry into the umbrell tino" category rather than separating them by national origin. The did not count Salvadorans by group until 2000. The 2000 census, ever, presents a mystery: in spite of anecdotal evidence from s providers that Cambridge's Salvadoran community was still sizabl census count of 567 Salvadorans and 361 "other Central Amer points to a significant decline from the "hundreds if not thous reported by the *Cambridge Chronicle* in 1991. In contrast, Mexica counted at 1,175 (up from 801 in 1990)—the second-largest na group among Latinos (after Puerto Ricans at 1,637). The "Mexica tion" of the East Coast Latino population has been widely recognize their presence in Cambridge in such numbers seems anomalous be none of the dozens of people interviewed for this research referr them at all. While there may be a number of professionals and stu residing in Cambridge who are Mexican nationals or Mexican Ameri it seems unlikely that they can account for such high figures and still invisible to those who live and work among Cambridge Latinos. V asked about her knowledge of Mexicans in Cambridge, Concilio H no's director Silvia Saavedra offered the following observation:

We don't have a lot of Mexicans. We have never had a lot of Mexicans. . . . T thing you have to be careful about is that the same way that the census asked

college degrees;[27] interviews with working-class Puerto Ricans, Dominicans, and Central Americans confirm this profile of Latinos' low socioeconomic status. Yet 1990 statistics (before the abolishing of rent control forced many low-income Latinos out of the city) noted that almost 23 percent of Cambridge's Latinos were occupying executive, administrative, managerial, and other positions that required higher levels of education than service or manufacturing jobs.[28] These seemingly contradictory statistics confirm Roberto Santiago's observation: "You know, there are two communities: the working community and the professional community." The "professionals" (to continue Santiago's generic term for professionals, entrepreneurs, artists, and academics) are individuals with some degree of higher education, although they can be generally divided into two categories: those born or raised in the United States and those who arrived as immigrants. Some of the former are the children of working-class Latinos who have attained higher educational levels than their parents. They know how to negotiate the city's social, economic, and political systems, but they still retain a connection with their working-class roots. The latter category is comprised of immigrants from affluent professional families who arrive in Cambridge already well educated. They hail from many national backgrounds, although anecdotal evidence suggests that a growing number of them are from South American countries rather than from the traditional sending areas, the Spanish Caribbean and Central America.

Indeed, with the exception of the mysterious explosion in the numbers of "Mexicans" referred to above, the greatest increase in Cambridge's Latino population can be seen in the "Other" category (i.e., other than Mexican, Puerto Rican, or Cuban). From 2,178 in 1980, the number of "Others" rose to 3,004 in 2000. In addition to the 3,004 Others were 378 Colombians, 567 Salvadorans, and 424 Dominicans, not counted prior to 2000, and 270 Cubans, whose numbers have remained relatively constant since 1980.[29] While the census data do not permit a correlation between Cambridge's growing category of professionals and the rapidly increasing category of "Others," the oral history interviews suggest that the latter are overrepresented in the professional rather than the working-class category.

Many of the professionals interviewed were immigrants who reported that they initially came in search of postgraduate education and ended up living in Cambridge because they liked the city's intellectual and cultural environment. Their education qualifies them to integrate into Cambridge's professional sector, but additionally, they arrive with a confidence in their ability to adapt and succeed that distinguishes them from their poor and working-class counterparts. One Uruguayan studying Business Administration at Bentley College noted, for example:

I don't think [my college education] was really different from what I could have gotten in the U.S. I didn't feel behind my colleagues in the U.S.

Moreover, in spite of shared connections to Latin American culture, they do not necessarily identify ethnically with other Latinos. As one professional from Puerto Rico noted:

It's difficult to connect with a Latino community because you don't know who makes that Latino community.... The Puerto Rican community here, the one that is already established, has a completely different social, cultural, and historical background than my background, because I come directly from Puerto Rico.... My connection with them—there's none.

Growing numbers of professional Latinos in Cambridge thus appear to be integrating into the city's economic networks, but generally as individuals rather than collectively representing an improvement in the experiences of the broader Latino community. Their connections with each other and with their working-class co-ethnics appear to be rather tenuous, so a Latino "community," like the one described by José Ortíz, may never again be a vital part of Cambridge's cultural landscape.

The transformations in class composition and relative power among Cambridge's various Latino groups were perhaps best symbolized by the political race between Dennis Benzan and Jarrett Barrios in 1998. Benzan's Puerto Rican mother and Dominican father (a cousin of the entrepreneur Rafael Benzan) had arrived in Cambridge in the 1960s and met in Columbia Terrace. Benzan grew up in the Terrace, and his parents were active participants in Concilio Hispano. After graduating from Howard University, he returned to Cambridge, and in 1996, at the age of 26, he was the first Latino to run for public office in Cambridge against his district's long-time incumbent, state representative Alvin Thompson, who was African American. Benzan's strategy was to register and get out the Latino vote, especially in the Port. He lost by 47 votes, but his active grassroots campaign demonstrated Latinos' political potential. Two years later, he ran for state representative again, but this time against another Latino, Jarrett Barrios. If Benzan was black, of working-class origins, and represented Cambridge's older Latino community, Barrios was more typical of the city's newer professional community: of Cuban ancestry, he grew up in Florida, came to Cambridge to study law at Harvard, and is white—and gay. After receiving a postgraduate degree at George Washington University, Barrios returned to Cambridge and joined a Boston-based law firm. There were no fundamental differences between the two candidates in terms of their desires to reach out to and support Cambridge's Latino population, but Benzan's primary constituency—working-class Latinos from the Port—had continued to dwindle, while

Barrios's—professional Latinos and well-educated progressive whites throughout the contested district—was expanding. Benzan lost the race.

## Looking to the Future

While Cambridge Latinos of the same national or class background may experience some degree of solidarity among themselves, they do not seem to share a perception of being part of a unified ethnic community. Dennis Benzan's conclusion that the community is in a "quiet crisis" is based on his observations of a decline in cohesion among working-class Cambridge Latinos and the resulting loss of voice in city affairs. He notes that because most of the former community leaders have moved out of Cambridge, the more recent working-class Latino arrivals have not had the opportunity to connect with their ethnic predecessors, so they do not know about—and thus cannot be empowered by—the community's rich history of political activism, nor do they have access to the store of social and political knowledge developed over time by their antecedents. The consequences of this social, cultural, and political rupture are being felt most acutely by the younger generation of working-class youth, whose mediocre education by the public schools is condemning many of them to invisibility at the bottom of the city's socioeconomic hierarchy.

Thus, even as recent census data indicate that Latinos in Cambridge are growing in numbers and prosperity and political and cultural developments—such as the election of Cuban American Jarrett Barrios to the State House of Representatives—suggest that some are also achieving public influence, the seemingly contradictory reality is that the outlook for working-class Cambridge Latinos is uncertain, and it does not appear that their trajectory will conform to patterns observed in other cities with growing Latino populations. Cambridge's once tightly knit ethnic enclave, the sort that was interpreted by the "mosaic" models as an indicator of successful incorporation, has been disrupted, and it is unlikely that it will be rebuilt. Moreover, simple numerical growth has not produced the developmental stages characterizing "ethnic succession" models, such as the one described by Hardy-Fanta and Gerson in other Massachusetts cities.

Clearly, then, there is no single path traveled by all Latinos as they settle in and adapt to their host cities: some patterns of incorporation may indeed reflect the influence of national and global forces, but the specific mode and outcome of immigrant incorporation in a particular place are indelibly marked by circumstances that are uniquely local. If the developmental trajectory of Cambridge's Latino community appears to complicate and problematize existing models of immigrant incorporation, it can be countered that the historical development and current character-istics of Cambridge's Latino community are too anomalous to be useful in efforts to identify broad trends and patterns in the development of Latino communities. After all, the city is one of the most expensive places to live in the country, and its economy is heavily reliant on two elite, world-class universities and an associated high-tech sector rather than on the sorts of businesses that typically provide an economic base for working-class Latino communities. But precisely because of its exceptionalism, the history of Cambridge's Latino communities serves to caution us against generalizations based on theoretical models without taking into account the power of place.

## Notes

1. Examples include Andrés Torres, *Between Melting Pot and Mosaic: African Americans and Puerto Ricans in the New York Political Economy* (Philadelphia: Temple University Press, 1995); Milagros Ricourt and Ruby Danta, *Hispanas de Queens: Latino Panethnicity in a New York City Neighborhood* (Ithaca: Cornell University Press, 2003); and Alejandro Portes and Alex Stepick, *City on the Edge: The Transformation of Miami* (Berkeley: University of California Press, 1993).

2. Sidney Mintz, "The Anthropological Interview and the Life History," in *Oral History: An Interdisciplinary Anthology*, ed. David K. Dunaway and Willa K. Baum (Nashville, Tenn.: American Association for State and Local History, Oral History Association, c.1984), 298.

3. Torres, *Between Melting Pot and Mosaic*, 1.

4. Compare Juan Flores, " '¿Qué assimilated, brother, yo soy assimilao!': The Structuring of Puerto Rican Identity" in *Divided Borders: Essays on Puerto Rican Identity* (Houston: Arte Public Press, 1993), 182–195.

5. Carol Hardy-Fanta and Jeffrey Gerson, "Introduction: A Statewide Over-view," in *Latino Politics in Massachusetts: Struggles, Strategies and Prospects*, ed. Carol Hardy-Fanta and Jeffrey Gerson (New York and London: Routledge, 2002), 1–21.

6. "Private Employment by Industry, 1972 vs 2000." *City of Cambridge, Massa-chusetts, Demographic and Socioeconomic Statistics* (Cambridge: Cambridge Community Development Department, 2001).

7. "Cambridge Detailed Racial and Hispanic Population, 1980–2000," *City of Cambridge, Massachusetts, Demographic and Socioeconomic Statistics*.

8. Alejandro Portelli, *The Death of Luigi Trastulli: Form and Meaning in Oral History* (Albany: SUNY Press, 1991), 47.

9. The interviews cited throughout this essay were collected by Kerry Biggs, Brigid Brannigan, Kathleen Flahive Ariana Flores, Meredith Gruen Andrew Hara, Sean Kennedy, John Keogh Galen Maze, Juliette Lizeray, Rachel Long, Rich Nightingale, Marisa Romo, and Radhika Thakkar. The final reports they wrote based on their interviews, from which I also drew, can be accessed at http://nils.lib.tufts.edu/archives/urban.html.

10. Until the end of the 1960s, Cambridge telephone books contained listings by street address and cross-listed by surname; also included were the householder's

occupation and names and occupations of spouse and children (thus revealing which units were vacant).

11. Ahsha Safai, "Immigrating to Public Housing: Haitian Immigrants and the Transformation of Washington Elms and Newtowne Court" (Master's thesis, MIT, 2000), 6–68.

12. Miren Uriarte, "*Contra Viento y Marea* (Against All Odds): Latinos Build Community in Boston," in *Latinos in Boston: Confronting Poverty, Building Community*, ed. Miren Uriarte, Paul Osterman, Carol Hardy-Fanta and Edwin Meléndez (Boston: Boston Foundation, 1993), 25.

13. Dolores Hayden, *The Power of Place: Urban Landscapes as Public History* (Cambridge, MA: MIT Press 1995), 9.

14. "Cambridge Resident Employment by Sector and Occupation: 1950–1990," *City of Cambridge, Massachusetts, Demographic and Socioeconomic Statistics*.

15. *Cambridge Chronicle*, July 17, 1969.

16. *Cambridge Chronicle*, June 22, 1972.

17. *Cambridge Chronicle*, November 20, 1975.

18. *Cambridge Chronicle*, February 8, 1979.

19. "Cambridge Resident Employment by Sector and Occupation: 1950–1980," *City of Cambridge, Massachusetts, Demographic and Socioeconomic Statistics*.

20. Peggy Levitt, "*A Todos Les Llamo Primo* (I Call Everyone Cousin): The Social Basis for Latino Small Businesses," in *New Migrants in the Marketplace: Boston's Ethnic Enterprises*, ed. Marilyn Halter (Boston: University of Massachusetts Press, 1995), 138.

21. Safai, "Immigrating to Public Housing," 71–80.

22. "Cambridge Detailed Racial and Hispanic Population: 1980–2000," *City of Cambridge, Massachusetts, Demographic and Socioeconomic Statistics*.

23. Uriarte observes that similar processes of professionalization occurred in Boston-based Latino agencies originally established as grass-roots organizations (*Contra Viento y Marea*, 24).

24. *Cambridge Chronicle*, September 3, 1992.

25. Hardy-Fanta and Gerson, 12.

26. Torres, *Between Melting Pot and Mosaic*, 4.

27. *Cambridge Chronicle*, February 11, 1999.

28. "Occupation by Race and Hispanic Origin, Cambridge 1990," Cambridge Community Development Department, 1991.

29. "Cambridge Detailed Racial and Hispanic Population: 1980–2000," *City of Cambridge, Massachusetts, Demographic and Socioeconomic Statistics*.

# 7

# Latinos in New Hampshire: Enclaves, Diasporas, and an Emerging Middle Class

Yoel Camayd-Freixas, Gerald Karush, and Nelly Lejter

The U.S. Bureau of the Census reports that New Hampshire had 20,489 Latinos at the start of this decade: 1.7 percent of a state with a 95 percent non-Latino White population.[1] Massachusetts next door had 430,000 Latinos. Why is this comparatively small Latino group in New Hampshire noteworthy?

Part of the answer lies in the almost total absence of Latinos in the state twenty years ago. New Hampshire was not a state of traditional Latino settlement. In 1980 New Hampshire was surpassed as the state with the fewest Latinos only by Maine, the Dakotas, and Vermont. By the year 2000, however, the Latino population had quadrupled, and the state now hosts growing Latino enclaves. New Hampshire has become part of an emerging national pattern of Latino settlement characterized by branching regional dispersal from traditional areas of concentration into new enclaves in nontraditional states and cities. This dynamic is known as the Latino Diaspora.

A second consideration is that the Latino Diaspora in the state also shows a new secondary pattern of Latino residential dispersal away from central cities into suburbia, small towns, and nonmetropolitan areas. This pattern is discernible in the state given its lower urbanization and relatively recent Latino communities. But it has not been reported in other states even though some are likely to show this secondary diaspora effect.

A third consideration is that the diversity in Latino residential settlement in New Hampshire also seems to involve a changing population profile. The traditional profile of Latinos in the Northeast has been that of urban working-class immigrants, often from agricultural backgrounds, settled in enclaves within central cities. But the Latino settlement in New Hampshire is driven not by traditional direct immigration from the Caribbean but by secondary migration from neighboring states. That is, these Latinos are much more likely to be migrants than immigrants. They are labor migrants but from more diverse national origins. They are more fluent in English, more assimilated, and occupationally and economically diverse. A major element that emerges from this profile is a socioeconomic diversity that suggests the emergence of a new Latino middle class.

This is a new development not only in New Hampshire but also in New England. Therefore, New Hampshire may serve as a case study on the evolution of a Latino middle class. Not that a Latino middle class does not exist elsewhere—the dynamic Cuban enclave in South Florida is an example. But South Florida is a well-established Latino community. A middle class is a new phenomenon in communities of more recent formation that emerge from the diaspora. In addition, this emerging middle class may drive some of the secondary residential dispersion evident in the Latino Diaspora. It is likely that a Latino middle class is emerging in other parts of New England, yet it is obscured by older settlements or a lack of focused analysis. An emerging Latino middle class has major political implications and can be expected to affect the relationship between Latinos and non-Latinos. The relatively small size of the Latino population in New Hampshire suggests that these effects will be gradual yet significant relative to population size.

The final considerations are contextual. First, New Hampshire is immersed in a dense northeast urban corridor stretching from Philadelphia through New York City, southern New England to southern Maine, and directly impacted by its dynamics. New Hampshire, at the edge of Northern New England, may serve as a barometer of changes expected in other formerly non-Latino Northern New England states like Maine and Vermont.

Similarly, understanding changes in Latino settlement and its implication for economic and social participation is becoming increasingly important. Latino kinematics are fueled by numbers. Early this millennium, Latinos became the largest minority group in the United States after a generation of relentless growth—a growth rate that accelerated in the 1990s. By the March 2002 Current Population Survey, the Latino population grew by another two million, reaching 37.4 million (13.3 percent of the U.S. population).[2] If this trend holds, the Latino population will grow by 67 percent this decade to 59 million in 2010. The changes from these emerging patterns will significantly impact millions of people and the communities where Latinos settle, which now include most of the United States.

## Latino Enclaves

The most common form of Latino settlement is the enclave. Latinos, like most Americans since the 1950s, are an urban population. The areas of dense Latino concentration coincide exactly with the major U.S. population centers. Latinos have typically settled in enclaves within the central cities of metropolitan areas, in seven traditional states: California, Florida, Illinois, New Jersey, New Mexico, New York, and Texas.[3]

Historically, ethnic enclaves have aided in the settlement and assimilation of immigrants. Little Italy and Chinatown are examples of economic enclaves. Enclaves are self-organizing community economic development engines that emerged in major immigrations. Therein, immigrant families found housing, work without English proficiency, and a familiar way of life that buffered them and mediated their incorporation into American society. Often it was their children who learned English and moved into the mainstream.    CUBA

Perhaps the most successful Latino economic enclave is the South Florida Cuban community. It is the counterpart of Little Italy and Chinatown on steroids. This is an ethnic economic enclave that started with small mom-and-pop businesses but grew to acquire geopolitical significance. The forty-year-old Cuban enclave is the strongest Latino economic base in the country. It works as a function not only of the Cuban-owned companies it hosts but also of the local, national, and international Latino companies it attracts as it projects into Latin America. Its magnitude is evidenced by a 2003 report on the five hundred largest Latino-owned U.S. companies by *Hispanic Business*. Florida, with one-fifth the Latino population of California, has as many firms in the Latino 500 as California, earning over twice the revenue ($8.9 billion), and a third of national revenues for the Latino 500.[4]

The Cuban enclave has also proven a powerful venue for the incorporation of Cuban immigrants. It was the primary mode of incorporation for 125,000 Cubans who arrived during the 1979 Mariel Crisis. Participation in the Cuban enclave was instrumental for these new Cuban immigrants to join the economic mainstream, whereas for non-Cubans it is indistinguishable from employment in secondary sectors of the economy—this preferential pattern is common to other U.S. ethnic enclaves.[5]

Enclaves have been and remain an important settlement path for Latinos. Historically, Latinos settling in the Northeast first concentrated in New York and New Jersey. By 1980 Southern New England had enclaves in Rhode Island, Connecticut, and Massachusetts. In Southern New England Latinos concentrated in established enclaves in cities like Boston and Hartford and branched into newer sections in cities like Springfield and Lawrence. This has been the expected geography for Latinos in New England; expected, because the established enclaves (e.g., Hartford) and the newer enclaves (e.g., Lawrence), follow a traditional pattern of settlement within the central cities of metropolitan areas. Often, their number and concentration are sufficient to forge basic economic enclaves that, while not as diversified or powerful as the South Florida enclave, host a foundation of businesses, jobs, and the rudiments of an internal economy.

In New Hampshire, Hillsborough is the largest county with 31 percent of state residents and containing the largest concentration of Latinos (59 percent of the state's Latinos); followed by Merrimack, Rockingham, and Strafford, which share 25 percent of the state's Latinos.[6] The fact that it borders Massachusetts may account for higher migration and high concentrations of Latinos. Hillsborough County includes the two largest municipalities in the state, Manchester and Nashua, with half of all Latinos in the state. Manchester and Nashua are new Latino enclaves and follow the traditional pattern of settlement within central cities.

## Latino Diasporas

Historically, the children of immigrants emerge from enclaves to join the economic and social mainstream. Demographic evidence suggests that Latinos may be emerging from their enclaves, but the picture is mixed. Unabated Latino growth is driving an interregional population expansion into nontraditional areas by growing new enclaves. Meanwhile, more acculturated Latinos may be mainstreaming, as suggested by residential dispersal away from enclave settlements.

The 2000 U.S. Census shows the first trend: Latino concentrations in every state. This is not a change as traditional enclaves remain, but a branching from traditional states into new enclaves in nontraditional states and cities. Using U.S. Census 2000 returns, analysts noted that Latinos are settling into nontraditional areas at very high rates.[7] New Latino communities arose in the South, North-Central, Northwest, and Northeast regions—just about everywhere we do *not* expect Latinos. This dramatic regional expansion is known as the new Latino Diaspora.

Latino diasporas represent an unexpected geography for Latinos who are establishing settlements outside traditional Latino states. The most pronounced U.S. Latino growth is now concentrated in these nontraditional areas. Diaspora kinematics are particularly strong in the eastern United States and may represent population expansion west to east and south to north.[8]

Nontraditional states experienced dramatic diaspora growth. For example, Atlanta, Georgia, grew a new Latino enclave that includes large numbers of Latinos not traditional to the East Coast—e.g., Mexicans/Chicanos, formerly found mostly in the Southwest and West. Nontraditional cities in traditional Latino states also experienced the effect:

e.g., dramatic Puerto Rican growth in Orlando, Florida. As a result, Latinos are now the largest minority in a majority of counties across the United States and also show dramatic growth in areas where they are not the largest minority (e.g., the deep South).

Latino diasporas are driven by growth. Historically, Latino growth is a function of high birth rates and net (im)migration.[9] But New England Latino growth is fueled by net interstate and intermetropolitan migration and New Hampshire's Latino growth is an extension of antecedent Latino growth in Massachusetts and other states.

New Hampshire is the fastest growing state in New England and all eastern states north of Delaware. Hillsborough County, where the Latino population grew over 100 percent last decade, and two other southeastern counties, drove the state's growth boosted by a net 1995–2000 gain in domestic migration of twenty-eight thousand, including many Latinos.[10] New Hampshire Latinos had the second highest growth rate in New England (81 percent)—far higher than the national Latino average (58 percent). New Hampshire has been slow to recognize this growing Latino presence; this pattern is common to other New England states with rapid Latino growth.[11]

Latino diasporas may also involve a secondary pattern of enhanced residential dispersal away from central cities and into suburbia, small towns, and nonmetropolitan areas. This dispersal may represent more acculturated Latinos mainstreaming away from the enclave. The pattern is discernible in New Hampshire, but it has gone unnoticed or has not been reported in other states, even though the evidence suggests that at least some areas should show this secondary diaspora effect.

For example, U.S. Census data show Latino residential dispersal. The 2002 Current Population Survey shows that Latinos in the United States are now evenly divided between those who live inside central cities and those who live outside them.[12] Similarly, in 2000 Latinos dispersed across most counties in New England. In northern New England many Latino groups are small (under a thousand residents) and settled in counties that have no central cities, only townships.[13] In Greater Boston it has been noted that Latinos settled in large numbers in satellite cities outside the urban core. The typical Latino lives on a block that is 46 percent Latino.[14]

The effect of residential dispersal is evident in New Hampshire. The twelve municipalities with the most Latinos account for 66 percent of all Latinos; the cities of Manchester and Nashua in Hillsborough County host half of all Latinos. The rest live in nonmetropolitan areas and small townships in every county.[15]

Nationally, the proportion of Latinos living in central cities is 46 percent,[16] which suggests a very similar pattern of enclave settlement between New Hampshire and national Latinos. Another 46 percent now reside outside the central cities. However, Nashua and Manchester are small and do not have a sprawling metropolitan area outside the central city like New York City or Boston; the areas outside Hillsborough central cities are nonmetropolitan. But the residential dispersal pattern for New Hampshire, if defined as Latinos residing outside central cities, would be 50 percent, thus similar to national data. One difference is that New Hampshire has four times the national proportion of Latinos in non-metropolitan areas. While this reflects the lower density and less urbanized character of the state, the fact remains that 40 percent of New Hampshire Latinos followed a dispersal pattern different than those that preceded them and typical for their counterparts in other parts of the country. Are Latinos who come to New Hampshire as a result of secondary residential dispersal different from Latinos elsewhere in New England? It is to this issue that we now turn.

## Population Profile

*Latino* is a term used to describe a group of nationalities that share common linguistic and cultural roots. Some people readily identify as Latinos and most accept the description, but many Latinos identify by national origin. National Latino groups originate in Mexico (and U.S. states formerly part of Mexico), Puerto Rico, Cuba, the Dominican Republic, and Central and South America. Historically, New England Latinos are mostly from the Caribbean: Puerto Rico, the Dominican Republic, and Cuba. This changed over the last decade. The origin of Latinos in New Hampshire is addressed by looking at migration, immigration, and fertility.

New Hampshire Latinos are overwhelmingly migrants: 70 percent were born in the United States or to American parents, and 30 percent are immigrants.[17] The predominance of native-born Latinos denotes a major change. Two-thirds of these migrants originate from New England states. This is consistent with the notion of a regional Latino Diaspora.

Latino growth in New Hampshire responds to net migration and indirectly to antecedent Latino growth in Massachusetts and other New England states. Massachusetts is the largest source of migrants to New Hampshire. Its 1995–2000 migration into New Hampshire was 60,731 persons; the largest outflow from New Hampshire was also to Massachusetts, resulting in a net migration to New Hampshire of 27,159 persons.[18] Latinos are part of this migration. Sources suggest that many Latinos move from dense population enclaves in areas like Lawrence to less-congested and affordable communities in southern New Hampshire.[19]

New Hampshire native-born Latinos fall into three groups: 27 percent born in New Hampshire, 53 percent in another state, and 20 percent outside the United States to American citizens (87 percent Puerto Ricans).[20] Among the 80 percent born in the mainland, two-thirds were born in the Northeast and one-third in other regions. Among Latinos born in the Northeast, two-thirds moved to New Hampshire from New England states, others from Northeast areas like New York and New Jersey. New Hampshire is experiencing vibrant migration from surrounding states and from other regions of the United States.

The migration status of school-aged and older residents is calculated based on respondents' 1995 place of residence. Place of residence is an index of relatively recent settlement that yields both migration and immigration data. Among New Hampshire Latinos in 2000, 63 percent were already state residents in 1995[21]: 30 percent lived in the same house, 26 percent in a different house but the same county, and 7 percent in a different county. This shows significant Latino residential stability and suggests that growth is taking place around a Latino community that is growing roots in New Hampshire.

While there is reliable information on where Latinos originate, there is little research on why they choose the state. Anecdotal evidence suggests one pull factor is available rental housing.[22] Some Latinos are fleeing rising rents in Massachusetts and look to New Hampshire for housing affordability, both for lower-cost rental housing and an opportunity to save and buy a home. In some cases they first settled in a southern New England city like Boston then moved to a city in Northern Massachusetts like Lowell. Other economic pull factors include better employment opportunity and affordable cost of necessities like food and car insurance.

Another pull factor is family reunification. Some Latinos move to join relatives already in the state. Often, these relatives praise the area's quality of life and job opportunities, describing New Hampshire as a good place to raise a family. This promotes immigration directly from the home country. Other family pull factors include reports of better schools, good municipal services like fire departments and police, and low crime. Anecdotal evidence also suggests some consistent downsides. These include unaccustomed rural and semirural settings, few minorities, unfamiliar surroundings, and experiences with racism and discrimination.

Less than a third of Latinos in New Hampshire are immigrants, mostly from nontraditional countries.[23] The predominance of immigrants from nontraditional countries denotes a major change. It also suggests that direct immigrant paths are established into new Latino communities, which may fuel enclaves created by the Latino Diaspora.

In the 2000 U.S. Census, 29 percent of New Hampshire Latinos were immigrants, lower than the proportion in Massachusetts, Connecticut, and Rhode Island. Trends indicate that the proportion of immigrants is decreasing and that of the native born rising. For example, migration status data for those who came to New Hampshire during the period 1995–2000 show that only 9 percent of New Hampshire Latinos were immigrants.

New immigrants fuel existing enclaves. Most new immigrants (81 percent) settled in the Nashua and Manchester enclaves. This suggests that the residential diaspora dispersal effect that involves some 40 percent of state Latinos may occur primarily among more established U.S.-born or naturalized Latinos.

Latino immigrants to New Hampshire originate in three regions. The traditional group from the Caribbean now only accounts for 31 percent of the total. Of these, over half are from the Dominican Republic, a group which is also overrepresented in Northern Massachusetts (e.g., Lawrence, Lowell). This suggests that these cities are important sources of migrants to New Hampshire and implies the existence of an established immigration link with the Dominican Republic driven by family reunification. The other Caribbean-origin immigrants are historically expected groups from Puerto Rico (37 percent) and Cuba (11 percent).

Most Latino immigrants to New Hampshire are not traditional to the Northeast: 41 percent are from South America and 28 percent from Central America. Most Central Americans are from Mexico (65 percent). This suggests new inflow links between New Hampshire and the western United States and Mexico. There are smaller proportions of immigrants from other Central American countries like Honduras, Salvador, Guatemala, and Nicaragua. Most South American immigrants are from Brazil (35 percent) and Colombia (30 percent), which also suggests new immigration links with those countries. There are also groups from Argentina, Venezuela, Peru, Guyana, and Ecuador. The resulting national diversity is extensive and more typical of larger cities. It suggests well-established immigration paths and predicts ongoing immigration.

Natural Latino population growth due to fertility and age, both major contributors to population growth and predictive of strong growth in the state, may not be as important a contributor as it has been elsewhere in New England. Net migration is a higher contributor.

The median age of Latinos in New Hampshire is twenty-five, and and the median age for non-Latino whites is thirty-nine. The New Hampshire Latino age distribution is bimodal, with a bulge of children and youth under eighteen and adults from their early twenties to late forties.[24] The bulge of children likely reflects the impact of natural growth, while the larger bulge of adults suggests migration of singles and families in their prime working years. Latino fertility rates are comparable to the United States after World War II—the parents of today's baby boomers. The fertility rate of more highly educated Latinas is virtually identical to non-Latinos. This is a caveat to the prediction of robust growth, as there is a high rate of college-educated Latinas in New Hampshire. These data suggest continued Latino natural population growth. However, new births will be surpassed by net migration and possibly matched by new immigration.

Most Latinos in New Hampshire were born U.S. citizens (70 percent), and 37 percent of the foreign-born are naturalized.[25] The Latino naturalization rate exceeds the U.S. average and is higher than that of Latinos with over twenty years of tenure in the United States. This 81 percent citizenship rate predicts well for political development. For example, in 2000 there were 16,497 Latino citizens, of whom 62 percent were adults. Therefore New Hampshire had 10,228 prospective Latino voters. While it is unlikely that these prospective Latino voters concentrate in the Nashua and Manchester enclaves and many are residentially dispersed, they represent a large and growing electoral force.

Given the high rate of citizenship among New Hampshire Latinos, it is not surprising that language is not a problem: 38 percent speak only English, which suggests a high level of assimilation; of the 60 percent who speak Spanish, four-fifths speak English well to very well, and only a small minority (12 percent) don't speak English well. The rates of assimilation and acculturation suggested by these data are high.

NH high assimilation rate

## An Emerging Middle Class

The socioeconomic profile of New Hampshire Latinos supports the notion of an emerging Latino middle class. This is observed by assessing the data on education, employment, earnings, income, and business and home ownership.

### Education

The proportion of college-educated Latinos in New Hampshire is over twice that of the national average[26]: 23 percent are college graduates or professionals compared to 11 percent of U.S. Latinos. This rate is also close to the average of all adults in the state (29 percent) and of U.S. adults (27 percent). The state's rate of Latino college graduates also outpaces all national Latino groups: Cubans (19 percent), Central and South Americans (17 percent), Puerto Ricans (14 percent), and Mexicans

(8 percent). Moreover, we observe a trend of college-educated Latinos settling in New Hampshire at a level higher than the expected share from any Latino nationality.[27]

## Employment, Earnings, and Income

New Hampshire Latinos are economically active, with high labor force participation and low unemployment.[28] Among Latinos sixteen years and older in 2000, 69 percent were in the labor force; 93 percent of those in the labor force were employed and 6.4 percent unemployed. The dependency ratio was .55—the nonworking population is about half the size of the working population, which reflects the large number of children. There are seasonal employment dynamics, and some 20 percent did not work for about ten weeks in the year, suggesting some problems of seasonal underemployment.

Median individual earnings of full-time Latino workers in New Hampshire were $26,682. Median earnings are much higher for families ($41,071) and households ($39,985). These data suggest that in New Hampshire Latino families, typically comprised of three persons, both adults work outside the home. A number of Latinos are poor or working poor. But Latino poverty is lower in New Hampshire: 21 percent of U.S. Latino families in 2002 lived in poverty compared to one-third fewer New Hampshire Latino families (14 percent). Most Latino poor in the state are children, primarily preschool and elementary school children.

The distribution of family income also shows strong evidence of upward mobility. Over 40 percent of New Hampshire Latino families had an annual income over $50,000. With the state's relatively low cost of living, this level of income can be expected to propel many families to home ownership.

## Asset Development: Businesses and Homeownership

Latinos in New Hampshire are developing assets commonly associated with intergenerational transfer of wealth, such as businesses and homes.

Small business growth and self-employment are driving Latino economic development nationally. Latino-owned businesses are 40 percent of all minority-owned firms. The Hispanic Chamber of Commerce reported 1.5 million Latino businesses in 1999 (up 76 percent in five years) and estimated their revenues at $160 billion; by 2003 this number grew to 1.63 million firms.[29] In New Hampshire, the ranks of Latino-owned businesses are also growing. About one-fifth have employees and show solid revenues. The most recent available data, from the U.S. Economic Census of 1997,[30] are now superseded by Latino growth. However, while the numbers are an undercount, business patterns should remain relatively accurate.

Most New Hampshire Latino firms are in service (42 percent), construction (11 percent), and retail (9 percent). These 735 Latino firms generated $117 million in 1997 revenue, employed 1,043 workers (not including owners), and paid them $26 million in wages. Many of these firms were sole proprietorship start-ups with no employees besides the owner. Statewide, 122 Latino firms (17 percent) had employees, generated $98 million in receipts, and paid average wages of $24,687 per worker; their average revenue was $804,402 each, whereas sole proprietorships averaged $30,276 each.

Industry details show a growing business sector of some weight. Latino businesses also seem to pay above average annual wages, and even self-employed sole proprietors seem to do fairly well. The most common Latino service firms offer business services, professional services like accounting or engineering, health and social services, educational services, and automotive repair. Those with employees averaged 1997 revenues of $348,000; professional service firms averaged revenues of $365,429 and paid higher wages: $61,200 per employee. Construction included a few construction firms and many independent trade contractors (e.g., plumbers, electricians). Those with employees generated $1.4 million each and paid average wages of $36,898. Latino Retail firms are mostly miscellaneous retail, bodegas, restaurants, car dealers, or gasoline stations. Retail firms with employees averaged $470,000 each; sole proprietors averaged $111,000 each. These data depict the emergence of a core Latino business community and entrepreneurial practices that sustain a growing middle class.

A major New Hampshire attraction is affordable housing. Latino settlement in enclave neighborhoods of urban centers like Nashua and Manchester is facilitated by available affordable rentals and ownership housing. Median monthly rent statewide was $642, which represents a manageable 26 percent of 1999 household income. Median monthly cost of home ownership was about 22 percent of household income.[31] Assuming a 35 percent benchmark (i.e., rents under 35 percent of household income are affordable), 70 percent of Latino households had affordable rents in 1999, while 30 percent paid too much. Since housing costs in southern New Hampshire where most Latinos reside have increased, the number of Latino households paying too much in rent may also have increased.

The 2000 census identified 5,457 Latino households in New Hampshire. Of these, 3,472 were rentals (64 percent) and 1985 were owned (36 percent). Latino home ownership rates are lower in central cities such as Manchester and Nashua where the home ownership rate is about half the Latino statewide average. Since these two cities include half of the Latino population in the state, the Latino home ownership rate outside of central cities is far greater.

Hillsborough County, where the major Latino enclaves of Nashua and Manchester are located, has the lowest Latino ownership rate in the state. Ownership rates are highest (over 70 percent) in Sullivan, Coos, and Belknap, followed by Strafford, Rockingham, and Merrimack (the counties of highest Latino concentrations after Hillsborough). All these are areas of residential dispersal away from Latino enclaves. The higher rates of Latino home ownership in dispersal areas are strongly suggestive of a difference in the character of enclave and diaspora Latinos.

## Conclusion

The prevailing evidence shows that New Hampshire has become part of a new national pattern of Latino settlement—the Latino Diaspora. The state shows branching regional migration from traditional Latino areas in New England neighbors into new enclaves in Nashua and Manchester. This is enhanced by the existence of multiple immigration paths into these new enclaves. These in-flows underpin local growth and are strongly predictive of continued growth. Data show a new secondary diaspora pattern of intrastate and interstate Latino residential dispersal away from central cities into New Hampshire's small towns and nonmetropolitan areas. This secondary dynamic seems to include a somewhat different group of Latinos; a group that may represent more acculturated Latinos mainstreaming away from the enclaves.

Diasporas are newer than enclaves and are not well understood. The New Hampshire data and evidence from other areas suggest that Latino diasporas may include two patterns: a growth-driven expansion from traditional states into nontraditional states and cities, and a secondary pattern of enhanced residential dispersal away from central cities and into suburbia, small towns and nonmetropolitan areas. It is not clear whether this secondary residential dispersal is a function of job opportunities (i.e., labor migration), gentrification, cost of living or quality of life opportunity, of growing socioeconomic diversity leading to mainstreaming, or a combination of these.

This analysis suggests that increased socioeconomic diversity and the enhanced aspirations of an emerging Latino middle class are a new factor. As Latinos grow and disperse, their impact on communities will increase both as a function of their size and the larger number of communities impacted. Whatever its governing dynamics, diasporas pose important yet differential implications for communities as they seek to adjust to Latino kinematics.

Summary population analysis shows a changing Latino profile. Latinos no longer fit a monolithic description as poor immigrants from agricultural backgrounds settled in central-city enclaves. Most Latinos in New Hampshire are migrants, fluent in English, more assimilated, and occupationally and economically diverse. Indicators in the areas of education, workforce, homeownership, and business strongly suggest a diverse and capable population.

An emerging middle class is a new phenomenon in communities of more recent formation arising from the diaspora; it is a new development not only in New Hampshire but also in New England. This trend is a factor driving some of the secondary residential dispersion in New Hampshire, as evidenced by home-ownership data. An emerging Latino middle class also has political implications. It will increase voter registration and participation and help support Latino candidates and social participation by Latinos.

Over the next generation Latino demographics will change the U.S. labor force and the political landscape. A Latino middle class may help soften these changes and buffer some conflictive reactions to Latino expansion, which is seen with alarm by those who fear that an immigrant minority may become a national majority. This fear is often framed as a threat to American culture with an anti-immigrant slant. Harvard's Samuel Huntington argues that Latino immigration threatens to fracture America's cultural identity, Latinos are more hostile to American traditions of assimilation than other groups, and encroaching Mexican immigrants are tantamount to a demographic *reconquista* of former Mexican territory annexed by the United States in the 1800s (i.e., he fears Chicanos may try to return the southwestern states to Mexico). He declares the challenges of this immigration are overwhelming—bilingualism, multiculturalism, religious diversity, dual citizenship—and cautions that "white nativist movements" (defined not as extremist militias or the Ku Klux Klan but those who fear a minority as the national majority) are a plausible response, particularly in times of economic hardship.[32]

Huntington's views may seem biased nostalgia for Anglo-Protestantism, and he fails to treat American history realistically. It is more characteristic of American tradition that the United States not only survives immigration but also flourishes as a result.[33] Yet his themes resonate with English-only and anti-immigrant movements. Clearly, Latino growth causes tensions and raises questions about the Latino character that are loaded and unanswerable.

But an emerging Latino middle class and profiles like those exhibited in New Hampshire may act as an antidote to anti-immigrant alarmism. Are Latino immigrants as successful as past immigrants adopting the American creed? Seemingly yes. Many New Hampshire Latinos are assimilated, and most are fluent in English. This hardly fits Huntington's image of Latinos hostile to American traditions. There are no encroaching Mexicans trying to return southwestern states to Mexico—if anything they kept the Southwest for the United States and are busy colonizing the east coast. Bilingualism is prevalent as a flow of new arrivals preserves language and a core culture, but bilingualism can be viewed as an asset, not a language barrier. The residential dispersal of Latinos seeking enhanced quality of life for their children is a mainstream American creed and familiar to non-Latino American families. Huntington's assimilationist monocultural melting pot has not materialized, perhaps because it never has before. Instead, U.S. consumers are adopting Latino tastes (music, dance, food) without undue conflict,[34] and quintessential American baseball is becoming a game between Dominicans. But creedal assimilation is evident among Latinos.[35] Creedal assimilation precedes cultural assimilation and may prove the more valuable contributor to American culture and identity in the long run.

## Notes

1. The authors are faculty at the School of Community Economic Development, Southern New Hampshire University. This chapter is part of a larger study by the authors, who gratefully acknowledge the work of Marucha Omwenga and Charles Rand on data analyses. We relied on summary file data and reports by the U.S. Bureau of the Census (Economics and Statistics Administration, U.S. Department of Commerce), including: *Population Estimates*, 2000 Census of Population and Housing, 2003; *Population Estimates and Projections*, 2000 Census of Population and Housing, October 2003; *Domestic Migration Across Regions, Divisions, and States: 1995 to 2000*, August 2003; Census 2000 Special Reports, www.census.gov/prod/2003pubs/censr-7.pdf; *U.S. Hispanic Population 2002*, Current Population Survey, PGP-5, March 2003; *Hispanic-Owned Businesses: 1997*, Survey of Minority Owned Business Enterprises, Census Brief, October 2001; *Economic Census 1997: Minority- and Women-Owned Businesses* (New Hampshire), www.census.gov/epcd/mwb97/nh/ NH.html#Hispanic; Marc Perry*State-to-State Migration Flows: 1995 to 2000*, www.census.gov/prod/2003pubs/censr-8.pdf, August 2003; Marc Perry*Migration of Natives and the Foreign Born: 1995 to 200*, www.census.gov/prod/2003pubs/censr-11.pdf, August 2003; Jason Schachter*Migration by Race and Hispanic Origin: 1995 to 2000*, www.census.gov/prod/2003pubs/censr-13.pdf, October 2003.

2. Roberto Ramírez, *U.S. Hispanic Population 2002* (U.S. Census Bureau, Population Division, Ethnicity and Ancestry Branch, 2003), www.census.gov/population/www/socdemo/hispanic/ho02.html.

3. Frank Hobbs and Nicole Stoops, *Demographic Trends in the Twentieth Century*, U.S. Census Bureau, Census 2000 Special Reports, Series CENSR-4 (Washington, DC: U.S. Government Printing Office, 2002).

4. Juan Solana, Joel Russell, Michael Caplinger, Cynthia Marquez, and Tabin Cosio, "2004 Hispanic Business 500," *Hispanic Business* (June 2004).

5. Y. Camayd-Freixas, *Crisis in Miami* (Boston Research & Development Group, 1988); A. Portes and R. Manning, "The Immigrant Enclave: Theory and Empirical Examples," in *Competitive Ethnic Relations* (New York: Academic Press, 1986), 47–68; A. Portes and A. Stepick, "Unwelcome Immigrants: The Labor Market Experiences of 1980 (Mariel) Cuban and Haitian Refugees in South Florida," *American Sociological Review* 50 (1985): 493–514; Jimy Sanders and Victor Nee, "Limits of Ethnic Solidarity in the Enclave Economy," *American Sociological Review* 52, no. 6 (1987): 745–773.

6. U.S. Bureau of the Census, Census 2000 Summary File SF 1; 100% data.

7. L. Belsie, "Hispanics Spread to Hinterlands," *Christian Science Monitor*, 93, no. 83 (2001): 1.

8. Y. Camayd-Freixas, G. Karush, and N. Lejter, *Latinos in New Hampshire: A Summary Profile.* (Manchester, N.H.: Community Economic Development Press, 2005).

9. Thomas Exeter, "The Largest Minority," *American Demographics*, 15, no. 2 (1993): 59.

10. Dave Levinthal, "New Hampshire Growing Fast," *Eagle-Tribune*, March 24, 2001, www.eagletribune.com/news/stories/20010324/NH_001.htm.

11. Y. Camayd-Freixas and R. Lopez, *Gaps in Representative Democracy: Redistricting, Political Participation, and the Hispanic Vote in Boston* (Boston: Hispanic Office of Planning & Evaluation, 1983); Y. Camayd-Freixas, E. Strom, B. Marcus, and L. Simmons, *Hispanics in Lawrence: Demographic Analysis* (Commonwealth of Massachusetts, 1985); Y. Camayd-Freixas, E. Strom, and R. Rivera, *Hispanics in Massachusetts: Population Trends and Policy Implications* (Massachusetts Legislature, Commission on Hispanic Affairs, 1986).

12. Ramírez, *U.S. Hispanic Population*, 2002.

13. U.S. Bureau of the Census, op. cit. (June 2001).

14. Brian MacQuarrie, "Ethnic Division Outside Boston," *Boston Globe*, December 14, 2004, B1, B4. The author quotes a study by Guy Stuart of the Kennedy School of Government and speculates that this may reflect "a significant immigrant network effect: people come and seek places where there are people from their country" (B4); he wondered how much this influx may be affected by real estate agent practices.

15. U.S. Bureau of the Census, Census 2000 Summary File SF 1; 100% data.

16. Ramírez, *U.S. Hispanic Population*, 2002.

17. U.S. Bureau of the Census, Census 2000 Summary File SF-3; population sample data.

18. U.S. Bureau of the Census (October 2003); (August 2003).

19. Based on conversations with local informants and media reports. Levinthal, "New Hampshire Growing Fast"; Kathleen Conti, "Latinos Find Haven in New Hampshire: Residents Drawn by Affordable Housing, Jobs." *Boston Globe*, November 9, 2003, www.rudymayer.com/ pages/local_NH_real_estate_news/ latinos.html.

20. U.S. Bureau of the Census, Census 2000 Summary File SF-3; population sample data.

21. Ibid.

22. Levinthal, "New Hampshire Growing Fast," and Conti, "Latinos Find Haven in New Hampshire."

23. The following analysis of immigration patterns is based on U.S. Bureau of the Census, Census 2000 Summary File SF-3; population data.

24. U.S. Bureau of the Census, Census 2000 Summary File SF 1; 100% data.

25. Citizenship and language data are drawn from: U.S. Bureau of the Census, Census 2000 Summary File SF-3; population sample data.

26. New Hampshire Department of Education, 2004.

27. Ramírez, *U.S. Hispanic Population*, 2002; Current Population Survey, 2002.

28. U.S. Bureau of the Census, Census 2000 Summary File SF-3; population sample data.

29. Bob Brooke, "Strength in Numbers," *Hispanic* 13, no. 1: 36–38; Joel Russell, "Past, Present, Future," *Hispanic Business* (2004), www.hispanicbusiness.com/news/newsbyid.asp?id=16372.

30. U.S. Bureau of the Census, Hispanic-Owned Businesses (October 2001); U.S. Bureau of the Census, Economic Census 1997 (2001).

31. U.S. Bureau of the Census, Census 2000 Summary File SF-3; population sample data.

32. Samuel Huntington, *Who Are We? The Challenges to America's National Identity* (New York: Simon & Schuster, 2004).

33. Alan Wolfe, "Native Son: Samuel Huntington Defends the Homeland," *Foreign Affairs* (May 2004), www.foreignaffairs.org/20040501fareviewessay83311/alan-wolfe/native-son-samuel-huntington-defends-the-homeland.html.

34. Russell, "Past, Present, Future."

35. Wolfe, "Native Son."

# 8 Brazilians in Massachusetts: Migration, Identity and Work

C. Eduardo Siqueira and Cileine de Lourenço

## Introduction

Brazilian emigration to the United States and Massachusetts grew vigorously between the mid-eighties and the late nineties and continues today. Brazilians have settled in many different cities and towns in the state throughout the last two decades, from the Metrowest area, especially Framingham, to the south and north of Boston. Although one can meet many new Brazilians daily in this state—a hint about the magnitude and geographic dispersion of this immigrant population—there is a scarcity of reliable information and data about the immigration experience of the Brazilian community.

This study covers several aspects of the Brazilian experience. We begin by tracing the first wave of immigration to Massachusetts, noting the work of anthropologists who have taken an interest in this topic.[1] Next we discuss estimates of the size of the population in Massachusetts and then examine why Brazilians choose to settle in Massachusetts. Thirdly, we look at racial and ethnic identity issues in the positioning of Brazilians as a distinct immigrant population in Massachusetts, a discussion that is partially based on a focus group with teenagers.[2] The chapter then continues with an examination of results of interviews with a convenience sample of immigrant workers.[3] The purpose of the interviews was to describe and analyze the workers' demographic characteristics, immigration paths, short and long-term plans regarding immigration to the United States, hazardous occupational exposures, and sociocultural obstacles in the work environment.

## Waves of Immigration and Reasons for Coming

Sales argued in *Brazilians away from Home* that Brazilian migration to the United States increased significantly in the mid- to late 1980s due to a combination of economic and political factors. The economic factor is the prolonged economic crisis in Brazil in the 1980s, which was a decade characterized by recession and low economic growth, also known as the "lost decade." During this decade, unemployment, inflation, and low wages pushed Brazilians to migrate to the United States, Japan, and Europe. By the end of the decade, three consecutive economic plans (Plano Cruzado I, Cruzado II, and Plano Verão) had failed to lift the economy. Sales described the last three years of the decade as the "triennium of disillusion," which pushed Brazilians to seek economic refuge in the United States. The political factor is the frustration and loss of hope that developed in the first few years after successful struggles against the military dictatorship, which led to a massive popular campaign for direct presidential elections in 1984–85.

During the "lost decade" of the 1980s Brazilian civil society mobilized millions of people throughout the country and reorganized labor unions, neighborhood associations, a variety of political parties, and nongovernmental organizations. All this effort culminated in the new Constitution of 1988, which framed a progressive body of legal concepts and social concerns to build a democratic future for the nation.[4] While politically the country moved toward democracy and the rule of law, the structural causes for the economic crises remained intact throughout the decade, frustrating the enormous social expectations that arose with the end of the authoritarian regime in 1985.

However, while economic and political conditions during the 1980s may explain why Brazilians decided to leave the country, they do not account for the specific pattern and flow that evolved. Ethnographic studies in Framingham and Governador Valadares (located in the state of Minas Gerais), show that these two communities have become the most important hubs that link Brazil with Massachusetts. It turns out that since the 1940s Brazilians in Valadares had been familiar with Massachusetts and developed networks that facilitated the emigration of thousands of Brazilian citizens to Massachusetts.

Valadares established its first social and cultural links with the United States during the Second World War because its soil contained large deposits of mica, which was commonly used for the production of radios in the United States. Despite the fact that Valadares was only one of the many counties in Brazil where jobs were scarce and prospects for social mobility few, it has become the major source of emigration from Brazil after the mid-eighties.

Informed by Massey's work with Mexican immigrants in the United States, Fusco and Scudeler[5] studied the social networks that emerged in Valadares. Sociologists who have studied immigration used the concept of social networks to explain migration between countries. Migration was defined as "a networking-creating process because it develops an increasingly dense web of contacts between places of origin and destination."[6]

According to Portes, the formation of these cross-national networks allow for the creation of a migration process that is self-sustaining, constant, and impervious to short-term changes. Therefore, migration is seen as a group-mediated decision whose timing and destination is largely determined by the social context of networks established over time.[7] There is evidence that the transnational network that linked the Valadares area and Massachusetts started as a circular migration of a few "mineiros" who came to Lowell to play soccer, went to Massachusetts to sell precious stones and gems or to Boston to study, or just decided to leave Brazil as a personal adventure.[8]

Data collected in a sample of households in Valadares by Fusco and Scudeler show that most immigrants to the United States were young (20–29 years old) and better educated than the average Brazilian, though they were less educated than the average American of similar age. Those immigrants had low proficiency in English, which partially explains why they are limited to low-skill and low-paying jobs in the United States. The majority of those who left Valadares in the mid-eighties are male and returned to Brazil within 6 years, while the majority of those who migrated more recently are female and stayed in the United States over 7 years. Eighty percent of the immigrants from Valadares only traveled once to the United States. This pattern of migration from Valadares suggests that each immigrant added his or her experience in the United States to a growing network composed of family, friends, and personal contacts. This expansion of the immigration network over time is typical of what has been called "chain migration" by immigration scholars.[9]

Thus the Brazilians of Valadares created a "daughter community" in Framingham, as well as smaller ones in the greater Boston area, by increasingly weaving a social net that has given them the help needed to settle in Massachusetts. Through an ever-expanding flexible network they found jobs for themselves and schools for their children. They identified houses to share, rent, or buy and churches to pray in. And, importantly, they found other Brazilians who could lend a hand to help out with their daily problems.

According to Brazilian government figures, there are more than 1.5 million Brazilians living overseas. The major receiving country is the United States, where 750,000 Brazilians lived in 1998. Massachusetts held the second largest concentration after New York, closely followed by Florida.[10]

Most Brazilian immigrants to Massachusetts before the 1990s were lower-middle-class males. This trend shifted in the nineties. Martes's survey of 300 Brazilians in 1996 showed an increasing migration of families.

Forty-eight percent were married, and 52 percent brought all their children with them to Massachusetts. Thirty-one percent of the respondents of her survey had the equivalent of a high school diploma, 12 percent had some college, and 16 percent had a college degree.[11] The continuous economic crisis combined with violence in urban areas in the early and mid-nineties to push upper-middle class families to leave the country and open businesses in the United States.

Confirming previous work by Sales and Martes, Jansen and Siqueira found that Brazilians' main motivation to migrate to the United States in the 1990s was economic: personal bankruptcy, reductions in wages, and worsening of their job conditions. Junior, for example, showed his disappointment with the contracting out of his previous high-skill job:

> My wage decreased a lot. I had a good status in my company [as a maintenance worker]. Everything collapsed. I became a regular Joe peon.[12]

Others explained that they came to the United States to save enough money to buy a house, a truck, or pay off debts in Brazil. Maria summarized her motive as representing the dream of many immigrants:

> I came to the U.S. with the same illusion of everybody else. To make more money, thinking that they would go back and never need to work for anybody else any longer...I came here to save money, go back, and build my own business.

Cláudia was a teacher whose financial resources kept decreasing while her debts increased. She was living in a financial crisis:

> I had no other option. I would either come [to the United States] or my family and society would call me a bad payer, an irresponsible person. Therefore, I had to take this option. I did not come to run away. I came to face this problem and be able to pay my debt.

Thus the main reason for coming to the United States is to rapidly accumulate money by working intensively for a short time, and then to go back to Brazil, which is typical of the sojourner experience of many immigrants to the United States. In addition, migrants are enticed by the perception that individual freedoms are respected in the United States Also figuring in their rationale is the attraction of U.S. economic, scientific, and technological progress and the opportunity to pursue educational goals by studying in a U.S. college or have their children receive a better education.

Another reason for Brazilian attraction to Massachusetts is the existence of personal networks. Lúcio expressed this view when he said:

I think that most come here because there is already somebody they know here. I think this is what makes people go from one place to another. Having somebody they know there.

José described how networks helped him:

I had never left Brazil, my home, and look where I am, first time that I leave Brazil. The main reason for me to come to America was having a place to stay, because the most important thing when you come to America is to have a place to stay. As Brazilians say, it's the so-called "ajuda."[13]

Other Brazilians come to Massachusetts because they believe that the state provides decent public services, such as public schools and health insurance, to immigrants. Ronaldo says that he came to Massachusetts because the state

provides better conditions for immigrants who arrive. Things such as health. My kids have good free schools. My kids have free busing. My kids have health and dental coverage. Thus, here I have better possibilities to see the light.

## Measuring the Population

There is considerable discrepancy between official and informal estimates of the Brazilian population in the state. On the one hand the 2000 U.S. Census estimated that there were 36,669 Brazilians.[14] But other sources, including the Archdiocese of Boston, have said that the true figure may be up to four times this number.[15]

Why would there be such a difference? Margolis has offered an explanation of the 1990 census undercount of Brazilians that remains applicable today.[16] Neither the 1990 or 2000 census mentions Brazil as a specific choice for country of origin under the categories Hispanic, Latino, or South American. Thus, Brazilians may have chosen to identify themselves as White, Other South Americans, Other Hispanic, or Latino. In addition, Brazilians may often avoid census outreach efforts for fear of deportation.

Another explanation, known to community representatives, is the fact that many Brazilians live in overcrowded housing units that violate maximum state occupancy laws and, to avoid penalties and fines, may underreport the total number of residents in each unit.

Other information, about business activity[17] and widespread settlement throughout the state,[18] suggests that the true count is well above the census count. But until more systematic estimation procedures are applied we cannot know for sure.

## Racial and Ethnic Identity

Salgado noted that:

> Important as it is to understand how U.S. racial and ethnic hierarchies, rela-
> tions, and ideologies affect migrants, reconfigurations of racial and ethnic
> identities in the United States must be linked with the racial and ethnic ex-
> periences of immigrants in their countries of origin.[19]

Based on our observations and conversations with dozens of Brazilian immigrants in Massachusetts, Brazilian immigrants' racial and ethnic perceptions respond to the complexities involved in identity construction in general and in the shifting positions adopted or discarded once exposed to U.S. racial and ethnic constructs. First-generation Brazilians, like other Latin Americans, come to the United States with an unstable but formed notion of what constitutes the Brazilian national identity. More importantly, they bring with them notions of racial classification that differ considerably from those existing in the United States.[20] Much as it has in the rest of Latin America, questions of race and national identity have occupied intellectual discourse in Brazil, particularly since the nineteenth century. In their attempt to understand the national character, the intelligentsia also prescribed notions of "Brazilianness" that have been transmitted through school books, novels, newspapers, political speeches, the media, and churches' pulpits.

Sales argues that Brazilians bring with them a certain "cultural baggage" that the scholar sees being reproduced and modified in the Brazilian immigrant community.[21] Yet neither Sales nor other Brazilian anthropologists who studied Brazilian immigrants in Massachusetts comment on racial perceptions as a key cultural element of this "cultural baggage."

Our observation, based on close contact with many Brazilians in Massachusetts, is that race and ethnicity are difficult subjects for Brazilians to talk about.[22] For example, when asked to respond to questions on race and ethnicity in U.S. Census forms, a group of Brazilian immigrant teenagers interviewed by Siqueira did not know how to fit their racial and ethnic identity within the categories available in those forms.[23] And they do not see themselves as Hispanics or Latinos despite considerable contact with this group in their high schools. These youth tend to self-identify as white or "moreno" (mulatto). Brazilian immigrants seem to have a great deal of difficulty in understanding U.S. racial and ethnic categories. Brazilians not only tend to conflate concepts such as race, ethnicity, and nationality, but also to overlook their African or indigenous hertiage. Brazilian racism against blacks and native Brazilian peoples may explain why we seldom hear Brazilian immigrants self-describe as "mixed race," which is the biological and cultural background of the majority of the Brazilian population.

Placing nationality over race or even denial of race altogether is consistently present in Brazilian immigrants' narratives of self-description. This preference to define oneself nationally rather than ethnically or racially is rooted in significant experiential and ideological factors.

First, most immigrants, particularly those who lack a full racial or ethnic consciousness, tend to confuse these three terms. Second, race relations in Brazil have traditionally been overlooked precisely because racial issues were presumably resolved by miscegenation during colonization and later attenuated by an ideology of racial democracy. These assumptions and the idea that racial issues were something of the past are inherited and perpetuated by successive elite-led nationalistic projects, including those forged in decades of dictatorships. The persistence of the ideology of racial democracy has brought enormous consequences for "afro-descendants" in that it prevented racial awareness and consequently the organization of a strong and coherent antiracism movement.[24] Although the Brazilian Black Movement has recently made gains at the public and institutional levels by addressing racism and socioeconomic disparity, the notion that race is not a problem in Brazil still persists.[25] Moreover, this ideology has promoted the internalization of racial constructs among Brazilians within and outside the borders of the nation-state.

The third significant factor in the discussion of racial and ethnic awareness has to do with temporality. Brazilians emigrated to the United States fairly recently and have not yet been completely immersed into American racial categorizations. This is an experience similar to other immigrant newcomers and first-generation Spanish-speaking communities. Coming from a place where racial categories are multiple and closely related to different shades of skin color, it is difficult for Brazilians to perceive racial differences as prescribed binary oppositions (white/black or white/nonwhite). In fact, American racial and ethnic categories tend to be rejected by most Brazilian immigrants as senseless because they do not match Brazilians' prior ideological, cultural, biological, and social experiences and discourses.

Brazilians work and live in close contact with other racial and ethnic immigrant groups, in particular Spanish-speaking Dominicans, Salvadorans, Guatemalans, Puerto Ricans, and Colombians. Differentiating themselves from these other groups has become an important part of the formation of their racial and ethnic identity in the United States. Responses from participants in our interviews of workers and from youth in our focus group session confirm Fleischer's findings that Brazilian immigrants do not see themselves as Hispanics.[26] We have observed an attitude of rejection among Brazilians, who seem to equate Hispanic with "otherness." This perception can be seen in this statement of one of the teenagers interviewed:

> They [Hispanics] and Brazilians, there is a big rivalry....I don't know why, because I do not know many stories about Hispanics, but maybe it was the upbringing of people. I do not even say the country, but the type of background. They [Hispanics] are illiterate. They are people who already live in a very poor area....So, the environment is full of problems, it is really low level.

Our teenage informants consistently defined *Hispanic* as a term appropriate for Spanish speakers, not Brazilians who speak Portuguese and have a different culture.[27]

In the same vein, most Brazilian immigrants do not seem to know the exact geographical origin of Hispanics, or they assume that all Hispanics are from Central America. The conscious or unconscious reproduction of negative views of Hispanics may be a self-serving ideology that Brazilians adopted to compete for jobs in the informal economy against other Spanish-speaking immigrants.[28] Whether out of unfamiliarity with the term or because of perceived negative connotations of the term, few respondents identified themselves as Hispanic.[29]

When asked how they think Americans view Brazilians in the United States, most of our informants pointed out that Americans tend to place Brazilians in the Hispanic category. While commenting on Americans' ignorance of the differences between Brazilians and Hispanics, the informants themselves tend to classify all Spanish-speaking Hispanics as a homogeneous social group, thus reproducing this imposed panethnic nomenclature. We also discovered that the confusion in the use of categories such as Latino, Hispanic, Latin American, black, white, and Brazilian reflects a lack of clear understanding of concepts such as race, ethnicity, and nationality.

When referring to their racial group identity, Brazilians often use the term "nosso povo é" (our people is) or descriptive statements such as "a raça brasileira é" (the Brazilian race is) followed by an adjective, such as *white* or *mulatto*. Answers given to racial self-identification questions tend not to be clear and demonstrate confusion between race and nationality. For example, informants may request further clarification about the meaning of the question "what's your race?" and at times may look clearly puzzled, not knowing what to answer. There are also instances when a dark-skinned informant self-identifies as of the "white" race, which is a trend also observed in Brazil.

It is reasonable to assume that this attitude on the part of Brazilian immigrants is related to their first-generation experience and the desire to reaffirm their national identity as a strategy for unity and survival. The vast majority of Brazilians in the Boston area are first-generation immigrants and undocumented, and they maintain strong ties with the home country. By asserting their identity they reinforce internal cohesion, repeating the experience of most first-generation immigrants to the United States.[30]

Thus, kinship ties are reaffirmed and icons such as the Brazilian flag and Independence Day are reinforced. The marginalized position of the immigrant in the host country makes it possible for them to access these icons and forge alliances with other individuals of the same "imagined community," that is, the Brazilian community. This is not to suggest that Brazilian national identity is static and unchangeable. Instead, we emphasize that some icons and national creations (such as historical traditions) do tend to be vibrantly remembered despite the fact they are continuously reconfigured and redefined in a new environment.

The nonadoption of Latino, Hispanic, and even Latin American ethnic identity by most Brazilian immigrants in the United States implies that Brazilians feel different from the rest of Latin America. The rationale used by average Brazilians to consider themselves as an unique ethnic group is based on language (Brazilians are the only Portuguese speakers in South America), colonial history (the only country colonized by Portuguese in the Americas), and a deep nationalism. In addition, the sense of a unique identity has been fomented historically by the elite-led aspirations for Brazil to be a regional power, economically and politically.

## Workplace Conditions and Issues

Information from a survey of workers in Lowell, Massachusetts, sheds some light on the conditions of Brazilians in the workplace.[31] Most participants are originally from the south of Brazil, whereas in other Massachusetts communities Brazilians tend to come from cities located in the southeast (especially the Valadares region). More than two-thirds of workers surveyed came from five states—Paraná, Santa Catarina, Minas Gerais, Rio de Janeiro, and São Paulo—that are part of the wealthier regions of Brazil: the south and southeast.

Seventy percent of the study participants have lived in the United States for less than two years, and only 5 percent have lived in the United States longer than ten years, a sign that this is a very recently settled immigrant population. The social network theory would suggest that the immigration of Brazilians to Lowell is related to friendship or family ties between new and old Brazilian immigrants in Lowell. We have not yet mapped out the social networks that could explain why so many Brazilians have recently chosen to settle in Lowell. Most of the older Lowell Brazilian residents came from Minas Gerais, not the south of Brazil. Yet the length of residence in Lowell of the new immigrants is similar to their length of time in the United States, indicating that most of those new immigrants emigrate directly to Lowell.

These laborers work long hours: 58 percent of study participants work over fifty hours per week, while 15 percent work for seventy hours or more per week. The great majority (over 80 percent) currently work cleaning houses or offices, in kitchens or serving customers of fast-food restaurants, or in other low-paid service jobs. Their current jobs are often their second or third job since immigration. Many of the study participants had previously worked in manufacturing jobs such as a juice or plastic factory before getting their current job. From these histories we estimate that three-quarters of the workers are employed in unskilled jobs. Only 4 percent work in high-skill jobs.

This job profile differs from their previous work experience in Brazil. None of the workers interviewed had ever worked as a janitor, cleaning houses, or in fast-food businesses. There is a significant contrast with the level of skills required for the jobs held in Brazil: 21 percent worked in high-skill jobs and 18 percent owned small businesses such as bakeries and auto-repair shops. This reported downgrading of skills on the job is consistent with Sales's findings concerning immigrants in Framingham.[32]

Respondents made unsolicited comments on job skills. Some quit a high-skill job hoping to find lucrative employment in the United States. Chico, for example, graduated in physical education and worked as a computer network support technician in a Brazilian university. He works in the stockroom of a warehouse in Lowell but states:

> I am not satisfied with my job, because I would like to do what I used to do before. I'd like to work in a computer laboratory again, work with computers, this is what I'd like... but I do not think about going back to Brazil. No. I suffered a lot over there. Fifteen years working in the university and studying... To go back all over again to make such little money!

Fernanda quit her business school and emigrated to Massachusetts, where she works as a cook in a fast food chain restaurant:

> I am not happy with my work because I moved away from my background completely.... I never worked with fast food in Brazil, so I feel like I am moving backwards. I do feel financially rewarded, but not emotionally. This makes me frustrated. Because it is very difficult here in America. I think that you make it financially, but your emotional side becomes very shaken. There is always some impact, something like that.

Ana voices her dissatisfaction with low-skill work. She is a psychologist who works in the United States cleaning the kitchen of a restaurant:

> What I do I do not like. I do stuff that is too simple for my skills. I have always been a thinker and always faced challenges. Moreover, because of this none of my previous jobs became a routine. Today I'm in a job that in addition to paying me little money became a routine. And the routine is terrible; it's tedious. That is why I don't like it. I don't see how I can grow in a job like that. And for me work and money is not all. Work has to make you grow as a human being.

About two-thirds of study participants express satisfaction with their jobs and feel financially rewarded. They feel respected by their bosses, despite their lack of documentation, legal workplace protections, and the downgrading of skills use. One of the plausible explanations for this apparent contradiction, given earlier comments of frustrations, is that the workers' initial expectations are based on their previous experience in Brazil, where employers generally treat low-skilled and service workers poorly. Compared to standards back home, these workers may get more money and feel that employers treat them better in Massachusetts.

On the other hand, a significant minority perceives that their bosses do not deal with them fairly or with respect. They say that they don't make enough money and are unable to use their previous training in their current position. For example, some state, Brazilians end up working as busboys or cleaning dishes while Americans wait tables and seat customers.

As with immigrant communities throughout U.S. history, organizations have arisen within the Brazilian community to address a wide range of needs, including workplace-related concerns. In the mid-nineties the Brazilian Immigrant Center (BIC) was formed. BIC's mission is to unite Brazilian immigrants to organize against economic, social, and political exclusion and for social change. The organization has provided English for speakers of other languages (ESOL) classes, organized leadership development and specific education and training for rank-and-file workers, and advocated for workers' rights in the workplace through legal and political mechanisms.

Recently arrived immigrants often work in unhealthy work environments, but the fear of being fired or deported often prevents them from seeking redress. In 2002 the BIC supported workers in resolving over seventy cases of workplace abuse, including workers' compensation cases. The BIC achieved this result through community pressure, direct negotiation with businesses, or in collaboration with the Massachusetts attorney general's office. Most of the cases the BIC addresses are related to nonpayment of wages or compensation for occupational injuries. Employers often violate labor laws by asking their employees to work overtime without paying legal overtime rates and may even not pay them at all.

Currently BIC has about three hundred dues-paying members and has sponsored workshops on worker and immigrant rights reaching nearly two thousand people. It also provided ESOL classes for over two hundred adults and participated in various fora, meetings, and demonstrations together with organizations such as Justice for Janitors, the Massachusetts Coalition for Occupational Safety and Health, and the Massachusetts Department of Public Health.[33]

In addition, the BIC and a few other Brazilian community organizations have lobbied local, state, and federal politicians as well as city and state officials to support immigrants rights. This coalition of groups, along with the Brazilian Consulate in Massachusetts, has promoted the annual celebration of Brazilian Independence Day (September 7) in Cambridge and organized several cultural festivals and sport tournaments.

## Sojourners, Settlers, and Immigrant Unity

Brazilians arrived in Massachusetts in large numbers in the last 15 to 20 years. Most view themselves as a separate national, racial, and ethnic group, as did other first-generation immigrant groups who have come to the United States. The affirmation of a distinct national cultural identity seems to be the dominant trend, which has also been the experience of other Latino immigrants to this country. Since this is a very recent immigration wave, one can now only speculate about the future: will Brazilians manifest a pattern of assimilation into mainstream America or a pattern of ethnic resistance into subsequent generations?

Scudeler[34] noted that among Brazilian immigrants from Valadares who returned home, about 36 percent had been in the United States for two years, 25 percent between three and five years, and about 32 percent between six and ten years. Up to now the published literature suggests that Brazilian immigrants are mainly sojourners or "birds of passage." Our own surveys ratify this impression. Yet, there also seems to be a sizeable proportion (one-third) that has lived in Massachusetts for over five years. These behave as settlers who strengthened their roots in the area by buying houses, starting small businesses, getting married and having children, and becoming permanent residents or American citizens.[35] These settlers still remain closely connected to Brazil and live as Brazilian transnational immigrants. They watch the "telenovelas" and news broadcasts of the Globo Television Network via satellite dish, eat Brazilian food at Café Belô and other local Brazilian restaurants, and travel regularly to Brazil for vacation or business. We believe that a fair description of the

Brazilian experience in Massachusetts is that there are both sojourners and settlers among the population. It is too early to conclude which group will predominate.[36]

Some Brazilian community leaders are aware of the need to create political and social mechanisms that will strengthen community solidarity and influence in the larger society. It is clear to many of those leaders that Brazilians are still an immigrant community "in the making" in Massachusetts.

The major challenge ahead is how to organize Brazilians independently without isolating them from other new immigrant communities in the state, such as Colombians, Salvadorans, or Haitians, which share with Brazilians any number of social and cultural barriers. Immigrant workers in Massachusetts tend to occupy similar service-sector job niches, such as janitorial and construction work, and are exposed to the same workplace hazards, abuses, and lack of health and safety protection. No matter where they come from, immigrants have a need to bond around a common agenda.

The obstacles to the unity of immigrant communities are many; they come from internal and external sources. Nationalism can enhance group strength, but it can make unity across groups difficult to achieve. Individualism, fear, and competition can also work against collective action and solidarity. Further study will document and analyze the process of Brazilian efforts at community growth and solidarity, both internally and externally.

## Notes

1. Teresa Sales, *Brazilians Away from Home* (New York: Center for Migration Studies, 2003); Ana Cristina Braga Martes, *Brasileiros nos Estados Unidos: Um Estudo sobre Imigrantes em Massachusetts* (Rio de Janeiro, Brazil: Paz e Terra, 1999).

2. The focus group was held with six Brazilian youths from Lowell in March of 2004. These were "cultural conversations" dealing with issues of identity and language.

3. Tiago Jansen and C. Eduardo Siqueira, "Brazilians Working in a Foreign Land: A Preliminary Study of Work Environment and Occupational Health Experiences of Brazilian Immigrants in Lowell, Massachusetts," unpublished report to the Committee of Industrial Theory and Assessment of the University of Massachusetts, Lowell, October 2002. Respondents answered a short survey and a set of open-ended questions during twenty minutes interviews.

4. C. Eduardo Siqueira, *Dependent Convergence: The Struggle to Control Petrochemical Hazards in Brazil and the United States* (New York: Baywood, 2003).

5. Wilson Fusco, *Redes Sociais de Migração Internacional: O Caso de Governador Valadares*, Textos NEPO 40, Núcleos de Estudos de População, Universidade Estadual de Campinas, Março de 2002; Valéria Cristina Scudeler, "Imigrantes Valadarenses no Mercado de Trabalho dos EUA" in *Cenas do Brasil Migrante*, ed. Rossana Rocha Reis and Teresa Sales (São Paulo: Boitempo Editorial, 1999).

6. Alejandro Portes, ed., *The Economic Sociology of Immigration: Essays on Networks, Ethnicity, and Entrepreneurship* (New York: Russell Sage Foundation, 1995), 22.

7. Alejandro Portes and Rubén Rumbaut, *Immigrant America: A Portrait* (Berkeley: University of California Press, 1996), 277–278.

8. Martes, *Brasileiros nos Estados Unidos.*

9. Charles Tilly, "Transplanted Networks," in Virginia Yans McLaughlin, ed., *Immigration Reconsidered: History, Sociology and Politics* (New York: Oxford University Press, 1990).

10. Heloisa Souza, "The Brazilian Community of New England: An Economic Profile," report prepared for the 8th Brazilian Independence Day Festival, 2002, available from author.

11. Martes, *Brasileiros nos Estados Unidos.*

12. All names from the study by Jansen and Siqueira are fictitious.

13. The word for help in Portuguese is *ajuda.* Here it means to have somebody to help recent immigrants when they first arrive.

14. U.S. Census Bureau, Census 2000 Summary File 3, Matrix PCT19.

15. The Archdiocese of Boston estimated in the early 1990s that there were around 150,000 Brazilians in Massachusetts. Martes says, in *Brasileiros nos Estados Unidos,* that this estimate was based on data collected from travel agencies and money transfer businesses in Massachusetts. She also notes that the Brazilian Consulate, other Brazilian churches, and community groups in Massachusetts uncritically accepted this estimate, which was not based on sound methodology.

16. Maxine Margolis, "Brazilians and the 1990 United States Census: Immigrants, Ethnicity, and the Undercount," *Human Organization* 54 (1995): 52–59.

17. Heloisa Souza's "The Brazilian Community of New England," an unpublished report, identified some 350 Brazilian-owned businesses in 40 cities and towns of Massachusetts in 2002.

18. Personal communication with Brazilian Consul in Boston, April 2004. There are settlements in Framingham, Cambridge, Somerville, Everett, Marlborough, and the Boston neighborhoods of Allston/Brighton and East Boston. Hyannis, Lowell, Peabody, Martha's Vineyard, and cities in the North Shore are some of the newest hubs of the community.

19. Gaspar Rivera-Salgado, "Transnational Political Strategies: The Case of Mexican Indigenous Migrants," in *Immigration Research for a New Century: Multidisciplinary Perspectives,* ed. Nancy Foner, Rubén Rumbaut, and Steven J. Gold (New York: Russell Sage Foundation, 2003), 138.

20. For a multifaceted discussion of ethnic identity of Hispanics/Lationos in the United States see Frank Bonilla, Edwin Meléndez, Rebecca Morales, and María de los Angeles Torres, eds., *Borderless Borders: U.S. Latin Americans, and the Paradox of Interdependence* (Philadelphia: Temple University, 1998).

21. Sales, *Brazilians away from Home,* 87–105.

22. Maxine Margolis discusses this issue in her work on the New York City community, *Little Brazil: An Etnography of Brazilian Immigrants in New York City* (Princeton: Princeton University Press, 1994), 235.

23. E. Siqueira conducted a group interview in 2004 with 6 Brazilian teenagers to collect qualitative information about ethnicity and identity formation. Unplubished data available from author.

24. Antonio Sérgio Guimarães, "Race, Class and Color: Behind Brazil's Racial Democracy," NACLA *Report on the Americas* 36, no. 6 (2001): 28–29.

25. Sheila S. Walker, "Africanity vs Blackness: Race, Class and Culture in Brazil," *NACLA Report on the Americas* 36, no. 6 (2002): 16–20; Héctor Tobar, "Racial Quake in Brazil," *Los Angeles Times*, October 1, 2003.

26. Soraya Fleischer, *Passando a América a Limpo: o trabalho de housecleaners brasileiras em Boston, Massachusetts* (São Paulo: AnnaBlume, 2002).

27. Fleischer, *Passando a América a Limpo*, 246. Fleischer's informants connected Hispanics with all sorts of negative stereotypes, associating them with criminality, gangs, drug dealing, and poor education, while viewing themselves as hardworking, peaceful, and better educated. Fleischer also comments that "it is no surprise that many Brazilians do not want to be identified as Latinos, as there is a fear of identifying with a minority group who they perceive as facing discrimination." Darién J. Davis, "The Brazilian-Americans: Demography and Identity of An Emerging Latino Minority," *The Latino Review of Books* (Spring/Fall 1997): 12. For a discussion among Brazilians in Massachusetts that generally argues in favor of accepting a Latino identity, see "Do We Fit Here?" *Boston Globe*, July 17, 2005, pp. C1, C7.

28. The authors have noticed that oftentimes Brazilian immigrants do not have strong arguments to support their prejudice against Hispanics. When Siqueira challenges this negative view of Hispanics with economic and historical arguments that demonstrate how this strategy can be counterproductive to Brazilian immigrant workers' long-term interests, many Brazilians tend to become defensive and realize that their opinions are based on hearsay and superficial impressions.

29. Oboler makes a similar assessment. Suzanne Oboler, *Ethnic Labels, Latino Lives: Identity and the Politics of (Re)representation in the United States* (Minneapolis: University of Minnesota Press, 1995), 2.

30. Portes and Rumbaut describe the same phenomenon with other immigrant groups, in Chapter 4 of Alejandro Portes and Rubén Rumbaut, *Immigrant America: A Portrait* (Berkeley: University of California Press, 1996).

31. Jansen and Siqueira, "Brazilians Working in a Foreign Land," 2002. Thirty-eight workers were interviewed. Fifty-four percent of study participants are female, while 46 percent are male. They are relatively young: 64 percent are younger than 40. Only 5 percent are older than 50. Two-thirds are married and 23 percent are single. Forty-one percent finished high school and 28 percent finished college in Brazil before coming to the United States.

32. Teresa Sales, *Brazilians Away from Home*.

33. http://www.braziliancenter.org, accessed July 2003.

34. Valéria Scudeler, "Imigrantes Valadarenses no Mercado de Trabalho dos EUA," 219.

35. Based on personal knowledge and experience the authors can affirm that the Brazilian population of Framingham and Allston have had the longest established residence in the state.

36. The changes brought about by security restrictions to obtain U.S. visas—and tighter enforcement of immigration regulations after the terrorist attacks of September 11, 2001—seem to have reduced the entry of new immigrants who would overstay their tourist visas. Whether this is a temporary phenomenon or not remains to be seen. Recently, community leaders claimed their members were being singled out for deportation more than other immigrant groups. Yvonne Abraham, "Local Brazilians Say They're Targeted Unfairly," *Boston Globe*, April 11, 2005.

# 9 Latino Catholics in New England

Hosffman Ospino

## Catholicism in New England

References to Catholicism in New England date back to the time of the Puritans and their nonfavorable attitude toward the Roman church. As Thomas H. O'Connor states in his history of Catholics in Boston, "if the English Puritans who followed John Winthrop to the Shawmut Peninsula had their way, there never would have been a Roman Catholic Church in Massachusetts."[1] The initial anti-Catholic sentiment would carry on throughout the centuries and challenge the establishment of the church in a territory that later on would become one of the major strongholds of the Catholic faith in the United States. Catholics in New England faced fierce resistance and opposition on the part of Protestant churches and organizations. Such antagonism was not limited only to Catholics who emigrated from England but was also extended to the French Catholic colonies bordering the states of Maine, New Hampshire, and New York. French Jesuits, or "Black Robes," were considered a dangerous menace to the newly established colonies, since they were perceived as secret envoys of Rome sent to disrupt the new colonies' stability.[2]

In the eighteenth and nineteenth centuries, thousands of Irish immigrants arrived in New England, most of them Catholics, thus changing the religious map of the region. Along with the Irish, throughout different periods, Catholics from Italy, Germany, Poland, Portugal, and other European nations arrived to become a powerful force that would transform the concept and influence of Catholicism in the northeastern region of the United States. Nevertheless, the anti-Catholic sentiment on the part of those already established was still present. Catholic immigrants were considered second-class workers, and their faith was perceived as a threat to the freedoms secured until then. Gradually, not without any struggle, Catholics began to influence the social, political, religious, and economic arenas of New England. Catholic churches were built in every town, especially in cities were Catholic immigrants concentrated for work reasons. For instance, in 1845 Lawrence, Massachusetts, had fewer than two hundred Catholics. By 1848, there were more than six thousand Catholics living in the "Immigrant City."[3] Catholics in Massachusetts founded diocesan and national churches on every corner, they organized one of the most remarkable Catholic school systems in the United States, many opened their own businesses, and the Archdiocese of Boston structured a vast organization to attend the social needs of both Catholics and non-Catholics. Finally, other Catholics set out to take an active role in politics. Boston quickly became a significant center of influence for Catholicism in the United States.[4]

Catholicism in New England was initially organized based on the experience, challenges, and expectations of the first European Catholic immigrants who came to the region. Today, the church confronts a culturally different wave of immigration bringing a different perspective to what it means to be a Catholic, namely the Latino experience.

## Latino Catholics: Changing Structures

The arrival of Latinos to New England has been motivated by various reasons. In the 1940s and 1950s, Puerto Rican immigrants established communities in several northern states, then becoming the largest Latino group in New England until today. Puerto Ricans arrived as part of a large migration due to the changing economic and political conditions that affected the island in the first half of the twentieth century. Many of them came to New England as agricultural workers and others joined the workforce in the industrial areas of the region.[5] Approximately 22,500 Puerto Rican farm workers were hired in New England in 1954.[6] Some Cubans came to New England following the aftermath of the beginning of Fidel Castro's communist regime in 1959 and later as part of waves of exiles who left the island in search of better living conditions. Immigrants from the Dominican Republic moved north from New York and also migrated from their island in search of better jobs and opportunities. In the 1970s and 1980s, immigrants from Central American countries fled from the hardships of cruel dictatorships, civil war, poverty, and violence. Many arrived in New England with the hope of finding better conditions in spite of the illegal migratory status that a large number of them share. Lately, Colombians, Ecuadorians, Venezuelans, and Peruvians, among others, continue to add to the numbers of Latinos who are transforming cities and neighborhoods. Each national group has brought its traditions, cultural expressions, language, and faith. For the external observer, it might seem that all Latinos are a monolithic group since they all speak a common language, seem to understand each other's cultural expressions, and generally identify as Roman Catholics.[7] However, Latinos are such a diverse group that a single-lens criterion does not suffice to appreciate the richness they bring.

Although the two Conferences of Bishops of Connecticut and Massachusetts have not issued any document on the pastoral care and presence of Latinos in New England, the dioceses in the region have taken concrete steps, particularly through the establishment of offices for the care of Latino Catholics. In some dioceses of New England, several offices for Hispanic Apostolate were created to meet the spiritual needs of the new arrivals; elsewhere, other diocesan entities have assumed this responsibility as part of a social concern. In those dioceses where the Latino population is small, there is not yet the need for an Office of Hispanic Ministry.

Certainly, the number of Latinos has seen a significant growth in all areas of the country. Compared to the 1990 census figures, the 2000 census revealed that the Latino population in New England has increased approximately 54 percent. The census also revealed that between 1990 and 2000 Latinos accounted for 40 percent of the nation's increase in population and that by 2040, there would be 80.2 million Latinos in the United States.[8]

These trends are reflected in the rising numbers of Catholic communities around the country. In 2003, 130 Catholic parishes in New England were reported to be offering regularly scheduled services in Spanish for Latinos. In 2000, there were approximately Latino 700,000 Catholics in New England, 12.4 percent of all Catholics.[9] Clearly there is a major cultural transformation taking place within Catholicism.[10]

## The Latino Religious Experience

The establishment of different Latino groups, varying by nationality or region of origin, in different parts of New England has created an interesting religious and cultural landscape. Each setting offers a microcosmic view of the Latino Diaspora: Puerto Rican, Colombian, Mexican, and so on, offering insights into the sociocultural milieus that comprise the Latino experience. Local businesses and churches in the neighborhoods are clear examples of this. It is interesting to visit Latino areas and find products displayed side by side that would never be available in any single part of Latin America or the Caribbean. In the United States they can be acquired with an easy facility. Buying a plate of food typical of a particular Latino country or purchasing a work of art made with the spirit of the land of the *abuelos* (grandparents) means unquestionably, a participation in the life of the community.

Churches also reflect this microcosmic character. Catholics from the Dominican Republic and Puerto Rico express the joy of their faith by means of an enthusiastic celebration of the Sunday mass. The combination of instruments, tropical rhythms, handshakes and hugs, and a sincere conviction that the church is their home, play a crucial role in the understanding of who they are as a community; likewise in parishes where most Catholic immigrants come from Central and South America. The masses reflect the spirit of these communities, whose spirituality tends to mirror different cultural traits, thus adding to the complex mosaic of the many Latino expressions of faith.[11] For Latinos, faith is more than a regular commitment to church services; rather, faith is a way of being. For Latinos, it is in the church, and more concretely at the moment of the liturgical celebration, that the manifestation of the unity of the community and actualization of what it means to be a Catholic Latino is most evident. Perhaps the words of a popular song help illustrate better that reality:

| | |
|---|---|
| No me importa de dónde tú vengas | No matter where you come from, |
| Pueblo o campo todo es igual, | Town or city it's all the same. |
| Si tu corazón es como el mío, | If your heart is like mine, |
| Dame la mano y mi hermano serás. | Hold my hand and my brother (sister) you'll be. |

The Latino religious experience offers new perspectives to the more traditional structures of Catholicism present in New England. This is the case of large cities such as Boston, Springfield, Hartford, and Providence, where it is not difficult to find parishes ministering to Latinos in their own language and helping them to become more active in the overall structure of the parishes and dioceses where they live.

## The Latino Catholic Experience

Catholicism prides itself on the universality and uniformity of its doctrine. For those who come from Latin America, there is no difference at all between what they regard as part of their Catholic faith before arriving in the United States and what they profess to believe now. However, a number of practices that are valued by Latinos within the context of their faith and their cultural traditions might seem unfamiliar to New Englander Catholics whose traditions of worship overall reflect a style that is more European in character. Frequently the lack of understanding about these traditions and practices on the part of many church leaders, the downplaying of the value that they represent for Latino religiosity, and the failure to understand their place in the life of the church create unnecessary tensions and unfounded misconceptions about the Latino culture.

Latino Catholics bring many "gifts" to the Church in New England: a multiracial identity, charismatic expressions, popular religiosity, strong sense of family values, and a spirit of fiesta, among others.

1. Multiracial Identity. It is true that most Latinos in New England communicate primarily in Spanish, mingle with Latinos from different countries with no apparent difficulty or sign of conflict, and often celebrate the cultural and religious expressions of other Latinos. For those who observe from the outside, this might give the impression that Latinos are a homogeneous, uniform group with no major differences. Latino Catholics are far from being so. In many Catholic parishes we find various Latino groups from different countries and ethnicities. Each group brings its own practices such as feasts of patron saints, Marian celebrations, popular devotions, and so on and invites other groups to celebrate with them. The racial factor remains always present, but I believe there is a sense of shared multiracial identity that differs significantly from past experiences in which national parishes were erected in the midst of ethnic and social tensions in the dioceses of New England. Nowadays in these dioceses there are not just Puerto Rican, or Dominican, or Salvadorian, or Colombian parishes. There are many parishes in which Puerto Ricans, Dominicans, Salvadorians, and Colombians, among others, worship together. Such diversity is undoubtedly a positive element that Latinos bring to the experience of Catholicism in New England. Unfortunately this very diversity, a departure from the melting-pot mentality, is often received with confusion and fear by the mainstream Church. Does it cause some elements in the Catholic Church to hinder Latino involvement in the leadership structure of the institution? I believe this is possible.

2. Charismatic Expressions. The different nationalities and various experiences of the Christian faith throughout the Latin American countries plus the necessary adjustments that immigrants undergo in order to live out their faith while remaining faithful to their traditions and practices in the United States come together in what can be described as the Hispanic/Latino religious experience. In the decades following the conclusion of the Second Vatican Council (1962–1965), Catholicism witnessed a significant revitalization. One of the strongest manifestations of this revival is the internal movement in the church commonly known as the *Charismatic Renewal*. The Charismatic Renewal among Latinos, understood not as one more group in the Catholic Church, but as the Church itself in a process of revitalization, combines both the liveliness of Pentecostal-like spirituality

and worship and the human warmth of Latino interaction.[12] This particular form of spirituality in the Catholic Church can also be found in non-Latino groups. Latinos incorporate into their masses a wide variety of musical instruments, rhythms from their countries of origin, expressive body language, and also a natural openness to share with others feelings of joy, sadness, distress, hope, and gratitude. The pipe organ, a fixture in many Anglo liturgies, figures rarely in Latino celebrations.

Not all Latinos subscribe to this type of spirituality, but it is a fact that the Charismatic Renewal has become the instrument in many parishes ministering to Latinos in New England. This is not a surprise. In countries like the Dominican Republic, Puerto Rico, and Colombia, the Charismatic Renewal has become widely known, thus affecting the organization and practice of Catholicism on a scale wider than local parishes. Most Latino immigrants and residents in New England are familiar with this movement.

3. Popular Religiosity. Latinos belong to a cultural tradition that is deeply religious. This religiosity is expressed in a variety of ways, both official and unofficial, to the point that it is not an easy task to group these multiple practices under the umbrella of one particular religious denomination or specific category. Popular religiosity is the natural expression of the religious experience of the people through practices that reflect the idiosyncrasy of a particular community of faith. Most Latinos share common ground in the practice of Christian traditions that have been developed for centuries under a mixture of particular historical conditions:

> Today's Latino popular Catholicism still bears the marks of its history, of its Iberian roots, and of the traumatic conquest of Amerindians and African slaves by Christians.... This religion's survival, in spite of five hundred years of efforts to suppress, educate, or convert it, reveals it as the enduring language of a subaltern people. Religious in expression, content, and experience, this language has long been the code through which hope and courage have been shared and maintained as plausible by generations of Latinos.[13]

Catholic expressions of popular religiosity can be identified in various areas and moments of the life of the people:

- Everyday Language. One often hears exclamations such as *¡Ay Virgen Santísima!* (Holy Virgin!) and *¡Santo niño de Atoche!* (Holy Child of Atoche—a Guatemalan expression).
- At Home. Small altars with images of Jesus and the saints, devotional candles, small statues of the Virgin or the saints, pictures of the Sacred Heart, and so on are popular.
- Family Celebrations. Masses are offered in thanksgiving for the arrival of a new member to the family or the celebration of a birthday; baptisms, first communions, and wedding receptions commemorate special

moments in the life of faith of the people. Such events are reasons for everyone to celebrate.

- Respect for the Dead. The *novenario*, which consists of praying for a deceased relative or friend for nine days after his/her death, is a key practice in the Latino culture. Normally a small altar is built at home with flowers, religious images, and the picture of the person for whom the prayers are offered. Every year a mass is offered for the soul of the deceased in hope that he or she will be in the presence of God. Children and young people are more likely to attend funerals with their families than they are in Anglo-Protestant cultures.
- Processions. During Holy Week it is customary to organize a live enactment of the stations of cross. Children, youth, and adults take part in this long procession remembering the moments of passion and death of Jesus. Other processions are also held on the feast of Corpus Christi, sometimes on Easter Sunday, on certain Marian celebrations, and on the feast of a patron saint.
- Marian Devotions. These hold an important place in Latino Catholic popular religiosity. The tradition of praying with the rosary is common in the homes of many practicing Latino Catholics.
- Associations. A variety of confraternities and associations are present in many parishes. It is through these groups that many Latino Catholics have their first encounter with the life of the parish in the new land and find themselves accepted in a particular group that shares their own faith.
- *Las Posadas.* In December, *las posadas*, a tradition widely practiced in Central America, becomes the perfect occasion not only to pray and prepare for the celebration of Christmas but also to share in the spirit of giving in the midst of traditional food and popular songs.

Certainly many of these expressions of popular religiosity are not exclusive of Latino Catholics in New England. Many of them belong to the collective tradition of Catholicism around the world. What makes them special is that it is through these expressions that Latinos preserve both their faith and culture as truly valuable elements of their heritage, thus enriching the experience of being a Catholic in New England. Such a stance surely challenges sectors with the same church and society that expect assimilation into models that overlook the vast potential of diversity and cultural pluralism for any institution.

4. **Strong sense of family values.** *La familia* continues to be of significant importance for most Latinos. The diversity of ideas in regard to the family in the United States is one of the first challenges that Latinos face upon their arrival in the United States. Generally for Latinos, the family is established around a monogamous, heterosexual relationship.

Marriage is still considered as a stabilizing factor at home, but the experience is that fewer couples actually get married "in the church."

The concept of family for Latinos is rather broad:

> For U.S. Hispanics, one's family is comprised, first and foremost, of those relationships intrinsic to one's inherited identity, namely, blood relatives. For Anglos, one's family is comprised, first and foremost, of those relationships which one *chooses* to have, namely one's spouse and children. Thus, when a U.S. Hispanic asks, "How is your family?" he or she will likely mean something very different from an Anglo who asks the same question.[14]

Every member of the Latino home plays a crucial role in the formation of the young and the adult community. The presence and advice of the elderly are fundamental for the development of the family. Usually the grandparents live with their children or at least nearby. For Latinos in general sending the elderly to a nursing home is not a priority.

Faith is sheltered and strengthened within the confines of the family. Children learn their prayers from their parents or grandparents at home, usually in Spanish. Sunday mass is a family event in which all the members of the family gather to worship. In many parishes with services in Spanish around New England, when one member of the family gets involved in one ministry, the other relatives follow in either the same ministry or one that suits better their interests. The sacramental life has been incorporated into what it means to be a Latino family. Baptisms, first communions, and weddings are family events in which all the members gather to celebrate. A concern for those involved in catechizing and ministering to Latino Catholics is that still many who request sacraments do so more as a part of traditional family practice or with a sense of superstition and less because they understand the theological content of the sacrament itself.

For many Latino Catholics the concept of family is extended beyond the circle of immediate relatives. At church, religious leaders, friends, and all others who come to worship are also considered family—particularly other immigrants with whom they can identify because of their migrant or legal status. Words such as *hermano* (brother) or *hermana* (sister) are addressed to any one in the group of prayer or the Sunday mass. Closer bonds are also created among those who come from a particular country. This is how parishes and churches in New England have become Latino microcosms in which everyone, regardless of differences, is part of the same family.

5. Spirit of Fiesta. U.S. Latino culture displays a sense of celebration that is closely connected to the religiosity of the Latin American experience. Latino Catholics focus on the celebration of the sacraments as events that affect the life of not only the individual but also the family and the

community in general. Baptisms, first communions, weddings, *quincea-ñeras*, patron feast days, silver and golden anniversaries, church in-augurations, Marian feasts, Christmas and Easter, and other occasions that are connected to the life of the church bring alive the spirit of fiesta that characterizes all Latinos.

The commercialization of what initially were religious holy days in-fluences Latino Catholics through the media, the school system, the workplace, and everyday routine. It is evident that Latino Catholics have adjusted their cultural perceptions to the more secularized ways in which such celebrations take place in the United States. In an attempt to gain acceptance by more people, mainstream culture often reduces the meaning of Easter to the Easter Bunny and the sharing of an abundant meal. During Christmas, everyone is concerned about giving and receiving gifts, and the word *Christmas* is almost avoided by the use of the expression "Have a happy holiday season." Although they have acceded to many of these practices, for a significant number of Latinos Easter and Christmas are still religious celebrations connected to the life of the community of faith.[15]

## Transnational Catholicism

The migration experience in the last fifty years has been shaped by the phenomenon of globalization in which access to information, faster con-ditions for travel, better communications, and breathtaking advances in technology rule the way in which we all live today. Latino migratory patterns exemplify this new transnationalism.

> Caribbean Latinos, especially mainland Puerto Ricans and immigrant Do-minicans, have been depicted as paradigmatic examples of groups engaged in deep transnationalism. . . . Significant numbers of Puerto Ricans and Domini-cans are said to live dual lives—engaging in double consciousness, cultivating dual loyalties, living serially between the islands and the mainland.[16]

The religious experience of Latino Catholics in New England has also been shaped by the phenomenon of transnationalism. Mexicans in the South were known for working in the fields seasonally and then returning to Mexico.[17] Churches and ministers would establish structures to min-ister to these temporary immigrants during the time they were in the country. Masses, prayer groups, and celebrations of sacraments were held in Spanish to attend to the needs of the immigrants. However, after the working season was over, many returned to their homes in Mexico, and the churches would return to their usual routine. In New England the experience of transnationalism of Latino Catholics has a different connotation. Although they come to New England with the hope of finding a better job, saving money, and then returning to their countries of origin, many end up staying for years or even establishing their own families and social structures permanently.

In this process, the church becomes a home base for building new relationships and pursuing their faith. Yet the ties with their families and friends and with their political and religious lives in their countries of origin remain firm. How does this occur? A few factors need to be taken into account.

1. Catholicism is a universal, *transnational* reality. Regardless of the place, language, or cultural setting in which Catholics practice their faith, the rites and doctrinal beliefs are the same. This homogeneity allows Latino Catholics to quickly relate to their religious practices back home, and also try to incorporate their learned experiences within the communities in which they now worship.

2. A good number of parishes have begun to serve Latinos in their own language. Most New England states have parishes in which services in Spanish are offered at least once a week. Prayer groups have been organized in these communities, many of them under the spirituality of the Charismatic Renewal, which has encouraged the formation of a network of preachers, both lay and ordained, who travel among parishes within the country and internationally. Often "healing priests" and lay preachers come from the Dominican Republic, South America, and Central America to lead retreats, Christian concerts, and celebrate mass. The events are hosted at small locations such as the local parish centers and large venues such as stadiums and concert halls. These preachers become a direct connection with the church in Latin America and bring back news and ideas from the United States. The process is reciprocal, with religious leaders going from local parishes in New England to Latin America.

3. The connection between the local communities in New England and Latin America is also visible in the economic support that groups of Latino Catholics offer to particular churches in other nations. Modest amounts of money are wired every month to support parishes in the countries of origin, to build new places for worship, to assist social programs, to pay for the formation of seminarians, and to buy commodities that would help priests, nuns, missionaries, prayer groups, and religious leaders do better work in their communities. Some of these benefactors make sporadic visits to see the progress of the works done with their contributions.

4. In the past, Catholic immigrants from Europe ensured that an adequate number of priests would accompany the communities in order to minister to them in their own language. Proximity to Latin America and

the facility of travel as well as the initial intention of many Latinos to return in the short run has resulted in a less-than-adequate supply of Spanish-speaking priests who minister to Latino Catholics in New England.[18] Local dioceses have recruited priests mainly from Bolivia, Colombia, the Dominican Republic, Ecuador, Mexico, and Puerto Rico.[19] Just a few of these priests were raised and educated in the United States. Some come to serve in these dioceses for limited periods of time and then return to their countries. A few decide to stay ministering to Latinos, although their dioceses of origin tend to be unhappy about this. Since many of the Latin American priests come to New England temporarily, many of them do not have the time to learn English and thus create connections with the wider Catholic community in the dioceses where they work. Most of them serve in their communities with the standards of ministry learned in their own countries. Thus, they prolong the Latin American way of practicing the faith and are less concerned with integrating Latinos into the domain of English-speaking Catholicism.

5. At the other end of the spectrum, some Anglo priests have learned Spanish and are able to minister to the increasing number of Latino Catholics who arrive in their parishes. Many of these priests have taken intensive Spanish courses abroad and others have learned the language on their own, pressed by the presence of their Spanish-speaking parishioners. Their efforts are greatly appreciated by Latino Catholics who yearn for a mass in Spanish. However, a number of these priests limit themselves to merely reading the mass and their homilies in Spanish, causing Latinos to look for more familiar and emotive ways of sharing their faith in prayer groups or gatherings at homes.[20]

An important mechanism for supplying Spanish-speaking priests in New England is the Society of Saint James Apostle, founded in 1958 by Boston Cardinal Richard Cushing.[21] This society is an association of diocesan priests who serve in South America. Priests from U.S. dioceses (mainly the Archdiocese of Boston) as well as European and Australian dioceses spend several years in South America serving in missions and working among the poorest of the poor. The society has continued its mission uninterrupted through today. A good number of the priests who have worked in Latin America have ministered to Latino communities upon their return. Their bilingualism and knowledge of Latin American culture enable them to become links between Anglos and Latinos in a time of changes for Catholicism.

6. Catholic literature in Spanish is not readily available in New England. Unfortunately for Latino Catholics, the variety of books on spirituality, sacred scriptures, and theology is limited. There are some religious bookstores that offer Christian resources in Spanish, both Catholic and

non-Catholic, but the availability is quite limited. This situation has created a small market of imports from Mexico, the Dominican Republic, and Puerto Rico. Catholic literature is purchased in these countries and brought to New England to be sold in parishes and at prayer groups, retreats, social events, and pilgrimages. This is not a big market, but clearly the lack of production of local resources in Spanish creates a high demand for Spanish literature and dependence on literature that often does not respond to the ecclesial reality of Latinos.

## Latino Catholics and the Institutional Church

Latino Catholics face an important challenge within the organizational structure of the church in New England. Most of the leadership within the different Catholic organizations is constituted of people who possess a good deal of formal education:

> Among Catholics ages 30 to 64, there are six times as many white, non-Hispanics who have a bachelor's degree than there are Hispanics with a bachelor's degree. The reverse is true with regard to Catholics with less than a high school education in the same age group: there are 2.4 times as many Hispanics as white, non-Hispanics. This large education gap is undoubtedly a factor in the low participation of Hispanics in Catholic church leadership. The fact that about 95 percent of Catholic lay ministers have at least some college education and 75 percent have a college degree adds credibility to this assertion. However, the education gap alone cannot account for white, non-Hispanic Catholics in lay ministry out-numbering their Hispanic brothers and sisters by 24 to 1.[22]

These numbers are clearly reflected in the participation of Latinos in the institutional apparatus of the church. Assessing participation in church leadership, it seems that Latinos in New England are repeating the historical paradigms in other settings: underrepresentation, tokenism, and indifference.[23] This situation becomes a challenge for both the church and for Latinos who expect to exercise more influence within the institution's organization.

Leadership roles in the Catholic Church vary notably in the organization of parishes and faith-based groups. Certainly many Latinos arrive in New England with the expectation that the church is run mostly by priests and religious men and women. This assumption is a product of their experience with the clericalist and paternalistic structures of the church in Latin America. Upon their arrival in the United States, they find a church in which lay leadership has a more active participation in the life and decisions of the parish or even the diocese. Their participation in their countries of origin rarely involves decision making on a large scale. More likely their role was restricted to leading a small group or serving in a particular ministry under the close tutelage of a priest or a nun. In the U.S. context, however, they find a church in which more responsibility is given to the laity. Positions such as "pastoral associate" and "director of religious education" include duties of administration that require adequate training, knowledge of English, and a better understanding of the mission of the church in the twenty-first century. Latino Catholics are scarcely beginning to realize this model of organization. Many opt for a quiet and passive participation in the life of their small communities. Others recognize that they lack the qualifications to fill these leadership posts, and choose to take up some responsibilities as volunteers. Ironically, their Anglo counterparts would be remunerated for basically the same work.

In some dioceses an auxiliary bishop or a priest with high rank has been assigned to ensure that the needs of Latino Catholics are met. The Archdiocese of Boston and the Diocese of Hartford have designated bishops to oversee the ministry to Latinos, among their responsibilities. In the rest of the dioceses a priest, a nun, or a layperson has been designated to serve as liaison to Latino Catholics, provide basic communications with other offices within the general organization, and help the different Latino communities to connect with local parishes. Some of these offices offer services and programs in Spanish. In some cases this contact person is not a Latino but is Spanish speaking.

Other diocesan offices have hired Latinos or Spanish-speaking personnel to expand their services. The diocesan offices of religious education in Boston, Bridgeport, Hartford, Providence, and Springfield hired staff members who organize and offer programs of faith formation in Spanish for catechists, lay leaders, and other ministers. As for the formation of lay leaders, the Archdiocese of Boston opened the Instituto de Formación de Laicos (IFL) (Archdiocesan Institute for Ministry [AIM]— Spanish track). The IFL offers a two-year program of intensive preparation for ministry among Latinos. The courses are taught all in Spanish mostly by a Latino faculty (clergy and laity) with graduate degrees in theology and education. During the fourth semester of the program, the students specialize in two areas of ministry at a parochial level, thus helping to improve leadership among Latinos. The Diocese of Hartford opened an Escuela de Evangelización (School of Evangelization) that offers training in different areas of spirituality and ministry to Spanish-speaking Catholics. The North East Institute for Pastoral Formation assists thirty-six dioceses, including the dioceses of New England, with programs of leadership and faith formation at the request of the different diocesan directors of Hispanic Apostolate. One of these programs is offered in Spanish in collaboration with faculty from the Catholic University of

America in Washington, DC. Also, the institute offers a program of cultural formation for priests interested in working more directly with Latinos. Boston College, through the Institute of Religious Education and Pastoral Ministry (IREPM), launched a series of graduate programs of formation for Latinos and those working with Latinos in pastoral contexts. Besides these large-scale efforts, parishes offer similar programs that respond to their local needs.

The formation of lay leaders is a positive initiative in the dioceses of New England. Perhaps these are the beginning steps that Latino Catholics need to take in order to assume a more active and defined role in the leadership of the Church. On the other hand, while the programs of formation for the laity are increasing, the number of Latino vocations to the priesthood and religious life does not keep up with the numbers of parishioners in the local parishes.[24] The scarcity of vocations is seriously affecting the church in the United States and Europe. Yet, there is no doubt that for Latino Catholics these trends contrast considerably with vocations in their countries of origin.[25]

Latino Catholics are also becoming visible through the media, where programming in Spanish is broadcasted weekly, oftentimes hosted by volunteer parish leaders. Usually the funding for these programs comes from local businesses and community members.[26] Some efforts have evolved into television programs in Spanish. Boston Catholic Television broadcasts several programs in Spanish, of which one is produced locally. In Boston, several parishes broadcast the Sunday Spanish Mass on public channels. The Diocese of Worcester broadcasts a Spanish mass and a program on Latino ministry and the diocese of Fall River airs a program about the family. Some dioceses in the region publish Catholic newspapers and inserts in Spanish to reach out to Latinos in the area.

## Looking to the Future

Latinos are on their way to becoming one of the strongest forces within Catholicism in New England. Two key challenges stand out on their immediate agenda: defections and institutional marginalization.

1. Defection. The numbers of Latino Catholics who leave the church in the United States is a concern for church leaders. According to Andrew M. Greeley, writing in 1997, approximately 600,000 Latinos left the church to join other denominations or renounced all religious affiliation.[27] Among the reasons cited are the lack of priests and qualified ministers to serve their spiritual needs, lack of services in Spanish, discrimination on the part of non-Latino Catholics, intense proselytism on

the part of Christian non-Catholic groups, lack of true commitment and knowledge of their faith, unfamiliarity with traditional Anglo services, and indifference on the part of Church hierarchy.

The cities and towns in which Latinos live are witnessing an upsurge of small Christian churches. For instance, as of August 2003, in Lawrence, Massachusetts, there were only four Catholic parishes serving Latinos, compared to more than thirty Christian, non-Catholic churches with services in Spanish.[28] Though small, the number of these churches continues to grow. Generally two hundred or three hundred people constitute these congregations, and the leaders do not necessarily subscribe to any of the more traditional Christian denominations. Most of these churches profess a Bible-centered understanding of Christianity fueled by a Pentecostal-like spirituality. They offer an atmosphere that Catholicism at first hand does not display: smaller groups, more personalized attention, doctrinal flexibility, and the opportunity of assuming leadership roles. Nonordained leaders can be seen preaching at the main celebrations and providing personal interpretation of the Bible. The rise of smaller, independent congregations is pressuring the traditional Christian denominations in New England to reach out more actively to Latinos.

2. Institutional marginalization. Latinos remain at the margins of church hierarchy and leadership even as they get more involved at the parish level and in diocesan events. They face the challenge of interacting as equals with other Catholics in the processes of planning, decision-making, and evaluation. There is an urgent need for Latinos and Anglos to seek common ground and to work together for the benefit of an institution that has historically thrived in the midst of diversity. Also, as many dioceses in New England struggle with scandals of sexual abuse by priests and poor administrative decisions, Latinos must continue to enter the structures of the organization to create heightened awareness of their presence and contributions.

The future of any institution is rooted in the quality of its leadership. Latino Catholics in New England face the challenge of inheriting a church that has been structured to respond to a culture in which education, dependability, and efficiency are praised as crucial values. Along with these premises, there exists a dim atmosphere of secularism combined with a moral and epistemological relativism, which presents Latinos with the perfect chance to bring the best from their own experience and use the best that has been advanced by U.S. Christian Catholics. Indeed, Latino Catholics should pursue a solid education in the faith and other academic areas, and thus become efficiently active in the life of their wider communities. Unfortunately the levels of education of many of the Latino leaders in Catholic parishes and dioceses in New England are not the highest. Latino leaders must compete in the market of the professional positions that are available in parishes and dioceses,[29] but many of them are not able to meet the standards established for these positions—college degrees, full proficiency in English, and availability to work in a job that often does not pay enough to support a family. In the end the positions are filled by more highly educated Anglos, who in spite of their good will, often are not equipped to understand the culture, language, and needs of Latino Catholics. The education of future Latino leaders in the church is a challenge that needs to be engaged seriously by the hierarchy and all pastoral agents. The church must face the future with hope, and not with fear or ambivalence.

## Conclusion

Latinos, the largest immigrant group in New England and the United States, have much to offer the larger society. Their presence is transforming not only neighborhoods, towns, cultural events, political structures, and the social milieu of many areas in New England, but also the organizational configuration of institutions like the Catholic church. It may be easy for the so-called established structures to look at the Latino presence as a problem or as one more concern that will soon fade. The fact is that the Latino presence continues to grow.

An example of how Latino growth is affecting Catholicism in New England is the pastoral plan of the Catholic churches in Lawrence. In the summer of 2002 the Archdiocese of Boston approved the first city pastoral plan in which the presence of Latinos became a defining factor in the process of deliberations. The plan stated:

> Since its foundation in the 1840s, Lawrence has been an immigrant city. The earliest immigrants came from Europe. The most recent waves of immigrants have come from the Caribbean. During the past 25 years, there have been significant demographic changes in our city, including large increases in the Hispanic population. The 2000 United States Census reported that Lawrence has 72,043 residents. According to the Census, 43,019 of those residents—60 percent of the population—are Spanish-speaking.[30]

The plan further affirmed:

> Since the majority of residents in Lawrence are Spanish speaking, and the vast majority of them identify themselves as Catholic, every parish in Lawrence will celebrate the sacraments in Spanish and English.[31]

Not all cities will become like Lawrence, with a population that is mainly Latino, and not all Catholic parishes in the dioceses of New England will opt for bilingual celebration of the sacraments and ministries; but for some cities this will be inevitable. The reality is that the trend of Latino migration toward New England is transforming structures that until recently reflected mostly Euro-American traditions.

Catholicism in the northeastern United States has never been uniform in its cultural expressions. Throughout history, the English, Irish, German, Polish, Italian, Portuguese, and other Catholics have shaped the practice of the faith with the richness of their culture and the hopes of their spiritual beliefs. Now is the time for Latinos to make their contribution to the history of Catholicism in New England.

## Notes

1. Thomas H. O'Connor, *Boston Catholics: A History of the Church and Its People* (Boston: Northeastern University Press, 1998), 4.

2. Compare ibid. 7.

3. Compare ibid. 83.

4. In 1866 the diocese of Boston had 116 priests, 109 churches, and approximately 300,000 Catholics. In this year Boston ranked as the second largest diocese in the country, after New York. Ibid. 125.

5. Compare Julio Morales, *Puerto Rican Poverty and Migration: We Just Had to Try Elsewhere* (New York: Praeger, 1986), 77–88.

6. Ibid. 82.

7. For a population count see note 9 below; for additional background data see U.S. Conference of Catholic Bishops, Secretariat for Hispanic Affairs, "Demographics," http://www.usccb.org/hispanicaffairs/demo.shtml#2. In New England it is possible to find immigrants from virtually all the Spanish-speaking countries in Latin America and the Caribbean in different communities throughout the region.

8. Compare http://www.usccb.org/hispanicaffairs/demo.shtml#2.

9. This estimate is derived by taking 80 percent of the 2000 census count of Latino population in the six New England states. For the choice of percentage see *Our Sunday Visitor's Catholic Almanac 2003* (Huntington, IN: Our Sunday Visitor Publishing Division, 2003), 421. For an estimate of Catholics in the New England states, see *Our Sunday Visitor's Catholic Almanac 2003*, 430–431.

10. Although the focus of this chapter does not include an analysis of the Christian, non-Catholic churches in New England, which will certainly be necessary in the near future, I would venture to assert that many of these churches are also being transformed by the presence of Latinos. On July 7, 2003, the *Eagle Tribune*, a local newspaper that covers the region of the Merrimack Valley in Massachusetts reported: "Ramos and his wife are part of a local and national trend: Latinos who are leaving the Church of their youth to join competing Christian faiths. The Southern Baptists, whose 16 million members make them the largest Protestant denomination, have about 2,200 Latino congregations, and they are adding about 300 new Hispanic churches a year. Other evangelical faiths winning converts include the Pentecostal Assemblies of God, Mormons, Seventh-Day Adventists and Jehovah Witnesses." Shawn Regan, "Evangelicals Wooing Hispanics from Catholicism," *Sunday Eagle Tribune*, July 7, 2002.

11. These observations are based on my research and experience, as I have been involved in Hispanic Ministry of the Boston Archdiocese, at parish and diocesan levels, for more than eight years. These and other observations are also part of my own research on the history and conditions of Latino Catholics in the Archdioceses of Boston, which I am putting together for publication in a forthcoming book.

12. "As a movement the Catholic charismatic renewal has projected a theologically conservative image, which is verified in fact partly because of its populist character. This conservatism is often less ideological and more the attempt of persons re-awakened spiritually to recover the sources of Catholic spirituality: the Scriptures, daily Mass, confession, spiritual direction...eucharistic adoration, and retreats." Compare "Catholic Charismatic Renewal" in *New Catholic Encyclopedia*, 2nd ed., vol. 3 (Detroit: Thomson/Gale Group; Washington, DC, in association with the Catholic University of America, 2003).

13. Orlando Espín, "Popular Catholicism: Alienation or Hope," in *Hispanic/Latino Theology: Change and Promise*, ed. Ada María Isasi-Díaz and Fernando F. Segovia (Minneapolis: Fortress Press, 1996), 322–323.

14. Roberto Goizueta, *Caminemos con Jesús: Towards a Hispanic-Latino Theology of Accompaniment* (New York: Maryknoll, 1995), 51.

15. This reality is confirmed by the increased numbers of people attending masses and religious services during these two times of the year. Along with this increased participation, the celebration of las posadas during Christmas and Good Friday practices during Holy Week add the tone of popular religiosity to the life of these liturgical seasons. I am thankful to the directors of Hispanic Apostolate of the different dioceses of New England for their observations on these issues and various others contained in this chapter.

16. Marcelo M. Suárez-Orozco and Mariela M. Páez, eds., *Latinos Remaking America*, (Berkeley: University of California Press, 2002), 6.

17. Suárez-Orozco and Páez cite the work of Wayne A. Cornelius, who argues that in the last two decades Mexicans have moved from a general transnationalism to habits of more permanent settlement. Compare W. A. Cornelius, "The structural embedd-edness of demand for Mexican immigrant labor," in *Crossings: Mexican immigration in interdisciplinary perspectives*, ed. M. Suárez-Orozco (Cambridge, MA: Harvard University Press, 1988), quoted in Suárez-Orozco and Páez, *Latinos Remaking America*, 7.

18. As of June 2003, there were 143 priests, both Anglos and Latinos, serving the different Latino communities in the nine dioceses of New England that have some form of Hispanic ministry. There are approximately 4,893 Latino Catholics per Spanish-speaking priest.

19. In 2003 there was a total of 55 Latino priests working in the dioceses of New England.

20. See note 11.

21. For a detailed account of the history and work of the Society of St. James Apostle, see the doctoral dissertation written by James Gaurneau, " 'Commandos for Christ': The Foundation of the Missionary Society of Saint James Apostle and the 'Americanism' of the 1950s and 1960s," (Ph.D. diss, Catholic University of America, Washington DC, 2000).

22. Ken Johnson-Mondragón, "The Educational Attainment of Hispanic Catho-lics in the U.S. and Its Impact on Pastoral Leadership in the Catholic Church," *En Marcha, Newsletter from the Department of Hispanic Affairs of the U.S. Conference of Catholic Bishops* (Spring 2003).

23. For example, see Anthony M. Stevens Arroyo, "The Emergence of a Social Identity Among Latino Catholics: An Appraisal," in *Hispanic Catholic Culture in the United States: Issues and Concerns*, ed. Jay P. Dolan and Allan Figueroa Deck, vol. 3 of the Notre Dame History of Hispanic Catholics in the U.S. series, ed. Jay Dolan (Notre Dame: University of Notre Dame Press, 1994), 115–116.

24. As of June 2003 there were fourteen Latino seminarians from all the dioceses of New England studying for the priesthood.

25. According to the 2003 *Our Sunday Visitor's Catholic Almanac*, there are 4,505 seminarians in Colombia, 493 in the Dominican Republic, 396 in Guatemala, 379 in El Salvador, and 96 in Puerto Rico.

26. There are about eleven Catholic radio programs in Spanish in the dioceses of New England.

27. Andrew M. Greeley, "Defection Among Hispanics (Updated)," *America*, 27 (September 1997): 12–13.

28. I am grateful to Mr. Joseph S. Giuffrida, assessor of the city of Lawrence, Massachusetts, for this valuable information.

29. For instance positions like director of religious education, pastoral associate, director of hispanic ministry, and so on. Many Latinos serve in these positions under different circumstances in relation to their Anglo counterparts: low salaries or no salaries at all, scarce participation in the main processes of decision making, and minimum interest for the needs of the Latino community in general because their voice is hardly heard or not considered relevant.

30. Lawrence Catholic Collaborative Committee, *Roman Catholic Presence in the City of Lawrence: Pastoral Plan*, 2002; See Introduction at http://www.saintpatrickparish.com/html/pastoral_plan_2002_introductio.html.

31. Ibid. The Sacramental Life of the Church, Goal 1, Objective 1.

In the late 1990s, the City of Boston recognized the growing population of Salvadorans with an official ceremony, honoring the country's national Independence Day. Here a multigenerational group sings the Salvadoran national anthem at the flag-raising event, held at City Hall Plaza. (Photo: *El Mundo*)

Since the late 1960s the annual Festival Puertorriqueño has been a central gathering event for Puerto Ricans and other Latinos in Massachusetts. It was originally organized in Boston's South End. Later it was combined with a parade through the principal barrios and culminated with a cultural event in Franklin Park. Here is a partial view of the 2003 festival. (Photo: Angel Amy Moreno)

In 2003 the Dominican Republic announced an active program to encourage immigrants in the United States to participate in the Dominican national elections. In cities throughout the Northeast, Dominican nationals turned out to cast their absentee ballots. Here a group from Waterbury, Connecticut, prepares to board a bus to Yonkers, New York, one of the polling sites. They pose with the "L" sign, indicating their support of presidential candidate Leonel Fernández. Fernández was elected that year. (Photo: Luis J. Pomales)

Since the 1940s, the U.S. Navy had conducted target practice on Vieques, a Puerto Rican island. Despite persistent opposition from Puerto Ricans, the bombings continued for decades. After a resident was killed accidentally during the 1999 bombing exercises, protest movements surged throughout the Puerto Rican diaspora. During 2002, in downtown Hartford, Connecticut, demonstrators call for an end to the Navy's military practices. The U.S. Navy withdrew from Vieques in May of 2003. (Photo: Valentín Rosario)

In 1999 four Hispanic members of the Boston Fire Department were sent to Honduras to help relief efforts during Hurricane Mitch. They delivered medical supplies and fire prevention equipment. Here, prior to leaving for Central America, a delegation presents a financial donation at City Hall. (Photo: *El Mundo*)

Mexicans are among the fastest-growing segment of Latin American immigration to the region. In December of 2004 the Mexican Consulate of New England sponsored a meeting of community leaders to identify challenges and action strategies for this population. (Photo: Leonardo Morales)

In Jamaica Plain, Boston, a neighborhood group demonstrates against plans to develop high-income residential sites. Affordable housing has become a contested issue, as areas once populated by lower- and middle-income families are eyed for other land uses. (Photo: *El Mundo*)

In Rhode Island during 2004, Grace Díaz became the first Dominican American woman elected to state office in the United States. She was elected as a State Representative from Providence. Here she is pictured, in white, celebrating her victory in the Democratic Party Primary, which took place prior to her winning in the general election. (Photo: Campaign for Grace Díaz for State Representative)

In 2004 residents of Chelsea, Massachusetts, organized a Latino Education Summit. The goal was to come up with a comprehensive strategy for improving the school system's capacity to help Latino student achievement. Here participants in a "working lunch break" discuss ideas on setting priorities. (Photo: Melissa Colón)

A partial view of a plenary session at the Third Latino Public Policy Conference, held in 2004 at the John Fitzgerald Kennedy Library and Museum in Boston, 2004. (Photo: Angel Amy Moreno)

Senator Edward J. Kennedy gives the keynote speech at the Third Latino Public Policy Conference, Boston, 2004. The conference was convened by the Mauricio Gastón Institute of the University of Massachusetts Boston and organized with a coalition of Latino community organizations. (Photo: Angel Amy Moreno)

A panel of Latino elected officials addresses a plenary session of the Third Latino Public Policy Conference. Seated left to right are: William Lantigua (Lawrence), Felix Arroyo (Boston), Roy Avellaneda (Chelsea), Juan Gómez (Worcester), and Jeffrey Sánchez (Boston). The moderator is Jorge Quiroga, television news reporter. (Photo: Angel Amy Moreno)

Latina and Latino youth who have excelled academically are acknowledged in a Boston citywide event in 2003. Education is a critical issue for the future of Latino communities. (Photo: *El Mundo*)

Photo gallery compiled by Angel Amy Moreno and Andrés Torres.

# Part III

# Identity and Politics

# 10 Descriptive Representation, Political Alienation, and Political Trust: The Case of Latinos in Connecticut

Adrian D. Pantoja

## Introduction

A major goal of the black, Chicano, and Puerto Rican civil rights movements was the elimination of electoral obstacles that kept African Americans and Latinos from having a meaningful voice in the governing process. Political activists and organizers believed the articulation of minority interests would largely be facilitated through the election of descriptive representatives who shared the goals and aspirations of the community.[1]

Descriptive representation, also referred to as symbolic representation, is a condition in which a citizen shares ascriptive characteristics such as race, ethnicity, and gender with his or her representative.[2] African Americans and Latinos achieved a potential breakthrough with the passage of the Voting Rights Act of 1965. The act, along with its subsequent amendments and court interpretations, resulted in a dramatic increase in the number of African Americans and Latinos holding elective office.[3] The increase in minority political empowerment not only came about by eliminating voting obstacles but through the creation of majority-minority districts, which are characterized as districts having a sufficient number of African Americans or Latinos to ensure they elect a representative of their choice.[4]

The rise of minority lawmakers has driven empirically minded researchers to examine the policy outputs resulting from increased minority representation as well as to analyze the behavioral and attitudinal effects they have on minority constituents.[5] This chapter builds on the latter studies exploring the representative-constituency political nexus from the constituent perspective. More specifically, I analyze the impact that perceptions of descriptive representation have on levels of political alienation and political trust among Latinos in Connecticut.

The analysis is carried out through a unique survey of Latinos done by the Center for Survey Research and Analysis (CSRA) of the University of Connecticut. The survey was randomly administered by telephone to

502 Latinos in 1998 and is representative of the state's diverse Latino population. Among the sample, 289, or 58 percent, identified as Puerto Rican, while the rest identified with some other Latino ethnicity. To my knowledge, this is the only survey with a significant sample of the Latino population in Connecticut. The questionnaire and data are available through the University of Connecticut's Roper Center (www.ropercenter. uconn.edu).

## Political Alienation, Political Trust, and Descriptive Representation

Democracies require their citizenries to possess certain political orientations and beliefs in order to ensure systemic stability.[6] Two critical orientations that are frequently used to measure the overall health of a democracy are political alienation and political trust.[7] Although both are murky concepts, political alienation can be defined as "a social condition in which citizens have or feel minimal connection with the exercise of political power."[8] Political trust refers to the faith or confidence people have in their political authorities, institutions, and regime.[9] The importance of these orientations is their association with behaviors that can threaten the stability of the regime. At best, politically alienated and distrustful citizens may simply tune out of politics. At worst, they may engage in more aggressive behaviors such protests or acts of terrorism.[10]

Contemporary research on political alienation and political trust has sought to determine whether these orientations are directed toward the political system or the incumbent administration.[11] This chapter does not engage this debate but rather seeks to identify the causes of these orientations.[12] A plethora of individual and political factors is associated with these orientations. The relative importance of each, of course, varies depending on the data used. Among the individual sources of political alienation and trust are a person's income, education, age, race, and sex. Much of the research shows that working-class and lower-class respondents, in general, manifest higher levels of political alienation and distrust.[13] Higher levels of education are inversely related to political alienation and distrust, while the effects of age are mixed.[14] Finally, researchers generally find that African Americans and women are more politically alienated and distrustful of government than white males.[15]

Because some find a weak relationship between individual demographic characteristics and these orientations, the research has also considered the political sources of these orientations.[16] For example, higher levels of political participation reduce alienation and increase trust, while disapproval of government policies and a pessimistic economic outlook contribute to feelings of estrangement and distrust.[17] Contextual factors such as the ideological leanings and partisan identification of representatives and presidential performance also play a key role.[18] Finally, and central to this chapter, researchers find that descriptive representation is inversely related to political alienation and positively related to political trust among African Americans.[19]

The "political empowerment" model is the framework most used to explore the behavioral and attitudinal effects descriptive representation has on black and Latino constituents. It argues that African Americans and Latinos are aware of their politically disadvantaged status and therefore tend to be more cynical, more alienated, and less trusting toward government. As African Americans and Latinos achieve a greater level of representation, we will observe increased political participation, efficacy, and trust in government.[20] Descriptive representatives through symbolic statements, gestures, and appearances send cues to their co-ethnic constituents that they will be more responsive to their special needs. In addition, as living symbols of the equal opportunity process, descriptive representatives provide a psychological uplift to the group.[21] The result is a politically efficacious or "empowered" constituency.[22]

While much of our knowledge on the effects descriptive representatives have on their constituents is informed by scholarship on African Americans, some are beginning to extend these models to the Latino electorate. The first of these studies by Pantoja and Segura finds support for the political empowerment thesis by noting that descriptive representation in legislatures decreases feelings of political alienation among the Latino electorate.[23] A second study by Barreto, Segura, and Woods observes that it leads to increased voter turnout among Latinos, and in a study of the 2000 presidential election by Barreto and colleagues, it is found that descriptively represented Latinos are more likely to be mobilized by candidates and interest groups.[24] Although these works have advanced our understanding of the nexus between descriptive representation and Latino political behavior, firm generalizations about their findings cannot be made since they solely analyze the experience of Latinos residing in the Southwest. These studies, as do most others, continue to overlook the experiences of Latinos in the New England states.

## Data and Variables

The data allow me to consider the individual and political sources of political alienation and political trust with the aim of testing the political empowerment thesis. The political empowerment model is typically tested through survey data, which are supplemented with contextual data noting whether a respondent resides in a district represented by a co-ethnic representative. The present survey, designed for other purposes, does not include an identifier enabling me to determine whether a respondent is or is not represented by a Latino. While I cannot measure actual descriptive representation, I can measure perceptions of descriptive representation. Specifically, respondents were asked whether they agreed or disagreed with the following statement: "Latinos have adequate representation in the Connecticut government." Respondents' answers were coded into a five-point scale ranging from "strongly agree" to "strongly disagree." At first glance the question appears to capture two possibilities. On the one hand, "adequate representation" could simply mean substantive representation or a derivation of policy outputs regardless of the race or ethnicity of representatives. On the other hand, it could be capturing symbolic representation, or the presence of Latinos holding elective office. However, because it is well established that voters use information shortcuts or cues such as race, ethnicity, or gender, to assess the "representativeness" of a candidate or institution rather than take the time to know the intricacies of public policies, it is more likely that the question, albeit imperfectly, captures an absence of symbolic rather than substantive representation.[25] In fact, most voters are unaware of the names of their representatives in Congress or other legislative offices, much less the policy positions they take, but are well of their race, ethnicity, or gender.[26] The question above constitutes the key independent variable in this study—Latino Representation. A high score, on the five-point scale, indicates a belief that there is an absence of descriptive representatives in Connecticut's government while a low score indicates the converse.

Two questions are used to measure each orientation—political alienation and political trust, yielding a total of four dependent variables. Political alienation is measured by the following two statements: (1) "People like me don't have any say about what the government does" and (2) "The government generally is run by a few people looking out for their own interests, not for the benefit of all." The first question captures a distinct dimension of political alienation, known as powerlessness, or the inability to influence government decisions. The second can be equated with normlessness, or the belief that government officials are violating long-standing norms or rules in an effort to serve some narrow interest.[27] Political trust is measured by the following two statements: (1) "In general, you can trust the people in Washington who run the federal government to do what is right" and (2) "In general, you can trust the people in Hartford who run the state government to do what is right." Respondents are asked to indicate whether they strongly agree, mildly agree, strongly disagree, or mildly disagree with each of the four statements above. Each question takes the form of a

TABLE 10.1. Political alienation and political trust among Latinos in Connecticut

| | Political powerlessness | Political normlessness | | Trust Washington | Trust Hartford |
|---|---|---|---|---|---|
| Strongly agree | 24% (119) | 25% (125) | Strongly agree | 18% (88) | 19% (97) |
| Mildly agree | 21% (106) | 32% (161) | Mildly agree | 32% (162) | 41% (206) |
| Neutral (volunteered) | 5% (27) | 3% (15) | Neutral (volunteered) | 3% (13) | 3% (13) |
| Strongly disagree | 23% (114) | 21% (103) | Strongly disagree | 22% (110) | 14% (70) |
| Mildly disagree | 22% (110) | 16% (78) | Mildly disagree | 21% (105) | 16% (78) |

five-point scale, with high scores indicating high levels of political alienation and high levels of distrust. The variables Powerlessness, Normlessness,
Trust Washington, and Trust Hartford constitute the dependent variables
in this study. For descriptive purposes, Table 10.1 shows the distribution of
responses to each of the questions.

When it comes to feelings of political powerlessness, Latinos in the
state are equally divided between those who feel empowered (45 percent)
and those who do not (45 percent). In terms of political normlessness, the
distribution is clearly skewed toward those who feel that government is
solely benefiting a few interests. Finally, when it comes to trusting the
federal government, Latinos in the state are once again divided, with only
50 percent stating the government in Washington can be trusted. However, the data show that Latinos are more trusting of the state's government, with 60 percent agreeing that they "trust the people in Hartford
who run the state government to do what is right." Although the survey
does not include a sample of white respondents for comparison, the results
clearly show that a large portion of Connecticut's Latino population feels
politically estranged and distrustful. Other questions in the survey also
reveal cynicism toward political officials and political parties. For example, 73 percent of respondents agreed with the statement "After they
are elected, political officials lose touch with the people." These sentiments are carried over to the political parties, with 72 percent agreeing
that "Political parties were only interested in our votes, not our opinions."
Another 70 percent agreed that "Political parties usually don't deliver on
their promises." These are troubling findings, since these orientations are
often associated with political apathy or the participation in other antidemocratic behaviors.

In order to understand the factors that foster or mitigate feelings of
political alienation and distrust among Latinos in Connecticut I use
multivariate analyses to isolate the relevant predictors and assess their

relative causal importance. Political alienation and distrust is not only endogenous to the presence or absence of descriptive representation. Each of the models includes an additional eight predictors, which are grounded in the literature.

The models include two additional political variables beyond the variable Latino Representation. The first variable, Attention to Politics, measures how much attention a respondent pays to political affairs. The variable ranges from 0, "never" pay attention to politics, to 4, "always" pay attention to politics. The second variable, Political Participation, is based on three questions. The first asks whether in the past year the respondent wore a campaign button, put a campaign sticker on their car, or placed a political sign in front of their house. The second asks whether they have signed a petition about an issue or problem of concern to the respondents. Finally, respondents were asked whether they have attended a political meeting, rallies, or heard a speech in support of a candidate. For each activity, individuals could indicate that they did or did not engage in such activity in the past year. The three questions are summed to form a three-point scale. Having an interest in and participating in formal politics is hypothesized to be inversely related to political alienation and distrust.

The social context, particularly contact with out-groups, is found to play a key role in shaping political behaviors and attitudes. While much has been written on the effects that contact with minorities have on white attitudes and behavior, little is known about the impact that contact with whites has on minorities.[28] The survey includes four questions measuring the degree to which respondents interact with Anglos in (1) the neighborhood, (2) at work, (3) among friends, and (4) at social gatherings. Each question ranges from 0, "all Latino," to 4, "all Anglos." The four questions are summed to create a scale ranging from 0 to 16. A high score in the variable Anglo Contact indicates greater contact with Anglos while a low score indicates greater contact with Latinos. I am agnostic as to the effect contact with Anglos will have on Latino levels of political alienation and trust.

Finally, the variables Income, Age, Education, Gender (Female), and U.S.-Born are included as controls. The variable Income is a measure of household income before taxes and takes on a seven-point scale, ranging from 0 (less than $10,000), 1 ($10,000–$20,000), 2 ($30,000–$40,000), and so on up to 7 (more than $60,000). Age is a continuous variable, which ranges from 18 years to 95 years. Education is based on a six-point scale, with 0 for "grade school or less," 1 for "some high school," 2 for "high school graduate," 3 for "some college," 4 for "completed college," and 5 for "postgraduate work." The variable Female is a dichotomous variable with 1 for "female" and 0 for "male." In general, individuals who are young and have low levels of education and income tend to display higher

TABLE 10.2.  Determinants of political alienation and political trust among
Latinos in Connecticut

| | Political alienation | | Political trust | |
|---|---|---|---|---|
| | Model I | Model II | Model III | Model IV |
| | Political powerlessness | Political normlessness | Trust Washington | Trust Hartford |
| Latino representation | .115** (.050) | .154*** (.051) | .216*** (.052) | .313*** (.053) |
| Political participation | −.308** (.121) | −.004 (.117) | −.120 (.121) | .106 (.124) |
| Attention to politics | .034 (.068) | .013 (.068) | −.041 (.069) | .047 (.071) |
| Anglo contact | −.040† (.026) | −.019 (.026) | .027 (.026) | −.013 (.027) |
| U.S. born | −.096 (.188) | .070 (.190) | .551*** (.192) | .489*** (.195) |
| Income | .009 (.045) | .001 (.044) | .018 (.045) | .031 (.046) |
| Age | −.008 (.006) | −.002 (.006) | .003 (.006) | .006 (.007) |
| Education | −.058 (.070) | −.062 (.070) | .149** (.070) | .107† (.069) |
| Female | −.055 (.169) | −.110 (.170) | .131 (.171) | .035 (.173) |
| Chi-square | 16.04 | 10.98 | 44.15 | 59.03 |
| Significance | .066 | .276 | .000 | .000 |
| Sample size | 493 | 493 | 493 | 493 |

Two-tailed probabilities: $^{†}p \leq .075$, $^{*}p \leq .05$, $^{**}p \leq .01$, $^{***}p \leq .001$

levels of alienation and distrust.[29] The evidence is mixed with regard to women. In some instances, women are found to be less politically alienated and more trusting of government.[30] Finally, the variable U.S.-Born is dichotomous, with 1 for respondents who were born in the U.S. and 0 for those born in other countries, including Puerto Rico. U.S.-Born can be taken as a measure of political socialization, with those born in the United States having more exposure to American government and institutions. A familiarity with American politics may lead to lower levels of alienation and distrust, or it may increase these sentiments.[31]

I run four models, one for each orientation, e.g., (Model I) Political Powerlessness, (Model II) Political Normlessness, (Model III) Trust Washington, and (Model IV) Trust Hartford. Since the dependent variables are measured on an ordinal scale, ordinal-logistic analysis is used to estimate the models. Table 10.2 has the results of the four models.

The political empowerment thesis is overwhelmingly supported by the data. The variable Latino Representation exerted a consistent and statistically significant influence across the four models. In other words, Latinos who perceived that the Hispanic population was inadequately represented in Connecticut felt more politically alienated and distrustful of the government in Washington and Hartford. While most of the other variables have signs in the theoretically expected direction, overall, the predictors are not as robust as anticipated. In Model I, only two additional variables were associated with political powerlessness—Political Participation and Anglo Contact. An increase in political participation lowered feelings of powerlessness, while increased contact with Anglos also had an empowering effect on respondents. The link between political participation and efficacy are well established by political behavior research.[32] Less clear are the reasons why increased contact with whites reduces feelings of political powerlessness among Latinos. One possibility is that the expansion of social networks leads to an exchange of ideas and values causing Latinos and whites to share similar political outlooks.

In Model II, only Latino Representation was associated with feelings of political normlessness. None of the other political factors or individual demographic characteristics were significant. Turning to Models III and IV, there is greater consistency across the predictors. Again, a perception that Latinos lacked political representation in Connecticut lowered trust in Washington's and Hartford's government. Additionally, respondents who were born in the U.S. were more distrustful of government, as were respondents with higher levels of education. At first glance, these findings may seem contradictory to theoretical expectations. Yet, they are consistent with the findings of Hibbing and Theiss-Morse who note that respondents who were most politically informed were also those who were most cynical toward certain political institutions.[33]

A politically alienated and distrustful Latino citizenry does not have to be a permanent feature of Connecticut's political landscape. The models demonstrate that increasing the number of Latino elected officials in the state can lower Latino levels of political alienation and distrust. I conclude this chapter by discussing strategies Latinos and other minorities can pursue to achieve political empowerment.

## A Strategy for Latino and Minority Political Empowerment

This chapter began by noting that one of the major goals of the black, Chicano, and Puerto Rican civil rights movement was the political empowerment of their people through the election of black and Latino representatives. It was believed that the presence of minorities in decision-making political institutions would change the policy priorities of government and in turn begin the process of uplifting black and Latino communities—political empowerment would result in social and economic empowerment. But beyond the change in legislative priorities, which has occurred, researchers began to note a change in the political behavior and orientations of minority constituents. Black and Latino empowerment were also associated with psychological uplift. Constituents having a descriptive representative participated in politics at higher rates, were more interested and informed about politics, and felt more efficacious and trustful toward government. The substantive and symbolic effects of descriptive representation are well supported by social science research and are reinforced by the data presented in this chapter. Latinos in Connecticut who believe there is a lack of Latino representation in the state feel more politically estranged and distrustful.

Since descriptive representation plays a key role in the empowerment of a minority community, what strategies can Latinos in and outside of Connecticut pursue to increase the number of Latinos holding elective office? Historically, the state's Latino community, most of which is of Puerto Rican ancestry, has successfully mobilized around ethnicity to promote voter registration, mobilization, and political representation.[34] As citizens, Puerto Ricans are not faced with what is perhaps the biggest obstacle for electoral participation facing other Latinos. As a result, Puerto Ricans in the state have long been politically active and viewed as a key constituency to the Democratic Party. The dramatic growth in the Puerto Rican population after the 1950s enabled the group to make significant political inroads into school boards, city councils, state legislatures, and recently the mayor's office in Hartford. The meteoric rise in the number of Puerto Ricans holding elective office in the state has been impressive and cannot be understated. Yet Latinos in Connecticut, like minorities elsewhere, remain grossly underrepresented relative to their population. With a population numbering over 320,000, Latinos make up 9.4 percent of the state's population,[35] yet none of the 36 state senators are Latino and only five Latinos are in the 151-member state house.

Because many Latino activists and advocacy organizations believe that the lack of empowerment is the result of low rates of electoral participation, most continue to advocate empowerment through citizenship, voter registration, and mobilization. Yet even if Latino voter turnout was similar to that which is found in Puerto Rico, existing electoral structures, namely the single-member plurality (SMP) system, will limit their ability to make further political gains. Under the SMP system the candidate that garners a plurality of the votes in a single district wins the office. This electoral arrangement has been found to disadvantage ethnic and racial minorities since majorities, usually whites, through racial polarized voting are able to defeat the minorities' preferred candidate, typically a black or Latino candidate.[36] Only when a sufficient number of minorities reside in a particular district and voter turnout is high are they able to elect "one of their own." To counter the effects of racially polarized voting, civil rights organizations have advocated the creation of majority-minority districts. This is a solution that has produced gains but has resulted in many unintended consequences that in the long run erode minority gains.[37] In fact, the drawing of racialized districts is now considered an "exhausted" strategy and in many instances, because of residential dispersion, it is impossible to draw a "Hispanic" or "black" district.[38]

In order to produce legislative bodies that are truly representative of America's diversity, I believe it is critical that ethnic/racial and social minority civil rights organizations and advocacy groups begin advocating on behalf of alternative voting systems such as proportional representation (PR), cumulative voting (CV), and limited voting to name a few. Under PR systems, which are common in Western Europe, officials are elected at-large in multimember districts according to the proportion of the vote their party receives. For example, if a particular party garners 30 percent of the vote, then it wins 30 percent of the seats in a representative body. PR systems essentially break the two-party monopoly and guarantee political minorities will obtain some level of representation.[39] Under a CV system, elections are held at-large and voters can cast as many votes as there are seats. If they chose to do so, they can cast all of their votes to a single candidate or divide them as they please. This method was employed in Alamogordo, New Mexico, in 1987. The result was the election of a Latino to the city council. The last time a Latino had held a seat in the city council was 1968.[40] Limited voting employs a similar logic to CV, but voters have a lesser number of votes to cast than seats open. These and other alternative electoral systems are widely used by other democracies and when applied in multiracial/multiethnic settings in the United States have dramatically increased the number of black, Latino, and female representatives to office.[41]

Whether minorities and majorities have the political will to advocate and implement these strategies remains an open question. What is clear is that the status quo and the old strategies will leave many groups, in particular ethnic/racial minorities, politically marginalized and disengaged, a situation that not only adversely impacts minority communities but democracy as a whole. For groups that have a long history of discrimination and political exclusion, the presence of minority representatives signals to constituents that their voices are being heard, that the system is legitimate and should be supported.[42] The absence of minority representatives also sends a powerful signal, suggesting the converse is true.

## Notes

1. Lani Guinier, *The Tyranny of the Majority* (New York: The Free Press, 1994).

2. Hanna F. Pitkin, *The Concept of Representation* (Berkeley: University of California Press, 1967).

3. David Lublin, *The Paradox of Representation: Racial Gerrymandering and Minority Interests* (Princeton, NJ: Princeton University Press, 1997).

4. Bernard Grofman, Lisa Handley, and Richard G. Niemi, *Minority Representation and the Quest For Voting Equality* (Cambridge: Cambridge University Press, 1992).

5. David T. Cannon, *Race, Redistricting, and Representation: The Unintended Consequences of Black Majority Districts* (Chicago: University of Chicago Press, 1999); Carol M. Swain, *Black Faces, Black Interests* (Cambridge, MA: Harvard University Press, 1993); Claudine Gay, "The Effect of Black Congressional Representation on Political Participation," *American Political Science Review*, 95 (2001): 589–602; Katherine Tate, *Black Faces in the Mirror: African Americans and Their Representatives in the U.S. Congress* (New Jersey: Princeton University Press, 2004); Lawrence Bobo and Franklin D. Gilliam, "Race, Sociopolitical Participation, and Black Empowerment" *American Political Science Review* 84 (1990): 377–393.

6. Gabriel Almond and Sidney Verba, *Civic Culture* (Boston: Little Brown, 1965).

7. Stephen C. Craig, Richard G. Niemi, and Glenn E. Silver, "Political Efficacy and Trust: A Report on the NES Pilot Study Items," *Political Behavior* 12 (1990): 289–314.

8. Mary Jo Reef and David Knoke, "Political Alienation and Efficacy," in *Measures of Political Attitudes*, ed. John P. Robinson, Phillip R. Shaver, and Lawrence S. Wrightsman, (New York: Academic Press, 1999).

9. Jack Citrin and Christopher Muste, "Trust in Government," in *Measures of Political Attitudes*, ed. John P. Robinson, Phillip R. Shaver, and Lawrence S. Wrightsman, (New York: Academic Press, 1999).

10. Edward N. Muller, Thomas O. Jukam, and Mitchell A. Seligson, "Diffuse Support and Antisystem Political Behavior: A Comparative Analysis," *American Journal of Political Science* 26 (1982): 240–264.

11. Arthur H. Miller, "Political Issues and Trust in Government: 1964–1970," *American Political Science Review* 68 (1974): 951–972; Jack Citrin, "Comment: The Political Relevance of Trust in Government," *American Political Science Review* 68 (1974): 973–988.

12. Stephen M. Weatherford, "Mapping The Ties That Bind: Legitimacy, Representation, and Alienation," *Western Political Quarterly* 2 (1990): 251–276.

13. James D. Wright, *The Dissent of the Governed: Alienation and Democracy in America* (New York: Academic Press, 1976).

14. Ada W. Finifter, "Dimensions of Political Alienation," *American Political Science Review* 64 (1970): 389–410; Robert E. Agger, Marshall N. Goldstein, and Stanley A. Pearl, "Political Cynicism: Measurement and Meaning," *The Journal of Politics* 23 (1961): 477–506.

15. Samuel Long, "Personality and Political Alienation among White and Black Youth: A Test of the Social Deprivation Model," *Journal of Politics* 40 (1978): 433–457; Paul R. Abramson, "Political Efficacy and Political Trust Among Black Schoolchildren: Two Explanations," *Journal of Politics* 34 (1972): 1243–1269; Harrell Rodgers, "Toward Explanation of the Political Efficacy and Political Cynicism of Black Adolescents: An Exploratory Study," *American Journal of Political Science* 18 (1974): 257–282.

16. James S. House and William M. Mason, "Political Alienation in America, 1952–1968," *American Sociological Review* 40 (1975): 123–147; Jack Citrin, Herbert McClosky, J. Merrill Shanks, and Paul M. Sniderman, "Personal and Political Sources of Political Alienation," *British Journal of Political Science* 5 (1975): 1–31.

17. Finifter, "Dimensions of Political Alienation."

18. Jack Citrin and Donald Philip Green, "Presidential Leadership and the Resurgence of Trust in Government," *British Journal of Political Science* 16 (1986): 431–453.

19. Susan Howell and Deborah Fagan, "Race and Trust in Government," *Public Opinion Quarterly* 52 (1988): 343–350.

20. Glenn F. Abney and John D. Hutcheson, "Race, Representation and Trust," *Public Opinion Quarterly* 45 (1981): 91–101.

21. Guinier, *The Tyranny of the Majority.*

22. Bobo and Gilliam, "Race, Sociopolitical Participation, and Black Empowerment."

23. Adrian Pantoja and Gary Segura, "Does Ethnicity Matter? Descriptive Representation in Legislatures and Political Alienation Among Latinos," *Social Science Quarterly* 84 (2003): 441–460.

24. Matt A. Barreto, Gary Segura, and Nathan Woods, "The Mobilizing Effect of Majority-Minority Districts on Latino Turnout," *American Political Science Review* 98 (2004): 65–75; Matt A. Barreto, Rodolfo Espino, Adrian Pantoja, and Ricardo Ramirez, "Selective Recruitment or Empowered Communities? The Effects of Descriptive Representation on Latino Voter Mobilization," paper presented at the *Annual Meeting of the American Political Science Association,* 2003.

25. Samuel Popkin, *The Reasoning Voter, Communication and Persuasion in Presidential Campaigns* (Chicago: University of Chicago Press, 1991).

26. Tate, *Black Faces in the Mirror.*

27. Finifter, "Dimensions of Political Alienation."

28. Susan Welch and Lee Sigelman, "Getting to Know You? Latino-Anglo Social Contact," *Social Science Quarterly* 81 (2000): 67–83.

29. Finifter, "Dimensions of Political Alienation."

30. Citrin et al., "Personal and Political Sources of Political Alienation."

31. John R. Hibbing and Elizabeth Theiss-Morse, *Congress as Public Enemy: Public Attitudes Toward American Political Institutions* (Cambridge: Cambridge University Press, 1995).

32. Stephen J. Rosenstone and John M. Hansen, *Mobilization, Participation, and Democracy in America* (New York: Macmillan, 1993).

33. Hibbing and Theiss-Morse, *Congress as Public Enemy.*

34. José E. Cruz, *Identity and Power, Puerto Rican Politics and the Challenge of Ethnicity* (Philadelphia: Temple University Press 1998).

35. Daniel Vasquez, "Latinos in Connecticut," Mauricio Gastón Institute for Latino Community Development and Public Policy, University of Massachusetts Boston, www.gaston.umb.edu.

36. Keith Reeves, *Voting Hopes or Fears? White Voters, Black Candidates and Racial Politics in America* (New York: Oxford University Press, 1997).

37. Kenny J. Whitby, *The Color of Representation, Congressional Behavior and Black Interests* (Ann Arbor: University of Michigan Press, 2000).

38. Swain, *Black Faces, Black Interests.*

39. Douglas J. Amy, *Real Choices, New Voices, The Case for Proportional Representation in the United States* (New York: Columbia University Press, 1993).

40. Richard Engstrom, Delbert A. Taebel, and Richard Cole, "Cumulative Voting as a Remedy for Minority Vote Dilution: The Case of Alamogordo, New Mexico," *Journal of Law and Politics* 5 (1989): 469–497.

41. Amy, *Real Choices, New Voices.*

42. Guinier, *The Tyranny of the Majority.*

# 11 Latino Politics in Connecticut: Between Political Representation and Policy Responsiveness

José E. Cruz

This chapter looks at the role Latinos play in Connecticut politics. It focuses on the state's three largest cities, which also have the highest Latino concentrations in the state: Bridgeport, Hartford, and New Haven. The chapter looks at the population and socioeconomic characteristics of Latinos as well as the level of representation the group has achieved. Examining the 2000 presidential campaign assesses the role that Latinos at the mass level play in the politics of the state. The role that the leadership segment of the community plays is assessed by reviewing the 2001 redistricting process as well as through interviews with Latino elected officials and activists. The interviews were semistructured and included twelve out of the twenty-seven Latino elected officials in the state and three key figures in the politics of the community: Yolanda Castillo, Américo Santiago, and Edwin Vargas Jr. Castillo and Vargas have been actively and prominently involved in Hartford and state politics for over two decades. Santiago was a state representative from Bridgeport for many years and was a crucial player in the 1991 and 2001 redistricting processes. Of the elected officials, six representatives were from New Haven, three from Bridgeport, and three from Hartford. Their names have been withheld at their request. The interviews were conducted by e-mail and over the phone during the winter of 2003 and the summer and fall of 2004.

## Population

Latinos are the fastest growing ethnic group in the state. Between 1992 and 2000, their numbers increased by 40 percent, from 228,000 to 320,000 residents. The growth of the state's total population during this period was only 6 percent, from 3.2 to 3.4 million. In 1992 Latinos were 7 percent of the state's residents. By 2000, they constituted 9 percent of the total and outnumbered blacks by more than ten thousand residents.[1] Of course, these figures are only heuristics that facilitate the analysis. In reality, Latino numbers could be higher than the census count. At the same time, their demographic edge over blacks may be less sharp given that Latinos can be of any race. Because the racial identity of Latinos is potentially fluid, the cultural and political implications of their greater numbers vis-à-vis African Americans are not clear-cut. In most cases, national origin and cultural background will trump race but this cannot be taken for granted.

The majority of Latinos in Connecticut in 2000 were Puerto Rican, accounting for 61 percent of the total. The second largest Latino group was "other," at 30 percent, consisting of a mixture of Central and South American nationals. South Americans and Central Americans were 10 and 4 percent of the total respectively. The second and third largest national subgroups were Mexicans (7 percent) and Colombians (3 percent). In 2000, three cities had the largest concentrations of Latinos in the state: Bridgeport, Hartford, and New Haven. Together these cities encompassed 38 percent of the state's Latino residents.

In Bridgeport, Latinos were 32 percent of the population in 2000. African Americans were 31 percent of the total and whites 45 percent. The proportions in Hartford were 41 percent Latino, 38 percent black and 28 percent white. Only in New Haven were Latinos the minority group in 2000—21 percent compared to 37 percent for blacks and 44 percent for whites. All cities, however, were minority-majority. The Central and South American element in these cities was weak in 2000. In all three, Puerto Ricans commanded solid majorities—72 percent in Bridgeport, 80 percent in Hartford, and 67 percent in New Haven, making Latino politics, in effect, Puerto Rican politics. Even though Colombians were the third largest subgroup in the state, their presence in these cities in 2000 was not strong. Cuban and Dominican numbers were higher across the board and Peruvians had a stronger presence in Hartford.

The presence of other non-Latino ethnic groups in the state was also weak in 2000. Massachusetts, for example, had more than twice as many non-Latino immigrants admitted as Connecticut did in that year. Of the 11,346 immigrants admitted to Connecticut during this period, the three largest groups were from India, China, and Haiti. Together they numbered only 1,635 or 14 percent of the total admitted.[2] The groups included in the racial categories recognized by the Census Bureau—American Indians, Alaska Natives, Asians, Native Hawaiians, and Other Pacific Islander—constituted minuscule proportions of the population both discretely and at the aggregate level. Nationals from Jamaica, Trinidad and Tobago, and other, non-Hispanic Caribbean countries were demographically significant but overall their numbers were still small—31,413 or 0.9 percent of the state's population in 2000.[3] Residents claiming a West Indian ancestry in 2000 numbered 49,435, including citizens and noncitizens, or 1 percent of the total state population.[4] The pattern was similar at the local level. West Indians had a significant presence but only relative to the very small numbers of other groups. In Bridgeport, only 8,375 residents claimed a non-Hispanic, West Indian ancestry in 2000, while 9,531 did so in Hartford. In New Haven, 2,367 made the claim. The West Indian proportion of the total population was 6, 8, and 2 percent in the three cities respectively.[5]

The impact of this demographic reality on Latino politics is not difficult to discern. For the most part, the political dynamic that shapes Latino political action revolves around conflict and cooperation between Latinos, African Americans, and whites. Given the strong demographic presence of Puerto Ricans amongst Latinos, the panethnic category is not much more than an artificial label for what are essentially Puerto Rican politics. Without Puerto Rican participation and support, Latino candidates in the state have very little chance of success. In New Haven, for example, Alderman Jorge Perez, of Cuban origin, has relied on Puerto Rican supporters to win election to office. In Bridgeport, the election of Peruvian Felipe Reinoso to the state legislature was possible as a result of a largely Puerto Rican effort; an initiative to establish a Peruvian political action committee was modeled after the Puerto Rican Political Action Committee of Connecticut, now defunct. In Hartford, Dominican Elvis Tejada was a stalwart of the Democratic Town Committee for the Third District—a Puerto Rican stronghold; the city's Club Duarte has benefited from the political advice of Puerto Rican political activists.

## Unemployment, Income, Poverty, and Educational Status

While in 2000 unemployment in Connecticut and at the national level was about the same, in Bridgeport, Hartford, and New Haven it was higher than at the state and national level. The city with the largest concentration of Latinos, Hartford, also had the highest unemployment rate. In the three cities the unemployment rate for Latinos was higher than the city and state rates. In Bridgeport, Latinos did slightly better than blacks but worse than whites. In New Haven, they did just as well as blacks but considerably worse than whites. Surprisingly, in Hartford, both whites and blacks had a slightly higher unemployment rate than Latinos but the difference was not significant.

Bridgeport had the highest median household income in 2000, yet it was 35 percent lower than the median for the state. The largest difference was in Hartford with a 54 percent gap. Half of New Haven residents received $0.56 for every dollar received by state residents as income. Latinos were worse off than blacks and whites in terms of median household income. While for whites in Bridgeport this indicator was only $5,000 higher than the amount for Latinos, in Hartford and New Haven the differences were $9,000 and $10,000 respectively.

The local poverty rate for individuals in Hartford was up to four times the rate for the state. For Latinos the poverty rate was 11 percentage points higher than the rate for whites in Bridgeport compared to a 16-point difference in Hartford and a 17-point gap in New Haven.

Of residents 25 years and over in the state, 84 percent had at least a high school diploma and 31 percent had a bachelor's degree or higher. Only 57 percent of Latinos had a high school diploma (with 29 percent of them being men, and 28 percent of them being women), and 13 percent had a bachelor's degree or higher. In terms of educational attainment, Hartford had the worst record: 61 percent of its residents 25 years and over had a high school degree or higher and only 12 percent had a college degree. The respective shares for Bridgeport were 65 and 12 percent. New Haven had the best record with a 74 percent rate for high school graduation or higher and a 27 percent rate for bachelor's degree or higher. Latinos in this cohort performed terribly in two of the three cities: only 29 percent were high school graduates in Bridgeport. In Hartford and New Haven the rates were 26 and 60 percent respectively. As for a bachelor's degree or higher, Latinos in all three cities had a low record of achievement. In Bridgeport, only 4 percent met the mark and in Hartford the rate was 3 percent compared to 10 percent for New Haven (see Table 11.1).

These statistics point to a stark reality of socioeconomic under-performance and disadvantage. But they also indicate very clear areas for policy intervention. The differences between the three cities would require different types of interventions but given the predominantly Puerto Rican character of the Latino population the differences would probably be more logistical than programmatic. Further, even though citywide indicators do not match Latino performance, it is likely that even place-based interventions focused on minority needs would benefit Latinos.

## Political Representation

According to the 2001 edition of the National Directory of Latino Elected Officials, Connecticut had twenty-six elected officials of Latino background—five state representatives, seventeen municipal officials, and four school board members. By 2004 the total was twenty-seven with the addition of one state representative from Waterbury as a result of the 2001

TABLE 11.1. Unemployment, income, poverty, and educational attainment among Latinos in Connecticut, 2000

| | Connecticut | Bridgeport | Hartford | New Haven |
|---|---|---|---|---|
| Unemployment | 4% | 6% | 9% | 8% |
| Whites | 3% | 5% | 9% | 0.06% |
| Blacks | 7% | 8% | 9% | 10% |
| Latinos | 7% | 7% | 8% | 10% |
| Median household income | $54,000 | $35,000 | $25,000 | $30,000 |
| Whites | $58,000 | $36,000 | $29,000 | $34,000 |
| Blacks | $35,000 | $33,000 | $25,000 | $26,000 |
| Latinos | $32,000 | $31,000 | $20,000 | $24,000 |
| Poverty status in 1999 | | | | |
| Whites | 5% | 15% | 23% | 18% |
| Blacks | 19% | 19% | 29% | 28% |
| Latinos | 25% | 26% | 39% | 35% |
| Population 25 years and over | | | | |
| high school graduate or higher | 84% | 65% | 61% | 74% |
| bachelor's degree or higher | 31% | 12% | 12% | 27% |
| High school graduates (25 years and over) | | | | |
| White males | 27% | 15% | 12% | 24% |
| White females | 29% (56%) | 17% (32%) | 13% (25%) | 26% (50%) |
| Black males | 36% | 15% | 16% | 38% |
| Black females | 33% (69)% | 19% (34%) | 22% (38%) | 32% (70%) |
| Latinos | 29% | 14% | 13% | 29% |
| Latinas | 28% (57%) | 15% (29%) | 13% (26%) | 31% (60%) |
| Bachelor's degree or higher (25 years and over) | | | | |
| White males | 21% | 5% | 7% | 15% |
| White females | 18% (39%) | 4% (9%) | 6% (13%) | 16% (31%) |
| Black males | 8% | 3% | 2% | 6% |
| Black females | 9% (17%) | 3% (6%) | 3% (5%) | 9% (15%) |
| Latinos | 6% | 2% | 1% | 4% |
| Latinas | 7% (13%) | 2% (4%) | 2% (3%) | 6% (10%) |

*Note:* In the columns with two figures, the percentage in parentheses denotes the combined rates for males and females.
*Source:* U.S. Census Bureau, American Fact Finder, Census 2000 Data Sets. http://www.census.gov

redistricting process. This number represents 13 percent of statewide and congressional officials, which relative to the Latino proportion of the state population (9 percent), constitutes a robust index of political representation. The same is not true relative to specific levels of government or in reference to the total number of elected officials in the state. For example, at the congressional level, in 2003 parity in representation would have meant one black and one Latino elected official. The Congressional delegation from the state, however, was 100 percent white even though whites were 82 percent of the population. Similarly, to achieve parity in the state legislature, the Latino delegation should consist of seventeen members rather than the six that held seats in 2004. In 1999, in the state's 203 boards, commissions, committees, and councils Latino representation was 2.7 percent—a mere fifty-four members out of 1,997 throughout the state.[6]

In 2004, the Democratic Party controlled the state legislature. In the Senate, twenty-one out of thirty-six officials were Democrats; the balance in the House was ninety-five Democrats and fifty-six Republicans. According to Democratic House Speaker Moira K. Lyons, the distinguishing characteristic of the Democrats was their willingness to welcome talented and hard-working people into the party. For his part, Robert Jackson, chair of the Hartford Democratic Town Committee in 1999, defined the Democratic Party as "the party of the people," while describing it as an organization that derived its strength from its respect for "individual differences, and [the celebration] of diversity, tolerance and fellowship."[7]

In 2004, the views of Latino elected officials concerning their relationship to the Democratic Party were mixed. According to some, at the state level the Democratic Party took Latinos for granted. In one instance, the party's attitude toward Latinos at that level was described as one of "benign neglect." In contrast, one Latino elected official in Bridgeport declared that the party was doing well by Latinos, that "positions have opened up. More can be done but we have to look out for ourselves. Make sure there is a quid pro quo." In New Haven, a former elected official stated, "They are definitely aware of our voting potential and have made some attempts to reach out. But nothing really substantial."

A counterpoint to this is provided by the existence of the Latino and Puerto Rican Affairs Commission, created in 1994 to review the impact of state legislation on the Latino community in the state and to encourage the political participation of Latinos in government. The commission also highlights the accomplishments and contributions of Latinos to the welfare of the state.[8] While the commission is dismissed by some as elitist and ineffective, it constitutes a valuable resource. For example, according to a survey conducted for the commission in April and September of 2000, Latinos in Connecticut do not consider themselves well represented politically. Most survey respondents were unable to name any Latino elected officials. Communication from elected officials was considered to be poor.[9] A follow-up survey, conducted in May 2002, indicated dissatisfaction with the number of Latino representatives at the state and local level as well as declining membership with the Democratic Party. While affiliation with the Republican Party remained constant between 2000 and 2002, the proportion of unaffiliated voters increased almost just as much as the proportion no longer identifying as Democrats. Just as in the 2000 survey, respondents in 2002 were not well informed about Latino politics in the state and did not consider themselves well represented.[10] These findings are only a small sample from a welter of information and data gathered by the commission that are invaluable both for political and policy purposes.

In the three cities that are the focus of this analysis, Latinos were 20 percent of municipal officials even though they were 31 percent of the combined population of the three localities. In a city-by-city comparison the contrast was not as stark except for Hartford—15 percent of municipal officials there were Latino compared to 41 percent of the population; in Bridgeport the ratio was 26:32 and in New Haven it was 19 to 21 percent. With the election of Eddie Pérez as Hartford's mayor in 2001 an important precedent was set. But this accomplishment did not bring the community that much closer to parity. Underrepresentation at the city level was compounded by party attitudes toward Latinos that ranged from slightly supportive to neglectful.

## The 2000 Political Campaign

When Elizabeth Dole came to Connecticut to campaign on behalf of George Bush she claimed that the former Texas governor would "attract more women to politics, cut taxes, and bolster education." Perhaps because her audience consisted of chamber-of-commerce types, not once did she mention Latinos or their issues in her remarks to the two hundred or so people present at the Metro-Hartford Chamber of Commerce luncheon where she spoke early in February of 2000.[11] Despite the audience, the omission was odd given the belief by most Republicans that under Bush the party was more likely to appear attractive to Latinos.

On Super Tuesday this belief did not pan out. Blacks and Latinos chose Al Gore eight to one. In the state's primary Gore beat Bill Bradley 55 to 42 percent. John McCain beat Bush, in part because of Bush's appearance at Bob Jones University, an anti-Catholic stronghold in the South. Gore won by securing the support of core Democratic constituencies, such as Latinos and blacks, whereas McCain was able to succeed because of his support among independents, crossover Democrats, liberals, prochoice voters, and Catholics.[12]

In May there was a reference to Latinos in the electoral campaign but it did not come from any of the candidates. Writing for the *Washington Post*, economist Robert Samuelson noted that during the 1990s the majority of immigrants were of Latin American origin (51 percent in 1997), half of whom settled in five metropolitan areas. One-third of that half (4.6 out of 14.3 million) did so in the New York—New Jersey—Connecticut metro area. According to the Census Bureau the Connecticut share of that third was 245,000. Samuelson mentioned that any plan to limit immigration by skill level would discriminate against Latinos, but his concern was mostly background noise during the campaign and less than a blip on the Connecticut radar screen.[13]

Near the end of June, Bush appeared to be moving ahead of Gore in the state. According to a poll conducted by Quinnipiac University, Bush managed to cut Gore's 9-point advantage down to a virtual tie, with Gore standing at 43 percent support and Bush at 42 percent.[14] Yet Gore was fundamentally concerned with winning New Jersey and preventing Bush from capturing the South.[15] Therefore, no special attention was given to the state and least of all to Latinos.

At the Republican convention in Philadelphia in July, Latinos were 3 percent of the delegates and at least one Latino delegate was from Connecticut. According to Santa Mendoza, most Republican delegates were ultraconservative. While in the state she was considered conservative, at the convention she fell within the moderate ranks.[16] Such small presence went largely unnoticed. At the Democratic convention, held in August in Los Angeles, the only trace of a Connecticut reference was when Ted Kennedy praised the choice of Joseph Lieberman for the vice-presidential slot as a clear sign of the party's commitment to civil rights.[17]

Early in September, Connecticut's eight electoral votes were counted among the 223 from states considered to be solidly or leaning for Gore. In 1996 Clinton captured 53 percent of the vote in the state and Gore was not expected to do any worse. "Solid Gore" is how the *Houston Chronicle* described the state at the same time that it declared the Northeast a write-off for Bush. Latinos were not regarded as a factor one way or the other.[18]

In October, there was a marginal reference to Connecticut's Latinos during the annual Supreme Court Preview at the College of William and Mary in Williamsburg, Virginia. "The only proposition that gained general assent," wrote Michael McGough in the *Pittsburgh Post-Gazette*, "had to do not with the philosophy of the next Supreme Court nominee but with his or her ethnicity. Liberal or conservative, pro-life or pro-choice, the next appointee is likely to be Hispanic."[19] And the prediction that circulated at the conference was that Judge José Cabranes, from Connecticut, would be tapped in the event of a Gore victory.

During the final stretch of the presidential race, the Democratic Party sent out special mailings to Hispanics in districts spread from southern California to Connecticut reminding them to support their Democratic congressional candidates, a reflection of the fact that the battle for control of the House of Representatives was as fierce as the battle for the White House.[20] Overall, however, as a loyal constituency in a heavily Democratic state, Latinos were pretty much ignored. In the end, Latinos gave Gore 61 percent of their votes nationally compared to 35 percent for Bush. In Connecticut, Gore's 242,544-vote advantage over Bush highlighted the insignificance of the Latino contribution to his victory.[21]

The perception of the majority of Latino elected officials interviewed for this chapter concerning the importance of Latinos in presidential races differs significantly from the reality described above. Two representatives expressed diametrically opposite views on this question. One thought that Latinos did not play an important role in the 2000 election while the other was convinced that their role had been very important. "I don't think we had ever seen as much attention being paid to the Latino voting bloc as the 2000 presidential election," the latter said. "It seemed like everyone wanted to speak Spanish publicly." In between these poles, the range of opinion included perceptions of limited impact as well as of marginality. The reasons offered for the limited electoral importance of Latinos ranged from small numbers, to insufficient organization, to low turnout rates. But it seems that the biggest impact Latinos have at this level is behind the scenes, through the work of and machinations between Latino and Democratic Party elites.

## Redistricting

After the dust of the 2000 election settled, redistricting emerged as a critical issue. In fact, as early as 1996 the Connecticut General Assembly determined that it was important to set guidelines for redistricting following the 2000 census because of an anticipated loss of a congressional seat. In 1997, the Task Force on Redistricting recommended, among other things, that a redrawing of district lines should minimize splitting towns except if this was necessary to meet the one-person, one-vote principle. The task force also suggested that coterminous lines between assembly, senate, and congressional districts were desirable but probably impractical.[22]

In 2001, a reapportionment committee composed of members from the senate and the assembly met several times to organize the redistricting process. The committee agreed to hold 5 public hearings throughout the state. Four were held in Bridgeport, Hartford, and New Haven. In keeping with the recommendations of the Task Force on Redistricting, the committee set targets of 151 districts for the assembly and 36 for the senate, taking into account population shifts and proportionality while respecting town lines. The public was encouraged and expected to submit redistricting proposals no later than August 31. The Reapportionment Committee's plan was due at the state legislature before September 15, the deadline for General Assembly action on the new districts. This deadline was not met and a new deadline of November 30 was set. At this point the responsibility for the plans was given to a reapportionment commission, which was constituted by the members of the committee plus one new member. The commission approved plans for the senate and the assembly before the new deadline, but the plan for Congress had to wait for approval until December 21, 2001.[23]

In March, State Representative Ken Bernhard from Westport wrote, "It will be an interesting and lengthy process to devise districts that are balanced in size and yet comply with the multitude of constitutional requirements that the courts have set in their judicial rulings over the years. Fortunately in Connecticut, the process may prove to be one of the most bipartisan and least acrimonious of any state in the nation."[24]

The transcripts of the public hearings held in Bridgeport, Hartford, and New Haven provide ample evidence to support Bernhard's prediction. During the first hearing, held in New Haven, representatives of the Latino community in Connecticut pleaded in the most polite terms for widespread access to information, for representation within the re-apportionment committee, and for districts that would give Latinos the opportunity to elect their own representatives. In Bridgeport, committee members were asked to work with local organizations, to keep Latino communities together, to use the redistricting process to facilitate parity in representation, and to provide information in English and Spanish. In one instance, committee members were told that due to past experiences Latino voters had little confidence in the political process. To restore that confidence all they had to do was to draw lines that gave Latinos the opportunity to vote for Latino representatives. During the last hearing, held in Hartford, committee members were chastised for not providing sufficient information to the public and for not heeding the request for racial and ethnic diversity within the committee.

These criticisms were offered with civility and were met with nothing but silence. Interestingly, the only Latinos to testify in Hartford were Lucía Gómez, a representative from the Puerto Rican Legal Defense and Education Fund (PRLDEF) based in New York City; Héctor Riollano, president of the Hispanic Democratic Club in Waterbury; Yolanda Castillo from the Connecticut Latino Voter's Rights Committee (CLVRC), who, even though a local Hartford resident, spoke in general terms on behalf of Latinos throughout the state; and Américo Santiago from Bridgeport, who spoke on behalf of the Fair Redistricting Partnership for the State of Connecticut, a group representing Latinos and African Americans. Unlike in New Haven and Bridgeport, no Latinos from Hartford spoke on behalf of their community in the city.

On July 17, the Latino Voting Rights Committee and the Committee for Fair Redistricting in the state of Connecticut presented redistricting maps to the reapportionment committee, including a plan for congressional districts. On August 23, the NAACP joined in and boundaries for 4 state senate districts were proposed—two for Hartford and one each for Bridgeport and New Haven—that concentrated black and Latino residents in order to increase the likelihood of minority representation in the state senate. A similar plan was presented for the state assembly. According to Yolanda Castillo, cochair of the CLVRC, "it is our goal to work with the Reapportionment Committee to make sure that this plan is given serious consideration and to recognize Latinos/as increased opportunity in Connecticut's democracy."[25]

In 1991, Latinos worked in concert to influence the redistricting process in the state. State representatives Juan Figueroa and Edna Negrón, from Hartford, and Américo Santiago, from Bridgeport, spearheaded the effort. According to Santiago, there was no collaboration with African Americans during that first round.[26] Yet, both Latino elected officials and the community came strongly together. With the assistance of PRLDEF as well as the Connecticut Civil Liberties Union, 3 demographically split assembly districts were turned into 4 with a solidly Latino demographic composition.

In 2001, the reapportionment commission took Latino proposals seriously and the effort was successful in a different way. This time around, Latinos were able to craft a broader coalition that included African Americans and other non-Latinos. The assistance of PRLDEF was once again critical. In the state assembly, results were mixed, while at the state senate level the initiative was not as successful, largely due to the unwillingness of the black incumbent in District 2 for Hartford, Eric Coleman, to relinquish his Latino constituency. Overall, results were positive. The community went from five to six state representatives as a result of the creation of a Latino district in Waterbury and representation was solidified in New Haven with the transformation of the 59th district from an influence to a majority Latino district.

## Prospects

To achieve parity in representation and policy responsiveness in Connecticut, Latinos must overcome significant hurdles. Party support for Latino candidates is inconsistent and often limited to advice and encouragement.

Financial support is typically minimal and too often nonexistent. Perhaps because local races are relatively inexpensive, lack of access to financial resources was mentioned as a significant challenge only by one out of twelve elected officials interviewed. At the state and congressional level the story is quite different. For example, after the consolidation of her district and that of Democrat James Maloney (5th and 6th), Congresswoman Nancy Johnson, a well-established representative with a twenty-year incumbency, spent $3 million in the November 2002 election to keep her seat.[27] Raising that kind of money is no doubt a significant challenge, even for a long-term incumbent. Yet, none of my interviewees mentioned money when asked about challenges at the state level. Instead, Latino elected officials think that it is more difficult to "get people to believe in themselves," to increase registration and turnout, to persuade voters that Latino candidates are qualified and trustworthy, to develop a statewide political strategy, to muster enough confidence to participate, and to manage conflict among elites.

The majority of respondents agreed that coalition building was important for political success at the state and local level but only three elected officials believed that it was a requirement. One indicated that there was no group that could be considered a natural ally. In his view, coalitions were important but only if their agendas were clearly defined. For another, veterans and senior citizens were the most important coalition partners while another mentioned local unions, nonprofit organizations, and the clergy. According to one elected official, coalition building was detrimental when it was not controlled by Latinos but engineered instead by "non-Hispanics, which recruit a few Hispanic leaders that will not question or challenge their agenda." Only three elected officials out of twelve believed that coalition building was a requirement for political success and of these only one mentioned African Americans as Latinos' most important partner. The view from Hartford, while not necessarily representative, was quite interesting. According to one Latino elected official there, success in 2003 was the result of efforts by a Democratic-Republican-Green coalition. When asked who was the most important coalition partner of Latinos in the city, the answer was: "It is hard to say. Usually people think blacks but a number of us are a little doubtful. It will depend on the situation. Right now Puerto Ricans can pick and choose because the [Puerto Rican] mayor is strong."

When asked if there was a systematic effort on the part of Latino elected officials to coordinate and share resources, ideas, and strategies among themselves, the most common answer was "no." In some cases, information sharing and consultation between individuals, limited efforts at the local and state level, and collaboration with black elected officials were acknowledged, but a lack of systematic attempts to develop a cohesive network of representatives with a clearly defined agenda was a commonly recognized feature. Information in this regard was not consistent. Some respondents declared categorically that no coordination efforts existed, while others suggested that there was an initiative underway to coordinate plans and develop a statewide strategy.

During the summer of 2004, Mayor Eddie Pérez confirmed publicly the existence of a statewide initiative—the Hispanic Democratic Caucus. According to Yolanda Castillo, the caucus began meeting in April 2004 and was composed of Latino elected officials and community leaders. The genesis of this effort can be placed at the end of the 2000 presidential campaign when Eddie Pérez negotiated with former Senate Majority Leader George Jepsen the establishment of a statewide Latino advisory group within the Democratic Party as a condition for continued Latino political support.[28] As of June 2004 the caucus had 3 objectives: to help elect John Kerry to the presidency, to elect a Latino to a statewide position, and to provide technical assistance and training to potential candidates to increase the number of Latino elected officials throughout the state.[29] By the end of October, Latinos obtained a charter for the caucus within the Democratic National Committee, effectively turning it into a pressure group within the party. On October 29, 2004, at a meeting held in New Haven, the group formally established a fundraising arm dubbed the Juntos ["together"] Political Action Committee of Connecticut.

Every single informant mentioned a different set of obstacles to using his/her position to benefit Latinos through public policies. These included lacking the voting power to institutionalize policy changes, the demands of other constituents, budgetary constraints, lack of mass-level support for policy goals, and patronage that excluded Latinos. Of twelve officials, only five mentioned fiscal constraints.

What do Latinos need to do to move ahead politically in Connecticut? According to informants, at the state level they need to make state agencies more accountable to the community, make the Democratic Party accept Latinos as credible candidates, seek such high-level positions as state treasurer and lieutenant governor, develop a cohesive network among elected officials, provide voter education in schools beginning at the elementary level, educate voters and support community self-help initiatives, and strike a balance between identity politics and inclusiveness. At the city level, political and civic leaders need to pursue a Latino-centered agenda, the community needs more visibility, and elected officials need to promote economic development projects, occupy more positions of leadership within the party, have a real presence within the community, be clear to their constituents about the limitations of their offices, make only promises than can be kept, understand that the community is diverse, and work jointly with other elected officials to assemble legislative majorities that will support a Latino agenda.

This smorgasbord of ideas hardly constitutes an agenda and even less does it represent a strategy for action. This is particularly troubling because Connecticut seems to be following the pattern in other states whereby Latinos achieve political representation but are not able to address the basic needs of the community. Once in office Latino representatives provide a voice for their constituents, some services, and sporadic redistributive measures, but they seem unable to impact the socioeconomic status of Latinos as a whole. In Connecticut this is true in terms of indicators such as unemployment, income, and poverty status. One important reason for this failure is the absence of a unified policy agenda and strategy. It is true that Hartford's mayor has publicly committed himself to increase homeownership from 25 to 30 percent and to add five hundred new or renovated housing units each year during the five-year period from 2004 to 2009.[30] But his is not a unified policy strategy for Latinos in the state.

On the positive side, the concerns expressed by informants should be part of ongoing deliberations among Latino elected officials and community leaders throughout the state. The Hispanic Caucus and its political action committee promise to provide both a forum and a vehicle for concerted efforts. As of November 2004, the target for action appeared to be the 2006 gubernatorial election. The appointment of Edwin Vargas Jr. as the Latino coordinator for outreach for the prospective gubernatorial candidacy of Connecticut Attorney General Richard Blumenthal had by then provoked a flurry of manoeuvres from Latino elites statewide vying for positions within the campaign. In the event of a Blumenthal victory these positions would serve as springboards for political appointments. In consonance with the goal of securing a statewide post for a Latino, prominent caucus members also began to lobby for the position of Secretary of State on the ballot.[31]

Whether this jockeying for position is matched by a serious and systematic agenda-setting process remains to be seen.[32] In light of the Hartford experience of the early 1990s, in which the lack of a policy strategy prevented the Puerto Rican political action committee from transforming political representation into policy responsiveness, current players need to know what they want to accomplish policy-wise and how to do so, before rather than after they find themselves in positions of power.[33] In this regard history should not repeat itself, especially in the more favorable context provided by a higher level of representation and a more powerful and respected Puerto Rican mayor in Hartford. In 2004, that context gave

Latino elites increased political capital. Still missing was a realistic strategy that paid attention not just to the goal of increased Latino political representation but also to the objective of policy responsiveness to Latino needs.


## Notes

1. U.S. Department of Commerce, *Statistical Abstract of the United States, 1996*, Table 35, http://factfinder.census.gov/bf/_lang=en_vt_name=DEC_2000_PL_U_QTPL_geo_id=04000US09.html accessed 8/1/03.

2. U.S. Department of Commerce, *Statistical Abstract of the United States, 2002*, Table 9.

3. U.S. Census Bureau, http://factfinder.census.gov/servlet/DTTable?_ts=86695083350, accessed 11/12/03.

4. U.S. Census Bureau, http://factfinder.census.gov/servlet/DTTable?_ts=86694999254, accessed 11/12/03. Non-Hispanic West Indian ancestry included Bahamian, Barbadian, Belizean, Bermudan, British West Indian, Dutch West Indian, Haitian, Jamaican, Trinidadian and Tobagonian, U.S, Virgin Islander, West Indian, and Other West Indian.

5. U.S. Census Bureau, http://factfinder.census.gov/servlet/DTTable?_ts=86694999254, accessed 11/12/03.

6. Office of the Secretary of the State of Connecticut, *Gender and Racial Diversity on Connecticut State Appointive Bodies, 1999* (March, 2000), pp. ii, iii.

7. Edward C. Sembor, *An Introduction to Connecticut State and Local Government* (Lanham, MD: University Press of America, 2003), 31.

8. Connecticut Office of Legislative Management, *Legislative Guide* (2000), 168.

9. Center for Research and Public Policy, *Latino Socio-Economic Study* (Connecticut General Assembly, Latino and Puerto Rican Affairs Commission, September 2000), 10.

10. Center for Research and Public Policy, *Third Latino Socio-Economic Study* (Connecticut's General Assembly's Latino and Puerto Rican Affairs Commission, November 15, 2002), 15, 21.

11. "Campaign 2000/Campaign Report," *The Boston Globe*, February 18, 2000, A28.

12. William Goldschlag with Thomas M. DeFrank, Timothy J. Burger, Richard Sisk, Helen Kennedy, and Marty Rosen, "Bush & Gore Flatten Foes Start to Eye Each Other and Big Day In November," *Daily News*, March 8, 2000, 3; Scott Shepard, Ken Foskett, "Gore, Bush take Georgia in 'Sea-to-Sea' Victory Romp; Democrats' Focus Turns Quickly to General Election; Campaign 2000," *Atlanta Journal and Constitution*, March 8, 2000, 1A.

13. Robert J. Samuelson, "Ignoring Immigration," *Washington Post*, May 3, 2000, A23.

14. B. Drummond Ayres Jr., "The 2000 Campaign: Campaign Briefing," *New York Times*, June 22, 2000, A28.

15. Judy Keen, "Signs Point to Tight Presidential Race, More Than Half the Votes in Electoral College Are up for Grabs," *USA TODAY* June 21, 2000, 1A.

16. Michael Kranish, "Campaign 2000, The Republican Convention, GOP Delegates; Discord Replaced by Desire to Win; Conservatives, Moderates Put Aside Differences," *Boston Globe*, July 31, 2000, A10.

17. David Von Drehle, "Rallying the Faithful for Gore; Bridging the Divide Between Old, New Democratic Parties," *Washington Post*, August 16, 2000, A1.

18. Alan Bernstein, R. G. Ratcliffe, and Bennett Roth, "Gore, Bush in Electoral Dead Heat; Midwest Shapes Up as Decisive Region," *Houston Chronicle*, September 3, 2000, A1.

19. Michael McGough, "Supreme Speculation," *Pittsburgh Post-Gazette*, October 1, 2000, E1.

20. Adam Clymer, "The 2000 Campaign: The House; Parties Wrestle to the Wire for a Majority in the House," *New York Times*, November 6, 2000, A28.

21. "Election: 2000 The Presidency," *St. Louis Post Dispatch*, November 8, 2000, 2.

22. Stewart MacWilliam Crone, *An Analysis of Potential Connecticut Congressional Redistricting*, (master's thesis, University of Connecticut, 1999), 7.

23. Minutes of Reapportionment Committee and Reapportionment Commission, Connecticut State Legislature, http://www.cga.state.ct.us/red/asp/RedistMinutes.asp, accessed 8/13/2004.

24. Ken Bernhard, "Redistricting Is the Next Complex Political Issue," http://www.bernhard.westport.ct.us/issues/Redistricting0301.html, accessed 8/13/04.

25. "NAACP Connecticut Chapter and the Connecticut Latino Voting Rights Committee Announce Joint Connecticut Senate Redistricting Plan," *Democracy Works*, http://www.democracyworksct.org/redistrictpress3.shtml, August 23, 2001.

26. Interview with Américo Santiago, September 22, 2004.

27. Sembor, *An Introduction to Connecticut State and Local Government*, 3.

28. Interview with Edwin Vargas Jr., October 29, 2004.

29. Interview with Yolanda Castillo, September 21, 2004; Abelardo King, "Eddie Pérez: 'En lugar de pedir limosnas, debemos sentarnos donde está el poder . . . y eso debemos conquistarlo con nuestro propio esfuerzo,'" *La Voz Hispana de Connecticut*, June 3–17, 2004, 3.

30. Brian McQuarrie, "Hartford's 'Strong Mayor' Has a Tough-Guy Past," *Boston Globe*, January 20, 2004, B1.

31. Interview with Edwin Vargas Jr., November 3, 2004.

32. Not to mention the fact that it may come to naught. As of this writing, there was a strong possibility that Senator Christopher Dodd would be the gubernatorial candidate in 2006. In that case, "he's the 800-pound gorilla, and he would be a great candidate and a fantastic governor," declared George Jepsen, reflecting the sentiment of most party leaders that Dodd would be their first choice in the gubernatorial race. See Raymond Hernandez and Alison Leigh Cowan, "Three Senators Consider Bids for Governor," *New York Times*, November 6, 2004, A1.

33. See José E. Cruz, *Identity and Power: Puerto Rican Politics and the Challenge of Ethnicity* (Philadelphia: Temple University Press, 1998), 176–193.

# 12 Immigrant Incorporation among Dominicans in Providence, Rhode Island: An Intergenerational Perspective

José Itzigsohn

## Introduction

This chapter describes and analyzes the ways in which Dominicans are becoming part of American life in the particular context of Providence.[1] Through this analysis, it also addresses contemporary debates on the processes and patterns of immigrant incorporation in multiethnic American cities. Immigrant incorporation is a multigenerational process, and for that reason the focus of the analysis is the differences and commonalties in perceptions and social practices between first- and second-generation Dominican Americans.

The Dominican community in Providence presents us with a good case to study the intergenerational process of becoming part of U.S. life. Providence is a small New England city. As many towns in this region, its economic base used to be manufacturing—indeed the Blackstone Valley was the cradle of the industrial revolution in America. Yet the manufacturing base is ever dwindling, although it has not completely disappeared. The economic base of the city has moved toward medical and educational services and tourism. These sectors do not offer the same economic mobility opportunities that the old manufacturing sector used to provide. Furthermore, employment in the remaining manufacturing sector is mediated by temporal employment agencies that do not offer job security or work-related benefits such as health care and pensions.

Providence is—and has been—a city of immigrants. In the past, the main immigrant groups were of European origin, mainly Italian, Irish, and Portuguese. There has been also an important presence of Cape Verdean immigrants in the city and region. According to the last census, Providence is today a minority-majority city. The minority groups are mostly of immigrant origin, mainly from Latin America and the Caribbean, East Asia, and Africa. Immigrants enter the labor market in the remaining manufacturing sector and low-skill services. Hence, they have lower incomes and higher rates of poverty. There is, however, a stratum of professionals, concentrated particularly in human services.

For the last four decades, the Dominican Republic has been one of the largest senders of immigrants to the United States. This is a remarkable fact given the small population of the country. Yet it is estimated that between 10 and 15 percent of the Dominican population lives abroad, most of it in the United States. Dominican immigrants are concentrated in New York, but—as with other immigrant groups—the trend has been toward residential dispersion. Providence is one of the sites of Dominican settlement, both in secondary migration from New York and in direct migration from the Dominican Republic.

Dominicans began to arrive to Providence in the late 1960s, but their numbers grew very quickly in the last two decades, a result of the recurrent economic crises that the Dominican Republic has suffered since the early 1980s. Today, Dominicans are leaving a powerful mark in all areas of life in Providence. In the economic realm, Dominican businesses are the main force behind the revitalization of the south side of the city. In the political realm, there are several Dominican elected officials and Dominicans have played an important part in the election of the current mayor of the city. In the cultural realm there are several Dominican media outlets, there is a large Dominican festival, and Dominican presence is felt in the sounds of everyday life in the city.

Dominicans are present in all neighborhoods of the city—with the possible exception of the east side, which is mostly white upper-middle class—but they are particularly concentrated and identified with the south side and its landmark avenue, Broad Street. This has also been the area of residential concentration of the black population of the city. This geographical proximity between Dominicans and African Americans opens possibilities for personal and cultural exchange but also for the development of intergroup competition. This is particularly notorious in the political sphere where Dominican candidates have competed with and often displaced African American office holders.

It is in this context that this chapter examines generational commonalities and differences in incorporation. The data show a curious pattern. Surprisingly, the attitudes of the first generation and the second generation toward several aspects of U.S. life are very similar. Yet their social practices differ widely. It is the argument of this chapter that the attitudes should be understood in the context of the social practices of the generational groups and that even if the two generations appear to have similar worldviews, their meaning is different. Furthermore, the data suggest that in contemporary multiethnic, multiracial cities, where minorities are majorities and there is no one hegemonic group but a multitude of different racial, ethnic, and immigrant groups, incorporation into American society depends on strong ethnic identities and the formation of panethnic solidarities. Finally, the chapter argues that in order to understand the immigrant experience it is necessary to explore seriously the race/class nexus.

## Immigrant Incorporation

The large-scale migration of the last four decades has created considerable popular and academic debates over the place of immigrants and immigration in American society. Are immigrants becoming part of the American mainstream, shedding those social and cultural traits that differentiate them from the receiving country? Are immigrants developing their own separated cultures and social networks beside mainstream society? Are they developing a counterculture as a result of exclusion and discrimination?

In the academic field, the analysis of the complex pattern of second-generation incorporation has been framed by two main positions. A group of scholars posits a bumpy path toward assimilation. These scholars argue that new immigrants will eventually follow the path of previous European immigrant groups in experiencing upward mobility and shedding their main identity and cultural traits and replacing them with a symbolic ethnicity concentrated around the celebration of holidays, festivals, and the eating of particular "Americanized" ethnic foods. Celebration of symbolic differences will take place in a context of a more or less homogeneous national identity. Proponents of this view argue that this scenario may take time—they point out, appropriately, that the process of assimilation of European immigrant groups was rougher and longer than it may appear looking at it from the vantage point of its results—but they find evidence that new immigrants are slowly shedding their distinctive characteristics and assimilating to American life.[2] This scenario, however, discounts the pervasive racialization that immigrants experience as well as the structural changes that have taken place in the American economy in the last decades.

A second vision argues that there are reasons to expect that the incorporation stories of new immigrants are different from those of previous immigrant waves. This theoretical position, known as segmented assimilation, posits that two structural elements are different between the current and previous wave of immigrants.[3] One difference is that of race: new immigrant groups are racialized upon their arrival to the United States and hence suffer discrimination and exclusion. Defendants of the first view argue that European immigrants were also racialized upon migration. While this is indeed true, it is questionable whether contemporary immigrants of color can follow the strategy of inclusion in whiteness that European groups followed. The other key difference is that the social structure of a service-based economy does not offer the same mobility opportunities that a manufacturing-based economy offered. As a result, the incorporation paths of immigrants depend to a large extent on the context of reception as well as on the resources of the immigrant community.

Segmented assimilation theorists further argue that the form of acculturation experienced by the children of immigrants is a key mediating variable in explaining and predicting their position in the U.S. stratification order. Portes and Rumbaut distinguish three different paths of acculturation among the children of immigrants, each path leading to different outcomes in terms of upward mobility.[4] The first path, named consonant acculturation, entails the adoption of middle-class values and norms, the shading of ethnic particularities, and the development of symbolic ethnicity. This path leads to upward mobility. Opposed to this path is dissonant acculturation, which involves the adoption of the outlooks and views of the underclass and the rejection of mainstream norms of hard work and investment in education. The expected outcome in this case would be downward assimilation and incorporation into a rainbow underclass.[5] The third path is dubbed selective acculturation and it involves the maintenance of strong ethnic identities and community attachments. The last path allows first-generation parents to exercise social control over the decisions of their children, and in this way it helps poor immigrant families avoid downward-leveling pressures that children find in inner-city public schools.

The segmented assimilation thesis accounts well for the current structural inequalities of American society, and it proposes a helpful classificatory scheme to understand the diversity of immigrant experiences. Yet the data suggest that the boundaries between the three paths described above are more porous than the current formulation of the theory allows. Furthermore, an exclusive focus on the structure of immigrant communities to explain patterns of mobility fails to address the economic and social reforms necessary to guarantee equal opportunity to poor immigrants and nonimmigrants alike.

An important issue in contemporary studies of immigrant incorporation is that of the development of transnational linkages and institutions by immigrant groups. An important body of research shows that immigrants do not shed their contacts with their country of origin. On the contrary, they develop extensive networks that connect the immigrant communities with their places of origin. Those linkages are important in the construction of the immigrant's symbolic worlds and have also been shown to have utilitarian uses for both local development and personal mobility.[6] It is not clear, though, to what extent those networks subsist beyond the first generation. Are the children of immigrants keeping their attachments and ties with the country of their parents or are their lives focused in their country of birth?

The Dominican experience in Providence provides an excellent opportunity to reflect on some of the questions raised by these theoretical efforts just described. Upon arrival to the United States, most Dominicans are racialized as nonwhites, sometimes seen as black, and sometimes seen as Latinos/as (which in this case is equivalent to a brown, mixed-race racial category). They also enter the labor market in its lower ranks in spite of the fact that many of them have skills and educational credentials; these assets are not recognized in the new society. The majority of the children of Dominican immigrants attend public schools in poor urban neighborhoods, which are not the best conduit for upward mobility. Hence the experience of Dominicans can help us understand the likely paths of incorporation of minority immigrants in the contemporary multiethnic/multiracial American urban centers.

Hernández has shown the structural poverty that affects the New York Dominican community, and Lopez has described the experience of exclusion felt by immigrant youngsters—particularly young men—in the public schools of that city.[7] It is not my present goal to replicate their analysis here. For the purposes of this chapter the available evidence indicates that the experience of Dominicans in the Providence labor market and in public schools resembles the New York situation—with the understandable differences between a major urban center and a small city.

The entry point of this chapter for the reflection on incorporation paths is an exploratory empirical analysis of the generational differences—or commonalties—in attitudes and practices among three generational groups of Dominican Americans: Dominican and American born as well as the group known as the one-and-a-half generation, that is, people who were born in the Dominican Republic but who spent their formative years in the United States. We will explore generational differences along several dimensions of the immigrant experience: the perceptions of American society, their language preferences, and their relationships with other ethno-racial groups. We will also explore commonalties and differences in transnational visions and practices.

The analysis presented in this chapter is part of a larger project to analyze issues of immigrant incorporation, identity, and transnationalism through an in-depth study of Dominican migration to Providence. The arguments developed here are based mainly in the analysis of a survey conducted in Providence among first- and second-generation Dominican Americans.[8] The survey attempted to capture the second-generation visions and practices

TABLE 12.1. Dominican intergenerational patterns: Description of the sample
(the numbers in parentheses represent column percentages)

| | Second generation | First and a half generation | First generation |
|---|---|---|---|
| Female Gender | 67 (66.3) | 19 (59.4) | 35 (70.0) |
| Age | 23.3 | 24.5 | 35.7 |
| Mean years of education | 13.0 | 13.3 | 13.4 |
| Married or living with partner | 7 (7.0) | 10 (31.3) | 28 (56.0) |
| Respondent has children | 33 (32.7) | 11 (34.4) | 35 (70) |
| Number of respondents | 101 | 32 | 50 |

but purposefully included a number of first-generation respondents in order to conduct a comparative study. There is no list of Dominican second-generation people, so it was not possible to conduct a random representative sample. In order to partially address this problem a list of second-generation people was composed through asking a large number of first- and second-generation residents. Out of this exercise a list of four hundred names emerged out of which one hundred were selected. Some of the selected names were in fact first-and-a-half-generation people, and for this reason I decided to include a small sample of first-and-a-half-generation respondents. The second-generation sample was completed through snowball sampling starting with the people who were randomly selected. The first-generation people were selected through snowball sampling with multiple points of entry. The final sample included 101 second-generation Dominican Americans, fifty first-generation immigrants, and thirty-two first-and-a-half-generation respondents.

The resulting sample, hence, cannot be considered to be representative, but its results can hint at some trends in incorporation that need to be further researched using other sources of data. The interpretation of the quantitative results will be complemented with qualitative data. In the frame of this project the author has conducted numerous qualitative interviews (this stage is still ongoing). The author has also participated—and participates—in the social and political life of the immigrant community, and this participation generates insights that helps put the survey answers in their socioeconomic and cultural contexts.

Table 12.1 presents some basic demographic characteristics of our sample. The sample consists of a majority of female respondents. It is also a sample of young people who are not married or living with partners. Yet in spite of the small percentage of people married or living together, one-third of second-generation respondents report having children. There are, as could be expected, important differences between the generational groups in age and marital status, with the first-generation sample being older and including a larger number of married people. The three generation groups have relatively high mean years of education. Yet the median for the second and first-and-a-half generation is twelve years of education, and the range for the second-generation sample goes from eight to eighteen years, indicating that our sample includes people who have completed graduate education as well as high school dropouts.

The remainder of the chapter presents the results of the sample and interpretative analyses. It is organized in three broad sections. The first one analyzes the experiences of incorporation of Dominicans in Providence, focusing on (1) their perceptions of mainstream society, (2) their language preferences, and (3) their relationships with other ethnic groups. The second section looks at transnational visions and practices among first- and second-generation immigrants. Finally, we look at the perceptions of belonging of immigrants and their children.

## Experiences of Incorporation

### Perceptions of Mainstream Society

Dominicans are leaving their mark on every area of Providence life. It could be argued that they have encountered in the city a welcoming place, where they developed a strong community and began to insert themselves in political and economic life. Yet the first generation finds itself working mainly in manufacturing and low-skill service jobs that do not pay very well. The second generation goes through a public school system that has all the well-known problems of urban school systems. There are, however, certain signs of upward mobility. A small segment within the first generation has moved toward the professional and managerial ranks, and those parents that can afford it try to send their children to private schools. Many of the youngsters find a way to higher education, particularly in the state university or in the community colleges. The Dominican community in Providence is a hard-working one but finds itself mostly in the ranks of the working poor.

Moreover, a look at the political and economic elites of the city and the state will show that they are still mainly white elites. The exclusive neighborhoods of the city are still mainly white neighborhoods, and wealth and ethno-racial belonging are correlated in space. So on the one hand immigrants and their children encounter a place that is friendly to their community life and social and political initiatives, but they also face an ethno-racial stratification system that is visible to the eye on all the areas of power. What kind of perception of American society does this situation elicit in first- and second-generation Dominican Americans?

TABLE 12.2. Dominican intergenerational patterns: Incorporation, by percentage (the numbers in parentheses represent column percentages)

| Generation<br><br>Perceptions of mainstream society | Second generation | First and a half generation | First generation |
|---|---|---|---|
| In the U.S. there is discrimination against minorities in economic opportunities | 91 (90.1) | 26 (81.3) | 41 (82.0) |
| Minorities in America have to work twice as hard as whites to get to the same place | 79 (78.2) | 23 (71.9) | 45 (90.0) |
| Dominicans suffer the same kind of discrimination as African Americans | 56 (55.4) | 21 (65.6) | 24 (48.0) |
| Dominican Americans can do as well as white Americans | 72 (71.3) | 17 (53.1) | 38 (76.0) |
| Language preferences | | | |
| Language you prefer to speak most of the time** | | | |
| English | 45 (44.6) | 11 (34.4) | 4 (8.0) |
| Both languages | 44 (43.6) | 18 (56.3) | 18 (36.0) |
| Spanish | 12 (11.9) | 3 ( 9.4) | 28 (56.0) |
| Language you speak with your closest friends** | | | |
| English | 54 (53.5) | 15 (48.4) | 4 (8.0) |
| Both languages | 40 (39.6) | 13 (41.9) | 25 (50.0) |
| Spanish | 7 (6.9) | 3 ( 9.7) | 21 (42.0) |
| In what language do you hope to raise your children** | | | |
| English | 1 (1.0) | 0 (0.0) | 0 (0.0) |
| Both languages | 90 (89.1) | 31 (96.9) | 33 (66.6) |
| Spanish | 10 (9.9) | 1 (3.1) | 17 (34.0) |

*Chi-square significant at $p < .05$ level.
**Chi-square significant at $p < .01$ level.

Answers to this question are addressed in Table 12.2. The table shows the responses to a number of statements concerning American society.[9] The table presents a clear picture. Large majorities of the sample think that there is discrimination in economic opportunities for minorities in the United States and that minorities have to work twice as hard as whites to get to the same place. Furthermore, a majority of the sample, although not as large as in the previous two items, believes that Dominicans suffer the same kind of discrimination as African Americans.

In all these dimensions of perceptions of mainstream society there are small differences in the answers of the different generations. For example, while only 78.2 percent of the second generation agrees with the statement that minorities have to work twice as hard as whites to get to the same place, a full 90.0 percent of the first generation agrees with this statement. Yet a chi-square analysis indicates that these differences are not statistically significant. This means that while there are differences between the answers of the different generational groups, from the vantage point of view of statistical analysis, the perceptions of mainstream society are basically similar across the generational groups.[10]

These results indicate the presence of a strong critical vision among all groups of the Dominican American community and at least a partial tendency to identify their experience with that of African Americans. First- and second-generation people are conscious of the racialization they experience and of the barriers that race imposes in U.S. society. Scholars working within the segmented assimilation paradigm relate critical views of American society with the experience of dissonant acculturation and lower mobility expectations. Some evidence would suggest that this is the case. There is a problem of school drop-out among Dominican youngsters. In the course of this research project we have also encountered people receiving public assistance and heard stories about relatives who have been deported or are in jail or in juvenile detention. These are undeniable realities. Yet the picture in this case seems to be more complicated.

The last row of the top half of Table 12.2 indicates that a large majority of second- and first-generation Dominican Americans—71.3 and 76.0 percent respectively—thinks that Dominicans can do as well as whites. It is important to note, though, that close to 30 percent of these generational groups do not agree with this statement. Interestingly, a much smaller percent—53.1 percent—of the first-and-a-half-generation respondents agree with this statement. These differences, however, are not statistically significant. Second-generation respondents were asked what job they expected to hold at age 35, and all the respondents had clear ambitions of professional or managerial jobs or of being owners of their own businesses. We do not know how realistic are those hopes, but qualitative interviews indicate that the recognition of racial barriers does not lead people into a rejection of expectations of mobility. On the contrary, the children of working-class immigrants attempt individual mobility strategies that may not include joining Ivy League schools or the upper ranks of management but entail obtaining associate or professional degrees that open doors to employment in human services or lower-level management in tourism or financial services. In the framework of this project we have interviewed several people that pursue this avenue of mobility, including teenage mothers. We have also encountered cases that have made it against all odds to the ranks of prestigious schools and high-paid professional jobs.

What these data indicate is that the lives of the immigrant working class are precarious, and there is not a clear boundary between those who try to make it through selective acculturation and those that fall into the more marginal sectors of U.S. society. Those boundaries cross the same neighborhoods, families, and sometimes even the same lives. The main problem of the immigrant working poor is one of lack of good schools, good job opportunities, and avenues for acquiring skills.

In some cases, the recognition of discrimination and structural barriers leads to participation in political and social organizations and collective actions directed to open up the system of inequality. This usually takes the form of participation in community nonprofit organizations, political mobilization, or church-based social activism. Those who attempt to deal with the predicament of exclusion through collective action are a minority, but it is always the case that political and social activists are a minority in each community. Yet through collective mobilization Providence's Dominican Americans have been able to elect some representatives and— acting together with other minorities and working people—channel some resources to their neighborhoods and defend some forms of public services, particularly in access to health for poor children.[11]

Segmented assimilation theorists, after appropriately alerting us to the importance of the structural characteristics of American society, shift focus onto the particular characteristics of the ethnic communities to explain their trajectories. The focus shifts to the formation of dense ethnic communities as an avenue for social mobility. The social control afforded by these enclaves shields the second generation and serves to transmit over time an immigrant ethos of thriftiness and strong drive to succeed. It is indeed the case that there are certain types of community structures that are more conducive to social control and to the transmission of parental goals. Yet I would argue that rather than focusing on the characteristics of the immigrant communities, it is necessary to shift the attention to the political and economic reforms that would create a level playing field in which immigrants would enjoy equal opportunity to succeed. While certain community structures may increase the likelihood of individual mobility, collective mobilization carries the possibility of creating a more level playing field for minority communities.

## Language Preferences

One of the most bitter debates on the issue of immigrant incorporation is that of language. Anti-immigrant groups have been recurrently trying to pass English-only initiatives as if the status of English as the language of the land was in danger. Yet most research indicates that the children of immigrants are learning English as previous generations have done.

This work looks at three indicators of language acquisition: the language people use to speak with their closest friends,[12] the language people prefer to speak, and the language people want to raise their children in. These results are presented in the bottom part of Table 12.2. The table presents expected differences and an important coincidence between the generations.

About half of second- and first-and-a-half-generation people speak in English most of the time with their friends, and about 40 percent speak in both languages. Similarly, about 45 percent of second generation people prefer to use English most of the time and a similar percentage prefers to speak in both English and Spanish. So people who were born or grew up in the United States are mainly English monolingual in their daily life or bilingual, and only a very small percentage prefers to use or regularly uses Spanish. Predictably, the first-generation respondents tend to prefer or to use mainly Spanish. Yet it is important to point out the relatively large percentages that feel comfortable in both languages. So here we see the process of cultural change at work. There are undeniable differences in the language practices of first and second generations, and those differences are visible and obvious to anyone who cares to share the experiences of immigrants. Yet a majority of first- and second-generation people hopes to raise children in both languages. While there are no differences here, one easily realizes that Spanish means in practical terms something very different for people from different generations. For first-generation people Spanish is their main language, and growing up in a first-generation household means growing up with the parents' language all around. Second-generation people themselves may not be fully fluent in Spanish, and since they prefer to speak English most or an important part of the time, children do not grow up in a household where Spanish is prevalent. Then what is the reason for insisting on transmitting the language to the third generation—or at least stating that they would like to do that? For second-generation people Spanish is a marker of identity. The society that second-generation people encounter is one in which they may encounter discrimination, and, as shown earlier, immigrants and their children hold critical views of American society. Under these conditions, maintaining identity symbols like language is, to a large extent, a form of reactive ethnicity.

Yet there is more to this—at least stated—attempt of language retention. Second-generation people growing up in multiracial and multiethnic cities encounter a society with many groups coming from many places in the world, as is the case in Providence. It is clear what the mainstream is in terms of language and goals: the "American dream" of upward mobility. This is achieved in English, and second-generation immigrants know it and know the language. On the other hand, there is not one central ethno-racial group. Whites are perceived as the mainstream, but they may be no more than the largest among many groups, none of which constitutes the absolute majority. In this case, the preference for language maintenance is also a form of preserving group and individual identity in what is basically a plural city where there is no clear group to "assimilate" into.

## Multiethnic Relations

The multiracial/multiethnic character of Providence poses the question of the relationships between different ethno-racial groups—an issue that is relevant not only for Providence. How do Dominicans relate to other ethno-racial groups in Providence? Particularly relevant for the city are Dominicans' relations with African Americans, with whom to a large extent they share urban space. Table 12.3 addresses this question. The table presents answers to questions concerning the relationships between Dominicans and whites, African Americans, and other Latinos.

The table shows a sort of common assessment between the generational groups concerning interethnic friendships. Less than half of each

TABLE 12.3. Dominican intergenerational patterns: Ethnicities, by percentage (the numbers in parentheses represent column percentages)

| Generation<br><br>Perceptions of relationships<br>with other ethno-racial groups | Second<br>generation | First and a half<br>generation | First<br>generation |
|---|---|---|---|
| Relations between white Americans and Dominicans are usually friendly | 43 (42.6) | 14 (43.8) | 22 (44.0) |
| Relationships between African Americans and Dominicans are usually friendly | 58 (57.4) | 18 (56.3) | 21 (42.0) |
| Relations between Dominicans and other Latinos are usually friendly | 68 (67.3) | 23 (71.9) | 40 (80.0) |
| Panethnicity | | | |
| Dominicans and Latinos/as are one and the same | 50 (49.5) | 16 (50.0) | 23 (46.0) |
| Latinos/a politicians represent the interest of Dominicans better than non-Latino/a politicians* | 52 (51.5) | 9 (28.1) | 19 (38.0) |
| When Latino/a political candidates run against non-Latino/a candidates Dominicans should vote for the Latino/a candidates because they are Latinos/as* | 16 (15.8) | 7 (21.9) | 17 (34.0) |

*Chi-square significant at $p < .05$ level.
**Chi-square significant at $p < .01$ level.

group thinks that relations between Dominicans and whites are usually friendly. Slightly more than half of the second-generation and first-and-a-half-generation respondents think the same about relationships between Dominicans and African Americans. More than two-thirds agrees that relationships between Dominicans and other Latinos/as are usually good. There are some intergenerational differences in the perceptions of inter-ethnic relations: the proportion of first-generation people who thinks that relationships with African Americans are usually good is smaller than the other two generational groups. On the other hand, a larger proportion of first-generation respondents think that relations with other Latinos/as are friendly. These differences, however, are not significant from a statistical point of view. What emerges is a sort of scale of closeness between Dominicans and other ethno-racial groups: Dominicans feel closest to other Latinos/as, somewhat close to African- Americans, and relatively distant from whites. This scale is shared by second-generation and first-and-a-half-generation respondents. First-generation respondents, on the other hand, feel the closest to other Latinos/as and feel equally distant from African Americans and whites.

The large proportion that feels closeness to other Latinos/as poses the question of the development of a panethnic consciousness. Dominicans share urban space and immigration experiences with other groups from Latin American and Caribbean origins. Although each group has a different history and there are important cultural differences between them, in the United States all people of Latin American origin are seen as being part of a common group and are often treated as such by governmental policies and initiatives, by civil society organizations, and by individuals. There is considerable evidence of the development of panethnic identities and panethnic social practices.[13]

Table 12.3 shows that about half of the three generational groups agree with the statement that Dominicans and Latinos are one and the same. One can look at this as evidence of the formation of panethnic consciousness, at least among important segments of the community—although it is necessary to point as well that a full half does not agree with the statement. In qualitative interviews emerges a sense of a layered identity: a strong sense of Dominican particularity, but also a sense of sharing something with other groups. It is a common occurrence in these interviews that when people are asked to define the commonalties with other Latinos they find themselves in a bind, as if it was something so self-evident to them that they never stopped to ask or think what is that unites the group. After thinking about this, respondents point to language and a vague notion of common culture or to common experiences of migration and the fact that other people perceive them as Latinos/as as the unifying elements. This panethnic layer of identity, to be sure, coexists with all sorts of stereotypes about people from other Latino/a groups.

The table also shows interesting generational differences in thinking about Latinos/as a political identity. Showing great political awareness, very few people would vote for a Latino/a candidate just because he/she is Latino/a, although first-generation people are more inclined to this type of automatic panethnic loyalty. Yet a larger proportion thinks that Latino/a politicians better represent the interests of Dominicans. And here there are a significantly larger percentage of second-generation people who think this way. The numbers point to the emergence of panethnicity as a political alternative for important segments of the community. To be sure, there are also an important segment of people who do not share this political identification, but what the data suggests is that for many first and second-generation Dominicans the Latino/a identity is part of their identification strategies and their everyday lives.

## Transnational Visions and Practices

Several recent studies have shown that Dominican immigrants build extensive networks between the immigrant communities in the United States and the Dominican Republic. Those linkages are embedded in the life of first-generation immigrants, and an important part of their resources and energies are devoted to transnational activities. Also, the Dominican Republic occupies an important place in the first-generation cultural frame of reference.[14] Little is yet known, however, to what extent those linkages and solidarities are transmitted generationally. Assimilation theory would expect second generations to break their identification and links with the country of origin. The following tables address this question. And they show something similar to what we saw in terms of incorporation. Different generational groups share similar transnational views, but differ in their transnational practices.

The upper part of Table 12.4 addresses transnational worldviews. What the table shows is large majorities of first- and second-generation people who share a transnational view. More than two-thirds agree that Dominican Americans are part of the Dominican nation and that they should help the Dominican Republic. There are larger proportions of first-generation people who agree with these views, and the differences are statistically significant, but the main difference is with people from the first-and-a-half generation rather than with second-generation people. There is a decline in terms of those who think that Dominican Americans should participate in Dominican politics, but 60.4 percent of the second-generation sample share this idea.

TABLE 12.4. Dominican intergenerational patterns: Transnationalism, by percentage (the numbers in parentheses represent column percentages)

| Generation | Second generation | First and a half generation | First generation |
|---|---|---|---|
| Transnational visions | | | |
| Dominican Americans are part of the Dominican nation** | 84 (83.2) | 20 (62.5) | 46 (92.0) |
| Dominican Americans should help the Dominican Republic | 83 (82.2) | 23 (71.9) | 46 (92.0) |
| Dominican Americans should participate in Dominican politics* | 61 (60.4) | 13 (40.6) | 35 (70.0) |
| Dominican Americans are as Dominican as those who live in the Dominican Republic | 62 (61.4) | 19 (59.4) | 39 (78.0) |
| Transnational practices | | | |
| Send money to family in the Dominican Republic** | 23 (22.8) | 11 (34.4) | 27 (54.0) |
| Invested in a house, land, or property in the Dominican Republic*[a] | 3 (3.0) | 4 (12.5) | 7 (14.0) |
| Member of a Dominican political party*[a] | 2 (2.0) | 3 (9.4) | 7 (14.0) |
| Member in social or sports clubs with ties to the Dominican Republic* | 8 (7.9) | 5 (15.6) | 11 (22.0) |
| Belonging | | | |
| The United States | 60 (60.6) | 14 (46.7) | 16 (32.7) |
| The Dominican Republic | 8 (8.1) | 1 (3.3) | 11 (22.4) |
| I feel equally at home in both countries | 30 (30.3) | 14 (46.7) | 22 (44.9) |

*Chi-square significant at $p < .05$ level.
**Chi-square significant at $p < .01$ level.
[a]The results of the chi-square test are problematic because more than 20 percent of the cells have expected counts lower than 5. I present them nonetheless to show the important differences between the generational groups in transnational practices.

Yet to what extent does this idea translate into social practices? The middle part of Table 12.4 looks at participation in several common transnational practices, and here the picture changes. A minority of people participates in the different activities shown in the table, with the exception of sending money to family in the Dominican Republic, which a majority of first-generation people do and a surprising quarter of second-generation people also reports as doing. Yet in terms of transnational practices we found important generational differences. Whether participation is high or low, first-generation people tend to participate much more than second-generation people in transnational social networks.

What we see is high transnational identification for the second generation but very little transnational participation. How can we understand this picture? Like all the coincidences between the generations, this has to be seen in its context. The meaning of transnational identification is simply different. Second-generation people adopt a transnational discourse as part of asserting their ethnic identity in the United States. Second-generation Dominicans have strong attachments to Dominicanness, but when they are asked to define it, is referred to as a heritage, pride in origin, rather than specific social practices. Dominican Americans use language, music, food, and celebrations as markers of identity. Yet their tastes in music and food and their language practices transcend the limits of the ethnic community, and their daily lives are often very similar to other youngsters from other racial and ethnic groups. Asked about their friends' ethnicity, 36 percent of second-generation respondents answer that most of their friend are Dominicans and 11 percent answer that most of their friends are Latinos. Yet 46 percent answer that their friends belong to all groups. Among the first-and-a-half-generation respondents, 63 percent answer that their friends belong to all groups. The same holds with regard to preferences for raising children in English and Spanish. What for first-generation people is an element of their daily life, for second-generation people is in part a form of reactive ethnicity and in part a way of asserting their uniqueness in a plural society where a strong group identity is important for many to forge a strong individual identity.

## Race, Class, and Incorporation

The results presented here show puzzling coincidences and differences between first and second-generation Dominican Americans. They coincide in many of their worldviews—such as in the desire to raise children in English and Spanish, a critical view of U.S. society, and a transnational attachment. Those worldviews are embedded in worlds of social practices that give them different meaning. The data shows that second-generation Dominican Americans prefer to speak English in daily life and do not engage in any significant way in transnational practices. The differences between the generations can be clearly seen in the bottom part of Table 12.4, which reports the responses to the question "which country most feels like home?" Sixty-one percent of second-generation people respond that they feel at home in the United States whereas only 33 percent of the first generation responds in that way. Important percentages of both generations indicate that they feel at home in both countries—45 percent of first-generation people. But what this table indicates is that the main referent for the formation of worldviews and practices for second-generation people is the United States.

It is in the context of multiethnic cities, neighborhoods, and schools and in the context of racialization that we need to understand the ethnic discourse of the children of immigrants. For them, the attachment to Spanish and to a transnational identity are part of asserting their place and identity in the United States. In contemporary multiracial/multiethnic cities and in conditions of social exclusion, the incorporation of the second generation entails the strengthening of ethnic, transnational, and—to some extent—panethnic identities. What do these results tell us about the process of immigrant incorporation?

From the point of view of assimilation theory, we can see that second-generation Dominican Americans choose to speak in English and see the United States as their home. Their everyday social practices do not differ much of those of their peers from other social groups. Yet they have critical views of American society and keep a strong attachment to their ethnicity and their country of origin. The modal pattern of incorporation of the second generation portrayed by the data seems to correspond to the selective acculturation path posed by segmented assimilation theory. Yet it is a more complex path than that theory would expect. It combines strong critical views of mainstream society with strong panethnic and transnational attachments as well as middle-class aspirations. Also the mobility trajectories of Dominican Americans in Providence—people who live in a similar context—include all the three scenarios described by segmented assimilation, sometimes within the same family.

To understand these experiences it is necessary to deepen the analysis of the race/class connection in contemporary American society and expose the structural barriers to mobility of the immigrant working poor as well as the inner workings of institutional racism. It is important to remember that the assimilation of European groups was finally achieved in the context of the massive postwar economic growth, with the opening of opportunities it created. It also coincided with the peak of the power of organized labor in this country, which forced a reduction in the income and wealth gaps in American society. Yet contemporary mass migration coincides with decades of increasing inequalities between haves and have-nots in the United States. It also takes place in a context in which pervasive institutional racism is hidden under a discourse of a color-blind society.

Furthermore, as in the past, there are important segments of public opinion that feel threatened by mass migration and mobilize against it. Huntington's recent book is a case in point.[15] The Harvard scholar takes issue with immigrants who keep their ethnic distinctiveness, arguing in particular against Mexican immigrants who allegedly refuse to shed their cultural distinctions, and affirms that Mexican culture is incompatible with what he posits as the key characteristics of an Anglo-protestant American culture. The empirical base for Huntington's claims is feeble, and in theoretical terms, his position is old nativism in a new bottle. The importance of the book—and its worrisome likely impact—derives from the fact that it elegantly articulates the anxieties and political views of considerable segments of public opinion who feel threatened by contemporary large-scale migration. This public opinion movement has led to attacks on the rights of immigrants and to the association of immigration with a security threat.

If we are concerned with the likely paths of immigrant incorporation we need to think about the social and economic reforms that would deal with the dual forces of class exclusion and institutional racism: How to build viable urban education systems? How to protect the income and working conditions of immigrant workers? How to offer opportunities to immigrant youngsters? How to stop the criminalization of young people of color? In other words, we need to focus the analysis on the structure of opportunities faced by the immigrant working class. Furthermore, we need to think about the type of coalitions and the forms of collective action that are likely to produce the necessary changes in American society so that everybody would have the opportunity to attain a decent life.

## Notes

1. The research reported in this chapter was funded by the Russell Sage Foundation (grant number 88-02-02). I want to express my thanks to the Russell Sage Foundation for its support of my research.

2. For a renewed version of assimilation theory see Richard Alba and Victor Nee, *Remaking the American Mainstream* (Cambridge, MA: Harvard University Press, 2003), and Joel Perlmann and Roger Waldinger, "Second Generation Decline? Children of Immigrants, Past and Present—A Reconsideration," *International Migration Review* 31 (1997): 893–922.

3. For segmented assimilation theory see Alejandro Portes and Rubén G. Rumbaut, *Legacies: The Story of the Immigrant Second Generation* (Berkeley: University of California Press, 2001).

4. Ibid.

5. There are several problems in crowning hard work or excellence in studying as the core values of the mainstream. These are undeniably part of the American culture, but they are part of a larger cultural repertoire. For example, from the robber barons to Enron, America has also had a fascination with other avenues to getting rich. Furthermore, the underclass shares other contemporary mainstream values such as consumption as personal fulfillment and judging the worth of people by their material possessions, and the much-criticized behavior of the marginal sectors of American society can be attributed in part to their objective difficulties in achieving these goals. Also, countercultural values are usually attributed to racialized groups. Yet research

has shown that countercultural practices and attitudes are not the province of any particular ethno-racial group. See, for example, Jay MacLeod, *Ain't No Making It* (Boulder: Westview Press, 1995).

6. For analyses of immigrant transnationalism see (among others) Nina Glick Schiller, "Transmigrants and Nation-States: Something Old and Something New in the U.S. Immigrant Experience," in *The Handbook of International Migration: The American Experience*, ed. Charles Hirschman, Philip Kasinitz, and Josh De Wind (New York: Russell Sage Foundation, 1999), 94–119; José Itzigsohn and Silvia Giorguli Saucedo, "Immigrant Incorporation and Sociocultural Transnationalism," *International Migration Review* 36, no. 3 (2002): 766–798; and Alejandro Portes, William Haller, and Luis Guarnizo, "Transnational Entrepreneurs: Alternative Form of Immigrant Economic Adaptation," *American Sociological Review* 67, no. 2 (2002): 278–298.

7. Ramona Hernández, *The Mobility of Workers Under Advanced Capitalism* (New York: Columbia University Press, 2002) and Nancy López, *Hopeful Girls, Troubled Boys* (New York: Routledge, 2003).

8. The survey was conducted between the fall of 2002 and the spring of 2003.

9. The statements were presented as a sentence, and the answers were presented in a scale that included 7 options: fully agree, agree, do not agree or disagree, disagree, fully disagree, do not know, and do not answer. For the purpose of the analysis, I created a dichotomous variable. One category included those who agree or fully agree, the other category included all the rest of the answers (including missing responses).

10. In statistical terms it means that we cannot reject the null hypothesis that there are no differences between the groups. Alternatively, when the results are statistically significant, it means that we can reject the null hypothesis and that we are confident that the differences found are real and not the result of chance in sampling.

11. For a discussion of different forms of Latino/a collective action see Agustín Laó-Montes, "Niuyol: Urban Regime, Latino Social Movements, Ideologies of Latinidad," in *Mambo Montage: the Latinization of New York*, ed. Agustín Laó-Montes and Arlene Dávila (New York: Columbia University Press, 2001).

12. Language used with friends is a better indicator than language used at home because it implies a measure of choice and refers to life conducted outside the home.

13. For an analysis of Latino/a panethnicity see José Itzigsohn, "The Formation of Latino and Latina Panethnic Identities" in Nancy Foner and George M. Fredrickson, *Not Just Black and White* (New York: Russell Sage Foundation, 2004), 197–216.

14. For an analysis of Dominican transnationalism see José Itzigsohn, Carlos Dore Cabral, Esther Hernandez-Medina, and Obed Vazquez, "Mapping Dominican Transnationalism: Narrow and Broad Transnational Practices," *Ethnic and Racial Studies* 22 (1999):316–339, and Peggy Levitt, *The Transnational Villagers* (Berkeley: University of California Press, 2001).

15. Samuel P. Huntington, *Who Are We?: The Challenges to America's Identity* (New York: Simon & Schuster, 2004).

# 13 Politics, Ethnicity, and Bilingual Education in Massachusetts: The Case of Referendum Question 2

Jorge Capetillo-Ponce and Robert Kramer

## Introduction

The second great wave of immigration to the United States, which began in the mid-1960s, has dramatically changed the ethnic composition of the nation. When the first great wave (1880–1930) reached its peak at the turn of the twentieth century, immigrants were close to 15 percent of the total population (14.7 percent in 1910). Today, immigrants have passed the 10 percent mark (11.5 percent in the year 2002). But unlike the first great wave that consisted mostly of populations from Europe, the present one has brought to our shores a much more diverse group of populations from Latin America, Asia, the Middle East, and Africa.[1]

As a result of the Civil Rights movement, bilingual education programs were set up, in the 1960s and 1970s, to respond to the need for a language policy that would enhance the educational and other civil rights of these millions of non-English speaking newcomers. The original reasons for their creation were both practical (give new immigrants help in learning English and becoming productive citizens) and ideological (recognizing that a real cultural democracy entails the respect for the language of minorities). At that time, large sectors of American mainstream society were sympathetic to the view that this influx of new cultures and ways of life would enrich American culture, bringing both skilled and unskilled workers into expanding industries and revitalizing decaying urban centers across the country.

But the dramatic increase in recent decades of our Spanish-speaking population (and in smaller but still significant numbers, of immigrants from Asia, Europe, Africa, and the Caribbean for whom English is not the mother tongue) has provoked a growing debate over the need to keep the supremacy of the English language as a necessary element of national cohesion and identity. This new attention to the language-ethnicity-migration connection has been the basis for an outpouring of books and articles by scholars, politicians, and journalists in the last decade, who have denounced both the lack of immigration control and the existence of bilingual education programs. This trend has also been characterized by the targeting, in particular, of Latinos. One recent and prominent example of this trend is Samuel Huntington's essay "The Hispanic Challenge," in which it is argued that the persistent inflow of immigrants from Latin America and their failure to assimilate into Anglo-Protestant culture threaten to divide the country into "two peoples, two cultures and two languages."[2]

The growing genre of anti-Latino and anti-immigrant literature seems to reflect a change of mood in large segments of the population, from a general understanding of ethnic and linguistic diversity as enriching our society to an attitude of concern about the effects of the large-scale influx of immigrants into the United States and their failure to assimilate rapidly into the mainstream culture. In short, the exponents of the new view consider that diversity does not mean enrichment but disunity and that the integration or assimilation of immigrants into American culture is being challenged by mass immigration. Growing diversity undermines the nativist belief that American culture is bound up with Anglo European culture and, more importantly to this study, with a specific language: English.

An important element of the new trend has been the emergence of antibilingual education movements in recent years, the most visible and influential one being "English Only," headed by California millionaire Ron Unz. Its platform is partially based on a fiscal rationale, that is, that bilingual education takes away precious resources from the budgets of school districts. But the emphasis has been on culture, specifically on what Unz and his followers call "separatism." They argue that by enrolling in bilingual education programs, Spanish-speaking immigrants are electing to bypass the process of acculturation and assimilation that turned previous immigrant groups into English-speaking Americans. And the campaign against what Unz and his followers consider a disuniting factor has already resulted in the passing of anti–bilingual-education laws in California, Arizona, and more recently, in Massachusetts.

This chapter constitutes an effort to contribute to the above mentioned debate over language, ethnicity, and immigration. Its focus is on the November 2002 vote in Massachusetts that included a referendum (Referendum Question 2) on whether or not Massachusetts should continue its thirty-year-old bilingual education policy. Our study offers an in-depth exploration of this question using three analytical tools: (1) an exit poll of 1,491 Latinos on their voting patterns the day of the election; (2) textual analysis of the debate in the mainstream print media; and (3) a study of the

opinions of native English-speaking Massachusetts residents, based on focus groups respondents.

We hope to illuminate the politics surrounding the bilingual education
issue and to take a fresh look at the present state of mainstream perceptions of ethnic/linguistic minorities and immigrants in general in the
context of an increasingly diverse Massachusetts. Our research suggests
that what posed as a referendum on bilingual education may have been, in
reality, a referendum on broader sociopolitical and economic aspects of
Massachusetts's society. These elements of our research are central to our
subsequent evaluation of the reasons for the polarization of the vote, of
the referendum's impact on identity politics and majority-minority group
relations in the state, and of a possible change of mood in the mainstream
population vis-à-vis ethnic and linguistic diversity.

## The Exit Poll

Even though Massachusetts is no stranger to racial and ethnic tensions, it
is also a state with a reputation for valuing immigrants and catering to the
needs of new groups coming into its society. In fact, it was in Massachusetts that the first mandatory transitional bilingual education law in
the United States was passed in 1970. But in November 2002, the Massachusetts electorate effectively ended bilingual education programs by
voting overwhelmingly (68 percent) to pass Referendum Ballot Question
2 (Q. 2), sponsored by the Unz group. Exit polling done at selected cities
in Massachusetts by the Mauricio Gastón Institute and UMASS Poll revealed, however, that out of a total 1,491 Latinos polled, a vast majority of
them, around 93 percent, had voted in favor of rejecting Q. 2 and keeping
bilingual education in place.[3]

These numbers show a polarization between an English-speaking,
mostly white majority and linguistic minorities on the bilingual education
issues. Latinos are by far the largest group using bilingual educational
services provided by the state. Less evident is the reason the referendum
drew so much mainstream support.

With the majority of voters lacking expertise in language learning
programs, the question arose: why did they vote as if they were convinced
that English immersion is superior to bilingual education? Answering this
question was problematic for two reasons. First, it is not certain that
Latinos were satisfied with the system of bilingual education in Massachusetts. Latinos, who voted almost unanimously against the referendum,
may have done so simply because they saw Q. 2 as a referendum on
themselves, as Latinos and immigrants.[4] Second, the Unz group appeared
on the surface to represent a commonsense point of view: the need to learn

English. The Unz campaign used simple but powerful slogans such as "English for the Children," but did not discuss how to accomplish the task.

In short, these two key elements in the vote on Q. 2 suggested that it had less to do with education and more to do with identity politics and dominant-minority group relations. Thus, our focus shifted toward the analysis of mainstream perceptions of bilingual education, the media coverage, and the two campaigns (for and against bilingual education), since these factors could shed further light on the polarized vote as well as the mainstream perceptions of an increasing ethnically diverse Massachusetts society.

## Mainstream Opinions: An Analysis of Motivational Types in Focus Group Sessions

In order to understand mainstream voters' perceptions of bilingual education and immigrants in general, we conducted focus groups in six urban areas around the state: Boston, Chatham, Chelsea, Holyoke, Stoughton, and Worcester. The focus groups pointed to a complex picture of perceptions of the vote and varied reasons for voting "yes" or "no" on Q. 2. Reasons for rejecting bilingual education ranged from pragmatic concerns over taxes or the perceived failings of the bilingual education system to more ideologically and emotionally driven rejections based on the primacy of English, or a "pull-yourself-up-by-your-bootstraps" mentality. Reasons for keeping bilingual education ranged from the belief that it is better to educate Limited English Proficient (LEP) students to solidarity with immigrants and minorities.[5]

We found in the focus group study a lack of general knowledge of the goals and implementation strategies of bilingual education programs and a scarcity or ambiguity of information for voters. When participants spoke of whether or not there should be bilingual education in general, positive answers were generally given with the stipulation that the programs work effectively or with the caveat that they should be reformed. When it was debated as a right, participants spoke as if they were talking about effective programs. Bilingual education in general, while it was acknowledged that all languages were being considered, was generally thought of as English and Spanish. Although many focus group participants felt that they weighed the educational evidence about bilingual education to some extent, their lack of expertise on curriculum development forced them to base their decisions on emotions, assumptions, and pragmatism.

The variation in views held by white native English speakers, African American native English speakers, and even the opinions of a few native English-speaking Latinos, suggests that concluding that the vote reflected anti-immigrant feelings within the mainstream population is far too simplistic. To better understand the complexity of this issue, we broke down the many themes arising from the focus group study into two motivational categories: (1) instrumental/pragmatic and (2) emotional/ ideological.[6]

The first type—instrumental/pragmatic motivations—is defined as the adoption of positions consistent with a means-ends rationality; that is, with the rational maximization of benefits for one's identified community. For example, someone voting against bilingual education because it will probably lead to higher taxes is exercising an instrumental or pragmatic motivation. We identified five of these instrumental/pragmatic motivational types in our focus groups:

1. Funding. Although there was no consensus that funding and taxes were the dominant reason for votes for or against the referendum, there was a feeling that bilingual education needs more funds to be effective.

2. Teacher training. Some felt that finding bilingual education teachers for so many languages is especially difficult. Consequently, many school systems may use teachers who are either not truly fluent in the language in which they are supposed to be teaching their subjects, knowledgeable in the subjects that they are supposed to be teaching, or both.

3. Tenure. Another major criticism was that students were kept in the programs too long, becoming dependent on the system and unable to transition into mainstream education. But at the same time participants were ambivalent on whether or not children can learn English in a year. This is relevant since Q. 2 proposed that a child spend one year in a "sheltered" or "structured" immersion classroom, where subjects would be taught almost entirely in English, yet with a curriculum and presentation designed for students learning the language that would only employ "minimal" native language instruction. After that year, students would normally be immersed into mainstream English classes. The consensus was that a student's ability to learn in a given amount of time was dependent on a number of factors—perhaps most importantly the age of the child and the educational supports he or she receives in school and at home.

4. Placement. Some participants questioned placement procedures, since some of the students are able to argue in English quite effectively while others that had recently arrived couldn't speak any English. Others felt that students with learning disabilities or disciplinary problems might have been placed into bilingual education to keep the "problem" students together.

5. English as a vehicle of success. Almost all participants shared, as a rational or pragmatic motivation, the expectation that speaking English is necessary for success in American society. While most participants felt that maintaining fluency in one's native language as well is optimal and some felt it as a matter of rights, it was generally agreed that English proficiency was the most important goal in educating LEP children. Another important educational goal was to develop effective citizens, which is dependent on English proficiency. A minority of focus group participants felt that cultural sensitivity in education was an equally important educational goal.

The second motivational type, emotional/ideological motivations, is defined as the adoption of positions based on values informed by popular conventional wisdoms, myths, and unsubstantiated beliefs, independently of their prospects for benefiting a specific community or for attaining greater efficacy or success. Take, for example, someone who has been through a bilingual education program or has had a child go through such a program. If this person is against bilingual education, then he or she may have a good reason for opposing the program. However, take someone who has never been through a bilingual education program, never had a child go through bilingual education, doesn't know people who have been through bilingual education programs, and has not studied the issue of bilingual education in depth. If this individual believes wholeheartedly that bilingual education doesn't work, it is likely that he or she has developed emotional or ideological positions based on conventional wisdom and unsubstantiated belief. We identified six kinds of responses that reflect emotional/ideological motivations.

1. Nostalgic optimism. Many participants mused that their grandparents would have viewed bilingual education as a luxury. Such a feeling is not necessarily anti-immigrant as many who hold it also hold a romanticized version of their ancestors' immigration to the United States and the way in which they "pulled themselves up by their bootstraps." The feeling was that newcomers should go through the same initiation process that past immigrants had gone through to become successful.

2. Language of the land. This sentiment was expressed by many participants. Whether this was an anti-immigrant expression, however, was contingent upon whether it was voiced in concert with the previous position ("nostalgic optimism"), or with the instrumental/pragmatic position "English as a vehicle of success." When related along with "nostalgic optimism," it seemed to imply that immigrants, for some unknown reason, do not want to learn English; whereas when espoused with "English as a vehicle for success" argument, it may be considered a pragmatic

view of the skills immigrants need to become successful in the United States.

3. Perceptions that bilingual education doesn't work. While many participants favored bilingual education in theory, they indicated that based on what they had heard, read, or seen, the program has been implemented so poorly for the past few decades that a change was needed. Since the referendum did not offer the possibility of reform, elimination of the program appeared to be the only option. Those who favored bilingual education preferred some kind of reform, but this response was excluded by Q. 2.

4. Belief that English immersion works. In contrast to nostalgic optimism, some participants with direct experience of language immersion believe in the efficacy of this approach. This sentiment was consistent with the educational goal of learning English. While other participants without any first-hand experience agreed with this position, yet another group (more sympathetic to a multicultural agenda) did not. They did not believe that the main educational goal should be English acquisition because learning other subjects would suffer or because students would be stripped of their native language and culture.

5. Belief that the native tongue can survive at home. Participants related stories of their friends or relatives who had come to the United States at different ages and had lost or maintained their native language. In general, the distinction came from the age at which people came to the United States. Some participants related stories of themselves or of other children of German, Italian, or French Canadian ancestry who had once spoken their respective languages but once they enrolled in English schools lost their ability after time. Yet others just took for granted that a native tongue would remain since it is the language of birth.

6. Conspiracy to maintain an underclass. The notion that eliminating bilingual education served the purposes of those who wanted to maintain an immigrant underclass was mentioned in Worcester in the context of government officials not caring whether bilingual education programs failed. But this notion was much more prominent in the Boston group, where there was near consensus that "the powers that be" are deliberately trying to strip people of their culture and to sabotage the educational and advancement opportunities of minorities, keeping them in a marginalized situation indefinitely.[7]

In addition to learning about participants' perceptions of bilingual education, our focus groups illuminated the complex nature of some of the perceptions and attitudes mainstream citizens held about immigrants and speakers of other languages in general, and how they felt when other languages were spoken in their presence. Several respondents pointed to occasions where people around them spoke Spanish, effectively excluding them from the conversation and creating an awkward social situation. Furthermore, the speaking of several languages in the workplace often led to frustrating and unproductive experiences, particularly in customer service situations where interactions were made difficult by language differences, as well as interactions between coworkers. For several respondents, this frustration was combined with an acute paranoia, where they felt that speakers of other languages were talking about them. This paranoia extended beyond social situations and was seen to be the cause of workplace conflicts as well.

## Mainstream Media Coverage and the Two Campaigns

The motivational categories described above offer a framework in which to place the breadth of opinions held by various representatives of the mainstream target group. Still, it is important to underline that tracing back the origins of the mainstream vote against bilingual education is a complex task. While most of the instrumental/pragmatic and emotional/ideological motivations exhibit a degree of negative or critical evaluations of bilingual education, focus group participants exhibited and attributed to others a mixture of motivations for voting one way or another. Some people felt everyone should learn English, whether it is for immigrants to have more opportunities or just because they believe English is America's language. Other participants felt that bilingual education was a good idea but was never implemented properly. Others just didn't want to pay for it. And in others there was an element of anxiety about the new immigrants' rate of assimilation.

In any case, opinions can be changed or reinforced according to the social context in which they interact with other opinions and influences. Thus, to achieve an overall understanding of the vote on Q. 2, we need to examine two key elements that had a central impact on the mainstream vote: the media coverage and the propagandistic character of the campaigns both for and against bilingual education.[8]

### Mainstream Media Coverage

While research on the effectiveness of bilingual education is inconsistent,[9] our analysis of the media coverage[10] of the debate surrounding Q. 2 revealed that media outlets in the state continuously pounded on this fact. It was common to see or read about how Unz opponents in Massachusetts, from politicians to grassroots activists to teachers and scholars, denounced

Republican gubernatorial candidate Mitt Romney for using what they called wildly optimistic and "misleading statistics on immersion in California," while Romney's spokesman Eric Fehrnstrom declared that the "Romney campaign had examined research from California and determined that immersion was superior."[11] Some articles questioned the training of bilingual education teachers, or the lack of program monitoring as the heart of the problem. Yet others questioned the idea that the path to faster English also led to better English, declaring English immersion "a myth," with immersed students still taking several years to become fluent in English. While focus group participants indicated that they might have been paying more attention to the media as voting day approached, this type of media coverage led to confusion about the effectiveness of bilingual education and English immersion.

Some focus groups participants mentioned seeing information in the *Globe* or *Herald*, while not seeing any in their hometown newspapers. The experience was different in the Worcester focus group, in which participants remembered having seen a lot about the debate in the *Telegram* and *Gazette*; in Chatham one participant thought that Q. 2 was, aside from the governor's race, the most promoted issue of the election. So while some had felt that there wasn't much information, and others felt that there was a plethora of information, it didn't seem that the information presented really made up anyone's mind. For the majority of participants, the simple message of "English for the children" resonated and voters responded. The probilingual message may have been much more confusing. The consensus was that with the exception of those who had already harbored strong feelings about the subject, almost everyone else went into the voting booth somewhat confused or conflicted about Q. 2, not having been helped to make up their minds by the media coverage. There was no discernible effect of the media coverage on stimulating political interest, even though attention to media might have risen as the vote approached.[12]

## The Two Campaigns

The anti-Unz campaign mobilized a loose coalition of teachers and principals, political activists, unions such as the Massachusetts Teacher Association and the Massachusetts Federation of Teachers, governmental organizations such as Boston's Office of New Bostonians and the Association of Community Organizations for Reform Now, and an umbrella organization, FACT (Committee for Fairness to Children and Teachers). The coalition used Q. 2 not only to urge Latinos to vote but mainly to unify the diversity of interests of the various pro–bilingual-education groups into one unified message and then project it onto the mainstream public. Our research shows that the coalition gradually discovered that projecting a unified message to convince voters presented many difficulties, precisely because of the abovementioned wide diversity of group interests.

Unlike previous get-out-the vote campaigns, this one featured Latino leaders. In Chelsea, for example, the Vota-Movils blared a Spanish jingle set to a salsa beat: *Latino sal a votar, una voz unida para triunfar* (Latinos, go out to vote, a united voice will triumph). It was a scene played out in Latino enclaves throughout the state. The democratic candidate for governor, Shannon O'Brien, as well as such national leaders as senators Kennedy and Kerry also supported the anti-Unz campaign, even if they did not make it a central issue as the Romney campaign did in support of English immersion. As a result, it is no surprise that Latino identity became directly linked to their rejection of Q. 2 and to supporting O'Brien as governor. Still, even though Latinos are the state's largest minority, comprising around 5.6 percent of the voting-age population, it was too small an electorate to make a difference on a statewide initiative.

Thus, the issue of maintaining bilingual education in Massachusetts moved on to the politically polarized spheres of identity politics and majority-minority relations. Latinos (by far the largest group using bilingual educational services provided by the state) may have voted as they did simply because they saw Q. 2 as a referendum on themselves, as Latinos and as immigrants. It also seems likely that they saw the passage of Q. 2 as a sign of group disempowerment in that the initiative took away a public service the Latino community had fought for and felt they deserved. Because of the political nature of the vote, this does not mean that Latinos necessarily thought that the Massachusetts bilingual education system had been especially successful.

Focus group participants felt that messages of the anti-Unz campaign were somewhat confusing. "Vote NO on 2" was a simple message, easily adopted by those already predisposed to vote no on Q. 2, and possibly aroused the curiosity of those who hadn't given the issue much thought as to why they should vote one way or another. Had the anti-Unz campaign placed more prominence on this slogan, it is possible it would have been more recognizable and effective. However, the "anti-Unz" buttons and bumper stickers and the "Don't sue the teachers" slogan were not very clear to our focus group participants.

It was not immediately clear to every participant who or what Unz was nor why Unz should be avoided. The Latino community, which had engaged in an intense effort of organizing against Q. 2, certainly knew what the symbolism meant; but the symbolism did not have wide appeal or recognition in the mainstream population.

Another unclear message of the anti-Unz campaign was the "Don't sue the teachers" slogan. Its basis was supposedly to influence even those not predisposed to supporting educational benefits for immigrants or limited English proficient children to at least try to keep their English-speaking teacher friends, colleagues, and neighbors safe from litigation. The anti-Unz campaign suggested that litigation could arise out of merely using a child's native language momentarily in class. Aside from the confusion over the legal liabilities facing teachers, this message did not resonate well with our focus groups. Some participants had not remembered hearing about it at all, others didn't really understand its point, and others had heard it but were not swayed one way or another by it. Some participants, who were very supportive of teachers or had been teachers themselves, felt that it was the wrong message. The issue should have been about children's education, not teachers' rights.

Aside from not eliciting sufficient sympathy among voters to defeat Q. 2, the fear-of-litigation angle may have backfired on the anti-Unz campaign by raising questions about teachers' intentions. The provision that allows for litigation against teachers, administrators, or school committee officials who willfully misrepresent to parents the option for placing their child in a bilingual education program by obtaining a special waiver is confusing unless one examines the regulations closely.[13]

Supporters of the Unz initiative, on the other hand, justified the need for such litigation, saying that teachers were keeping immigrant children in bilingual programs longer than necessary. If teachers were following policy, why should they fear litigation? So the argument went.

To counter the vocal grassroots efforts of the anti-Unz movement and the positive (if lukewarm) support of the O'Brien campaign, Mitt Romney introduced English immersion as a central issue in his campaign. The Unz campaign was supported by a coalition of educators, academics, and politicians, and relied on Romney's television and radio ads that stressed the need to end the "failed practice of bilingual education." The effort in support of Q. 2 avoided pep rallies and demonstrations and focused on debates, media interviews, and low-key addresses to target groups.

The Unz campaign used both economic logic and historical stereotypes of bilingual education (which have become conventional wisdom) to project the idea that supporting bilingual education had nothing to do with being a liberal or a democrat. By identifying with "English for the children," both liberals and conservatives alike could feel as though they were doing what was best. And to offset Latino activism, the Unz campaign enlisted Lincoln Tamayo—a former principal of Chelsea High School—who became a major Latino figure in the pro-Unz camp and its most visible spokesperson. His presence might have confused the mainstream population about where the Latino community stood on the issue, leaving the impression that Latinos were not unified in opposition to Q. 2. Only later did the Gastón/UMASS poll verify the overwhelming support of bilingual education among Latinos.

The Unz campaign strategy was effective; the referendum won in 328 of the state's 351 communities, including urban centers, blue-collar towns, and wealthy suburbs. It even passed in cities with large Latino populations, such as Holyoke and Chelsea. It was defeated in Boston, as well as in such liberal towns as Amherst, Brookline, and Cambridge. Besides these "core liberal" towns of Massachusetts, Q. 2 passed almost everywhere else in the state.

In addition to having a clear mainstream message ("English for the Children") that voters throughout the state could identify with and support, the Unz campaign had greater economic resources at its disposal. According to reports filed with the Office of Campaign and Political Finance covering the period from August 1, 2001 to October 15, 2002, the probilingual anti-Unz campaign raised $206,664, and the Unz anti-bilingual-education campaign raised $442,100, more than 60 percent of which came from California.[14]

To understand the overall complexity of the vote on Q. 2, it is crucial to look closely not only at voter motivation but at the different approaches that each campaign utilized. The Unz campaign utilized a low-key approach and a simple message that appealed to the mainstream. The more activist-oriented, coalition style of the anti-Unz campaign may have appeared more radical to the mainstream public. While the anti-Unz campaign had initially sought to influence mainstream voters, it appears that polls taken a few weeks before the vote, showing clearly how well the "English for the children" message was resonating with mainstream voters, seemed to force the anti-Unz coalition to change strategy. It then focused on bilingual education's main constituency, the Latino minority, which had already been mobilizing to protect the future of bilingual education. This last-minute change may have had caused further confusion among potential mainstream voters. Although it is not clear that the anti-Unz campaign was responsible for turning people against bilingual education, the comments of many participants in our focus groups suggests that the diffusion of the message confused many voters and weakened the overall impact of the campaign.

## Conclusion

The mainstream motivations exhibited in our focus group study were shaped mainly by the media coverage and the approaches that each campaign used to influence public opinion. Understanding this helps to appreciate how the Unz campaign exploited the fears of mainstream voters. It used a low-key approach and a simple message with general appeal that reinforced the unsubstantiated but widely held belief that by eliminating bilingual education, voters might begin to mend the fractures in present-day America. The Unz strategy gained the center of the political spectrum and decisively outmaneuvered the multicultural, activist-oriented style of the anti-Unz campaign, which was characterized by disparate messages that were perceived as "more radical" by the general public.

The vote on Q. 2 suggests that the mood of mainstream Massachusetts has shifted away from sympathy with ethnic diversity as a means of enriching our society to an attitude of concern about the effects of the recent large-scale influx of immigrants into the state. Most participants in the focus groups were sympathetic with a pull-yourself-up-by-your-bootstraps ideology. They were willing to "tolerate" high levels of immigration as long as the newcomers paid their own way, did not receive special considerations or "breaks" such as bilingual education, and assimilated at a relatively rapid rate.

By no means are we stating here that these attitudes have consolidated into one coherent or conscious ideology. In fact, the focus group study shows that, in general, participants did not realize the consequences of voting in a particular way on a program that they had little or no interest in. But most of the instrumental/pragmatic and emotional/ideological motivations of participants did exhibit a degree of negative or critical evaluations of bilingual education and of immigrant groups in particular. And the mainstream vote did have a profound impact on linguistic minority groups, especially Latinos, who use and value bilingual education programs.

We end this chapter by highlighting two central themes in our research: (1) the factors leading to the polarized vote, and (2) the connection between identity politics and the challenge of achieving cultural democracy.

Accounting for the polarized vote leads to the analysis of the role of the media, the campaigns, and the referendum process. While the mainstream media, in their search for "objectivity," obsessively reported on the pros and cons of maintaining bilingual education in the state, it avoided altogether the issue of minority rights. The result was narrow coverage about the efficacy of a specific program instead of a wider and more fruitful debate on the advantages of recognizing and treating linguistic minorities as equals rather than ignoring their right to preserve their language and culture.

The Unz campaign understood very well after its victories in California and Arizona the power that negative perceptions of bilingual education can hold in the minds of typical American voters. Its propagandistic approach based on historical stereotypes of bilingual education exploited many of the negative or critical evaluations of bilingual education in the mainstream population. This approach was successful because it made it possible to disguise intolerance in the attire of common sense. It successfully projected the idea that the main objective of the campaign was to promote greater educational achievement through English learning, and it downplayed the restriction on the rights of linguistic minorities.

The "English for the children" camp may have been short on logistics or implementation strategies, but its message resonated with both the liberal and conservative public. Eliminate bilingual education because it doesn't work, they argued, saying that it was neither educating children effectively nor teaching them English, thereby leading them to a life of disadvantage. Everyone could be persuaded by the argument that English proficiency for all is essential: well-intentioned liberal voters desirous of changing a system that was failing immigrant and minority children, xenophobes who disliked paying extra taxes to support programs for "them" to learn in "their native languages," and everyone in between.

The perception that the implementation of bilingual education programs has been largely a failure is perhaps the major obstacle for open educational debate. Undecided mainstream voters seemed to have had an easier time identifying with the conventional wisdom that these programs don't work than with the success stories that proponents noted. The lack of standardization in program curricula, teacher requirements, and training further undermined the program's reputation. Many may have voted against what they perceived as poor implementation rather than the principle of bilingual education. Politicized information about funding, questionable teacher training, length of program and dependency, systemic fragmentation, and dubious selection criteria apparently fueled voters' opposition to the program.

While the Unz campaign successfully argued that the burden of proof was on bilingual education to justify its effectiveness, the anti-Unz campaign was unfocused and lost the opportunity to demonstrate that pluralism in language as in other cultural qualities is desirable and that there are benefits to be gained from improving the interaction between dominant and minority groups. Instead of using a propagandistic approach based on direct attacks on Unz, instead of trying to prove that the Unz group was antiminority, instead of mounting a case for the defense of teachers against litigation, the pro–bilingual-education camp could have used a pedagogic approach based on the careful analysis of the intolerant character of the Unz campaign and based on making bilingual education more effective. Finally, this approach could have touted bilingual education as a symbol of greater mainstream respect for the culture of minorities.[15]

The polarized vote on Q. 2 is an example of how a prime tool of democracy—the referendum—can be used, wittingly or unwittingly, to provoke intolerance in the mainstream population and, in this case at least, to undermine minority rights. In theory, referenda, by triggering media coverage and campaigns for and against a specific issue, increase political knowledge, political efficacy, and political participation. But as we observed with the focus groups, participants manifested considerable confusion about central aspects of Q. 2, and neither the media coverage nor the strategies of the two campaigns had a measurable effect on civic education or on increasing the mainstream population's understanding of bilingual education. Nor did the process promote political efficacy by offering citizens a direct say in policy making. Q. 2's wording was confusing and incomplete because reform was never an option.[16] Reform would have been the best way to achieve political efficacy and avoid polarization. In regard to political participation, we should not confuse what actually happened with increased citizens' interest and popular participation. In reality, the outcome was polarization of the political discourse, resulting in a vote characterized by a vulgar majoritarianism.

The second main theme we addressed is the connection between identity politics and the political discourse. Our research indicates that most political learning and political participation took place among members of the group with the largest stake in the vote: the Latinos of Massachusetts. With the campaigns going head to head, it became obvious that the bilingual education debate strayed far from being about education and became more about Latino ethnic identity and relations between the dominant and minority groups in the state. Thus, for Latinos the vote was an uneasy introduction to the American political system, especially if they understood it as an assault on their language and parental choice. Voter turnout rate increased in Boston by 41 percent from 1998, in part due to greater Latino participation.[17] Thus, Q. 2 might very well have brought about a turning point for Latino activism. And increased activism may translate into the development of other avenues in which to seek acknowledgement of their rights and their distinct cultural heritage.

We must realize that treating members of minority groups as equals means recognizing the worth of distinctive cultural traditions. Achieving this goal will require that public institutions promote educational programs that acknowledge rather than ignore cultural particularities.

Referenda can be an important element in this educational process, but perhaps they need to take place more regularly and be more fully institutionalized (particularly the funding aspects). And perhaps these referenda need to be part of a broader process of citizen participation and cross-cultural acculturation that includes a continuous dialogue between majority and minority groups, so that they achieve their intended goal of increasing political knowledge, political efficacy, and political participation. These changes might prevent the polarization of political discourse that we saw on Q. 2, and they might promote better ways of handling emotional issues such as bilingual education, so that we enhance the rights of cultural minorities and the overall democratic process.

## Notes

1. This is an expanded version of the study "Challenges to Multiculturalism" published in *New England Journal of Public Policy* vol 20 (Fall/Winter 2004–2005): 139–147.

2. Samuel Huntington, "The Hispanic Challenge," *Foreign Policy*, March/April 2004, 30.

3. For a complete analysis of the results of the exit poll see Jorge Capetillo-Ponce, "The Vote on Bilingual Education, and Latino Identity in Massachusetts," *Gastón Institute Report*, Spring 2003, 1, 8.

4. It is interesting to note, on one hand, a survey of 198 Latino leaders conducted by students of UMASS Boston and the Gastón Institute on April 23, 2004, indicated that 74 percent felt that bilingual education programs needed reform, while only 16 percent said that bilingual education was working fine. Both groups said that it should not have been eliminated. On the other hand, we want to underline that Q. 2 became a rallying point for the Latino communities of Massachusetts. By promoting the maintenance of bilingual education programs, Latino leaders and bilingual education activists were able to raise voter awareness and to mount voter-registration campaigns throughout the state. As a result, Latino identity became directly linked to their rejection of Q. 2 and their support for Shannon O'Brien for governor.

5. For an explanation of the methodology used in this study as well as other aspects that are briefly described in this section, see the report by J. Capetillo-Ponce and R. Kramer, "The Mainstream Voters Focus Group Project: Native English Speakers' Views on Bilingual Education and Referendum Question 2" at the Gastón Institute's home page: http://www.gaston.umb.edu.

6. Our motivational types generally follow Max Weber's classificatory ideal types. Our first type follows closely Weber's instrumental rational type, which occurs when means and ends are systematically related to each other. Our second type has elements of Weber's value-rational type, which is behavior undertaken in light of one's basic values and beliefs. As in Weber, our types are "pure forms" that provide a common reference point for comparison.

7. In the Boston focus group, which was mostly African American, feelings toward the vote itself differed from those of English-speaking participants in other urban areas. What these responses point to is not only a higher degree of solidarity among English-speaking minorities with linguistic minorities and the immigrant underclass

but also a perception of the vote as an issue pertaining to ethnic majority-minority group relations.

8. In this context, "propagandistic" means expressions of opinion or actions by groups deliberately designed to influence opinions or actions of individuals or groups without careful scrutiny and criticism of the issue at hand. In this case we refer to propaganda that alters public opinion on matters of large social consequence, such as the elimination of bilingual education programs.

9. It is inconsistent because, first of all, there is the notable lack of standardization and of evaluation criteria leading to a wide range of opinions on effectiveness and to great difficulties in framing meaningful comparisons with other types of programs, such as English immersion. And second, because this is such a politically charged topic, the goals and opinions of both proponents and critics always vary significantly, causing activists, politicians, and educators on both ends of the political spectrum to selectively choose available research. For more on this subject see Lorna Rivera's "A Review of the Literature on Bilingual Education," *Gastón Institute Report*, Fall 2002.

10. Research was based on textual analysis of 150 newspaper and television pieces about the debate from March 2002 to November 2002, using the Lexis-Nexis database.

11. Anand Vaishnav, "California Bilingual Reform has Pros, Cons," *Boston Globe*, October 27, 2002, metro section, p. A1.

12. Other than through print and electronic media, the other main sources of information that people mentioned were mailed voter registration materials, schools, Latino organizations, and the anti-Unz campaign.

13. The Unz initiative was complex in its provisions yet limited in its options. It begins with a confirmation of English as the language of Massachusetts and a call for immigrants to learn it quickly. Section four contains the main arguments, stating that all children should be taught in English, and that "English learners" should go through a "sheltered immersion" program that should not last longer than a year. Section five outlines the conditions under which section four ceases to apply: if parents sign a waver, which, if granted, allows their child to enter bilingual education programs. Parents can apply for the waiver if the child is already relatively proficient in English, if the child is ten years old or older and his or her teachers believe a bilingual program would be better, or if the child has "special individual needs." Section six, one of the more controversial points, allows for any teacher, administrator, or elected official to be sued, in certain cases, for failing to implement the new regulations.

14. The lack of economic resources in the anti-Unz camp could have been a decisive factor. Unz lost a similar campaign in Colorado after a $3-million donation by Colorado billionaire Pat Stryker. The anti-Unz campaign in Colorado had predicted chaos if thousands of ill-prepared immigrant children were to enroll in mainstream classrooms. Bilingual education backers derided the ads for exploiting the fears of white voters, but they worked.

15. This approach, at the very least, would have questioned the entrenched anti-bilingual-education (and in some cases anti-immigrant) opinions and motivations within the mainstream population, in addition to countering the resulting polarization in the vote by projecting the message that cultural democracy is not simply a radical view held mainly by activists and certain minorities.

16. Some focus group participants pointed out that the wording of Q. 2 and its accompanying description was unclear. For instance, a "no" vote on the referendum was to keep the bilingual education system the way it was, and a "yes" vote was to

change or eliminate the system, which is less than intuitive since the question was a referendum on bilingual education. Others expressed that had the referendum offered a choice between elimination and reform rather than elimination and no change, their vote might have changed for reform.

17. According to BostonVote Analysis. See Cindy Rodríguez, "Election 2002: Activists encouraged by Latino Turnout," *Boston Globe*, November 9, 2002, p. B1.

# 14 The Evolving State of Latino Politics in New England

## Amílcar Antonio Barreto

With a new millennium comes the realization that growing Latino communities will alter the American political system. The demographic Latinization of the United States is no longer limited to the four traditional enclaves or regions: the Southwestern states, southern Florida, metropolitan Chicago, and greater New York City. Government figures reveal that this trend also applies to New England. Except for southwestern Connecticut, we are not discussing a demographic spillover from the New York City region. Latinos are migrating to New England in ever-increasing numbers—particularly in Massachusetts, Connecticut, and Rhode Island. Over time this community will assert a greater influence over New England politics—both the politics of popular social movements as well as the formal electoral arena. Future Latino political participation will increase along with the size of this community. Still, participation in the formal political process will be tempered by the citizenship status of many of the area's Spanish-speaking immigrants. Latino political participation will also depend on the compactness of Latino settlement patterns.

Nonetheless, this increased political participation may generate negative responses from non-Latinos. Recent debates over the status of bilingual education in Massachusetts are indicative of the fact that Anglo resistance to this wave of Latin American immigration and Latino migration will manifest itself from time to time. Such a backlash may trigger, as the example of the Canadian province of Quebec illustrates, a surge of ethnic resistance that may manifest itself in the form of more overt nationalist sentiments. Ironically, those fearing the growing Latino presence in New England may be generating a self-fulfilling prophecy.

## A Remarkable Decade: 1990 to 2000

New York City is usually selected as the prime focus of Latino political studies in the north Atlantic states. A second alternative would be Philadelphia, and a possible third choice would be Hartford, Connecticut.

These cities represent the most numerically significant Latino enclaves in the north Atlantic states. Continual migration and remigration to and from New York City and the island of Puerto Rico has popularized a term known as the *guagua aérea*, or "air bus." Federal census data released in 2000 indicates that the Latino presence in that metropolis continues to expand though the composition of New York City's Latino community is far more heterogeneous than previously imagined. Latin New York, a term once synonymous with Puerto Rican New York, is quickly being transformed due to immigration from other parts of Latin America and the gradual migration of many Puerto Ricans from New York City proper to its surrounding suburbs.

Recent trends also reveal that New England, particularly the region's three southern states, may become a new and noteworthy focus of Latino studies in the United States. The last decade witnessed a remarkable increase in New England's Latino population. In 1990 there were 568,240 Latinos in New England, corresponding to 4.3 percent of the region's population. Ten years later the census bureau counted 875,225 Latinos in New England—a 54 percent increase.[1] Thus, by 2000 Latinos encompassed 6.3 percent of all New Englanders. When compared to non-Latino regional population growth the 1990 and 2000 numbers appear extraordinary. There were 12,638,703 non-Latinos in 1990. A decade later there were 13,047,292 non-Latinos—a growth rate of only 3.2 percent. Connecticut's Latino community grew by more than 100,000 inhabitants. In neighboring Massachusetts the Latino presence expanded by more than 150,000 residents. Rhode Island's Latino community almost doubled in this period. Despite more modest growth rates in Maine, New Hampshire, and Vermont, the region's three northern, and most rural, states still experienced appreciable rises in their Latino communities.

These demographic growth patterns acquire a rather important symbolic significance when one realizes that Latinos have displaced African Americans, regionally and nationally, as the largest minority. Still, one must keep in mind that Latinos may identify themselves in a number of racial categories including black. Until 1990 African Americans remained the largest minorities in the two most populous New England states, Connecticut and Massachusetts—8.3 and 4.8 percent respectively. A decade later that status vanished; Latinos outnumbered African Americans even in these two states. Latinos were poised to comprise almost 10 percent of the state populations of Connecticut and Rhode Island. None of the six states experienced significant enlargements in the black populations.

Just where are these new Latinos coming from? The region's single largest group remains Puerto Ricans. Though its formal status has changed over the past century of U.S. rule, it remains an American territory subject to the authority of the federal government lacking any voting representation in Congress.[2] Puerto Ricans were naturalized *en masse* by Congress in 1917. As U.S. citizens, unlike all subsequent Latin American immigrants, Puerto Ricans would have unfettered access to the U.S. labor market. Still, large-scale Puerto Rican migration to the U.S. mainland did not transpire until the 1940s when manufacturing plants throughout the Northeast and Midwest recruited workers from this American overseas territory to satisfy labor shortages in the wake of World War II. Significant waves of Puerto Rican migration to Hartford materialized in the 1950s.[3] In the case of Boston the establishment of a sizeable Puerto Rican presence would not take place until the 1960s.[4]

New England's largest Puerto Rican settlements were established in the industrial centers of Connecticut and Massachusetts. By 2000 Puerto Ricans constituted over 5 percent of Connecticut's population and 3 percent of Massachusetts's population. The presence of Puerto Ricans is a pivotal factor when discussing Latino electoral politics since these U.S. citizens can immediately vote or run for office. Since the 1980s Puerto Rican migration to the U.S. mainland has been channeled, increasingly, to smaller cities and away from the traditional urban centers.[5] Increases in New England's Puerto Rican community are largely attributed to natural population increases rather than migration from the island of Puerto Rico or Puerto Rican migration from other parts of the United States.[6]

Most Puerto Ricans settling in the United States bypassed New England. The same holds true for Cubans. Like Puerto Rico Cuba was also a Spanish colony until 1898. Unlike its sister island to the east, Cuba was granted its independence soon after the U.S. invasion. Large-scale Cuban migration came in the wake of the 1959 revolution and most Cuban migrants settled in southern Florida. Cubans made no significant demographic increases in New England in the 1990s. Logically, political instability in the wake of a post-Fidel government may spur an influx of new Cuban immigration.

In contrast Mexican immigration to New England is showing vibrancy. According to the 2000 census figures the percentage of Mexicans in Connecticut, Massachusetts, New Hampshire, and Vermont doubled in the last ten years. In Rhode Island the percentage of Mexicans tripled during the same period. In each case Mexicans constitute less than 1 percent of the state's population. The absolute numbers we are discussing remain small. However, the pay scale of jobs—even the lowest-paid ones—in this region compared to wages in Mexico and other parts of the United States will continue to attract Mexicans far from Southwestern border states and the Midwest. Despite Mexico's distance from New

England, this country will likely nourish the regional Latino community for decades to come. Mexicans potentially could outnumber Puerto Ricans in New England before the end of the twenty-first century.

Mexican migration and immigration patterns represent a fascinating trend within the Latino community. No single people will invigorate the Latinization of the United States more than Mexicans. Their numerical potency is such that the terms *Latino* and *Mexican* will become virtually interchangeable in the western two-thirds of the country. As Latino settlement patterns increasingly traverse that boundary, so will our perception of Latinos along the Atlantic seaboard. Demographic patterns will likely create two distinct Latino realities in the United States—a Mexican-dominant Latino realm west of Appalachia and an increasingly heterogeneous pan-Latin American/Latino reality in the Atlantic states.

A part of the story, one that is not completely transparent from recent census figures, is the rise in the "other" category. Political strife, socioeconomic instability, guerrilla insurgencies, and gang violence throughout Latin America in the 1990s have promoted the exodus of thousands of immigrants from Central and South American countries. In the case of Colombia, the disintegrating authority of the state is producing a brain drain and capital flight, both of which are targeting their sights on the United States.[7] Within New England, East Boston, Massachusetts, and Central Falls, Rhode Island, are developing significant Colombian enclaves.[8] About one-quarter of Latin American and Caribbean immigrants to New England during the 1990s came from the Dominican Republic.[9] Spanish-speaking South Americans—Colombians, Peruvians, and Ecuadorians—represented 15 percent, while Central Americans—Guatemalans, Hondurans, and Salvadorans—were 9 percent of the region's Latin American and Caribbean immigrants.[10] Economic and political instability in Argentina and Venezuela in the past decade will undoubtedly enlarge this "other" category in the 2010 census figures.[11]

The New England state with the largest increase in the "other" Latino category was Rhode Island. Almost 6 percent of the state's population is now comprised of "other" Latinos. Dominicans represented 45 percent, Colombians were 17 percent, and Guatemalans comprised 14 percent of the state's legal Latin American and Caribbean immigrants in the 1990s.[12] Despite a substantial growth in Puerto Rican population—from 1.2 to 2.4 percent of Rhode Island's population—"other" Latinos in Rhode Island outnumber Puerto Ricans by a factor of two to one. There is likely an overcount of Puerto Ricans in New England, as may be the case in other parts of the country. Latin American immigrants fearful of federal authorities and the possibility of deportation might claim Puerto Rican ancestry or ethnicity in order to benefit from this group's citizenship status. Furthermore, the number of legal residents omits the unknown and presumably significant number of undocumented inhabitants.

Territorial compactness has a major impact on participating in the realm of formal or electoral politics. When it comes to electing legislators, the prevailing system employed to select lawmakers in the United States remains the single-member district. These districts advantage geographically concentrated groups, while proportional representation systems accrue votes for candidates or parties regardless of constituent residence. Table 14.1 provides some insights into the growth and geographic concentration of New England Latinos.

The data in Table 14.1 break down the 1990 and 2000 census numbers for Latinos by state at the county level. The first row corresponds to Connecticut's eight counties ($N = 8$). The county with the smallest Latino presence—Litchfield County in the state's northwest corner—was 1.1 percent Latino (column 1) in 1990. Litchfield is also Connecticut's most rural county. In 1990 the county with the highest Latino presence, Hartford County in this case, was 8.2 percent Latino (see column 2). Column 3 reveals the median percentage Latino for the state's counties. Column 4 displays the standard deviation for the 1990 county-level data. Standard deviations provide us with a snapshot of just how concentrated Latinos were in 2000. Columns 5 through 8 repeat the same series of data for the 2000 census. There are two distinctive patterns in the region. Latino growth patterns in Maine and Vermont remain dispersed. By contrast, Latino growth patterns in the other four states shows a propensity toward further geographic—largely urban—concentration.

Let us begin with Vermont—the state with the smallest Latino presence in terms of absolute numbers. Out of its fourteen counties the one with the smallest Latino presence was less than 0.5 percent Latino. The county with largest Latino presence was 1.3 percent. Those figures remained essentially identical for both the 1990 and 2000 census. The standard deviation of 0.3 tells us there is very little variation among the state's counties. This is not surprising given that Vermont is a largely rural state. On the other end of the spectrum is Rhode Island. The county with the smallest Latino presence in 1990 was 0.8 Latino in 1990 and 1.1 percent the following census. A remarkable feature in the 2000 data was the demographic expansion in the county with the largest Latino presence. In 1990 the county with the most significant Latino presence—Providence County—was 6.6 percent Latino. By 2000 that percentage increased to 13.4 percent. Furthermore, the county-level standard deviation more than doubled from 2.2 percent in 1990 to 4.7 percent in 2000. Rhode Island's Latinos—as is the case in Connecticut, Massachusetts, and even New Hampshire—are a largely urban community, and are becoming more so.

TABLE 14.1. Latinos in New England by county: descriptive statistics, 1990–2000

| | Percentage Latino 1990 | | | | Percentage Latino 2000 | | | |
| --- | --- | --- | --- | --- | --- | --- | --- | --- |
| | Minimum | Maximum | Median 1990 | Standard deviation | Minimum | Maximum | Median 2000 | Standard deviation |
| Connecticut (n = 8) | 1.1 | 8.2 | 3.7 | 2.7 | 2.1 | 11.9 | 6.1 | 3.8 |
| Maine (n = 16) | 0.2 | 0.9 | 0.5 | 0.2 | 0.5 | 1.1 | 0.6 | 0.2 |
| Massachusetts (n = 14) | 0.8 | 11.0 | 2.5 | 3.3 | 1.0 | 15.5 | 2.9 | 4.9 |
| New Hampshire (n = 10) | 0.4 | 1.7 | 0.6 | 0.4 | 0.5 | 3.2 | 0.9 | 0.8 |
| Rhode Island (n = 5) | 0.8 | 6.6 | 1.3 | 2.2 | 1.1 | 13.4 | 1.7 | 4.7 |
| Vermont (n = 14) | 0.4 | 1.3 | 0.5 | 0.3 | 0.4 | 1.3 | 0.8 | 0.3 |
| New England (n = 67) | 0.2 | 11.0 | 0.8 | 2.4 | 0.4 | 15.5 | 1.1 | 3.7 |

*Sources:* www.census.gov/main/www/cen1990.html; www.census.gov/main/www/cen2000.html.

## Exclusion and Protest

It is impossible to divorce studies of Latino politics from broader discussions of race, culture, and ethnicity in the United States. The growth of
Latino communities in the second half of the twentieth century should
have fostered significant increase in Latino participation in the formal
political process. This was not the case. Cultural stereotypes stained
Latinos from the beginning. Studies of American political values in the
1950s and 1960s describe the United States as one of the few countries
with a participatory political culture.[13] Such scholarship presumed that
Anglo American culture was individualistic, suspicious of the government
power, egalitarian, and populist.[14] Because of their dissimilar culture,
Latinos themselves were blamed for their own low levels of electoral
participation. Low levels of electoral involvement were also blamed on the
paternalistic attitudes of Puerto Rico's commonwealth government.[15]
Interestingly these scholars ignored the fact that electoral participation
rates on the island of Puerto Rico surpass those of mainland Americans.

A new generation of scholarship has painted a different portrait of the
American political scene. Large-scale Latin American migration and
immigration coincided with the demise of the notorious urban political
machines.[16] Doused in patronage, these corrupt inner-city institutions
also integrated immigrants into the American political process. Newly
arrived European immigrants were offered employment and a fast track to
citizenship. In return, immigrants were expected to reciprocate by voting
for the party's candidates. Hence, low levels of Latino political participation are not a matter of culture but a result of institutional defi-
ciencies.[17] Post–machine-era parties were not interested in mobilizing
Latinos, fearing the consequences of energizing this potential electoral
bloc.[18] When Latinos asked to participate, they were made to feel unwelcome.[19]

Latino political activism in the Northeast developed, for the most part,
outside the formal party structure. Hence, it was more willing to challenge
fundamental sociopolitical tenets as exemplified by support for radical
movements. In New England the Marxist and proindependence Puerto
Rican Socialist Party organized activities in Boston and Hartford.[20] The
most extreme, and least common, form of antisystem politics came in the
form of espousal of Puerto Rican independence through violent organizations such the *Macheteros* (Machete Wielders) and the *Fuerzas Armadas
de Liberación Nacional* (Armed Forces of National Liberation).[21] Intense
resentment incurred from social and economic marginalization cultivated
support for political extremism within the mainland Puerto Rican community.[22] That frustration was channeled through militant support for

independence. But a new generation of activists is opting to fight for their *barrios* within the United States.[23] Such a new focus does not obliterate interest in the issues "back home."

Indeed, Puerto Ricans throughout New England joined the successful campaign to demilitarize the island of Vieques—site of the former U.S. Navy's bombing range in eastern Puerto Rico.[24] Organizers of the July 2000 Puerto Rican Festival in Boston used the gathering to demand the Navy's withdrawal from Vieques and organize vigils outside the John F. Kennedy Federal Building and the J. Joseph Moakley Federal Court-house.[25] The organization *Todo Connecticut con Vieques* (All Connecticut with Vieques) organized rallies in front of symbolically strategic buildings, such as the U.S. Armed Forces Recruitment Center in Hartford, Con-necticut.[26] In concert with their brethren in Hartford, Puerto Rican acti-vists allied with the group *Todo Worcester con Vieques* (All Worcester with Vieques) prepared their own protests in front of Worcester City Hall in April and August of 2001.[27] Parades and protests have become political events depicting a select image of the community to insiders as well as outsiders. Not surprisingly, the vast majority of Vieques protests in New England were located in Connecticut and Massachusetts, the states with the most sizeable Puerto Rican communities. The effectiveness of transnational political activism was demonstrated when the U.S. Navy in 2003 formally declared an end to its use of Vieques as a site for military practices. For many transnational communities, such as Latinos in the United States, the struggles over *here* are symbolically linked to struggles back *there*.[28]

## Electing Latinos

While informal politics will remain an integral part of Latino activism the increasing size of Latino communities will impact the formal political process. The number of Latino officer holders in the region is increasing, though not in proportion to demographic developments. This is not to say that Latinos cannot be elected from ethnically diverse districts. Still, the probabilities of that happening are not very high. At the moment there are no Latino governors, federal senators, or congressmen in New Eng-land. Let us examine the issue of ethnic representation using the region's congressional delegation.

As a region, New England has twenty-two seats in the House of Rep-resentatives speaking for almost fourteen million residents.[29] This cor-responds to approximately one congressman per 630,000 inhabitants. The 2000 census counted almost 900,000 Latinos. Were the ethnic repre-sentation proportional to the community's size there should be at least one Latino in the House from New England (assuming a fictitious all-Latino district). Were the region's Latinos geographically concentrated there would be enough to constitute the majority in two congressional districts. This gives us an idea as to how imbalanced single-member districts can be. Of course, this principle applies to political minorities—such as Republicans in Massachusetts or Democrats in New Hampshire—as much as it does to ethnic minorities.

Outside of municipal legislatures, perhaps the first major signs of Latino inroads in the formal electoral politics will be in state legislatures. This was demonstrated recently in Massachusetts, for example. In the 2002 mid-term elections, Jarrett T. Barrios, the grandson of Cuban immigrants and a two-term member of the state House of Representatives, became the first Latino elected to the forty-member Massachusetts State Senate.[30] He joined three Latinos in the state's 160-member lower chamber. Two were new members, William Lantigua and Jeffrey Sanchez, and one was an incumbent, Cheryl A. Rivera. Representative Lantigua is Dominican. Both Sanchez and Rivera are Puerto Rican. The Latinos elected to the Massachusetts state house in 2002 can thank, to a significant degree, not only the increase in the absolute numbers of Latinos in this state, but also the increase in the standard deviation of Latinos (see Table 14.1). A higher standard deviation is indicative of greater geographic concentration in particular pockets, facilitating the election of politicians in single-member district systems. The three lawmakers—Lantigua (Lawrence), Rivera (Springfield), and Sanchez (Boston)—were elected from districts in major Latino strongholds.

The Latinos in the Connecticut House of Representatives were Juan Candelaria, Marie Lopez Kirkley-Bey, Evelyn Mantilla, Lydia Martinez, Felipe Reinoso, and Assistant Majority Leader Minnie Gonzalez. Representative Reinoso is originally from Peru. The other Connecticut state lawmakers are Puerto Rican. As José Cruz has noted, Puerto Ricans in the Northeast represent the bulk of Latino elected officials.[31] However, with the increase in immigration from the Dominican Republic, Mexico, and other Latin American countries, that trend may apply more to New York, New Jersey, and Pennsylvania and less to New England. On a related note, Michael Jones-Correa's study of Latino politics in Queens, New York, suggested that many Latin American immigrants resisted formal political participation and naturalization fearing how their fellow co-ethnics and families back home would view their actions.[32] The increased presence of non-Puerto Ricans in New England state legislatures may reveal a greater acceptance, if not resignation, that the move to North America is a permanent one.

In 2002 Rhode Island's two Latino state representatives, León Tejada and Anastasia Williams, were reelected. Illustrative of the Latino population in that state, neither are Puerto Rican. Tejada was born in the Dominican Republic; Williams was born in Panama. Voters in Rhode Island also elected the state's first Latino state senator, Juan M. Pichardo, in 2002.[33] (In 2004 Tejada was defeated by Grace Díaz, who became the first Dominican woman elected to a state legislature). Senator Pichardo is also the first Dominican American state senator anywhere in the United States. His election may be symbolic on more than one front. During the primaries Senator Pichardo defeated an 18-year Senate veteran, Charles D. Walton, Rhode Island's first and only black senator. In 1990 Latinos as a percentage of the state's population surpassed the percentage of African Americans by a small margin. One decade later and the state's Latino population almost doubled while Rhode Island's African American community grew by a small margin.

Still, Rhode Island's Latinos, a community comprising 8.7 percent of the state's population, comprised less than 3 percent of membership of the legislature's lower chamber. This ratio is rather startling when we compare it to that found in neighboring Massachusetts and Connecticut. Latinos in Massachusetts make up 6.8 percent of the state population but only 2 percent of the membership in the state legislature's lower house. In Connecticut Latinos are 9.4 percent of the population and 4 percent of the members in the state house of representatives. Although the more than two-to-one ratio of percentage of Latinos to percentage of Latino lawmakers in Connecticut is far from ideal, it is still much better than the ratio in Rhode Island, where it is almost three to one, or in Massachusetts, where it is more than three to one.

There is not much difference between Connecticut's Latino population (9.4 percent) and Rhode Island's (8.7 percent). Yet one cannot aptly appreciate the dynamics of Latino politics in the United States without understanding the cultural diversity within Latino communities.[34] Puerto Ricans comprise 5.7 percent of Connecticut's inhabitants, while they are only 2.4 percent of Rhode Island residents. In Hartford, Connecticut, Eddie Pérez, a native of Puerto Rico, was first elected mayor in 2001. This city is about 41 percent Latino and 33 percent Puerto Rican. Whereas Rhode Island's considerable Colombian and Dominican residents must first secure permanent residency and later become naturalized before they can register to vote, the same does not hold true for Puerto Ricans. Instead of comparing the ratios of Latinos as a percentage of a state's population to the percentage of Latino elected officials (in this case, in a state's house of representatives) let us compare the percentage of Puerto Ricans to the percentage of Latino office holders (regardless of country of origin). When we do this to the data from Connecticut, Massachusetts, and Rhode Island, we come up with a ratio of close to one to one in all three states. When it comes to electing Latinos into office in New England, we cannot ignore a rather critical variable, namely the Puerto Rican population.

New Hampshire's only Latino state representative, Carlos E. González, a Republican, is a native of the Dominican Republic. It may seem a bit unusual to imagine the election of a Latino in a state that is less than 2 percent Latino. However, one must take into account the unique nature of New Hampshire's lower chamber. Most state houses of representatives in New England have 150 to 160 members. Rhode Island is an outlier; its state lower house has only seventy-five members. New Hampshire represents the other end of the spectrum with a 400-member lower house. The exceptionally large number of representatives in New Hampshire allows even the state's small Latino community to elect one of their own. No Latinos were elected to the Maine or Vermont state legislatures.

As was mentioned earlier, the most significant increases in Latin American immigration to New England are due to Mexicans, Dominicans, and other Central and South Americans who are noncitizens upon arrival. The chronic underrepresentation of elected Latino officials in the region will likely persist for the time being, even in Latino enclaves. Underrepresentation is not only a problem in terms of lack of input in the formal political process; it also leaves a community vulnerable to scapegoating. For the foreseeable future Latino activists will have to fight on several fronts. They must drive home the message that securing citizenship is a vital asset, register these new citizens to vote, and then mobilize them on election day. Latino political activists will also have to keep a close eye on the shape of district boundaries. After all, there is an important difference between a district that has a "majority of minority residents" and another that has a "majority of minority voters."[35]

## Bilingual Education

The Latino demographic expansion of the 1990s and the election of Latinos to the state house certainly did not deter the resurgence of the debate over the public role of the English language. There may not be an overt official language policy in the country, but there is a "covert" policy favoring English.[36] The connection between the English language and American identity antedate the American Revolution. At the center of the language debate in the United States lies a preoccupation over the defining characteristics of American culture.[37] One of the few object cultural markers used to classify Americans is the language of the majority. There is a prevalent suspicion in American society that Spanish-speakers do not want to learn English.[38] Many also fear that the linguistic battles in neighboring Canada could materialize in the United States. Ironically, the current debate in New England could help to generate precisely the linguistic tensions that English language proponents wish to deter.

Language resurfaced as a political issue in the 2002 Massachusetts gubernatorial race. Republican candidate Mitt Romney favored a ballot initiative—Question 2—abolishing the state's bilingual education program. This ballot question, promoted by California businessman Ron Unz, would replace existing bilingual education programs with a single year of English-language immersion. Romney's Democratic opponent, Shannon O'Brien, opposed the proposal, as did the state's incumbent governor, Republican Jane Swift.[39] For many Massachusetts Latinos the ballot question had a clear anti-immigrant and anti-Latino subtext.[40] A *Boston Globe* postelection analysis of suburban communities suggested that fears of an anti-immigrant backlash, in the form of opposition to bilingual education, were not unfounded.[41] Bilingual education opponents selected Massachusetts as the next battleground in the American language crusade for rather symbolic reasons. Unz underscored that a victory in a traditionally liberal state such as Massachusetts, a state thoroughly associated with educational institutions, would mark a major coup in its own right and a stepping stone toward changing the face of bilingual education at the federal level.[42] This ballot initiative won with the support of 68 percent of the state's electorate.[43]

Support for this language initiative confirms earlier studies proposing that a substantial majority of Americans, regardless of partisan affiliation, favored various English-only or English-first proposals.[44] Some scholars claimed that the presence of a large Latino population had no direct relationship to support for English-only laws.[45] Still, there was no denying that ethnic affiliation—Latino versus non-Latino—had a pronounced outcome in the vote. A University of Massachusetts at Boston exit poll of twelve thousand Latino voters highlighted tremendous opposition in the community to Question 2—92 percent opposed it.[46] Paralleling the results of the ballot initiative, 87 percent of these Latino voters claimed to have voted for Democratic challenger Shannon O'Brien. Preliminary estimates claimed that the voter turnout rates in predominantly Latino precincts nearly doubled those of the last gubernatorial election in 1998.[47] In the end Republican candidate Mitt Romney won the Massachusetts governorship, and Question 2 passed. But the association between the candidate, the party, and this initiative could linger for Massachusetts Latinos. Massachusetts's Question 2 could become the functional equivalent of California's notorious Proposition 187.

That 1994 ballot question—one backed strongly by the state's Republican governor Pete Wilson—was a measure limiting immigrants' access to a host of social services. Many perceived it as an anti-immigrant and anti-Latino measure and it served to galvanize Latino electoral participation.[48] Four years later Latino support proved instrumental in defeating the Republican Party's gubernatorial candidate Dan Lungren.[49] Politicians in New England could learn valuable lessons from their counterparts on the West Coast.

## Lessons from Quebec

Students of Canadian politics have long been familiar with the term *Quiet Revolution*—a period of fundamental transformations in Quebec politics and society. This transmutation was quiet in the sense that it took place largely without violence. Yet it was certainly a revolution that irrevocably altered relations between the country's two largest linguistic communities. The emergence of the *Parti Québécois* (PQ) in the late 1960s—a party committed to Quebec's separation from Canada—was one of the first tangible signs to Anglophone Canadians that a fundamental shift in French-English relations was well underfoot. A new generation of French political activists defiantly challenged the privileged status of English in Canada and the domination of the Anglophone business elite within Quebec.[50] Prime Minister Pierre Trudeau admitted that: "Anglo-Canadian nationalism produced, inevitably, French-Canadian nationalism."[51] Canada's largest linguistic minority stated emphatically that it would no longer tolerate its second-class status. The PQ certainly challenged the economic dominance of the province's powerful English-speaking minority—a minority, accused by Québécois nationalists of governing like the whites of Rhodesia or South Africa.[52]

This example bordering New England leaves open the question whether Anglo American nationalism could fuel a stronger and perhaps more militant sense of Latino identity in years to come. Policies and attitudes perceived as anti-Latino, coupled with a budding Latino presence, hold the potential to foment antagonistic Anglo-Latino relations. Unlike Francophone politics in Quebec, we are not discussing the possibility of Latino separatism in New England, nor anywhere else in the United States. Indeed, even in those regions where Latinos constitute sizeable proportions of the population there are no serious calls for the creation of independent Latino homelands. Even the Aztlán movement within the Mexican American community was less a call for the Southwestern states to separate from the United States than an act of defiance protesting Latino social, economic, and political peripheralization.[53] The only American jurisdiction where secession is a sincerely debated public policy alternative is Puerto Rico.

Thinly veiled apprehensions about Latinos in general rise to the surface when federal policy makers discuss Puerto Rico. Despite more than a century of American rule, this island remains Spanish-speaking. In 1989 Senator J. Bennett Johnston of Louisiana expressed deep reservations about language and the island's status. The senator was worried that giving Spanish a co-official status in a prospective Puerto Rican state would accentuate the island's heritage, underscoring that "It doesn't want to be American."[54] His comments insinuated that Latino and American are mutually exclusive. And yet Senator Johnston was far from alone on this issue. More recently, congressmen John Duncan of Tennessee and Bob Goodlate of Virginia expressed similar views.[55] California Congressman Steve Horn unequivocally described Puerto Rico as "another Quebec."[56] For Harvard professor Samuel Huntington, unassimilated Latinos represent the most significant threat to the disintegration of the United States.[57]

These commentators fail to realize that most ethnic problems in the United States are due to the dominant society's refusal to embrace minorities rather than the minority's refusal to blend into the mainstream.[58] George M. Fredrickson said, "American nationalism has often been circumscribed by implicit or explicit racial limitations that belied its universalistic promises."[59] The paradigmatic American is still presumed to be white, protestant, middle-class, and Anglophone.[60] Yet cultural amalgamation, though often conflictual, rarely impacts one group without impacting the other. Indeed, the "Hispanization of the United States" is concurrent with the "Anglicization of Hispanics."[61] Consequently, and ironically, xenophobic attitudes toward Latinos could spur in New England the kind of alienation that eventually led to Quebec's Quiet Revolution.

## Conclusion

Although far from shores of Florida and the border states of the Southwest, New England is undergoing a silent but irrefutable demographic transformation. Latinos are now the area's largest minority, and this trend will likely continue for the foreseeable future. Interestingly, this demographic change has yet to manifest itself in the political arena. When discussing Latino issues, clearly we cannot ignore the significant barriers to greater participation, such as citizenship status. Still, those who habitually blame the victim fail to take into account the long-established practices of key institutions. With the exception of Cuban Americans, the Republican Party until recently has ignored Latino voters. On the other hand, the Democratic Party, particularly its urban branches, often shunned

Latinos in the post-machine era for fear of having to cut the proverbial pie into thinner slices. Furthermore, the existing electoral system favors territorially compact groups. Latinos are concentrating in key pockets, particularly in southern New England. But while some continue settling in established enclaves, other Latinos are spreading out, even to rural parts of the region.

Latinos are just now beginning to see co-ethnics elected into office. Most of these new Latino executives and lawmakers hold positions in local government and usually represent heavily Latino districts. In addition to territorial compactness, an important variable in the likelihood of electing Latinos is not just the proportion of Latinos to non-Latinos in a district but also the proportion of Puerto Ricans. Unlike other immigrants from Latin America, these U.S. citizens can vote and run for office upon arrival. In all likelihood we shall continue to see Latinos active in the one realm where institutional barriers do not hamper their activism. This is the arena of informal politics—demonstrations, protests, and grassroots activism of various kinds. New England activism on behalf of the Vieques demilitarization campaign is but one recent example. Nonelectoral political activism will surely remain a hallmark of Latino politics. In time, greater political participation will also show itself in the formal political arena.

Students of politics can learn valuable lessons outside the social sciences. Newton's third law of motion states that for every action there is an equal and opposite reaction. If Latino growth patterns in New England represent action, its opposing force may be Latinophobia. Most overt manifestations tend to be mild, at least in New England. Often they employ subterfuge. As opposed to a direct assault, anti-Latino admonitions manifest themselves, for example, in attacks on bilingual programs or initiatives. Behind such measures is a conjecture: to be American is to be Anglo, if not ancestrally, at least in language. Its converse is that to be Latin is to be foreign; this applies to both objects and people. With a thinly cloaked predisposition against non-Anglos, English-language advocates in New England could learn valuable lessons from their northern neighbors. Francophone pride in Canada was traditionally a mild ideology, at least in the political sense. Since its birth in 1867, the Canadian Confederation advocated cultural autonomy, not separation. That changed in the 1960s, a decade that witnessed the emergence of a defiant Québécois nationalism. This revolt did not emerge by itself. Québécois nationalism was the natural end result of Anglo-centric Canadian nationalism. As New England's Latino communities grow, its English-speaking establishment will be left with an important decision—whether to embrace and accept diversity or attempt to marginalize it. The various forms of future Latino political participation may depend as much on the reactions of the area's majority as on the actions of Latinos themselves.

## Notes

1. www.census.gov/main/www/cen1990.html; www.census.gov/main/www.cen 2000.html.

2. The Commonwealth of Puerto Rico sends a Resident Commissioner (a non-voting delegate) to the U.S. House of Representatives. All the other Puerto Ricans in Congress represent districts in states.

3. José E. Cruz, *Identity and Power: Puerto Rican Politics and the Challenge of Ethnicity* (Philadelphia: Temple University Press, 1998), 4.

4. Carol Hardy-Fanta, *Latina Politics, Latino Politics: Gender, Culture, and Political Participation in Boston* (Philadelphia: Temple University Press, 1993), 5; James Jennings, "Puerto Rican Politics in Two Cities: New York and Boston," in *Puerto Rican Politics in Urban America*, ed. James Jennings and Monte Rivera (Westport, CT: Greenwood Press, 1984), 75.

5. Francisco Rivera-Batiz and Carlos E. Santiago, *Island Paradox: Puerto Rico in the 1990s* (New York: Russell Sage Foundation, 1996), 132–135.

6. Ibid.,135.

7. Juan Forero, "Prosperous Colombians Flee," *New York Times*, April 10, 2001, A1 and A8.

8. Cindy Rodríguez, "Exodus to Eastie," *Boston Globe*, November 1, 2000, B1.

9. Enrico A. Marcelli, *Legal Immigration to New England During the 1990s* (Boston: Mauricio Gastón Institute for Latino Community Development and Public Policy, University of Massachusetts Boston, April 2002).

10. Jamaicans and Haitians represented about a quarter of the region's Latin American and Caribbean legal immigrants. Brazilians were about 6 percent. Ibid.

11. Economic and political crises in South America are also fostering immigration to Europe and, for Jewish Latin Americans, to Israel. Sophie Arie, "Economic, Political Unrest Fueling Argentina's Exodus," *Boston Globe*, February 10, 2002, A8; Simon Romero, "Descendants of Venezuelan Immigrants Flee to 'Old Country,'" *New York Times*, May 22, 2002, A10.

12. Marcelli, *Legal Immigration*.

13. Gabriel A. Almond and Sidney Verba, *The Civic Culture: Political Attitudes and Democracy in Five Nations* (Princeton, NJ: Princeton University Press, 1963).

14. Seymour Martin Lipset, *Continental Divide: The Values and Institutions of the United States and Canada* (London: Routledge, 1990), 26.

15. Nathan Glazer and Daniel P. Moynihan, *Beyond the Melting Pot: The Negroes, Puerto Ricans, Jews, Italians and Irish of New York City*, 2d ed. (Cambridge, MA: MIT Press, 1970), xix–xx.

16. James Jennings, *Puerto Rican Politics in New York City* (Washington, DC: University Press of America, 1977), 46.

17. José R. Sánchez, "Puerto Rican Politics in New York: Beyond "Secondhand" Theory," in *Latinos in New York: Communities in Transition*, ed. Gabriel Haslip-Viera and Sherrie L. Baver (Notre Dame, IN: University of Notre Dame Press, 1996), 269–270.

18. Jennings, *Puerto Rican Politics*, 85–86, 115.

19.  Michael Jones-Correa, *Between Two Nations: The Political Predicament of Latinos in New York City* (Ithaca, NY: Cornell University Press, 1998), 77.

20.  Angel A. Amy Moreno de Toro, "An Oral History of the Puerto Rican Socialist Party in Boston, 1972–1978," in *The Puerto Rican Movement: Voices from the Diaspora*, ed. Andrés Torres and José E. Velázquez (Philadelphia: Temple University Press, 1998), 246–259; José E. Cruz, *Identity and Power: Puerto Rican Politics and the Challenge to Ethnicity* (Philadelphia: Temple University Press, 1998), 84–85; Hardy-Fanta, *Latina Politics, Latino Politics*, 38–39.

21.  See Cruz, *Identity and Power*, 167, and Ronald Fernandez, *Los Macheteros: The Wells Fargo Robbery and the Violent Struggle for Puerto Rican Independence* (New York: Prentice Hall, 1987).

22.  Amílcar A. Barreto, "Towards a Theoretical Explanation of Terrorism," in *Democratic Development and Political Terrorism: The Global Perspective*, ed. William J. Crotty (Boston: Northeastern University Press, 2005).

23.  Luis Aponte-Parés, "Lessons from El Barrio—The East Harlem Real Great Society/Urban Planning Studio: A Puerto Rican Chapter in the Fight for Urban Self-Determination," in *Latino Social Movements: Historical and Theoretical Perspectives*, ed. Rodolfo D. Torres and George Katsiaficas (New York: Routledge, 1999), 43.

24.  Katherine McCaffrey, "Forging Solidarity: Politics, Protest, and the Vieques Support Network," in Torres and Velázquez, *The Puerto Rican Movement*, 332.

25.  Cindy Rodriguez, "Lively Festival Celebrates Puerto Rican Heritage," *Boston Globe*, July 31, 2000, B3; José Martínez, "Feds Oust Squatters from Vieques Bombing Range," *Boston Herald*, May 5, 2000; Adrian Walker, "The Shrapnel from Vieques," *Boston Globe*, May 31, 2001, B1.

26.  Ron Zapata, "Seven Arrests Made in Protest of Vieques Bombing," *Associated Press State & Local Wire*, June 27, 2001.

27.  Chris Echegaray, "Navy Tests on Vieques Spurs Rallies," *Worcester Telegram & Gazette*, Worcester, MA. August 3, 2001, B1; George B. Griffin, "Vieques Bombings Makes Ripples at City Hall," *Worcester Telegram & Gazette*, Worcester, MA. April 28, 2001.

28.  Amílcar A. Barreto, *Vieques, the Navy, and Puerto Rican Politics* (Gainesville: University Press of Florida, 2002).

29.  Federal House seats: Connecticut, five; Maine, two; Massachusetts, ten; New Hampshire, two; Rhode Island, two; and Vermont, one.

30.  Senator Barrios is also the first openly gay state senator in Massachusetts.

31.  José E. Cruz, "Los puertorriqueños y la política en los Estados Unidos: Una evaluación preliminar," *Revista de Ciencias Sociales* 1 (1996), 99.

32.  Michael Jones-Correa, *Between Two Nations: The Political Predicament of Latinos in New York City* (Ithaca, NY: Cornell University Press, 1998), 92.

33.  Edward Fitzpatrick, "At the Assembly: Minorities Hopeful Despite Few Gains," *Providence Journal-Bulletin*, December 1, 2002, B1.

34.  Ronald Schmidt, Edwina Barvosa-Carter, and Rodolfo D. Torres, "Latina/o Identities: Social Diversity and U.S. Politics," *PS: Political Science & Politics*, 33 (2000), 566.

35.  Frank Phillips, "Minorities Welcome U.S. House Map Plan," *Boston Globe*, September 25, 2001, B2.

36.  Harold F. Schiffman, *Linguistic Culture and Language Policy* (London: Routledge, 1996), 14–15.

37.  Ronald Schmidt, *Language Policy and Identity Politics in the United States* (Philadelphia: Temple University Press, 2000), 88–91.

38. Carol L. Schmid, *The Politics of Language: Conflict, Identity, and Cultural Pluralism in Comparative Perspective* (New York: Oxford University Press, 2001), 98.

39. Scott S. Greenberger, "Bilingual Ed Splits Rivals for Governor," *Boston Globe*, November 25, 2002, B1.

40. Michele Kurtz and Cindy Rodriguez, "Debate Over Immersion Roils Latino Community," *Boston Globe*, November 2, 2002, A1, B5.

41. Anand Vaishnav, "Dissecting Bilingual Education's Poll," *Boston Globe*, November 10, 2002, B9.

42. Ed Hayward, " Voters decide on Bilingual Ed," *Boston Herald*, November 6, 2002.

43. Anand Vaishnav, "Dissecting Bilingual Education's Poll Defeat," *Boston Globe*, November 10, 2002, B9.

44. John Frendreis and Raymond Tatalovich, "Who Supports English-Only Language Laws? Evidence from the 1992 National Election Study," *Social Science Quarterly* 78 (1997), 354–368.

45. Ibid., 354–368; Raymond Tatalovich, "Voting in Official English Language Referenda in Five States: What kind of Backlash against Spanish-Speakers?" *Language Problems and Language Planning* 19 (1995), 47–59.

46. Cindy Rodriguez, "Activists Encouraged by Turnout of Latinos," *Boston Globe*, November 9, 2002, B1.

47. Ibid.

48. Christine Marie Sierra, Teresa Carrillo, Louis DeSipio, and Michael Jones-Correa, "Latino Immigration and Citizenship," *PS: Political Science and Politics*, 33 (2000), 538.

49. Zachary Coile and Elizabeth Fernandez, "New Allies, Old Friends put Demos on Top," *San Francisco Examiner*, November 9, 1998, A1.

50. Marc V. Levine, *The Reconquest of Montreal: Language Policy and Social Change in a Bilingual City* (Philadelphia: Temple University Press, 1990), 39–40.

51. Pierre Elliot Trudeau, *Federalism and the French Canadians* (New York: St. Martin's Press, 1968), 163.

52. Pierre Vallières, *White Niggers of America* (Toronto: McClelland and Stewart, 1971).

53. David G. Gutiérrez, *Walls and Mirrors: Mexican Americans, Mexican Immigrants, and the Politics of Ethnicity* (Berkeley: University of California Press, 1995), 185.

54. United States Senate, *Political Status of Puerto Rico. Hearing Before the Committee on Energy and Natural Resources* (Senate Hearing 101–98, part 1. Washington, DC: Government Printing Office, June 1–2, 1989), 371.

55. *Congressional Record* 144, no. 19 (Washington, DC: Government Printing Office, March 3, 1998), H695, H799.

56. *Congressional Record* 144, no. 20 (Washington, DC: Government Printing Office, March 4, 1998), H785.

57. Samuel P. Huntington, *Who We Are?: The Challenges to America's National Identity* (New York: Simon & Schuster, 2004).

58. Walker Connor, *Ethnonationalism: The Quest for Understanding* (Princeton, NJ: Princeton University Press, 1994), 21.

59. George M. Fredrickson, *The Comparative Imagination: On the History of Racism, Nationalism, and Social Movements* (Berkeley: University of California Press, 2000), 63.

60. Suzanne Oboler, *Ethnic Labels, Latino Lives: Identity and the Politics of (Re)-Presentation in the United States* (Minneapolis: University of Minnesota Press, 1995), 26; Bonnie Urciuoli, *Exposing Prejudice: Puerto Rican Experiences of Language, Race, and Class* (Boulder, CO: Westview, 1998), 15–16.

61. Ilan Stavans, *The Hispanic Condition: Reflections on Culture and Identity in America* (New York: Harper Collins, 1995), 9.

# Selected Bibliography

Amy Moreno, Angel. "An Oral History of the Puerto Rican Socialist Party in Boston, 1972–1978." In Torres and Velázquez, *The Puerto Rican Movement*, 1998.

Baker, Susan S. *Understanding Mainland Puerto Rican Poverty*. Philadelphia: Temple University Press, 2002.

Bluestone, Barry, and Mary Huff Stevenson. *The Boston Renaissance*. New York: Russell Sage Foundation, 2000.

Bonilla, Frank, Edwin Meléndez, Rebecca Morales, and María de los Angeles Torres, eds. *Borderless Borders: U.S. Latinos, Latin Americans, and the Paradox of Interdependence*. Philadelphia: Temple University Press, 1998.

Boston Foundation. *Latinos in Boston: Confronting Poverty, Building Community*. Boston: The Boston Foundation, 1992.

Caraballo Ireland, Elba R. "The Role of the Pentecostal Church as a Service Provider in the Puerto Rican Community; Boston, Massachusetts: A Case Study." Ph.D. diss., Brandeis University, 1991.

Center for Research and Public Policy. *The Latino Socio-Economic Study*. Hartford: Connecticut General Assembly, Latino and Puerto Rican Affairs Commission, 2000.

Cruz, José. *Identity and Power: Puerto Rican Politics and the Challenge of Ethnicity*. Philadelphia: Temple University Press, 1998.

———. "Pushing Left to Get to the Center: Puerto Rican Radicalism in Hartford, Connecticut." In Torres and Velázquez, *The Puerto Rican Movement*. Philadelphia: Temple University Press, 1998.

Darder, Antonia, ed. *Culture and Difference: Critical Perspectives on the Bicultural Experience in the United States*. Westport, Connecticut: Bergin and Garvey, 1995.

Darder, Antonia, and Rodolfo D. Torres, "Latinos and Society: Culture, Politics and Class." In *The Latino Studies Reader: Culture, Economy and Society*, ed. Antonia Darder and Rodolfo D. Torres. Oxford: Blackwell, 1998.

De la Garza, Rodolfo O. Louis DeSipio, F. Chris García, John García, and Angelo Falcón. *Latino Voices: Mexican, Puerto Rican and Cuban Perspectives on American Politics*. Boulder: Westview Press, 1992.

Delgado, Richard, and Jean Stefancic. *The Latino/a Condition: A Critical Reader*. New York: New York University Press, 1998.

Duany, Jorge. *The Puerto Rican Nation on the Move: Identities on the Island and in the United States*. Chapel Hill: University of North Carolina Press, 2002.

Flores, Juan. "Pan-Latino/Trans-Latino: Puerto Ricans in the 'New Nueva York.'" *CENTRO Journal* 8 (1996): 173–186.

Flores, William V., and Rina Benmayor. *Latino Cultural Citizenship*. Boston: Beacon, 1997.

Foner, Nancy, Rubén G. Rumbaut, and Steven J. Gold, eds. *Immigration Research for a New Century*. New York: Russell Sage, 2000.

García, John. *Latino Politics in America: Community, Culture and Interests*. Lanham, Maryland: Rowman & Littlefield, 2003.

Glasser, Ruth, "From 'Rich Port' to Bridgeport: Puerto Ricans in Connecticut." In Whalen and Vázquez-Hernández, *The Puerto Rican Diaspora*. Philadelphia: Temple University Press, 2005.

———. *Aquí Me Quedo: Puerto Ricans in Connecticut*. Connecticut Humanities Council, 1997.

Guarnizo, Luis. 1998. "The Rise of Transnational Social Formations: Mexican and Dominican State Responses to Transnational Migration." *Political Power and Social Theory* 12: 45–94.

Hamamoto, Darrell Y., and Rodolfo D. Torres. *New American Destinies: A Reader in Contemporary Asian and Latino Immigration*. New York: Routledge, 1997.

Hardy-Fanta, Carol. *Latino Electoral Campaigns in Massachusetts: The Impact of Gender*. Boston: University of Massachusetts Boston, 1997.

———. *Latina Politics, Latino Politics*. Philadelphia: Temple University Press, 1993.

Hardy-Fanta, Carol, and Jeffrey N. Gerson. *Latino Politics in Massachusetts: Struggles, Strategies and Prospects*. New York: Routledge, 2002.

Hernández, Ramona. *The Mobility of Workers Under Advanced Capitalism*. New York: Columbia University Press, 2002.

Itzigsohn, José, Carlos Dore Cabral, Esther Hernández Medina, and Obed Vázquez. "Mapping Dominican Transnationalism: Narrow and Broad Transnational Practices." *Ethnic and Racial Studies* 22, no. 2 (1999): 216–40.

Jennings, James, and Mel King, eds. *From Access to Power: Black Politics in Boston*. Cambridge, MA: Schenkman Books, 1986.

Jennings, James, and Monte Rivera, eds. *Puerto Rican Politics in Urban America*. West Port, CT: Greenwood Press, 1984.

Levitt, Peggy. *Transnational Villagers*. Berkeley: University of California Press, 2001.

———. "Migrants Participate across Borders: Toward an Understanding of Forms and Consequences." In Foner, Rumbaut, and Gold, *Immigration Research for a New Century*. New York: Russell Sage, 2000.

Mass Institute for a New Commonwealth. *Mass.migration*. Boston: Mass, Inc. 2003.

———. *The Changing Workforce: Immigrants and the New Economy in Massachusetts*. Boston: Mass, Inc. 1999.

Matos Rodríguez, Felix V. "Saving the *Parcela*: A Short History of Boston's Puerto Rican Community." In Whalen and Vázquez-Hernández, *The Puerto Rican Diaspora*. Philadelphia: Temple University Press, 2005.

———. "The Browncoats Are Coming: Latino Public History in Boston." *The Public Historian* 23, no.4 (2001): 15–28.

———. Matos Rodríguez, Felix V. "Saving the *Parcela*: A Short History of Boston's Puerto Rican Community." In Whalen and Vázquez-Hernández, *The Puerto Rican Diaspora*. Philadelphia: Temple University Press, 2005.

Meléndez, Edwin, guest editor. "Latinos in a Changing Society: Part I." Special issue, *New England Journal of Public Policy* 11, no. 1 (1995).

Meléndez, Edwin, and Miren Uriarte, eds. *Latinos, Poverty and Public Policy in Massachusetts*. Boston: Mauricio Gastón Institute, 1993.

Montero-Sieburth, Marta, and Ralph Rivera, guest coeditors. "Latinos in a Changing Society: Part II." Special issue, *New England Journal of Public Policy* 11, no. 2 (1996).

Oboler, Suzanne. *Ethnic Labels, Latino Lives*. Minneapolis: University of Minnesota Press, 1995.

Piore, Michael J. *Birds of Passage*. Cambridge: Cambridge University Press, 1979.

Portes, Alejandro and Rubén G. Rumbaut. *Legacies: The Story of the Immigrant Second Generation*. Berkeley: University of California Press, 2001.

———. *Immigrant America: A Portrait*. Berkeley: University of California Press, 1996.

Rivera, Ralph, and Sonia Nieto, eds. *The Education of Latino Students in Massachusetts: Issues, Research, and Policy Implications*. Boston: Mauricio Gastón Institute, 1993.

Rodríguez, Clara. *Changing Race: Latinos, the Census and the History of Ethnicity in the United States*. New York: New York University Press, 2000.

Sales, Teresa. *Brazilians Away from Home*. New York: Center for Migration Studies, 2003.

Small, Mario Luis. *Villa Victoria: The Transformation of Social Capital in a Boston Barrio*. Chicago: University of Chicago Press, 2004.

Suárez-Orozco, Marcelo M., and Mariela M. Páez, eds. *Latinos: Remaking America*. Berkeley: University of California Press, 2002.

Sum, A., I. Khatiwada, J. Motroni, and N. Pond. *Moving Out and Moving In: Out-Migration and Foreign Immigration in the Northeast Region and New England During the 1990s*. Boston: Center for Labor Market Studies, Northeastern University, 2002.

Torres, Andrés, and José E. Velázquez, eds. *The Puerto Rican Movement: Voices from the Diaspora*. Philadelphia: Temple University Press, 1998.

Torres-Saillant, Silvio, and Ramona Hernández. *The Dominican Americans*. Westport and London: Greenwood Press, 1998.

Uriarte, Miren. "A Challenge to the Racial Order: Boston's Latino Community." *Boston Review*, September–October, 1992.

———. "Organizing for Survival: The Emergence of a Puerto Rican Community." Ph.D. diss., Boston University, 1988.

Uriate, Miren, Phillip Granbery, Megan Holloran, Susan Kelly, Robert Kramer, Sandra Winkler, with Jennifer Murillo, Udaya Wagle, and Randall Wilson. *Salvadorans, Guatemalans, Hondurans, and Colombians: A Scan of Needs of Recent Latin American Immigrants to the Boston Area, Summary of Findings*. Boston: Mauricio Gastón Institute, 2003.

Uriate, Miren, with Maria Estela Carrion, Charles Jones, Natalie Carithers, Juan Carlos Gorlier, and Juan Francisco Garcia. *Rhode Island Latinos: A Scan of Issues Affecting the Latino Population of Rhode Island*. Boston: Mauricio Gastón Institute, 2002.

Westfried, Alex Huxley. *Ethnic Leadership in a New England Community*. Cambridge, MA: Schenkman Publishing, 1981.

Whalen, Carmen Teresa, and Victor Vázquez-Hernández, eds. *The Puerto Rican Diaspora: Historical Perspectives*. Philadelphia: Temple University Press, 2005.

# Notes on Contributors

**Amílcar Antonio Barreto** is an associate professor of political science at Northeastern University, where he teaches international law, Latino politics, and nationalism. He is the author of three books, including *The Politics of Language in Puerto Rico* (2001) and *Vieques, the Navy, and Puerto Rican Politics* (2002).

**Yoel Camayd-Freixas** is a professor and the chair of the PhD and Advanced Practitioner Masters programs in policy at the School of Community Economic Development, Southern New Hampshire University. He is also director of the Applied Research Center at the university, where he serves as principal investigator on several sponsored research studies.

**Jorge Capetillo-Ponce** is an assistant professor of sociology at the University of Massachusetts Boston and a research associate at the Mauricio Gastón Institute. His research focuses on social theory, race and ethnicity, media, international relations, and Latino studies. His latest publication is *Deciphering the Labyrinth: The Influence of Georg Simmel on the Sociology of Octavio Paz.*

**José E. Cruz** is an associate professor of political science at SUNY-Albany and the author of *Identity and Power: Puerto Rican Politics and the Challenge of Ethnicity* (Temple University Press, 1998). He directs the New York Latino Research and Resources Network, a research consortium focusing on health, education, immigration, and politics.

**Cileine de Lourenço** is an associate professor of Latin American studies and Spanish at the Department of English and Cultural Studies, Bryant University. She has written about representations of race, class, and gender in Latin American cinemas, and she is coauthoring a book on identity construction among Brazilian immigrant women in the Boston area.

**Ruth Glasser** received her PhD in American studies from Yale University in 1991. She currently teaches in the Urban and Community

Studies Program at the University of Connecticut. She is the author of *My Music is My Flag* and *Aquí Me Quedo: Puerto Ricans in Connecticut,* and she is a coeditor of *Caribbean Connections: The Dominican Republic.*

**Phillip J. Granberry** worked with community-based organizations assisting U.S. immigrants before becoming a PhD candidate in public policy at the University of Massachusetts Boston. His dissertation is entitled "Individual, Institutional, and Environmental Determinants of Social Capital, and Its Influence on the Earnings and Health of Mexican Immigrants in Los Angeles County."

**Megan Halloran** is a PhD student in public policy at the University of Massachusetts Boston. Her focus is on education and policy issues related to individuals with disabilities. She is a certified teacher of children with special needs and a founding member of the Aspergers Association of New England.

**Deborah Pacini Hernandez** is an associate professor of anthropology in the Department of Sociology/Anthropology and the director of the Latino Studies Program at Tufts University. Her research areas include comparative Latino studies, Latino community studies, and ethnic and racial identity in Caribbean and U.S. Latino popular music and culture.

**José Itzigsohn** is an associate professor of sociology and ethnic studies at Brown University. He studies the incorporation of Latino/a immigrants. He is working on a book on Dominican immigration to Providence. Through this case study, the book will address contemporary debates on identity formation, occupational mobility, and transnational linkages.

**Gerald Karush** is a professor of computer information systems at the Graduate School of Business, Southern New Hampshire University, and a senior research fellow at the Applied Research Center, where he is involved in several research studies. His principal areas of experience include computer technology, economic development, demography, and market and evaluation research.

**Robert Kramer** is a postresident doctoral candidate in the Public Policy Program of the McCormack Graduate School of Policy Studies at the University of Massachusetts Boston. He holds an MS in Public Policy from the University of Massachusetts Boston and an MA in Community Social Psychology from the University of Massachusetts Lowell.

**Nelly Lejter** is associate dean for administration and an adjunct instructor in sociology at the School of Community Economic Development,

Southern New Hampshire University. She is also a senior research associate at the school's Applied Research Center, where she is involved in several research studies.

**Enrico A. Marcelli** is an assistant professor of economics at the University of Massachusetts Boston and the 2003–2005 Robert Wood Johnson Health & Society Scholar at Harvard University. His research and teaching focus on the causes and consequences of Latino immigration to the United States and the social determinants of health.

**Angel A. Amy Moreno** is a professor of humanities and social sciences at Roxbury Community College. An oral historian and master photographer, he has curated fine art and photo exhibits throughout New England and Puerto Rico. His awards include the Boston Latino Best Photographer Award and the Distinguished Historian Award by the Senate of Puerto Rico.

**Hosffman Ospino** is the coordinator of academic programs in Hispanic ministry and adjunct faculty at the Institute of Religious Education and Pastoral Ministry at Boston College. He is a doctoral candidate in theology and education at Boston College. He is working on a book about Latino/a Catholics in Massachusetts.

**Adrian D. Pantoja** is an assistant professor of political science at Arizona State University. He studies Latino political behavior and public opinion, immigration, and ethnic/racial politics. His research has appeared in a variety of journals and edited volumes. He is pursuing several projects on the Dominican diaspora, transnational ties, and immigration.

**C. Eduardo Siqueira** is currently an assistant professor in the Department of Community Health and Sustainability at the University of Massachusetts Lowell. He holds a doctoral degree in Work Environment Policy from the University of Massachusetts Lowell. Dr. Siqueira graduated in Medicine at the Federal University of Rio de Janeiro, Brazil.

**Michael E. Stone** is a professor of community planning and public policy at the University of Massachusetts Boston. His book *Shelter Poverty: New Ideas on Housing Affordability* has been called "the definitive book on housing and social justice in the United States." He is coauthor of *Housing: Foundation for a New Social Agenda* (forthcoming).

**Andrés Torres** is research associate at the Center for Puerto Rican Studies, Hunter College, City University of New York. Previously he was a professor of economics and Latino studies at the College of Public and

Community Service, University of Massachusetts Boston. He directed the Mauricio Gastón Institute from 1998 to 2005. He is the author of *Between Melting Pot and Mosaic* and coeditor (with José Velázquez) of *The Puerto Rican Movement*.

**Miren Uriarte** is a sociologist at the University of Massachusetts Boston and a senior research associate at the Mauricio Gastón Institute. She researches the Latino experience in New England and has published in the areas of demography, education, and social welfare. She has also published studies about Cuba and other parts of Latin America.

# Index